Congratulations Clarabelle!

SONGS I HEARD MY MOTHER SING

Charlton Speer
aka Pa
10/22/2007

Songs I Heard My Mother Sing

Charlton Lyons

True tales, told in rank disorder,
of the writer's generation of mainly decent people
and of his family and of himself, such being
the terminal moraine left by an age long past
and soon to be forgotten with the rest.

As the heart holds her memories close
lest they fly,
To live on in my heart is not yet to die.

AuthorHouse™
1663 Liberty Drive, Suite 200
Bloomington, IN 47403
www.authorhouse.com
Phone: 1-800-839-8640

© 2007 Charlton Lyons. All rights reserved.

No part of this book may be reproduced, stored in a retrieval system, or transmitted by any means without the written permission of the author.

First published by AuthorHouse 9/24/2007

ISBN: 978-1-4343-4059-7 (sc)

Front Cover Painting: Portrait of Marjorie Lyons painted circa 1916 by the Polish artist Maurice Fromkes

Printed in the United States of America
Bloomington, Indiana

This book is printed on acid-free paper.

Written for

Scout

whose perfectly beautiful being lived back in there,
just there, behind her perfectly beautiful eyes,
eyes which in death, as they were in her life,
I know to be still fixed upon my face.

Dulce et decorum est pro patria mori:

    Carmina – Liber Tertius – Carminum II
        Quintus Horatius Flaccus

To give up one's life for one's country
is surely a sweet and fitting way to die.

CONTENTS

The Stories

Opus 1

Prelude in a minor key	1
Introit	5
Sonata for solo eccentric	11
Adagio for broken heart strings	24
Chant in D: The Thinking Artist's Decalogue	30
Introduction and Allegro: Picture at an Exhibition	
Introduction	31
Allegro: The Portrait of Marjorie Lyons	34
Le Tombeau d'Alexander Pope	39

Opus 2

Menu-ette	46
Requiem for two innocents come from Lebanon	57
Recitativo secco	67
Bagatelle	72
NOLA	79
Ride a cock-horse …	82

Opus 3

The obbligato	88
Over there, over there … (Pa's War Letters)	112

Opus 4

Traditional: Michael Hall of Wisconsin	121
An early trio	141

Opus 5

Der Wanderer	165
Dei Forelle	181
Away to Rio!	190
Introduction, Two Step and Galop for the End of Time:	
Harbach and Fellner	206

Opus 6

Variations on a Theme by Chaucer   217

Opus 7

Humoresque   261
Octet for male voices:
    The Society of Orpheus and Bacchus   271
The Colonel McCabe March   279
The moon shines tonight on pretty Redwing   286
Come to the church in the wildwood …   300

Opus 8

Harold in Jersey   304
Escales: Ports of Call   318
Landkjending: Land-Sighting   325
The Swan's Song   332

Opus 9

Pavane for a Dead Prince: Plot N Row 7 Grave 17   340

The Pictures

Front cover: The portrait of the author's mother, Marjorie Lyons, painted circa 1916 by the Polish artist Maurice Fromkes. This portrait is the subject of the author's story herein, *Introduction and Allegro: Picture at an Exhibition,* a true story, as, saving only a few tall tales readily recognizable as such, are all those you will be hearing the author tell.

Back cover: The author's pool in the summer of 2006 as seen from Scout's grave. It is here beside this pool that for a time you and he will spend some early evenings together before super, coming to know each other as he spins the tales of times gone by that constitute this book.

Front matter: *L'Allegro* and *Il Penseroso*, being the author as he was in the summer of 1926 when he was four years old.

Harry Hall, the author's maternal grandfather. Circa 1940   Page 23

Mr. and Mrs. H. P. Hall, the author's maternal grandparents. Circa 1930s. They are standing beside "The Sassbox", their little cottage on Lake Chetek, Wisconsin.   Page 23

Ernest John Lyons, the author's paternal grandfather, with his older sister, Mary Ella. Circa 1880.   Page 27

Army mug shot of the author. December, 1943.   Page 94

The author - Bad Heilbrunn, Germany. May, 1945.   Page 104

The author again - Bad Heilbrunn, Germany. May, 1945.   Page 104

Michael Hall of Wisconsin. Circa 1890?   Page 122

Mary Scally Hall, wife of Michael Hall. Circa 1890?   Page 122

A rapids in the Chippewa River. Circa 1890?   Page 127

Marjorie Lyons and her younger sister, Norma, (in costume and character). Circa 1902.   Page 131

The Michael and Mary Hall farmhouse located out on Eagle Prairie, Wisconsin. Circa 1890?   Page 133

The author with his nurse, Palestine, and his baby brother, Hall. Spring of 1924.   Page 142

The author's brother, Hall Lyons, with Bud Johnson, the author's friend from boyhood, and Hall's command, LCT 1326, on Okinawa. June of 1945.   Page 150

Some impressions of Yale as he knew it in 1941:
line drawings by Jack Moment done more than
forty years later.   Pages 179-180

A day's catch on Lake Chetek, Wisconsin. Circa 1920.   Page 184

The black dog Scout and the author posed among the boosters
at The Doctors' Lounge on The Promised Land.
January of 2,001.   Page 261

Peggy Lyons with her dog Meg, and her husband. 1980.   Page 262

The Society of Orpheus and Bacchus, a male quartet.
Spring of 1942.   Page 272

Nan Merriman singing at a banquet honoring
the author's father. January 23, 1953   Page 286

Charlton Lyons, Sr., the author's father, with his
graduating class, the Tulane Law School. 1916.   Page 289

Marjorie Lyons, schoolteacher, Pollack, Louisiana. 1918.   Page 291

Charlton Lyons, Sr., Attorney-at-law, Shreveport. 1922.   Page 292
285?

Charlton Lyons, Sr. with Ike in Shreveport. 1952   Page 293

Charlton Lyons, Sr. with Ronald Reagan at the 1964
Republican National Convention.   Page 295

Charlton Lyons, Sr., with Ronald Reagan and
Tom Stagg in New Orleans. 1964.   Page 295

"Auf Wiederschen" The author at age seventy-nine,
apparently making a fashion statement at the tag end
of the twentieth century. Late December, 1999.   Page 334

A view of the American military cemetery that lies
near Margraten, Netherlands.   Page 352

                The Acknowledgments
                            Beginning at page 353

                   The Appendices

Appendix A.   Pages 361-363
A letter from the author to Fred Hall Ryan dated May 13, 1945 and written shortly after the arrival of his firing battery in the Bavarian village of Bad Heilbrunn.

Appendix B.   Pages 363-364
The text in its entirety of a very short "society column" which appeared in late December, 1904, in a Chippewa Falls, Wisconsin newspaper.

Appendix C.   Pages 364-367
The text of a piece written circa 1906 by one Thomas McBean and published in a Chippewa Falls, Wisconsin, newspaper, soon after Michael and Mary Hall had sold the farm and taken up residence on Bridge Street in Chippewa Falls.

Appendix D.   Pages 367-371
An undated, four page "letter home" written, and illustrated, by Susybelle Lyons in the 1950s while she and her husband were in Havana, Cuba.

Appendix E.   Pages 372-381
A "biography" of Charles Richard Spencer as compiled, at a time unknown to the author, by a person described as "researcher Professor Richard Sheppard of Magdalen College, Oxford."

Appendix F.   Pages 381-392
A transcript of all but the first page of an eight page, single-spaced, typewritten document, containing, in English translation, extracts from many, and perhaps most, of the reviews appearing in South American newspapers of certain of the concerts given throughout South America by The Yale Glee Club in the summer of 1941.

Appendix G.   Pages 392-393
A press release, undated but issued around the time, late in August of 1945, when the author, an officer then serving with the 609th Tank Destroyer Battalion, was departing Camp Atlanta outside Rheims, France, for Le Havre to board the Victory ship, *U. S. Victory*, for return to the States.

Appendix H.   Pages 393-395
An Associated Press release which was prominently displayed in the New Orleans morning newspaper, *The Times-Picayune*, of September 8, 1945 and which advised the names of troop ships arriving that day from Europe in three east coast ports, and also announcing the arrivals that had taken place the previous day, beginning with the arrival on September 7th of the *S.S. Victory*, the ship on which the 609th Tank Destroyer Battalion, including the author, returned to the States.

Appendix I.   Pages 395-397
An E-mail message from the author to Jack Moment sent on Wednesday, March 09, 2005 concerning his sighting on March 24, 1945, of the air-borne armada on its way to its assault on the Germans across the Rhine, with Charlie Higgins and Jack Moment both on board.

Appendix J.   Pages 397-400
Three documents relating to the last days and hours of Charles Alfred Higgins, Jr. The first of these, the text of a letter to the author from Jacqueline Haun dated August 29, 2005, relates also to Charles Richard Spencer.

L'*Allegro*

Il Penseroso

The next voice you hear will be his —
but in the year 2007 and at the age of eighty-five.

Opus 1

Prelude in a Minor Key

The bitter cold of it! Someone said that in Verviers he'd seen rats sticking to the sidewalk. But we shouldn't worry much about them, he said—so were the cats. There were maybe a dozen of us that morning, all 2nd Louies fresh from the States, blowing on our frigid hands and stomping the frozen earth with frozen feet. Standing there beside a six-by-six army truck, and waiting for something—it doesn't matter what. Looking hopefully up and down that dirt road the way country dogs used to do eighty years ago when I was a boy.

When did we first become aware of them? Well, retrospection doesn't say, but most likely we heard their thrumming first—the incantatory throbbing of their motors as they mumbled their way toward us out of the west. Then we would have seen them, there in the sky, to the northwest and not flying high either, because my memory clearly has them at only two or three thousand feet, and heading toward the river Rhine, lying just there at the horizon to the east. Those planes, they were not swarming in a ball as bees do but came in a long, thin line stretched out across the sky, patiently following one another in the dutiful way that passenger pigeons were once wont to do. That's what I was told when I was a boy—told by old men who'd themselves seen those pigeons passing in the long trains of their enormous numbers.

We wouldn't have paid them much mind, not at first. Just a few flights of transports, maybe sent to drop supplies? No, I think not. But what we saw at first was only their beginning. A forlorn hope like those sent out before ancient armies to engage the enemy in those lonely, single combats which were once the necessary preludes to the grand melee and battle royal.

But as I watched them flying north of us across the sky, first for long minutes, but then, as it seemed to me, for hours, coming in their never ending numbers, I slowly waked to the fact that I was witnessing something highly extraordinary, some military operation of enormous, unprecedented magnitude and consequence.

For these were not combat aircraft, none of them were. I could see no bombers among them, and although fighters were doubtless high up there somewhere, an umbrella watching down, I never saw even one. No indeed, they were all cargo aircraft, C-47s, C-46s and lots of British transports I could not have named. Many of them certainly had gliders towed behind, and of course I must have seen those gliders, too, but for some reason, I paid them little notice at the time. It all seemed so eerie as they passed us by, all those thousands upon ghostly thousands of aircraft, flying in a column slowly towards we knew not where.

Not for a great long while, hours and hours it seems in memory, not until the last of all those great birds had passed in solemn procession on out of sight in the east, did we depart on our several ways, all as replacements assigned to various combat units. I myself was heading south to rejoin the Tenth Armored Division and to take the place of a very selfless man who'd only just met his fate—a friend of mine in college whose wholly unexpected identity I was not to learn until just a year ago, three generations, or some sixty years, after the fact.

Whatever it was, the long passage of that vast, spectral army of the air, it was an ill-boding never to be forgotten and I never have.

So when you asked me just now—and you're certainly not the first—what memory is most striking when I think back on the war, well, it's the sight of all those planes passing. That apparition I saw that late March morning in 1945, in far eastern Belgium, towards the end of our virtuous war. The war that was fought by almost the whole of my generation, and on fronts scattered all round the earth, all those long years ago. I can still feel the cold of that morning—that silent cold. It was the silence and cold of the morgue.

For more than forty years after VJ Day, saving only a year or two after we got home, there wasn't much talk of the war. Like most of us, I rarely even thought about it. But as you know, beginning with the fiftieth anniversary of Pearl Harbor, there was a whole new interest taken in it, and for more than fifteen years now, you read about that war everywhere. Books and other accounts of it at every hand. Just those battle pictures on The History Channel, they're still able to fascinate three whole generations of men and boys.

I have no present recollection whether or not, at that time in 1945, I knew anything at all about that great air armada—other, of course, than what I'd seen of it myself. But it was a scene that struck a chord in me. I could feel it in my bones. A dominant seventh—a chord that would hang there, suspended and unresolved, for almost all of the rest of my life. But not so long ago, just a couple of years, I learned, through the benevolence of serendipity, that what I had seen passing me that morning had been, in fact, the perfectly enormous operation I'd sensed it to be. It turned out to be almost of the magnitude of the Normandy invasion itself. I learned that it's even been given a name. *The Airborne Bridge Across the Rhine*. That's what history has come to call it.

Never heard of it? Well neither had I. That is, not until one day in March of 2005, sixty years later to the month and not far distant from the very day. That's when I first learned about it. Learned that two very close and dear old friends had been up there in that sky as I watched. And I learned it at first hand from someone who knew the whole story, because he'd been one of them. Oh, yes, one of those two old friends happily turned up after many years and told me that they'd been up there that day, the two of them. And he told me just what had lain in wait for them, as they left me behind and flew on toward their rendezvous with the Fates, there at that bridge they laid across the Rhine.

One of my friends was a Signal Corps Officer who'd volunteered himself aboard the mission so that he could stand in the cargo door of a C-47 and take pictures of the battle royal he knew would be coming. The other, a paratrooper with the 17th Airborne Division, was aboard one of those gliders I must have seen up there—a glider carrying, along with my old friend, three or four enlisted men and a 75mm pack howitzer. That paratrooper, like me, a Lieutenant of Field Artillery, had not long before graduated with me from the Field Artillery School at Fort Sill, and before that, he'd been one of my two roommates our freshman year at college. And that Signal Corps officer, just the year before that, in 1939-1940, he'd been my roommate at Lawrenceville. Lawrenceville, you ask? That was the boy's boarding school in New Jersey from which all three of us had together graduated in June of 1940 and from which, the following fall, the three of us, with two other friends, had gone together on to Yale.

I guess it's just the fate of those of us who find ourselves still among the living—the last leaves clinging to the tree of life, if you will—to have had to watch all the rest turn red and fall.

Well, I see it's supper time now but I'm so glad we had this first visit together here around the pool. There can be others, you know? That is, if you don't mind listening to an old man's mind rummaging about in yesterday's attic? I ought to warn you, though— the past doesn't seem to return to me in quite the order in which it arrived. But that's OK, I guess, because stories aren't always best told in their proper order anyway. Not even in the five books of Moses. What was it the rabbi said about that? There's no early or late in the Torah? Wasn't that it? Same with *The Book of the Thousand and One Nights.* Just one true tale after another, tumbling along like the tumbling tumbleweeds. That's all I can promise.

What do you say? Do you think you might want to come again tomorrow evening? Just a bit before supper, could you? Sit here again with me, while we talk? You see, I've never talked much about the past. Not about my past. Not to anyone, not even to my children. But here lately I've been having all these memories and I'm feeling the need to share, to tell someone, while I still can. Before they disappear. So that's why I'm so glad you happened along.

But now, about those planes. Even after all these years, I've never forgotten them. Never been able to get the memory of them out of my mind. They didn't look like warplanes, you see. Oh, but they were! Oh yes, they certainly were! So there's an infinite sadness that comes with my memory of all those spectral aircraft passing. And my two friends up there with them. Up there above, passing me by, in that slow, solemn and stately procession. It was something like watching a courtly dance. Like watching a pavane.

Introit

Ah, you've come again! I'd hoped you would. Here, have a seat near me and we'll talk a while. Let's see now—you said last evening you'd like to hear the story of my life. That's what you called it, didn't you? Sure you did!

Well, you ought to be ashamed of flattery as bald-faced as that. But it's OK, I guess. That's' what friends are meant for, isn't it, to flatter each other? Anyway, it kept me awake last night—well, for three minutes, it did, while I was trying to imagine why you'd ever want to hear about me. The very thought of it bores me to death! You have no idea, a life as colorless and marginal as mine, so without incident? Why, you just can't imagine! Fact is, we're all the same, you know. Of no importance, living, and soon forgotten, dead.

But past is prologue, so why don't you begin by reading my obituary? Here! Here's a copy of it I brought out for you. Just the usual obit, the same old hoop skirt stuff. What's a hoop skirt obituary? Well, what's a hoop skirt? Why, it's just a—a "come-on". A tantalizing something that covers everything but reveals nothing. Here you are. Won't take you long. My life's story in two pages.

Shreveport, LA – Charlton Havard Lyons, Jr., after a long, full and exceptionally happy life, died here on [month, day and year.] Following a private family graveside service and interment, an Episcopal service in celebration of the gift of life will be held at St. Mark's Episcopal Cathedral, (day of the week) (date) (time of day), the officiant to be _____ .

The family will be happy to visit with friends _____ and again at the church following the service.

On December 11, 1921, five days before the death of Camille St. Saens, Charlton was born to Marjorie Hall Lyons and Charlton Havard Lyons. He graduated from South Highlands Grammar School in 1935, from The Lawrenceville School, Lawrenceville, New Jersey, in 1940, from Yale University in 1943 and from Tulane University Law School in 1948.

As did his whole honorable generation, Charlton volunteered for military service soon after Pearl Harbor and served in the United States Army, first as an enlisted man and later as an officer, including wartime service in Europe as an artillery forward observer with the Tenth Armored Division.

Charlton was a life long communicant of St. Mark's Episcopal Church, with service on its vestry. His community, educational and cultural involvements included service on the Board of Trustees of Centenary College and for a time its Secretary and on the board of The Community Chest and as a chairman of its annual fund drive.

And, through membership on their boards, he also served the Genevieve Orphanage, American Red Cross (Caddo Parish Chapter), The Courtyard Players (a Shreveport theatre-in-the-round of more than sixty years ago) and the Shreveport Country Club. He was a founding partner of The Strand Partners and, in the early 1950s, while serving as a member of the Board of Directors of the Shreveport YMCA, worked closely with Mr. M. E. Mischler, its then Secretary, in the planning of a major enlargement of the services and facilities of that organization, having himself drafted and secured the passage of the amendment to its articles of incorporation resulting in the first Metropolitan YMCA. He served on the boards of the Shreveport Symphony and of the Shreveport Opera Association, of which he was its second president.

Charlton's life was filled with an abiding love for music and reading and theatre. He first came on stage locally in 1933, playing the role of "A Boy With An Accordion" in "The Crime At Blossoms" at The Shreveport Little Theatre. His final stage appearance was at Marjorie Lyons Playhouse at Centenary College in the summer of 2004, a span of more than seventy years.

From 1948 until the last of his several abortive "retirements" in 1998, Charlton worked in several disparate business ventures but, by his own lights, was for the most part just an old fashioned oilman, working with a long list of dear office friends at Lyons Petroleum, digging for buried treasure.

Charlton is survived by his wife, Peggy McClure Lyons, and his six children, Susybelle Lyons Gosslee, Stafford Lyons, Charlton

Havard Lyons, III, Sally Scott Lyons Wood, Laurie Wilkinson Lyons and Marian Lyons McGoldrick and by eleven grand children and _____ great grandchildren.

That's right, I'm the sole author of it. Wrote it all myself. That way, my wife and my children won't have to do it. Anything they'd write would be twice too long anyway. Cost too much. I couldn't afford it. That's my opinion, not theirs. Why is it people spend all that money on obituaries anyway? It's just a flag made to be flown for a day, that's all it is. And all that money spent just to embalm the inconsequential in saturnine and engrave the ephemeral in July lard! Beats the hell out of me!

Look there! It says I was born in 1921, so naturally we don't share the same past. But otherwise we're much alike, you and I. Doesn't your whole future lie out there ahead of you? Well, so does mine! So we're not only sitting here together, we've arrived together at the very same place in life. I can see that plain as day, can't you?

So you'd like it if I shared my past with you, is that it? Well, I can't wait. Not everything, of course. Just a bit of it. It might learn you something—keep you out of trouble some day, right? And as for me, it might just be the thing that keeps me alive a while longer. You remember Scheherazade, how she hornswoggled The Reaper, just by telling him stories? That's what kept *her* alive.

You and I, we've just met, but I think we're going to become great friends. That's why I'm going to trust you with a small confidence about myself. Something I'm not too proud of. I've been a reader all my life. From early childhood. Oh, yeah, that's bad stuff and I'm guilty—guilty as homemade sin, but there's something about me that's even worse. From some deep grammar born in me—by the way, do you by any chance happen to be a Chomskyian?—I've always sensed the reading of something as being just the mirror-side of the writing of it.

Yes, I know. I don't blame you for coughing and moving away from me a bit. Some people, when they get terrible old like me, they develop peculiarities. Get a little goofy? *Fey*, they used to call it. Don't hear that word any more. Don't know why. Plenty of us around. Of course, some of us don't even know that we're peculiar.

But that's not me. Oh, no, I *know* I am! So you might as well hear the nutty stuff right off. That way, you won't be so surprised when it comes out later on.

But honestly now, can't you see that? The reading and the writing of the same text as being like the obverse and the reverse of a coin? Haven't you sometimes, as you read, put yourself at least subliminally, or subconsciously, in the position of the writer of the very stuff you've got your eyes on, pondering, as the writer might have done, the effectiveness of a plot hook, or considering how to point a paragraph, eliminating the colons and semicolons, so that it will be something heard by the reader's ear—heard as talking, talk like ours right here for instance, and not something seen by his eye, as writing on a page? Now really? Haven't you had that experience?

Or perhaps you're on to him and can see that that writer is judging the effect on you—*you* the very reader he visualizes, of some subtle narrative strategy he has in mind. Wasn't it Byron who never pointed his poetry himself but left that to others? I think he did that to be sure that he'd only hear his poetry in his ear and not see it in his eye. Hear the song in the air and not lose the music through looking down at the notes he'd put on the page. Why sure, he had to!

Or, putting it in a slightly different context, consider a mature audience in a playhouse. Like any experienced reader, that audience out there is always aware, at one and the same time, not only of the character, the persona, the mask being played on stage, but, at least subliminally, of the *person* of the actor just behind that mask. And all this, without let or hindrance to the fullest participation in the performance by that same audience.

And the actor, consider him. If you're in the audience, I can assure you that despite those seemingly unfocussed and unseeing eyes up there onstage, that stare launched out over you to a distance of a thousand yards, the actor, for his part, is in fact ever and keenly alert to each person of the audience. Every sound, every movement, every expression out there in the gloom is registered up there on the stage, becoming instant cause for elation or alarm.

So an audience should never, *ever* delude itself into a false sense of its own anonymity, for the players, the actors, they know you—every one of you out there in the shadows. You're part of the art of theatre—a part as essential as the players themselves. You're half the dialogue between the stage and the house. And isn't that true of all art? Isn't art just a dialogue between two suites of sensibilities?

Wish I could think what it was that Walter Pater had to say about art and music. It was something that went straight to the heart of the matter. Oh, well, maybe it'll come to me later.

By the way—would you care to hear how I came to end the war, down in the far south of Germany, in Garmisch, living for a few days next door to Richard Strauss? No? Well—maybe another time?

Oh, my! I seem to have maundered off the subject again. Unless of course, that *was* the subject. Let's see now, what was it you were talking about? Oh, yes, you were saying something about reading being just the mirror image of writing. Or was I the one who said that? Anyhow, I couldn't agree with you more. And that leads me to another confession.

Now, here you'll have to forgive me if I look away—if I don't look you quite in the eye, because this is somewhat embarrassing for me, but to tell you the truth, I've always aspired to be a writer. An author. Yes I have! And from boyhood, too! Well, no—not just an author—a *published* author. All my life I've wanted nothing more than to go to my grave, to be buried with the knowledge that I had done with my life at least one worthwhile thing. You know, like writing something that might actually be *printed*? That someone might even care to *read*? Oh, of course I've always known that such a thing would never happen to me, but now—now that I've gotten old, I'm not so sure. In fact, I think I might just have that old aspiration of mine quite within my grasp.

Because, you see, my wife and all six of my children have sworn—that's right, they've given me their solemn pledge—that when the time comes and after fair trial held and judgment rendered and I'm sent down below, my obituary, the one you have there, the one I wrote myself in my own hand, would be the obituary that was published in our local paper. Of course now, they're free to make an addendum or two, fill in the blanks, but they've promised me that what I've written there *will* be published, and published largely unaltered. They took that oath before a magistrate, too, so I know that it's certain to happen. And, you know what?—I can hardly wait!

So you see, there's a great day coming and it's not far off! That great day when, *florissant en haut mon panache, mon flambeau de gloire,* I bid you all farewell and take leave of the world and lay myself down to rest. And on that great day, I'll find myself secure in the peace that comes from knowing—knowing with a certitude that is absolute—that on the morrow, before I'm to be buried away and forgotten, our morning paper will be out on the streets, and that in it, the people will be reading *my* obituary, the very one I wrote myself, and that I'll be going to my grave a completely satisfied and happy man—certain in the knowledge that I had indeed become a published author.

Sonata for Solo Eccentric

His rather small feet, side by side in the grass, are shod in old fashioned high-top, black leather shoes, thin soled from long wear and showing a few cracks, yet nicely polished and laced up to the top-most eyelets. The laces tied neatly into twin bow knots. Below the cuffs of his trousers are seen some four or five inches of the underwear that covers his bony old shins and reaches on down his skinny old ankles and through his shoe tops to his feet. He wears such underwear, those long johns of his, all year round. It's woolen, too, but lightweight on this late afternoon of a summer's day. It's 1936 and the heat of the great Dust Bowl of the thirties, now in full bloom, touches even here where we are, in far Northwestern Wisconsin, on the banks of Lake Chetek.

He's wearing a suit, one of the two he owns, not the black one but the dark gray one he wears every day. His suit coat lies unbuttoned and open, but not his vest which is all buttoned up, every button top to bottom. So is the collar of his shirt, buttoned up for his four-in-hand tie. And so, too, is his fly, buttoned neatly up. Sitting there on his straight-backed, wooden chair, he would give every appearance of being a well buttoned-up and rather distinguished old gent. And perhaps that's what he himself believed he was, but it's just as likely that that's only what he'd have us to believe.

The vest came with the suit of course, as did two pairs of pants. Back in those days only bespoke suits came otherwise. There's a hip pocket sewn into his trousers and there's something in it all right, something quite thick. Wonder what it is? It could be a wallet but we can't be sure of that. At least not yet. If so, he's a very rich man.

Sewn into the front of his trousers, top right, there's another pocket, the little narrow watch pocket certain to be found in all trousers worn by the men of his day. But of course there's no watch in it, for there in plain view, one end fixed through the top button of his vest is a gold chain and we immediately suspect that the other end of that chain will lead to his watch, its thin gold case planted out of sight in a vest pocket, the petite pocket sewn into its left side.

Clusters of gray hair peer out from under a somewhat misshapen black fedora hat perched just a wee bit jauntily on his head, a nice large head with little jowl. He's sixty-seven years old as we see him, not fat, not at all, certainly not cadaverous, either. Well, I suppose he does appear to be pushing a bit of a paunch around these days. His gaze seems fixed upon something out there across the lake.

Under that hat is an actor's face, handsome, broad and open, and set in it are those fathomless azure eyes. There's an enormous gravity in that face, in those level eyes, steady and unblinking. That's a face in which one can certainly trust—or so one would think.

But notice! His eyes are unseeing, focused on nothing. Oblivious even of that last evidence, a faint trace still remnant in the earth along the lake shore not ten yards away, of that annual trek his family made beginning sixty-five years before, of that long journey that required the full length of a mid-summer day, of that wagon ride from the farm just north of Chippewa Falls to this very spot of land. Granted it's not the Camino Real, but they're still visible, those two parallel tracks first made there by his father all those long pioneering years ago and for his family they're an already historic trace. For it was to these very family-hallowed grounds that his father brought his large Irish family to camp out for a few summer days. Brought them the twenty miles up from the farmstead he'd acquired at the end of the Civil War. For underfoot, among the scattering of white and yellow birch, lies the silent but visible, and thus irrefutable, testimony of the earth that the first feet, after only those of the Indians, to touch down here were those of his father.

Surely he must be looking at *something,* one would think, but it's something visible only to him. Something far back in time, some ghost or other, something only his memory sees. Who knows what?

Now he's enjoying a few last puffs on his pipe, a gnarly black briar stuck in his jaw. Presently, after the fire in the pipe has died away to ash, without taking his eyes from the lake, his right hand takes the pipe from his jaw and taps out the dottle on the heel of his left. The pipe now on his lap, he takes from a trouser pocket a clasp knife, opens it and reams a bit of the crust out of the bowl before using it to clean his nails. The knife back in his pocket and the pipe back on his lap, he reaches again into a pocket and comes out with his pipe tobacco, not in a leather pouch, no, but in the paper wrapper in which it came. It's what he's always smoked, Granger Roughcut.

Then suddenly he lays aside his interest in another smoke and takes from his hip pocket a bottle. Could it be—? Yes, yes it is, it's a pint of liquor! Sure and it's Irish too, Irish whiskey, and like the tobacco, still in the bottle he bought it in, for this old man of long ago, he's Irish to the bone and his being Irish, you'd know there's nothing peculiar about him, nothing peculiar at all. He takes a nip. And by and by—another. Time passes.

Everything at last put away, he takes from a trouser pocket a black leather coin purse, three compartments with snaps at the top which he opens one by one. He counts his money. Several silver dollars, a small fortune then, some smaller coins and, like so many men of that time, a gold coin. His is a twenty dollar gold piece. He carries no folding money this day. The purse goes back into his pocket and out comes his pocket knife again and with it this time he pares his nails. He carefully considers its edge before wiping the blade on his trouser leg and putting it away. All men of that long ago time carried pocket knives like his. A knife was the tool that made the day possible, a pocket knife and a good whet rock.

He reaches across with his right hand to take his watch from his vest pocket, opens it and looks at the time. Before returning his watch to its pocket, he removes from his right coat pocket the large, red bandanna handkerchief he always keeps there. He then proceeds to carefully polish the watch, holding it up in the fading light before putting everything away.

Like most old men of his time, he's been bred up in the country and so carries there on his person everything he needs, but, in the case of our *particular* old gentleman, what he carries is also the most of everything he owns.

He is Henry Patrick Hall. He's called Harry by the many who know him abroad in the world, but Uncle Hal by his numerous collateral relatives, the descendants of his five sisters. His one brother, Joe, when only sixteen but already a logger, had on

June 2, 1890 drowned in the Chippewa River. That mighty logging river was then in the full spate of the spring thaw and choked with the winter's logging coming down. Our Joe was struck by a log and drowned while rescuing a friend. That friend was himself drowned in that same river just one year later and to the very day. And so ended the short career of the great uncle I never knew, Joseph T. Hall. Just a boy who was known in his life by only a few and now by no one still living. A ghost long ago forgotten but whose name I bring briefly back for one last remembrance.

Harry's wife and three children call him Dad and their direct descendants call him Grandfather Hall, of course. Grandfather Hall was born soon after the Civil War, on September 15, 1868. Born in his parents' farmhouse just north of Chippewa Falls. It was a farmhouse pitched out on what was then an uncommon piece of ground for that densely forested and glacier-pocked part of the world, a bit of true prairie and the site of a crossroads cluster then known as Eagle Prairie. When my grandfather was born, all of Northern Wisconsin was still best thought of in just the terms that poetry gives us—that is, as a vast forest primeval, dark with the murmuring pines and the hemlocks. Grandmother Hall is known both as Annie Laurie and Aunt Laura. She came from back east, from Newport, Vermont, born there on May 1, 1876 as Laura Ann, or Annie Laurie O'Rourke. She and Grandfather Hall were married on June 5, 1894. Annie Laurie had only just turned seventeen.

Soon now, my grandmother comes out and calls him in to the dinner she's prepared on her little black, cast iron cook stove. And yes, it was fired with wood as were still then half the cook stoves in the county. But you shouldn't think of that as primitive. Oh, no! Primitive was what my grandfather's own parents had found, Michael and Mary Hall, when, long, long before, just after it had become a state, they came into that country of the Ojibwa, that's to say, the Chippewa. Came there with nothing. Nothing, that is, but a tenacious Irish will and all those same hopes and aspirations that fueled the settlement of the whole of our Midwest, then in its full career.

But now, when my grandmother calls Dad to dinner, he slowly rises and turns to climb the two stairs to the nearby screen door and enters their little white cottage, the cottage my grandmother calls The Sass Box. The cottage in which they live for all but the coldest winter months of the year. The cottage that is provided for them by their eldest daughter, Marjorie, and her husband, Charlton.

Through a window in The Sass Box we notice three coal oil lamps on a table there, mantles cleaned, wicks trimmed and ready to be lit for the night. Electricity is slowly crawling its way down the dirt road that comes here from the nearest town a mile or so away, called Chetek, but it won't reach The Sass Box for another year yet, not until 1937 will it. As we watch, one of those kerosene lamps comes to life and a warm, golden glow lights up the dusk inside.

Now he's gone, he and my grandmother have disappeared into their little white cottage and into my memory. We will never see him again. Not him, nor yet the likes of him. Not ever.

You should know that my Grandfather Hall was not always so without apparent distinction as I've described him here. Fact is, he had been for much of his life a self-conceived minstrel of the specifically Irish sort, wandering here and there, regaling with song and story audiences small and large wherever he found them, in road houses, bath houses and flop houses, at harness races and ball parks, in *Bier Stube*, bar room, and tavern, in great halls, lodge halls, grange halls, pool halls and saloons scattered everywhere about Northern Wisconsin. He was, in complete truth, a man of some considerable, if only local fame. Famous as a raconteur, a teller of tales and performer of miracles in roles in all dialects. A singer, too, a tenor with a high Irish voice, sweet, tender and reaching. He'd been quite something in his day, but now he was something else.

Wisconsin, of course, was settled by immigrants from all over Europe—honorable, *legal* immigrants—and within each of those disparate new nations of new Americans was heard its own distinctive brand of spoken English, its own dialect, and from his childhood my grandfather heard them all. And such was the genius of his ear and voice that he could reproduce them all, every one. He could call them up again at will. The Swede, the Italian, the German, the German Jew, the Norwegian, the Scotsman, the Bohemian—they peopled his stories. He owned them. Well no, not the Frenchman.

Not the Spaniard, either, so there mustn't have been very many of those two breeds living anywhere close around.

James Whitcomb Riley is no doubt a name now remembered only by the odd antiquarian, but in his day Riley was mid-America's best loved poet of rural America. A poet who would himself go about the country reciting his own homely, strongly-metered narratives to countless crowds of plain, uncommon country people, who were deeply moved by it. My mother said that on more than one occasion Riley had been present himself when her father performed some of Riley's stuff. I use the word *performed*, because that's what my grandfather did. He did not *recite* those stories that Riley told, oh, no! The ones my grandfather used were typically *contes*—that is, tales told in verse, and told in the first person, and, right there before your eyes, he would *become* that person, the very person Riley obviously knew so well and was there, live, in his verse. Riley was heard to say, *When I read my poems aloud to people, I just wish I could read them the way Harry does.*

Now Grandfather Hall *did* drink, that's true enough. He drank to friends who were with him and to friends who were not. He drank to wherever he was and to whatever the occasion. In fact, he drank to anything and everything and, yes—yes, one might as well go ahead and say it. Sometimes, if there were nothing more opportune to hand, he'd even drink to excess. So deep did he drink in fact, that everyone who knew him became certain that his early death would be the inevitable dire consequence of it all. *Harry hasn't long to live*, the Greek chorus chanted. *Liquor's gonna kill him soon, and liquor's gonna kill him sure.* Nor, as people will, did they keep those views to themselves. Oh, no, the rumor of it went far and wide. *Fama crescit eundo.*

It was along about this time that my mother became much concerned over her father's consumption of alcohol and sent him over to the little town of Chetek to see Doc Adams. When he'd returned from his appointment with Doc Adams, *Well, Dad, what did he tell you to do?* That's what my mother asked him. *He told me that every time I feel like taking a drink, I should just eat an apple instead, that's what he told me. But now, Marjorie, you don't really expect me to eat a peck of apples every day, do you?*

By the way, you never hear the word *peck* anymore, do you? People no longer even have a sense of what it means—how much a peck is. That's because it's a word from my grandfather's world, an agrarian world which our country has now left far behind.

It's true. Demon Rum would sooner or later have put an end to Harry—that is, had not some other, quite different and far more lethal agency intervened and done him in before the liquor did. But as fortune would have it, and as we know fortune usually does, in the event he defeated those expectations, because a fortnight before his eighty-eighth birthday, on August 25, 1956, kicking and dragging his feet, he passed over the Rainbow Bridge. His body is buried in the old Lyons-Hall plot at Forest Park Cemetery here in Shreveport—why don't we call it *hometown* from now on?—and with him lie his wife and all three of his redheaded daughters. I don't know where his dog Tex is buried, but him and that little black and white cur, they were a very loving couple.

Of course it was not he who provided this final resting place for his family. It was again his eldest daughter and her husband, because—how shall I say this? Ah, yes! Harry Hall was a man not known to have often found gainful employment. In fact, he never did himself provide any kind of home for his family, not that I know of. Not even the last dwelling place of all of them on earth, the family plot at Forest Park. For you see, he was the kind of man known in those far-off days as *a poor provider,* and for all of my mother's early life she, with her mother and sister, Norma, lived as permanent residents on the farm her grandparents, Michael and Mary Hall, had settled in the Civil War.

My mother, Marjorie Hall Lyons, was the first of his three daughters and she was born March 27, 1895. Never in God's world could mere reason have predicted the future that the good fortune dispensed by the Fates had prepared for my mother, that little red-haired baby girl, raised up on a prairie not so far from the northernmost waters of the mighty Mississippi.

But I see that just talking about my grandfather has pulled the cork out of my bottle, so maybe you'd like to hear about something else? I had another grandfather you know? Oh, you would? You'd really like to hear more about Uncle Hal?

Well, I did know him for a far longer period of time than I knew my Grandfather Lyons, my father's father, so I knew him much better—knew him in the round, as they say. I knew him quite well myself, of course, but there were many things about him I learned, indirectly, from my mother, so I'm glad you're interested.

There's someone else my mother told me a lot of fascinating stuff about. That was Uncle Hal's father, Michael Hall, my great grandfather. He was born in Ireland long before The Famine and by 1859 he'd somehow made his way to northern Wisconsin. I'll tell you about him sometime. He was a character straight out of Willa Cather and not like his son at all.

My mother said that as a boy, her father had a job in the winter delivering mail to and from the lumber camps up the Chippewa River. The Hall farm was close to the Chippewa and he'd use the river to get to those camps with the mail. He skated, she said. On ice skates Can't you just imagine my grandfather as a boy in winter, skating up and down the Chippewa River on the ice! Likely up the Flambeau, too, with a mail pouch on his back. I guess that's so. My mother said he did it, but with my Grandfather Hall one never knew. Not for sure. Come to think of it, though, I guess he did, because he sure learned somewhere how to skate on thin ice. In fact, he became something of a genius at it, because for all of the thirty-five years I knew him, that's the way he chose to pass the days—and nights, too, from all I heard—skating on ever thinner ice.

Something I heard two older cousins say. It was something exchanged just between themselves, but I heard it. They said that my Grandfather used to cause the family a lot of trouble because he had a hard time keeping his fly buttoned up. I hadn't been told as yet about such a thing—I was still too little—but I knew with the instant, perfect and uncanny certainty of biological endowment what act it was my Grandfather would unbutton his fly to perform. And that, somehow, a woman would be the object of its intention.

I think I mentioned that he was a poor provider—never earned a good living. Have you ever heard that term, *a poor provider*? No, I thought not. It's dropped out of use. Save possibly as an archaism or in some derivative sense. It's too judgmental. And we can't have that, can we? Oh, no, it's quite wrong, quite wrong to put the faculty of judgment, imperfect as it is, to use. No, no, mustn't do that! What leaves the culture, soon leaves the language. You ask any linguist, they'll tell you.

Other than skating with the mail, I never heard of my Grandfather Hall being gainfully employed at anything. Well, I *do* have one stubborn little memory, back there in a far, dark corner of my head, and she's waving at me madly, trying to attract my attention. And she's right, I do have a childhood memory of him being off somewhere in South Carolina, cruising timber. And that makes sense, too, because I've known quite a few *poor providers* in my time, and they all seemed to do their *poor providing* from some place of unemployment situated at a distant remove from all the folks back home.

Oh, sure, my Grandfather Hall was a rascally kind of fellow, but he never intended any harm by it. That's just the way he was, and when I was little, I stood in great awe of all that and thought him, in his way, just rather *wonderful*. I still do.

It was just in his nature to want to demonstrate how short a trip it is from fact to fiction. Tell you the kind of thing he'd do. My mother was, among other good things, a good gardener. Flowers, vegetables, didn't matter. Now, long ago in the South, even after the war—but let me stop here. It would be natural for you to think I mean the Civil War, but not so. Nor do I mean the First World War. I mean the *Second* World War, because when you hear anyone of my generation mention the war, they'll be talking about the one we fought. That is, if they'll talk about it at all.

Let's see, where was I? Oh, yes, my mother kept a garden at our house on Erie here in hometown, an azalea garden for the most part, but there was lots of other stuff there, too, including a variety of *spiraea* we called bridal wreath. If you don't know it, *spiraea* is a flowering plant found even more than a hundred years ago in every southern yard or garden irrespective of its pretensions. Now, in the early spring, when the azaleas and *spiraea* were both blooming in my mother's garden—I can see them still, the long white sprays of the bridal wreath, crescent to the ground—that's when my mother's friends, great ladies in their broad brimmed garden hats, would on Sundays come to see my mother's garden. And when they arrived,

Grandfather would be waiting for them, turned out in his best suit and with his walking stick in hand, for he'd taken it upon himself to take them on the kind of tour of Marjorie's garden which only he was capable of conducting.

I can see him now, pointing with his cane to this and that. Pointing with the elaborate ceremony, sometimes amounting to disdain, he could bring to any scene. Explaining that and this with the air of one possessed of an infinite authority. And, ironically, most of what he told them about the plants and trees and flowers was quite true, for he *was* something of an authority and *did* know what it was he was talking about. All the while, I'd be hanging around the outskirts of the crowd, watching the show unfold, waiting for our arrival at the first of the plantings of *spiraea*. For it was there, at the *spiraea*, that he would deliver himself of one of the great lines in all of theatre. *Now, ladies—them there is Marjorie's diarrhea bushes, so I wouldn't crowd too close up if I was you.*

Did you know that in old times people used *spiraea* as a home remedy? Well they did, used it like aspirin. When they didn't feel good, they'd just go out and break off a couple of shoots and rub their gums with the broken ends and right a way they'd begin to feel better. Because *spiraea's* got the same kind of acid in it that aspirin's got. In fact aspirin's named for *spiraea*. *Spiraea*? *Aspirin*? Hear it?

I remember one time my mother was waiting for us when we arrived back after a tour of the garden. One of those ladies spoke right up. *Oh Marjorie, your father is the most remarkable man! How fortunate you are to still have him with you! How blessed!* Hearing this and fearful of what it might mean, my mother stood frozen, waiting for the worst, a demurring smile painted on her face. Mind you, the word was demurring, not demure. There was nothing demure about my mother. Ever! But you could clearly see the apprehension that lay there behind that smiling mask. It was there in her eyes. *My God, what's he done now?*

But it turned out not to be so bad after all. *He's so remarkable, Marjorie, the most remarkable man we've ever met. And to think that Andrew Jackson was president when he was born. One hundred years! One hundred years old and he doesn't even have a limp!* My grandfather was then about sixty. But he couldn't help it, he just loved to fool folks and he was very, very good at it.

And not just folks, he could fool fish as well. That's another thing I liked about him. I've got a picture somewhere of all the fish he caught in Lake Chetek in just one day. A day's catch, I think it says. Grandfather told me that all those beautiful fish were caught by just him and two other fellows. Can't call their names but he talked about them a lot. Two close friends of his from long ago and now I can't even call their names. I'll show you that picture some day, if I can ever find it.

I was the one who took him fishing the last time he ever went. He was pretty old, but he wanted to go just one more time and he wanted me to take him. Said he'd get out of the boat at a place he knew up Ten Mile and fish from the bank. He was wearing his suit of course and his hat and he brought with him a long, stiff cane pole he'd rigged to fish the way he'd always fished. A stout line the length of the pole and a big hook tied to it. He was wearing a pair of knee-high rubber boots, cow lot boots is what we used to call them. That's all. No bait, no landing net, no creel, nowhere to put a fish if he'd accidentally catch one, something I much doubted he'd do. But then you never knew about him. One thing I did know, I knew better than to volunteer any suggestions, ask any questions. I was then— oh, about twenty and he'd wised me up considerable. You're wondering what happened, aren't you? Well, I'll tell you.

I cranked up our old Elto kicker—that's an outboard motor— and ran the two miles to where Ten Mile Creek comes in and let him out on the bank. He said for me to come back and pick him up in an hour or so. So I went off fishing by myself and when I got back he was sitting there on the bank, waiting. I pulled in and told him I was sorry he hadn't caught anything. That's when he gave me his look of utter disdain. How long has it been since you received a look of disdain? Can't remember, can you? It's out of fashion. Not that people don't feel disdain any more, they just don't show it. Hide it! That's why you can't trust them.

Grandfather told me to row down the bank a-ways so he could pick up. And then I started seeing them, those fish he'd caught. They were hanging from the trees, one by one, as we moved along. All nice dinner table bass, two, three pounds. I think he'd caught maybe six or eight. But I strike a blur here so I can't be sure. I had maybe one. He'd caught all those fish using little green leopard frogs he'd caught with his hands along the bank, one by one as he needed another for his hook. He'd move very quietly down the bank, you see, fishing that frog as he went, pull it off the bank into deeper water or drop it on a lily pad out there, move it around a bit so a bass could sense the motion, maybe see the frog up there through the translucence of the leaf, and then let the frog jump himself off the pad and if there was a bass anywhere around that bass was history.

He didn't need a sack for his fish either. When he caught one, he'd just walk over to the nearest tree, find a little limb sticking out at just a nice height, and he'd prune it to a stub with his clasp knife and hang that fish on it through the gills. That way, his hook was always in the water. He was a fisherman whose likes we're never going to see again.

He'd sit outdoors every evening before supper, smoke his pipe, have a nip, look out across the lake. He was thinking of something of course, but of what? I studied him as best I could, but he remained as inscrutable as the Sphinx I was to stand before many years later, when Peggy and I were there in Egypt. So what on earth was it he was thinking about, as I watched him all those years and years ago? When I was a child and when I was a boy and even as a grown man—he didn't die till 1956—I'd look at him and wonder. What is it, do you imagine, that's there inside that large, actor's head of his? What ghosts are there, behind those rheumy eyes? What memories? What's he thinking about now, do you suppose? And now that I've become an old man myself, I think I've got a pretty good idea of what it was.

I've got a couple of pictures here of my Grandfather Hall for you to see. I'm not quite sure when they were taken but 1940 wouldn't be a bad guess. This first one is a pretty good likeness of him. That's just about how he looked. The other one includes my Grandmother, too, and here you can see them both, Uncle Hal and Aunt Laura, standing beside The Sassbox. If you'd known them the way I did, you'd want to reach out and try to give them a big hug right now. Grandfather wouldn't let you but Grandmother would.

Adagio for broken heart strings

There was nothing in my father's father, my Grandfather Lyons, that resembled in the slightest my Grandfather Hall. Like my parents, the two of them came from opposite ends of the Mississippi Basin, but they might as well have come from opposite poles of the universe. But when I put my mind to Grandfather Lyons, and call him back to life, I see that, after Palestine, he was the first love of my life.

He was Ernest John Lyons, born at Abbeville, Louisiana on April 22, 1865. That was one week after the assassination of our virtuous President Lincoln. Not for another eighty years, not until May 8, 1945, would we again see so clearly that virtue can sometimes be made to prevail. In 1893 my grandfather married Joyce Bentley Havard, my father's mother and the grandmother I never knew. In 1934 my Grandfather Lyons died in the bedroom next to mine, a painful, lingering, humiliating and altogether terrible death. I'll never forget lying awake at night, listening to those groans of agony coming from his room. Wondering to myself why I'd ever said it. But then, right after, why what I'd done had been so wrong.

In those days, just as most of us then were born at home, so most folks died there, too. Often the same home, sometimes even the same bed. My parents had brought him up here from Melville, to our home over there on Erie Street, to pass the end of his life among us before they closed his eyes. But I didn't know that then. How could I? I, who was just a boy and knew death only as a fiction? And anyway, is death ever any better understood by any of us than is time by a mule? When I was little, my parents seemed to see me as far more mature than I knew myself to be, so it would not have occurred to either of them to stand between me and any of the realities of life. Certainly not the inevitability of the end of it. So I was there in the next room when he died. But I'd already suffered his loss before that.

You see, for three blessed years I'd been my grandfather's inseparable companion, so it was awful, awful hard on me when, a few months before he died, all that changed and his door was closed to me at night just because of something I had said. I was only a little boy and couldn't really have been expected to know better than to say what I did, but even if it hadn't been my fault, I know that I was left hating myself for it anyway.

And so it was that, as soon as he came to live with us, we became close, my grandfather and me, and I began to know that wonderfully quiet, patient and gentle man. Because, after supper, before bedtime, I'd spend an hour every night with him in his room. One night he'd read to me and on the next we'd play chess. But that third night! Ah, that was the one that means the most in memory, because that was the night he'd tell me tales—strange and wonderful stories of that magical place called South Louisiana. That Cajun country into which he'd been born and where he'd lived his life.

The stories I loved best were the ones about the Atchafalaya swamp. More than half a million acres of it, sprawled out around the lower Atchafalaya River. Nothing like it anywhere in our country. That's where the Mississippi itself wants to go. Not the long, flat way past New Orleans, but down the Atchafalaya River, straight downhill to the gulf, and one day it will. Everybody knows that.

My grandfather told me that as a young man he'd go with others like him out into that swamp to gather Spanish moss. It grew there everywhere in rank profusion, in what was then a great virgin forest of bald cypress trees. A great forest like that of northern Wisconsin and like the forest that was Wisconsin, soon to be lumbered off. He said that when they'd pulled it down into their bateaus and raked the snakes out of it, they'd haul that moss off by boat to a landing and sell it. I think it was used to stuff cheap bed ticking, but I'm not too sure about that part of it. I remember feeling those snakes crawling all over me when I'd go to bed at night. Those snakes kept me awake. Cottonmouths, he called them. And oh, yes, there were alligators, too. Gators were everywhere then, just as they are now once again. But just imagine that! Raking those snakes out of that moss the way my grandfather did!

Of course, being a little boy, I thought that every word he was telling me was the truth. And most of it was, because as the Fates would have it, on account of my lifelong romance with oil, I would myself, and not thirty years later, go deep into that same

Atchafalaya swamp. I'd spend a lot of time there, me and our little company of very independent oilmen. We were Lyons Petroleum back then and we weren't in there to gather moss. Rosebuds neither. Certainly not snakes. We were there to drill deep wells—two, three miles deep into the crust of the earth, in search of buried treasure. We drilled in oil fields called Bayou Long and Mystic Bayou, and another one that I forget. That's right, there was a field we drilled in that was actually called Mystic Bayou, and it was right in the dead-middle of that swamp.

Half way between Bayou Long and Mystic Bayou we had a little oil field camp. It was built high up on pilings because the water level fluctuated with the seasons the way that nature meant it to. Hard by our camp, there was a stretch of canal and when I didn't go in the long way by boat, that's where I'd grease our little float plane down. But you don't want to hear about all that!

Oh, you *do*? *Well, now*—!

All right then, we'd go in there with drilling rigs, with sky-tall derricks reaching up over draw works mounted on great submersible barges—barges towed to location by tugboat from far off through meandering bayous and straight, dug canals and sunk on location to the bottom. When you were up there high on the drilling platform of one of those rigs, looking from that marvel of modern engineering out into that great, gray swamp, you felt yourself to have arrived at the still point between nature's yesterday and man's tomorrow—the still point of the turning world.

Of course there'd be time on my hands out there, with nothing to do and that's when I'd go fishing, I sure would! And that's when I'd be off exploring that whole phantasmagorial Pleistocene world. Literally losing myself in it. For one thing, you had to keep a constant watch for snakes. Brown water snakes, some of them, but mostly cottonmouths. Alligators, too. Snakes and alligators were everywhere you looked in that vast, watery world and that was only fifty years ago.

But in that very mystical place, in the solitude of a southern summer's day, there was much else besides. That is, if you had the eyes to see it. Over here would be the lilt and swoon of a kingfisher's flight. Over there, a solitary great blue heron flies. Just look at her! Look there at that elderly lady, like an ancient archaeopteryx, slow-waltzing her long, bony shanks across the grand ballroom of her own primordial sky. And everywhere were the cypress. We're in a great cypress swamp, I told you that. It was a place where, only yesterday, one could still see, here and there, still standing, the odd patriarch bald cypress tree, spreading its oriental arms. You just can't imagine how it was! I wish you and I could go back there again. I'd show it to you, I sure would. Then you could see what I saw.

You've seen pictures of my Grandfather Hall, but now look at this photo of my Grandfather Lyons. I believe he was in his early twenties when this was taken. In 1888 maybe? He was the youngest of eight. Standing beside him is the next youngest, his sister Mary Ella.

That's a young man you're looking at and he's strong and fit. Not at all the old man I knew only when he'd reached the end of his life, reduced to the humiliation of seeing his parchment skin falling away from the bones. When he was suffering his own excruciating hemorrhoids. But when this picture was taken, those snakes would never keep *him* awake at night!

And those tales he told, they were the tales of his youth and I loved hearing him tell them. They were true, too. Well—one wasn't! That damned Indian story! He wasn't at all like Grandfather Hall. He wasn't the kind to make things up. If it weren't for that cock-and-bull story, it wouldn't ever have happened. Or if I'd just known enough to keep my mouth shut. But anyhow, he was my wonderful, dear Grandfather Lyons, and now I'm the only person left alive who ever knew him.

Why I'm suddenly thinking of it, I have no idea, but I wrote a stage play once. It was a genre play and in it every character—well, all save one—is struggling to recover from the death of someone, or some thing they'd loved very much. You might even say that death was the protagonist of the play. But it was a comedy with lots of laughs—or at least I thought so. Every night I'd watch those audiences pretty close and I listened to the people as they talked in the foyer during the interval, and it seemed to me that only a handful of them ever realized that the play had anything to do with death. I was rather proud of that. Comedy *does* have that uncanny ability to camouflage what's really going on. Even our fine director, my friend Bob Buseick, turned suddenly to me about ten days into rehearsals and said, *My God, Charlton! It's about death! This play is all about death!*

I called it *Under Hunter's Moon* and it's set in a quail hunting camp. A hunting camp is, of course, nothing more than a sty in which the male chauvinist pig forgathers with his ilk. Both by universal consensus and by any reasonable standard, we hunters are swine. That's what we are—*swine*! You ask anybody, they'll tell you. Well, no, not just *any*body. Don't ask Ortega y Gasset or Tolstoy. They were both hunters. And whatever you do, don't ask Puccini! Puccini was a duck hunter so inveterate that he refused to live anywhere that wasn't pretty close to water, and the companions of his heart were those hoggish hunters who, like him, chose to live around the lake and would bestir themselves only to lay in wait for the wild and wily duck.

Anyhow, in this play, we're out in the Texas Panhandle. That's another place I'm familiar with. Maybe I'll tell you about the Panhandle some evening. It was a very strange sort of experience, writing this play was. My sense of scene was so strong that the play actually peopled itself. Those characters simply appeared out of my sub-conscious—walked right out on stage, straight out of the purple sage and mesquite, arriving one by one, unannounced, half of them in the dead of the night as though from the grave. They took charge, too. Right off. Showed me everything. Worked it all out among themselves, there on the stage of my mind. I just sat quietly in the dark of the house and watched them, as they held me spellbound.

But now, about my Grandfather Lyons. Listening night after night to my grandfather dying in the next room—that was a terrible, terrible ordeal for me. There he was, someone I loved so much, and I could hear him dying. There was only a thin wall between us, but it had become impenetrable. There was no way I could get through it—no way I could get to him, because he'd made it clear to me that I was no longer welcome there in his room on the other side. I knew that he had said everything to me that he was ever going to say. But I still had things I wanted to say to him. That all happened a long, long time ago, but it left the first of a number of permanent scars that a long life has left on me. Some memories are wounds that refuse to heal. I was eleven years old when my grandfather died. And he left without telling me good bye. Someday I might feel more like telling you all about it, but not just now.

Oh yes, now I know what made me think of that play. It was what Bubba said about ghosts.

BUBBA

Ghosts? Look here—ghosts ain't nothing but memories. Memories powerful enough to where a man can see em. That's all ghosts is.

Under Hunter's Moon - Act II
A play in two acts – 1992.
By Charlton Havard Lyons, Jr.

A Chant in D: The Thinking Artist's Decalogue

1. Thou shalt never frustrate the emergence of thy wind, from neither end, shalt thou.

2. Thou shalt ever give close and critical attention to thy preparation of thy impromptus and improvisations.

3. Thou shalt never engage thyself in self-deception; self-indulgence, yes, by all means and at every opportunity; but self-deception, no.

4. Thou shalt never under-exaggerate, as that is the one fault sure to destroy thy very credibility as artist.

5. Thou shalt see to it that thy every show of modesty be false.

6. Thou shalt never eschew the classic, literary, mnemonic adage, apt alliteration's artful help.

7. Thou shalt take care that thy performance be not over-rehearsed.

8. Thou shalt ever take pride that thou, the artist, by common consent a moron, art at least a *thinking* artist, and hence that rarest of the breed, an oxymoron.

9. Thou shalt save back the seed for the sewing of the fallow field.

10. Thou shalt never *ever* squat whilst sporting thy spurs.

11. Thou shalt never frustrate the emergence of thy wind, from neither end, shalt thou.

(Yes, I know, but is this not the very sort of self-indulgence required of us by the stern Commandment No. 3, supra? And besides, isn't it really kind of neat? I mean, in its own humble way, of course?)

Introduction and Allegro:
Picture at an Exhibition

Introduction

That portrait of my mother you saw the other night in the foyer of the theatre at Centenary, that's what you asked about, right? Well, yes—you see, back in 1956, when that theatre was built, Joe Mickle, Centenary's President, insisted that it be named after my mother. And not only because she had been a wonderful leading actress here and in Dallas and Houston in the twenties and thirties, but because of her long and ardent support of all theatre here in hometown. Her interest in theatre, as it was in music, too, of course, was personal, intense, almost wholly untutored, so far as I know, and abiding in her all her life. She knew with a sure instinct born in her what good theatre was and when she saw it, she promoted it, including the good theatre she saw being done at Centenary by the gifted director, Joe Gifford. That's why it's named The Marjorie Lyons Playhouse, or in theatre circles here, the MLP.

Something else. The MPL was designed by my parents' old friend, the architect Sam Wiener. You likely missed the plaque now hanging by the box office which the American Institute of Architects presented to the theatre in 1997. After a long evaluation of the many outstanding buildings built here in the twenty-five year period beginning in 1947, the MLP was judged the crowning architectural achievement of that period.

But now about Fromke's portrait of my mother. In the spring of 2003 my friend, Bob Busieck, at that time head of Centenary's drama department, asked me if by chance I had a portrait of my mother suitable for hanging in the lobby of the theatre. He wanted one to hang beside a memorial to Joe Gifford, whose genius was the real inspiration for the theatre. Mary Bozeman, a former student of Joe's and herself a professional theatre person, commissioned that plaque memorializing Joe which you must have seen there in the foyer beside my mother's portrait. And I did have such a portrait, one I'd owned for thirty years, the one you saw.

When I showed it to Bob, he thought it perfect and said that if it was OK with me, he'd like to hang it in the lobby where you saw it. He wanted to have a little ceremony, unveil it on the opening night of the 2003 summer musical, *1776*. I was delighted of course. Then I mentioned to Bob that there was a rather interesting story behind that painting, the story of how my father had acquired it. Bob asked me if I would write a little something about it to put in the play bill for *1776*. Well, being as you've noticed, rather long winded by nature, I found *a little something* to be well beyond my limited talent for compression, but I did write a short version of the story of that painting. It was I, you see, who had to do it, for I was the only one who knew what my father had said. What he'd written and left behind. So, to mint a fresh conceit, I alone was left to tell the tale. Maybe the telling of tales is all that's keeping me alive these days.

On opening night, a little ceremony was indeed held and the plaque for Joe and the portrait of my mother were both unveiled. And that account, in which I have quoted much of my father's own direct and felicitous language in his own description of it, was indeed made an insert in the program for the musical that summer.

But you wanted to know, Did she actually look like that? Was her hair really such a blazing red? Such a ferocious fire? Couldn't help but notice, could you? Well, it's certainly true that the subject of a portrait, of any painting for that matter, may be a fiction. *The Great Gate of Kiev* which we see in Hartmann's painting and hear in Mussorgsky's piano music or in Ravel's orchestration of it, was never seen in Kiev, or anywhere else. Hartmann was an architect as well as a painter and neither his sensational design, entered in an architectural competition for a commemorative gate for Kiev, nor any other was ever actually built in Kiev.

But oh, yes! Yes indeed—Marjorie Lyons really *did* exist and her hair was every bit the blaze of bright yellow fire you saw in that portrait of her. It must have been one of those serendipities that follow genius-at-work when Fromkes found just the perfect pigment for that precious gold of her hair. I'm sure it's a pigment no longer to be found anywhere in the civilized western world. But *he* found it—the true color of my mother's own hair. A color never to be seen again anywhere in the world, save only in that portrait you saw.

I'm not aware of any attempt to photograph or otherwise reproduce that portrait in color. But you know, I might just try. I know someone who might be able to do it. Fletcher might. My friend, Fletcher Thorne-Thomsen.

Anyhow, here it is. The story I wrote for Bob. The story of how that portrait of my mother comes now to be a picture at an exhibition.

L'Allegro:
The Portrait of Marjorie Lyons

The story of a painting, it's provenance, how it was immediately lost to her posterity, how it was long searched for by her husband, Charlton Havard Lyons, how by him finally found and acquired and, at the last, come home to rest in the theatre which bears her name.

It was in the spring of 1917 that Maurice Fromkes, born in Poland on February 19, 1872 and died in Paris, France, on September 16, 1931, found himself in New Orleans, Louisiana, and while there painted portraits of three young women then students at Newcomb College. One was Clarisse Claiborne, a New Orleans beauty. Another was Elizabeth Learned, a belle of Natchez, Mississippi. The third was Marjorie Hall, hair of burnished gold and not long off her grandfather's farm in the far reaches of northwestern Wisconsin.

The painting of Marjorie Hall was a profile in oil. Wearing a blue, mandarin coat, Marjorie is looking at a Vandyke crayon sketch, details which, of course, she remembers with perfect clarity.

As the three girls were engaged by the artist, he took with him when he left New Orleans all three of those paintings. The whereabouts of the portraits of Miss Claiborne and of Miss Learned are to this day unknown. That the portrait of Marjorie did not also disappear forever into that same oblivion is the subject of this story, a tale which begins long, long ago, on August 28, 1917, at a wedding on the banks of Lake Chetek, a lake carved by the Wisconsin, the last of the great glaciations, the same lake to which Michael Hall, Marjorie's grandfather, had, beginning soon after the Civil War, brought by ox cart his large Irish family to camp for a summer week. For it was on that August 28th that Marjorie Hall married Charlton Havard Lyons.

Soon enough, Marjorie told her new husband of those three paintings and, again soon enough, he formed an attachment to that portrait of his wife, a likeness of her he had never seen, save through her eyes. Time passed, lots of time, almost half a century before

Charlton, knowing nothing of its whereabouts, finally began his patient search. Through friends in New York, inquiry was made at most of the leading galleries. None knew anything of the Fromkes portrait of Marjorie. Eventually, the Manager of one of the galleries—the Milch Gallery—did recall having several years before received a letter regarding a Fromkes' painting, a letter from a woman unknown. And so on his next trip to New York Charlton called at the Milch Gallery.

"Did the Manager by any chance still have that letter?"

"Oh, no, I'm sure we don't—not possibly. That letter came several years ago and we don't keep letters like that very long."

But Charlton, pleasantly, persistently: "Where do you keep your old letters?"

"In the basement."

"Would you mind if we went through your old letters together?"

"It's useless, utterly useless. A letter that old? Never!"

"Mister, this is a matter of the very greatest importance to me Please, please, let's go through those letters.

"Well, all right, but it'll be a waste of time."

And so it was that the Manager and Charlton descended into that place of long forgotten things, that oubliette, if I may, and began their search through the gallery's dusty files of old correspondence. Shortly the Manager looked up.

"Well, I'll be damned! The name of the client who wrote that letter is Mrs. Helen Blair. Here's her letter. She lives in Los Altos, California."

"I thank you, sir, and with all my heart."

As it happened, Charlton had planned to attend a meeting in San Francisco scheduled about three weeks later. He and Marjorie made the trip together. Charlton called Mrs. Helen Blair at the address shown in her letter. A woman answered and said that Mrs. Blair did not live there anymore.

"Do you own a Fromkes painting?"

"Never heard of Fromkes and I don't own any paintings."

"Who is Mrs. Helen Blair?"

"She is my mother."

"Where does she live?"

"Connecticut. Old Lyme, Connecticut."

Charlton and Marjorie returned home to Shreveport but Charlton was soon again in New York and called Mrs. Blair in Old Lyme. After introducing himself, Charlton asked, "Mrs. Blair, do you own a Fromkes portrait?"

"Yes, I do. I'm looking at it right now."

"Is it a profile of a red-haired girl looking at a Van Dyke crayon, the subject wearing a blue Mandarin coat?"

"Yes, it is."

"Would you mind if I came to Old Lyme and looked at that portrait?"

"No, but not now. This place is frozen over and I'm leaving on the first train that runs and I'll not be back until next summer. Call me in about three months. Now Mr. Lyons, when you come, are you going to try to pressure me into selling that painting to you?'

"No, Mrs. Blair, I would never pressure a lady, but I think it is fair to tell you that I would very much like to own it and I have ten grandchildren who feel the same."

"Mr. Lyons, that won't get you a thing. I have eleven grandchildren and each one of them adores that painting and, to tell you the truth, so do I." End of conversation.

Three months later (we are now in the summer of 1962) Charlton called Mrs. Blair and a day was set when he would come to Old Lyme, Mrs. Blair giving him the train schedule from New York and offering to meet him at the station. So come now with me and listen, as Charlton speaks to us in his own words.

"The train arrived at Old Lyme at about 11:30 a.m., on time. A lady of some 65 stepped up and asked, "Are you Mr. Lyons?" She was most unusual and interesting, plainly but neatly dressed. Wore a rather large straw hat. Her appearance indicated that she spent much time in the sun, perhaps gardening. We got in her car—a modest car—and she asked me if I had had lunch. I had not. She then suggested that we have lunch at an old inn on the outskirts of town. When they got out of the car, she picked up a wicker basket, 8 inches wide and a foot long. I thought it contained our lunch. I was wrong.

We sat down. She opened the basket. On one side was a bottle of scotch, on the other a bottle of bourbon.

'I drink scotch, Mr. Lyons, but you being a southerner, I thought you'd like bourbon?'

'Very thoughtful' I said 'but the scotch would please me very much.'

Hard for me to do at lunchtime, but we had a couple of drinks and I hadn't come so far to make myself objectionable. After a delicious luncheon, we drove to her home some ten miles in the country. Her home? A little gem! And a garden that only Marjorie could improve upon. We sat down and we talked and we talked and we talked. Politics, religion, family, trips. She, I learned, and not to my surprise, was a Republican and an Episcopalian.

During all this great, long while, more than two hours, not one word had been said about the portrait. By either of us. True, she'd shown me the portrait but I'd simply said,

'That's the portrait, no doubt of it.'

Finally, Mrs. Blair said, 'Mr. Lyons, what are you going to do about the portrait?' I thought she meant, how much would I pay for it? But I was never more wrong. I replied, 'Mrs. Blair, that is for you to say, the portrait is yours.' 'Oh, no, Mr. Lyons! You should have it, I want to give it to you.' I wanted to pay for it of course, and suggested an appraisal by an art dealer in New York. But Mrs. Blair refused to accept any payment at all, but she did finally agree that I could make a contribution to her church in Old Lyme, St. Anne's Episcopal Church."

There was more to the story of course, much, much more, but we might draw the curtain here on this little drama, The Portrait of Marjorie Lyons, a drama just 28 inches high and 32 inches wide. Draw it closed or open, either way you like. At the end, after he had had the portrait completely and beautifully renovated and had brought it home with him to Shreveport, Charlton received one final word from Mrs. Blair, a letter dated October 17, 1962.

"Dear Mr. Lyons,
Your letter came just before I left home to come here to New Hampshire, and I had no chance to answer. However, I did

send the check to the assistant treasurer of the Building Fund for the Church and it was most gratefully received. Am sure that you will receive an acknowledgement. My appreciation for the amount of the check is great, and I think you were most generous. I would never have dared to suggest as large an amount. Therefore, from the point of view of St. Anne's, I guess I was wise.

I hope that you and Mrs. Lyons, as well as your children and grandchildren, have many, many years of pleasure from the lovely portrait.

Congratulations on your appointment as a national committeeman.

With renewed thanks for your generosity, I am

                                            Very sincerely,

                                            Helen Blair"

Le Tombeau d'Alexander Pope

THE ZEBRESS
Or Lines on a Lady

By Charlton Lyons, Jr.

A woman's hid in every verse that's writ,
And she sultana reigns omnipotent.
At once besparkled rhymes her eyes inspire:
Her eyes, these rhymes, reciprocally require.
Twin fires ingeminate their own alarms;
Twin twins reduplicate the other's charms.
The rhythms of her walk the like demand
Of verse. How graceful is her treading scanned!
Behold proportion's noblest form and grace,
How irony is imaged in her face.
Preposterous though her catechism be,
Reversing first and last, kind and degree,
Instructs she yet her one consistency:
Where clearly wrong, affection is her plea.
But hark! How that the minstrel means his song:
If he sings right, she's virginal to wrong.
Two pangs this poet feels of perfect joy:
When inspiration flames and flames destroy.
So twice in life his woman's faults grow dim;
Both when she weds and when she widows him.
As ceaseless as her talk my numbers flow;
Of neither weary will I ever grow.

The Yale Literary Magazine – Fall - 1942
The Oldest Monthly Magazine in America
(By courtesy of the poet.)

It was late the other evening when you asked me if I'd ever written poetry, remember? And I told you I didn't know how to answer because I just wasn't sure what's poetry and what's not, right? Then you allowed as how I was nuts, and that's when I told you to take a number. To be perfectly frank, I was glad to hear it because that's what convinced me I could rely on you for the truth.

But since you asked the question, here's something you might look at. Found it under glass in the Beinecke Rare Book Room. I had a short story in that issue, too. But here's something I wrote my freshman year at Yale. *The Zebress*. It's a little homage to Pope, so you might see it as being not *really* poetry at all. Anyhow, take a look at it, while I go and bruise up some mint and handcraft you something kind of special. Now don't wander off somewhere, because I'll be right back!

Behold! A matched pair! A mint julep for you and one for your horse. You say it *looks* too much like poetry *not* to be poetry, that's what you think? Well, just two hundred years ago, toward the end of the eighteenth century, there were lots and lots of folks who would have said that certainly was *not* poetry. That it wasn't even *like* poetry. Too much like Alexander Pope, they'd say—pretentious doggerel, stuff like that. Pope was burnt toast by then, you see. But when I wrote it, that's just what I wanted to hear—that it was like Pope. Because at that particular time, I had Pope's voice in my head and I couldn't hear anything else. Pope'll do that to you.

When I was at Yale, I had a teacher the first year named Maynard Mack. Just ten of us in the class and Maynard taught us how to read Pope. Well—how to *read*. Maynard was more than my teacher, really, he made himself my friend. Teachers'll do that, good ones. Sometimes. What you're looking at there, I don't know if it's poetry or not. Don't much care either, because I wrote it as an obeisance—my obeisance to Pope. As homage to him and to Maynard, too. Remind me to tell you about a way of reading that was conceiving itself at Yale while I was there. It came to be called *New Criticism*, but this was in 1940 that I wrote that poem, and I rather doubt that it was called *New Criticism* quite that early.

About that poem, as I say, it was my attempt to honor Pope by imitating him. At that time, I was an extraordinarily sincere young man. So think of it as my *Tombeau* to Pope. You've heard Ravel's piece, *Le Tombeau de Couperin*? Yes, you hear it a lot. *Tombeau*, of course, is French for tomb, and people do place flowers on their tombs in memory of their dead. But here, despite that title, Ravel wasn't writing in memory of Couperin and Couperin's time, so much as he was in memory of his own friends who'd died in the *First* World War.

Remember Horace? *dulc'et décor'est pro patria mori*? Since I first began to look back at my life, that sort of thing's been in my mind a lot. Because I lost friends myself in our war, and I'm afraid that every single one of them has now been long forgotten by everyone but me. I think about one in particular. One who was killed when not long out of my sight. So I'd give almost anything if I could do something myself—something like what Ravel did in memory of his friends who died in his war. If only I could just find a way to express the way I feel about all those friends of mine who gave away their lives in ours. If only I could see them once again, long enough to embrace them just a little minute and tell them how well they did.

Of course, Ravel did want also to call up the music of Couperin's time, and he does that simply by calling his ghost up from the grave. Pope, of course, was composing his music at the same time that Couperin was composing his. And me—I'm trying to do somewhat the same thing for Pope. Trying to let the poem speak of Pope by playing his kind of music, in hopes of calling up his ghost.

But there's more to it than that. *Tomb* is not the *only* meaning of *tombeau*. *Tombeau*'s got another meaning. One specific to music. A meaning in which it was used long before Ravel was born, but of which Ravel was certainly well aware. Back in Couperin's time, *Tombeau*, was a word which, among musicians, meant a piece of music written to memorialize something or someone. So you might say that *The Zebress* is my *tombeau* to Pope.

Pope was only four and a half feet tall. Even Kant was six inches taller than that! But short as he was, Pope was himself, the very height of reason. That's why they named the whole damned century after him. The age of reason. Mankind's always been balanced on a seesaw between reason and emotion anyway. Both of them swear they're just seeking equilibrium. Homeostasis. That's what they *say*, but damned if they do! Reason's a Poland China and passion's a Chester White. Hogs can't see *anything* as grey. Bet you didn't know that. You may recall me telling you that Pater had said something rather interesting about music, but that I couldn't remember what it was, remember that? Well, I finally thought of it and I've printed it up for you and here it is. Go ahead, take it home with you. Stick it up on your ice box door. Study on it and it'll change your life.

All art constantly aspires towards the condition of music.

> Walter Horatio Pater
> *The School of Georgione*

Pater's absolutely right, too! Music *is* the elixir of life—the drug of choice. That's because it goes, unmediated, straight into the arteries—right into our own consanguineous blood. Because music's native in us, you know, it's there at our birth. We're born with the same sure foreknowledge of its materials and design as that possessed by the bird who goes about building her nest with no mother to guide her, no how-to book in her hand. People are born to dance and sing. Music's our natural language, the one language we all can speak. Write it down.

One of my five daughters, Marian, the youngest, when three could hear a song sung once around our piano and the next night sing it herself, dead square in the middle of every note. My daughter Sally Scott was the third of the clutch of them and she was a natural mathematician. For Sally, mathematics was simply something she'd learnt elsewhere and before.

And there's something I saw myself when I drove down one year for the final campfire at the girl's summer camp that Sally loved. My God! You wouldn't believe so much raw emotion! That was the year their tears put out the final campfire, and I'm not under exaggerating! Sally had picked up a stray guitar while she was there and taught herself to play it, and she played and sang to me in the car all the six hours home. And you wonder how such a thing as that can be? Just one reason. We don't come aboard wholly ignorant of seamanship and sail.

Tell you something kind of wonderful about Sally. Funny, too. When Sally was a little girl, maybe nine or ten, her mother and I took her to see the movie *Psycho*. That was my first wife, Susybelle, she was the fine mother of all my children. Of course *Psycho* was not appropriate for a child her age, but Susybelle and I didn't know that. We thought it was just another movie. But as matters worsened—you remember Norman's mother at the end?—I became more and more concerned about the effect Norman and his ma were having on Sally, but what could I do? So as we were walking up the aisle after the movie ended, I asked her, *What did you think of the movie, Sally?* She knew without thinking what she thought of it, *That boy certainly did love his mother!* Even as a little girl, when Sally would drink, she drew the bucket from deep in the well.

Remember when I was talking about those two different hogs, reason and passion? Well, music's both of them. It's the whole hog, if you like. Because it's classic and it's romantic and all in the same breath. It's reason and passion, form and feeling, number and chaos. And yeah, Apollo and Mercury, too. Whatever you like! It's only music that can compass the poles, can quit us of this surly, old, pedestrian earth and bear us high, high aloft, as on the wings of angels, towards the stars. *Per aspera ad astra*, what?

Suffering *zee langueur*, are we? Don't blame you. Got carried away there. Happens sometimes. That third julep'll do it to you every time. Oh, I see. You're just tired of hearing so much talk about music? Me too. So—how about a complete change of subject, something entirely new and different? All right, now. How would you like to hear about the week Richard Strauss and I spent as next door neighbors in Garmisch? Right after the war ended? Not now, hunh? Well then, let's go off in another direction. Why don't I sing you a song before you have to head for home?

OK now, here's a brisk little ditty. It's something I dreamed up the words to all by myself. You'll be the first one to hear it. Oh? Likely, also the last, you say? Well, like I said, you're now the truth teller around here.

Anyway, I've set this to an old familiar tune that's just right for it. No, not the Star Spangled banner, that's too tough for most people to sing—you need to be a highly trained musician. You know, someone like me. Careful now, I've got to pitch this just right.

> I went to the musical fair,
> The fife and the drum were there.
> The bold bassoon, to a ragged time tune,
> Was crooning his aubade air.
>
> Charlton Lyons – 2006
> (By courtesy of the lyricist)

Opus 2

Menu-ette

Here's that recipe I promised you. It's one of my best, a barbecue sauce. Wonderful on everything from pickled peacock's tongue to Post Toasties. Superb on chickens. Doves, too. Spare ribs? You bet! Get those baby back ribs now! Don't get those others!

<u>The Lyons' Oily-chops Barbecue Sauce</u>
Place in a large sauce pan, warming it as you go so as to produce a fluid interlarded with the solids:
- 1 pound of oleo (or butter, but oleo's just fine)
- 1 large bottle of A-1 Sauce
- ½ bottle of <u>good</u> commercial Worchester Sauce or better yet, an equivalent volume of the homemade Worchester Sauce for which the recipe appears later below
- 1 lemon – all of the juice and ½ of the shell
- Chopped fresh garlic to taste
- 4 satisfying dollops of Chili Sauce
- 1 bay leaf
- 1 onion – after removing the dry, wrapper leaves just drop the whole onion right in there—plop!,
- Salt, Black Pepper and Tabasco to taste

Do Not <u>Cook</u> This Sauce At Any Stage!

Just before use on cooked or cooking meats, sprinkle chopped parsley (fresh if at all possible!) liberally over the sauce, now cozy-warm, nut-brown and almost finished in the pan.

NB: This sauce freezes very well and keeps for long periods of time. Also, and importantly, two nationally known writers on food and food preparation have opined that although no scientific proof is as yet in place, there already exists a large and ever mounting mass of anecdotal evidence to the effect that this sauce is a specific both against borborygmus and against erectile dysfunction.

The Worcestershire Sauce your grandmother always wished she could make.

1-tablespoon olive oil
6 ounces fresh horseradish, peeled and chopped
2 medium onions, diced
2 jalapeno peppers, seeded and finely diced
6 cloves garlic, peeled and chopped
¾ teaspoon coarsely ground fresh black pepper
2 cups water
4 cups white vinegar
3 cups dark molasses
1 ounce anchovy fillets (8 to 12), chopped
12 whole cloves
1 tablespoon salt
1 lemon, peeled and chopped
1 lime, peeled and chopped
tamarind to taste

Place the oil, horseradish, onions, jalapenos and garlic in a large pot, and sauté over medium heat until the onions are translucent. Add the black pepper, water, vinegar, molasses, corn syrup, anchovy, cloves, salt, lemon and tamarind. Mix thoroughly and bring to a boil. Simmer over low to medium heat for 1 hour, or until the mixture coats the back of a spoon.

Strain through a fine sieve into a medium saucepan. Reduce by half over low to medium heat. The sauce should have a slightly syrupy consistency. As it cools, it will thicken. When covered, it can be refrigerated up to two months.

Makes 3 cups.

Seems like weeks now, we've been sitting here around the pool in the evening, me talking about olden days and you coaxing me to stop talking about it and write it down. Make a book of it, you say. Tell you what Samuel Johnson said. That's Dr. Sam Johnson. Well, Boswell says he said it, so I guess he did. Sam said that the man who writes for any reason other than the money that's in it, that man is a blockhead. Now, you wouldn't want people going around calling me a blockhead, would you? Course not, I didn't think you would. What's that? Oh, you think I just might not come off looking so bad after all, do you? Well, there *was* a time when I was a dreamer. But that was a long time ago. From about 1935 until after the war. A dreamer of very dreamy dreams. Thought I'd be a writer, sure did.

Speaking of Johnson, here's something else I seem to remember about him. Didn't he express a strong aversion to biographies that began with a pedigree and ended with an obituary? Sounds like him anyway. What do you think his reaction would have been to a life story which actually *began* with an obit? Just a thought.

But as a boy, what I happened to be doing was what I liked doing. Didn't matter much what it was. As a young man, too. I went to law school after the war, and all the way through I thought I'd practice law. Not transactional law of course! No, no! Litigation! But as things turned out, I became neither a writer nor a lawyer. No, in both instances I finally decided that I'd work for a living instead.

But you'll be glad to know that I didn't flat turn my back on that book thing of yours. No, I thought about what you said and the first thing I decided was that if I were ever to write a book, I ought to write it in the first person, don't you think? What say? Oh, no, no, you misunderstand! Not the first person singular! Everyone does that. No, I meant, in the singular first person. That would be more like me. I've even taken a step or two in that direction. Looked around, just in case.

That's right, I've been thinking I might find a use for the money, because money's a pleasant thing to have on hand, you know? But what worries me about writing a book is that it would be just my bad luck for it to become a huge commercial success and there I'd be—suddenly faced with a humongous income tax problem. Which is something I don't need right now. I mean an income tax problem. Right? So I've definitely decided not to write that book. Nope, I've got to pass it up. Heck-fire, I just can't afford all that extra income.

But while I was thinking about it, I did make my own study of the market place, and the first thing I did was read up on the book business. Book publishing, you know. Because there's nothing fancy or high-brow about it. It's just another cottage-industry. Bunch of people in it just for the money, and right quick I found that the most merchantable item in the whole damn business is the *how-to* book.

This will surprise you but people are not much interested in things of the mind. If they can't see and touch it, well, it just doesn't exist. They're interested in the right-here and the right-now, that's the fact of it. Did you know that there are more than fifty thousand new titles published every year in this country? Imagine that! Oh, no, I'm not much given to self-deception and I can tell you that any book I'd write would be just like me—remaindered! A big, fat anachronism. Out-of-print. Even my natural readership won't be buying it, for crying out loud! Too long past their bedtime. They're all fast asleep now, their graves scattered about all over the earth.

But anyway, I did go to my favorite book boutique, Tower Book Shop, looked around there and then I went to that Barnes and Noble. You never in your life saw such a great surfeit and clutteration of books as they've got in there. Laying around all over the place! Half naked! Right on top of each other, too! Look, I'm going to get us both just one more cup of kindness. Be right back.

There you are! Cheers! Let's see now—oh yeah, we were where I was looking around in that book store. Now, I've always heard they breed like rats in there, those books do, and I can believe it. Do it at night. After lock up, when they've got the whole place to themselves. Can't you just see them in there, in that Barnes & Noble, all piled up together in the dark, all those books with nothing to do all night long but fornicate around, this way and that, recombining all that DNA into be-jillions of little baby books to flood a market that's already full fathom five? Can't you just see it? You think I'd exaggerate about a thing like that? No way!

Makes you feel awful sorry for all those trees they batten on, too. Cause that's when they go into their feeding frenzy. After the sex. Devouring whole trees, whole forests of trees, perfectly good trees, too, chopped down before their time only to be transmogrified into wood pulp fiction. And now you want me to add my own innocent little baby book to that repulsive pile of lascivious, lecherous lust? Hell no! I won't do it and wild horses couldn't make me!

But I did come to one conclusion about that book business. It's all about money. And money's a people-thing, and what the people want, that's where the money is. So what kind of books do people want anyway? You're right—they do! You guessed it right off. Cook books! Can you believe it!

So while my mind was off its chain—you know, doing my free-ballooning thing about writing for money?—I decided I'd better consider doing recipes. A cook book. And while I was making all that money, I might as well serve humanity at the same time and memorialize about forty of my own best recipes. Some of them old family recipes, too. Never given out. Worth a fortune. I ought not do it, I suppose—give away those cherished family secrets, but there's plenty of money in it and anyway, if I don't do it, they're sure to be lost to posterity forever. I've got to think about that, don't I? High culture? The culinary arts? They've got to be worth some sacrifice. Right?

Nowadays, a book—doesn't have to be a cook book—any book ought to have at least two or three recipes in it. Somewhere right up front, too. In the first few chapters. I can see that book jacket now, just look there! The blurb on that jacket says it right out loud. This book's got just what you want, folks—*recipes.* And look there at the photo of the author! See, he's in full, living color, standing there in front of his barbecue pit. And that barby's stainless steel, too, wouldn't you just know it? Industrial strength! Oh yeah, he's proud as punch. Thinks he's a maharajah, looking so spiffy there in his cooking costume. Tall white hat on his head, silly shit-eating grin on his face. That's the way they all look on those book jackets these days, all those published authors? You noticed?

And let's see now, what else have we got here? Oh yeah, that barby! Look at her, that barby's smoking up a storm. Flames shooting out every which way. She's already hot as a firecracker and if they don't do something quick, she's going to erupt for sure! Blow right up! But that cat's cool, see. He's no more concerned than Pliny was just before the eruption of Vesuvius or—or Shadrach, Meshack and Tobedwego in the face of the fiery furnace.

And look at him! Look at that rascal! You see, he knows he's a published author, so what's he doing? He's trying to out-smoke that barby—sure is! See the smoke curling up from that big, fat, handmade cigar he's got there in his left hand, you see that? And oh, my! Just look! Look what he's got in his other hand there! He's holding one of those big, fat foot-long hot dogs and he's smoking that sucker too. And what's that he's got there on the fire? Chickens! He sure has. Broilers! Now that picture there, that's nothing but pure, literary genius. Sell ten thousand copies and you better believe it! First day!

Now I grew up when chickens were raised on the ground. Not on wire in those chicken factories they keep now. You bought them live, too, feet tied up till their time came and their necks were wrung and they were left to flop around on the ground. And they'd some of them get up on their legs, too, they sure would, and they'd run around all over the place for a while—with their heads off, mind you. Like— like, well, just like chickens with their heads cut off. Sometimes be ten minutes before they'd go down for the count. That's the way I saw it done as a boy. Up there in Northern Wisconsin.

Down South here, you saw chickens in people's yards everywhere out in the country. Half the people out there on the land had a hen house. Guinea fowl, too. Not just in the country, either. Even as late as 1948 when I came back here from law school to go to work in the oil field, chickens were being kept on the sixth floor roof of one of our principal office buildings right down town. The Ricou-Brewster building. Our little old offices were on the eighth floor of the building directly across the street. The Giddens-Lane

Building, and we could look down and see them. Forty or fifty of them down there. White Rocks and Rhode Island Reds. Mr. and Mrs. Ricou lived in that building, had an apartment in it, and one of them was up there on that roof, two—three times a day, throwing scratch. And that was right here where we are, in Shreveport. The very centrum of hometown city, directly across from the courthouse.

Lots of people had chicken coops then. Fine people, too. Kept chickens so they could have fresh *huevos rancheros* and chicken salad. People used to think nothing of it. But now they do. Just last year, right here in hometown, a doctor and his wife started keeping three or four hens in a coop in their yard. Just pets for their children you know? Well, someone new moved into the neighborhood and started squawking about it. That lady squawked a heap louder than those chickens ever did. Raised herself up a little cabal and took it to the planning commission and there was a big debate there before the commission ruled against her. Almost unanimous, it was. So then she appealed it to the city council and the council, they turned around and voted against the chickens. Four to three. Can you imagine that? Voting *against* chickens? But then I suppose that on most days of a man's life, the fish don't bite, the ducks don't fly, and reason sleeps.

And don't think this was some minor little dust-up either! The testimony in the minutes of that one city council meeting ran to some one hundred and seventy column inches in our newspaper! Some of it was quite acrimonious. Ad hominem, even ad personam. Only one member of the council had troubled to go see those chickens for himself. Fact is, nowadays not more than a handful of the folks here in hometown have ever *seen* a chicken coop. The clerk couldn't even spell it. Everywhere in those minutes it's spelled *coup*. And at another place in those minutes we are informed that a neighbor had testified that a *fowl deed*—so help me!—was being perpetrated against those innocent chickens. It's not only the chicken that's fallen into parlous times but orthography itself.

Last I heard, the chicken owners had taken the council to court. I tell you, people living in that very real world that existed during the first third of my life, people still in touch with nature, had they sat through that hearing, would have walked out, well assured that our hometown had become simply a safe haven for public and private insanity.

That doctor and his family live in a beautiful old home not four blocks up Fairfield Avenue from where a friend of mine used to live. Randolph Marston. He's dead now, of course, but he kept a fresh Jersey cow almost till the day he died. Kept it there in his yard. What did you say? In the front yard? Hell no, not in the front yard! In the back yard! Just cause Randolph kept a cow don't mean he came from one of those places way far back there in the woods where the owls don't hoot. Hell, no! Randolph lived in a handsome mansion, there at the intersection of Fairfield and Kings Highway. Right in the midst of some of our finest old homes, if you don't mind! A milk cow in Randolph's front yard? I'm going to tell Randolph what you said. That is, if I ever run across him again.

I make a joke of it, but sometimes I have the saddest thoughts when I talk like this about those ways we had. Hard to believe that so much time has slept itself away while my back was turned, but it has, and now it seems always on my mind. You see, never again will I hear my father whistle up the dogs so we can go bird hunting. No more will any of us hear the slow, rhythmic ka-chunk of the felling axe coming through the winter woods. And oh my God!—that rush, that sense of life lived to the glorious hilt that came over you when you found yourself going like sixty down a dirt road, riding the rumble seat of a roan-red 1932 Ford coupé. And all of that was only yesterday. What ever happened to olden times? What happened to those days of auld lang syne? *Ubi sunt?*

Ubi sunt? Come on now, you know what I'm talking about. You don't? *Ubi sunt?* Well—first off, it's Latin of course. And it's elliptical, I mean, there's some more to it, I can't remember what. But it just asks a question, that's all. Where are they? That's all it says, at least when read word for word. Where are they? But it means more than that, a lot more. What's happened to everybody? That's what it means. Where'd they all go? What happened to it all?

There are whole libraries of books that do nothing but ask that question, but Latin does it in just two words. If I were ever to be dumb enough to write that book you keep throwing up to me, I'd probably also be dumb enough to title it *Ubi Sunt*. Or some other title equally certain not to sell. So, just who is it you think is out there that wants to hear some windy, superannuated old fart blow it out his barracks bag?

But Latin's dense, you know. Lean, hard, efficient. Not fat, like English. That's why Latin's such a fine voice for poetry. The language those old Roman writers used was their sword, their *gladius*. No, no, Latin wasn't meant to waive grandly about in the heroic air. It was meant for stabbing. One deft motion, straight to the heart of the matter. That's why those old poets didn't have to go back again and again, revisit, rewrite, rewrite, compress. They never had to squeeze the fat out of what they wrote because it was lean to the bone to begin with.

As I say, English is just the opposite. The fattest language ever spoke by man. Corpulent to the power of X. Just take my old 1953 OED in there! Nothing in it but words. Three linear feet, gorged with English words. Why, it's nothing but a yard-long, suet sausage! And not a picture in it! Can you believe that? Not one!

But you know what? I've always had a sweet tooth for fat. I just love it, don't you? Now don't be ashamed to admit it, because the whole history of man is nothing but the record of his ceaseless search for fat. And when I say fat, I mean, specifically, *animal* fat. That's the drive that's made man the king of the beasts. That's right, our search for animal fat. Well, salt's been nice, and honey, too, but mostly fat.

And that's one more reason I should never undertake that book you've been flattering me to write. I wouldn't be free to blather away. I'd have to go back and wring the lard out of it. Because if I didn't—well, you know what the critics would say! No, I'd want my writing to be more like me, more like the way I talk. You know—slathered with lard? I wouldn't want to write *writing* anyhow. I'd write *talking*. That's more in my line of work—talking is. You know what I mean?

Speaking of chickens, do you know the etymology of orange marmalade? How it got that name? No? Well, way back there, people used to save their kitchen scraps—throw them out in the yard for the chickens, did you know that? Well, they did. Now, I heard this from a professor of agronomy, and him being a full professor,

I'm satisfied it's true. He said that one day a lady out in the country had an orange go sour, so she threw it out in the chicken yard, where she kept an old hen and a bunch of little biddies, and by and by one little chick happened over, and when she saw that orange lying there, she hollered out, *come on over here, kids, and see the orange mama laid.*

Did you know that Louisiana is now the only state in the Union where cock fighting is still legal? That's right, the free state of Louisiana. In the great majority of states, cockfighting is not only illegal, it's a *felony*. But it's legal here, and if you're wondering how such a thing could be, go down to Baton Rouge and sit in while our legislature's in session. Oh, our politicians are forever mouthing off about our state's *image*. How we're *perceived* by the media. A bunch of cockfighting Neanderthals who have succeeded in institutionalizing political corruption and enthroning our own peculiar mix of red-neck roister and Mediterranean decadence—that's what the rest of the country says about us. Of course, that *does* make our politicians put on their worry faces. And they *are* worried, too. But about how we *appear*. They're not one damn bit worried about who we actually *are*! Or who *they* are either—our legislature.

To show you how queer-headed people have become in this important matter of chickens, they're selling some now they call *free-range* chickens. That just means they're raised on the ground the way all chickens used to be. Well, that's only how they say they raise them! Who knows what they actually *do*. But no matter, they cost you extra anyhow. Now these free–range chickens I'm talking about, they're not *live* chickens—you understand that? No, they're dead as salt mackerel. You can't wring their necks. Nothing like that. People wouldn't know how to do that anyway.

But now I think about it, people could learn how, couldn't they? Learn all over again. Sure they could! Grocery stores could conduct classes, you see. Right out in front of the store. On the parking lot. Perfect place! Conduct classes on wringing chickens. Award certificates of proficiency when they'd worked their way up to wringing a dozen in twelve minutes, one a minute. All of them got to be flopping and running around out there on the tarmac at the same time for it to count. Naturally, there'd have to be judges for that, and them judges, they'd all be out there, too, flouncing around in their chicken costumes. Synchronizing their stop watches. And them and all them chickens, why they'd be running around out there together, all over the place. Have their tail feathers sticking straight up. Stuff like that. Draw a hell of a crowd, too, sure would! Wouldn't you be there?

Hey! Where you going? Come on back, now. That was just some of that nutty stuff I warned you about, remember? It comes out sometimes when I've been drinking. When I feel like indulging myself in the odd flight of fancy. But look here, I don't really see what's so damn wrong with an old man humoring himself once in a while, do you? Even an old fossil can remember what it was like to be young— when he'd sometimes dance a little jig, and do it for no good reason at all, other than just the sheer hell of it.

Well, OK, I understand. But be careful on your way out to the street. It's getting dark out there!

Requiem for two innocents come from Lebanon

Have you ever been to Lebanon? No? Well, I was there once. It was in the late summer of 1974, a third of a century ago and just before the eruption of that long revolution that laid waste that little country and sacked and burnt Beirut. That was also during the time that my life was fraught with a five year passage across that vast and stormy sea called self-elected single-hood. If you've never found yourself in that boat, you're forever wondering whether you'll ever find your way safe across those treacherous waters to the further shore. I finally did, thank God! But anyhow, during that tumultuous time, I took myself off twice to Europe, just to look about over there again. That's when I went to Beirut, and it was worth the trip just to see the souks, for Beirut was then the fragile, polyglot, many cultured, at once marginally, and highly, civilized capital of the Near East. Think of it as being then the Paris of that far corner of the world.

It began right here, around this pool. I was sitting right here when I was invited by two young and very attractive Lebanese friends I'd only just met, to come over and visit them in their country. A young couple from Lebanon vacationing in this country, Vera and Tony Frangieh. They had become friends in Beirut of my good friends, Bob and Phyllis Oakley, who'd sent them here to hometown to spend a few days with Bob's mother, before they headed on west.

But let me stop off here a minute and tell you a bit about Bob and Phyllis. Both enjoyed long and distinguished careers as Foreign Service Officers before they retired, but at the time of my visit there, Bob was serving as head of the Political Section in the American Embassy in Beirut, and his desk was then much concerned with Arafat. Arafat and the PLO were, in fact, headquartered close by, on the outskirts of Beirut, and, as you can imagine, very confidential exchanges were then taking place between our Secretary of State, Kissinger, and Arafat. Exchanges even the existence of which neither would have wanted revealed. Exchanges in which Bob would sometimes act as our unofficial contact with Arafat and the PLO.

Bob went on later from Beirut to the State Department and the staff of the National Security Council and followed that with services as our Ambassador, first to Zaire, then to Somalia and, finally, to Pakistan. While in Beirut, Phyllis, although herself a handsome, very able, beautifully spoken and experienced Foreign Service Officer, could not serve as one because she was married to Bob. But soon after their tenure in Beirut, the rules were changed and Phyllis resumed the career she had given up to marry Bob. Phyllis would twice become Assistant Secretary of State for refugees, and also for intelligence, an experience she couldn't tell me very much about, since it involved some of the hush-hush of sword and dagger,

But it was here in Shreveport that I first came to know a little, and to like a lot, their young and delightful friends, Vera and Tony Frangieh, both so innocent, it seemed to me. They loved lazing around my pool here so much that they came over almost every day during their brief stay. Now as fortune would have it, I had plans myself to leave in a few weeks for Vienna and a ten day stay down in Graz, Austria, visiting with Stafford, one of my five daughters, who was there with her opera-singer husband, and when Tony and Vera heard this, they urged me to come from Vienna down to Beirut. As did Phyllis and Bob. So that's how I came to leave Austria—in August, wasn't it?—and visit Lebanon, both as Vera and Tony's American friend and as the Oakley's house guest in their quarters nicely situated on the *Corniche* that runs along the Mediterranean between the Embassy and the American University to the south.

I was there in Lebanon only ten days or so, but I quickly learned that although the actual violence was as yet of a relatively low order for Lebanon, the intrigue itself among all factions was intense and mounting and that the country was in fact already a tinderbox ready to burst into flame. And of course soon after I left, it did explode into a civil war that lasted for the next fifteen years or so.

Despite that, I was able to visit nearly the whole of its seacoast, from Tripoli all the way down to Sidon. Even Sidon was not a particularly safe place to be. I mean, one didn't want to wander about in there. Certainly not on foot, so my tour of Sidon was made entirely through the windshield. But Tyre, now! Tyre was out of the question! Even back in those days, no one in his right mind went down to Tyre!

As I say, soon after I left Lebanon that whole Byzantine place turned to welter and waste. Nor was that the first time I had found myself escaping just ahead of the terror. Back in the nineteen fifties, possibly a year, maybe longer, before Castro seized Cuba from Fulgencio Batista, I was in Havana seeing two old friends there. Two brothers, Joe and Tony Benitoa, who'd been for five years my friends and classmates when I was a boy at boarding school in the East. The Benitoas were closely related to the Batista regime. In fact, Tony Benitoa's wife was Batista's daughter, so they were in grave danger when, not long after I left Havana, the Cuban revolution broke over them. Joe and Tony and their families did somehow manage to escape out of Cuba alive. But my other foreign friends, Vera and Tony Frangieh, they were not so fortunate. So, twice now in my life it's been *après moi, le deluge*.

This'll give you some idea of how things were in the Lebanon of those days. I remember very clearly an evening dinner party at which the Oakleys and I were guests. Our host was a former Lebanese Army General who held aspirations for the presidency as successor to Tony's father. I guess I forgot to tell you. Tony's father, Suleiman, was the President of Lebanon, and so, young though he was, Tony was a person of some distinction. And, as I discovered only last year, his was not a distinction based solely upon that of his father but one he'd earned himself. Earned by his own gun, even before I knew him.

Anyway, our host's apartment constituted the top floor of a small apartment building of perhaps four or five stories and when we arrived, there were numerous guards stationed all around the building. All in uniform. Heavily armed. Live ammo. That's true! Live ammo!

We dined al fresco. Perhaps thirty of us at tables set out on the veranda which surrounded two sides of the apartment and onto which the large principal room let out. Soon after we were seated and as we were being served, machinegun fire was heard coming from close by. If you've ever heard it, you know that the sound of machine gun fire coming from close by is rather difficult to disregard. I myself knew instantly what it was of course but so, obviously, did everyone else, as they all became suddenly silent, looking towards our host, who arose and left us sitting there. You see, this was not something new to these people. They lived with it every day and so they just sat there in silence, patiently waiting. Can you imagine living everyday in the midst of all that?

Presently, the General quietly returned to his place and the buzz of talk slowly resumed. It was strange, I thought, that our host had made no announcement, no explanation for the gunfire. But no, the word had instead been very quietly, very discretely, very knowingly, passed from table to table. No need for us to worry. Just the usual gunfire being let off by their Palestinian guests, venting their frustrations from an encampment close by. They were, of course, that little nascent army in mufti that the world would come to know as Hezbollah.

Phyllis and Bob were wonderful hosts, taking me with them everywhere. So were Tony and Vera, who came around half the days I was there. I remember Tony taking me to the presidential palace so that I might meet his father, Suleiman Frangieh. Tony's father was not only the president of the country but a sovereign of the whole Frangieh clan, a clan of rough mountain people constantly engaged in some kind of war, if not with the competing Gemayel clan, then among themselves. The Gemayels were yet another clan of Maronite Catholics and they, too, had produced presidents and other political leaders, for under the Lebanese constitution, their country's President is *required* to be a Maronite Christian. A very exotic place, politically and otherwise.

Think of those clans as the Hatfields and the McCoys. Or better yet, the Shepherdsons and the Grangerfords, the family names Twain devised specifically to invoke the mythopoeic power of Abel and Cain. *The Sea of Grass* comes to mind. The whole scene reminiscent of Shakespeare. The Capulets and the Montagues. But in Lebanon there was no prince to halt their bloody encounters. No ruler threatening death to those seeking justice with the sword. So *lex talionis*, and in its most atavistic form, was then the law of the land. Retributive justice, not by the state but by the clan.

I'm wondering—is that law something with which we humans are not actually born but must be carefully taught? Or is it a part of that deep grammar, that suite of precognitions with which we most certainly *do* come into this life? Good question. One, no doubt the subject of many a doctoral dissertation. Sure to be. Personally, I think it can't be answered. That's what makes it such a good question. Don't you agree? That's the awful truth of the matter—we're not at all sure *who* we are.

One day Tony and Vera and their little daughter—she was very, very small and as dear a little child as you ever saw—took me with them up to Tripoli, where they kept a *pied-à-terre* and where, for the first time and at first hand, I saw a very different Tony from the one I had first come to know around the pool here. The Antoine Frangieh who was the President's son. The son, in fact, to whom his father, Suleiman, owed his presidency. But that was something about him I didn't know at first. I saw him then simply as a very nice young man who'd come here from the Near East for a visit.

But there in Tripoli, I realized that Tony was something much more than that. That he was in fact an important, if irregular, functioning part of the fabric of their still-Byzantine polity, because awaiting Tony in his apartment when we arrived were some dozen or so suppliants, each of whom it was Tony's duty to receive and to hear out. Sorry if I seem to make fun, but I can best picture them for you in just the way I first set eyes on them, sitting about on the floor, wearing their Jesus shoes and robed as they were when playing supporting roles to Peter O'Toole in *Lawrence Of Arabia*. Each a character straight from central casting. Look-alikes of Omar Sharif or Anthony Quinn, and every one of them in costume and character.

The scene was so surreal that no one could forget it. Tony himself, dressed in the Western style, sitting there as though on a throne. And the way the set itself was dressed. You see, Tony, like every male of the Near East, both then and now it seems, was obsessed with weapons and hung all about that apartment was a huge collection of them. Guns of every caliber, sort and variety, every fashion and age. Blunderbusses were there, as I recall. Tony could even sport a few rocket launchers! It's true, he did! They were, in fact, an especially fetching feature of the décor.

Everything in that scene was vintage *Lawrence*. Everything, that is, but the three of us, Vera and Vera's beautiful little daughter and me, sitting apart on our straight-backed chairs. Or maybe it was we who were the most surreal. Maybe it was we three who were most needed to lend the scene its final, oriental truth as *Lawrence*.

Just imagine that little girl sitting there, all dressed up for her parents' new friend from America. Wearing her flowered frock, her little white shoes dangling from her feet as she sat so patiently there beside her mother. Although she remained silent as a little owl, she was especially proud of those new shoes. I knew that because she was forever moving them about in little ways that I'd be sure to notice. I had had five daughters myself, five little girls like her, so I well knew that it's in the nature of little girls—well, grown women suffer from it, too, of course—to expect us men, on our own and without benefit of instruction, to register all sorts of such important feminine niceties. Why they continue to expect so much of us when their whole experience is to the contrary is a question for the ages.

Then, with those formalities done and favors granted or withheld, the four of us drove up into the mountains that rise steep above Tripoli, to the Frangieh's family home. Well, their *fortified stronghold* above Zgharta. That's where I met Tony's mother. I don't recall her name, but she was a gracious and lovely lady. My French proving marginally better than her English, we used French instead. It was a most cordial visit, with something to eat and drink.

It must have been that music on the radio just now that brought Vera and Tony back to mind, because, as I listened, they reappeared before me and I could see them again, as real as they were in life, two lovely, innocent, half naked young people, splashing and paddling happily about at my feet. Just as though it would never end, right out there in the pool, when in fact their brief, unfortunate lives were, even as I watched, drawing to a sudden and bloody close.

For soon enough after I'd come away home, they were cruelly murdered. At the behest of Bashir Gemayel, their family's fortress was breached and overrun and Tony and Vera cut down. And Tony's lovely mother? Yes, she also was killed. All of them, even their family dog, done in by their faithful fellow Christians, the

Geymayel clan. And oh, their precious little daughter, so proud in her pretty little girl's frock and her little white shoes! My god, but I hate to tell you this, but yes, they did—they slaughtered her, too!

So you see, in no time at all of the five of us who'd been together there in Zgharta, I was the only one left alive. But I can still see that little girl. See her sitting there so quietly in her new white shoes. I don't know why it is but I can still see her. As plain as day.

Then, last summer, in 2006, when Israel began its attack on Hezbollah, I made a search of Tony and his family. Much of what I discovered was rather a surprise. None of it should have been, as all of it bore the stench of their politics of retaliation. Here's just a sound bite—a wee glimpse at what I found.

In Lebanon, the President is elected by the National Assembly and at the presidential election that had been held in August of 1970—that was some four years before I was there—Tony's father, Suleiman, was one of the two candidates. After the third ballot the vote was exactly split between Suleiman and his opponent, Elias Sarkis. This was a large surprise, as Sarkis had been heavily favored to win. But with the Speaker abstaining, as was the custom, the count stood at 49 votes for each.

That's how things stood when Tony, leading a gang of heavily armed thugs, broke past the guards and into the forum and forced the Speaker at gunpoint to reconsider the custom in the new light cast by his self-evident self-interest—which, in short, he did, breaking the tie by voting for Tony's father, who thereupon became President. Following that demonstration of the high and ancient art of effective political rhetoric, Tony was placed in command of the Frangieh clan's private army, the Marada Brigade, a position he held until his death.

It might—or might not—reassure you that justice was done to hear that the death of Tony and all his family, save only his son, did not go un-avenged. Oh, no! When the killing of his son went down, Tony's father swore revenge and, soon enough, Bashir Gemayels' daughter was killed by a car bomb, and then later, in 1982, Bashir was himself assassinated.

Yes, I did mention Tony's son. Tony and Vera had a son, but I never saw him. He was named Suleiman, after his grandfather, and was much older than their little daughter. But Tony's son, Suleiman, was away at school at the time of the slaughter and so was spared the fate of his little sister and his parents. In fact, until fairly recently he not only held high office but had aspirations for the Presidency as well. This Suleiman, Tony's son, I see sometimes described by the media as *dapper*. But Bob says he's venial and thuggish and much of the press says the same. Like his grandfather, he has been a staunch ally of Syria, on the tines of whose fork—political, economic and military—long suffering Lebanon has for many years been skewered.

So you see, this town of Zgharta, this Lebanon, being, in essence, Sicilian, has for generations had its own local, internecine civil wars, continuous among the clans and even within the Frangieh family itself, which is split apart and readily spills its own blood. And these being human animals little different from us—yes, like every one of us—there's nothing to be done about it. Nothing at all.

It's a sad tale, but as I told you, if we are to talk, then I'll have to tell you things as they come to mind. And that's what was in my mind when you arrived. I'm sure it was that music I heard. The sadness of it, that brought them back to memory. What *was* that music that flooded over me and raised those two lovely figures up from the dead? I know you can't see them there in the pool. No, of course not, but I can. Vera and Tony, bobbing about, filled with the joy of their holiday here in this strange, free land they'd heard so much about. Their images are still in here, embedded on the inside of my eyes. Can you understand that at all?

Ah, of course! *Satie*! That's what was playing. *Gymnopédie*, the first one, the one you hear most often. I've heard it played in a hundred different arrangements, but this one was new to me. It was a brass quintet and maybe the most chilling of all. I'm not musician enough to know if that's a key change there at the end of the second chorus or just some kind of accidental. You know, something Satie flatted into blue. Probably just a change of key. Anyhow, it was there at that sudden, unexpected, heart-wrenching note at *Gymnopédie's* excruciating end, that I suddenly saw Vera and Tony again out there in the pool just the way they were. And that seems like only yesterday. I'd forgotten how real a ghost can be.

It's the despairing acceptance of the sorrow of man's inevitable fate that I always seem to hear in that music. That's what called them up, Tony and Vera, there in the pool looking at me. No, not *at* me, *through* me, and with unseeing eyes, as though I were the ghost. Not outrage, oh, no! Acceptance! The heartbreak that lies there just under Satie's clear, level, amused but undeceived and uncompromising, infinitely caring gaze. And all of that richness in a bare handful of seemingly simple notes. Infinite riches in a little place. And the title itself. *Gymnopédie*! Those two bare and lovely Attic shapes I saw out there, aren't they what Keats saw on that urn?

Anyhow, seeing them there has made me think of Higgins. I haven't seen him lately, but he still comes, of course. Even after all these years, so don't you worry, he'll be back.

Look just over there across the pool and under that pear tree. That's where my dog's buried. That way, when I'm sitting here in the evening, she's always in my sight, Scout is. That's why I've put that chair over there. There beside her grave—you see it? And that little cocktail table? That's for me, too. That's so I can go over in the evening sometimes and sit with her. Keep her company for a while. Just a little minute, you know? Close to sunset, the way we used to do. Maybe you've had a dog like that? If you've had the experience of the love that a dog can give, then you know. But if you haven't—well then, all I can say is that I'm sorry. So sorry for all that you've missed.

And when Higgins comes, right there is where he stops. Right there beside her grave. He just stops a while and looks across the pool at me. All the time we were in school together, and even in college, Charlie never came down here to hometown. Never did. Not once. Not while he was alive anyway. So he never sat around this pool either, of course. I don't know how he found me, but he did. But then I found him, too. Took me a devil of a long time, but I did. With Jacqi's help, I did. That's Jacqi Haun, she's the archivist at Lawrenceville, the school where Charlie and I were roommates. It was she who discovered where Charlie's buried. Maybe I'll tell you about that some time, too. Who knows?

But anyway—nowadays, when Charlie comes, Scout knows it, and she gets up out of her grave and stands over there beside him.

She died just two years ago, you see, so she still looks something like her old self. That beautiful, glistening, jet black she was, so alert and oh, my! so lovely still. But Charlie now—he's a different matter. He's been dead for so long that when he shows up, I don't see him now the way he was. Not in his own true colors, I mean. Not like I see Scout. No, he's in what you might call—what's that word I hear nowadays? *Grayscale*! That's it! Charlie's in grayscale when he comes, but other than that, they're much the same, really. Higgins and Scout. Neither of them ever speaks to me now. I mean—we don't seem to talk the way we used to do. But that's all right, we can look. So that's what we do now, look at each other. Just the three of us. Across the pool.

So, yes, Charlie does still come. Now and again. Sometimes he brings Mr. Spencer with him, but mostly he comes alone. And I've got an idea that when he comes now, it's just to make sure that I'm still all right.

Recitativo secco

You've been wanting me to tell you about my father, so maybe now's a good time to begin. Papa was born in Abbeville, Louisiana back in 1894. Abbeville's as French as it sounds, Cajun-French, of course, and not far from the Gulf. But that was never Papa's home. He was only born there, and until he left home at sixteen to work his way through college and law school, he lived with his family in another South Louisiana town, the little river town of Melville.

I've been twice to Melville lately, and but for the ivy covered corpse of the two-room Bank of Melville, of which my Grandfather Lyons was president, and a few other scattered remains from my father's boyhood, Melville would appear to be now much as it was when Papa was a boy. Even a full generation after Papa's, in the early thirties, when I passed part of a long, hot summer there myself, it could not have been much changed. That is, except for a reach of railroad track and the addition of a good gravel road into town.

This was in the summer of 1933 and prohibition had just been voted out. I can clearly remember that Saturday morning when the first beer truck was due to arrive from the brewery in New Orleans. I'm a little kid in the midst of several hundred men. I can see them now. They're of all ages and every one in overalls. Standing there in the dirt of the main street, silent, patient and very thirsty. Some have been there since daylight. Many have arrived on foot from miles around. And most of them are out of work. But all have come for but one purpose. And there I am, too, unselfconsciously among them.

Now, you mustn't suppose for a moment that during all that long drought of prohibition, men like these would have suffered much from want of moonshine. Not them! A few fired their own screw and the rest knew where to go. The best booze came from Opelousas. Everybody knew that. Opelousas corn—corn liquor. But this was going to be beer, and it was going to be legal, and I'd like to think that, being basically honest men, they felt the difference might be of some importance. Well, at least refreshing.

As I said, Melville is a river town and the river that runs past it, straight and narrow, swift and deep, before letting out into its own great swamp some twenty-five miles downriver, is the mighty Atchafalaya itself. I said deep? Deepest river anywhere in the world! Melville's not far south, either, of another little place important to my father's family history, and yes, it bears the same French suffix. It's called Cheneyville, and it's the old Stafford-Havard home place, Greenwood Plantation. It's still there at Cheneyville and, after two hundred years, *mirabile dictu*, it's even now still in family hands.

Melville is where Papa's maternal grandfather, my own great grandfather, Charlton Wright Havard, and his wife, Sallie Morris, lived most of their life together. This great grandfather of mine, *Captain* Charlton Havard, owned two or three steamboats and, although they were no doubt small vessels, members of the working class presenting no serious challenge to the mighty *Robert E. Lee*, he did in his youth command one or two of them himself, so *Captain* was, for him, not merely an honorific but an earned estate. The Captain Havard we have here also owned several plantations and so, for those parts in them days, he was a man of substance, a station in life fundamentally different from, and not at all to be confused with, the novelist's but-to-be-pitied man of property. But my father's own parents, though for the time by no means poor, poverty being a relative thing then as it is now, were people of a means much more modest than those of the Captain.

Here's a letter I want to read to you. Papa wrote it near the end of the war. It sounds a bit strange nowadays, but funny, too, especially at the end. Although it does reveal something of who my father was at that time in his life, it's greater interest may lie in the expression it gives to that remarkable ethos with which were imbued so many of those men of my father's generation who bred up the boys of mine. It's dated February 26, 1945 and addressed to me and my brother Hall and to my cousin, George Logan. Hall and George were then far out in the Pacific and I was on board ship to the ETO.

Dear Charlton, George and Hall,
This is late Sunday afternoon and I am having some quiet moments in the office. My mind naturally turns to you. I am thinking

of the things that you should do when you return to insure successful lives. There are some minimum things that are vital. I shall dictate them as they run through my mind:

Honor and integrity are the first requisites. Your word must be your bond. If you are steadfast in matters large and small, you will very quickly gain and keep the respect and confidence of your associates and the public. Nothing spreads more quickly than infidelity. More important than these external factors is the inward and satisfying self-respect that a man gains from calling balls and strikes, even against himself. I am happy to say that all of you possess these ingredients to a maximum degree.

A particular business should be selected, and, having once made the choice, you should apply yourself to it assiduously. Nothing is to be gained from changing from business to business, haphazardly. Of course, occasions may arise that justify change. I evolved from the law business to the oil business. To be justified, an analysis should show that the change is based upon opportunity for improvement on a large scale. The point is that one should hold to his own business as a general rule and only fundamental and impelling reasons should justify a change.

Having selected a business, continually study its subject until you are proficient and expert. This study should continue throughout life. Others will be impressed by your proficiency, and that gets business. Only continuous hard work can accomplish this result.

Read the lives of great men. They are inspiring. Read books on past and present business and political subjects. Few do. You will then be in position to discuss knowingly the important subjects of the day. Those who do not read will be glad to listen to you. Also, reading broadens the mind and character.

Make it an important part of your business to meet people. Work with the Community Fund, Red Cross, etc., you will never get much business from strangers until you have established a reputation. If you have what it takes, as you meet people you will impress them with your qualities and business will result.

Become an activating influence in public affairs. Man was placed upon this earth to be something besides a brute force. One's existence can only be justified by being an aggressive force for good.

Justify your existence by being on the positive, not the negative, side of life. Such conduct will result in both business advantage and disadvantage; as some enemies will be made but the result will be a plus. Business advantage and public approval may result from this course but in the inwardness of man, public approval is a very superficial thing. The great important thing in life is the satisfaction of the soul that comes from pursuing a course that is right, affirmatively opposed to all things that are wrong. Right and wrong are general terms but are easily distinguishable by the simple fact that where there is doubt the issue must be resolved as wrong. If you have no doubt about a thing being right, it will usually be right. On that rock and that rock alone, can man justify and dignify his destiny on earth.

Each day should be lived as though it were a life. Each day should be lived as though it were our last day on earth: all to the end of being deeply considerate and helpful to our fellow travelers. My own view is that everyone performs to his maximum efficiency with the mental and physical tools with which he is endowed. The drunkard does not wish to be a drunkard. He makes a constantly tortuous mental effort to release himself from the drinking habit. He is unable to do so because, perhaps, some tissue in his brain is not as strong as it should be. Men do their best as water seeks its level. The more fortunate in ever-thankfulness should stretch forth the helping hand to the less fortunate. We are not entitled to take pride unto ourselves for the big things we think we do. They are really impersonal. We have simply been born with the body and mind that is capable of overcoming difficulties and of accomplishing more than another. These powers are not something that we have created ourselves. We have had nothing to do with their existence. They have come from a higher Power. Of course, there are restraints and balances that must always be kept in mind when man deals with man, but the ultimate object should be to always be considerate of the feelings of others, and we should be considerate, understanding, and helpful in our human dealings but we should never permit ourselves to be imposed upon.

If, when comes the great end-day of life, one can, in true conscience, feel that the net result of his contribution has been on the side of rendering happiness and lasting benefit to mankind, then, and then only, shall he have merited existence.

I might also say that if your trousers are carefully hung at night and not worn on consecutive days, pressing costs can be reduced as through this means trousers can be worn several times without repressing. Pants hung on a chair lose their crease at once.

Also, brush your teeth often and hard. That stimulates blood action, the teeth feel well and alive. A lick and a promise won't do. As one becomes older, the importance of good teeth is appreciated more and more. While young, have your teeth examined and cleaned at least three times each year, later, more often.

Damned if I haven't used a lot of words!

Love,

Papa

Bagatelle

Since last evening when I read you that war-time letter of Papa's, it's been on my mind that I may well have given you an impression of him that is not only incomplete but very likely misleading. Anyway, there's more to tell, a lot more, and I'll begin with a bit about his boyhood down there in Melville, Louisiana, where from the age of twelve he jerked sodas after school and for two summers worked as water boy for a railroad gang. Papa would sometimes tell me things about those days. Not often but sometimes, and when he did, I'd hang on every word.

I suppose that rail gang for which he hauled water must have been working on that new railroad then being built down at Krotz Springs, twelve miles below town. In fact, I think I remember Papa telling me that. Although a hundred years ago when Papa was a boy, railroads had already had a long history in our country, new lines were still being laid out everywhere and new track spiked down, so that by the time I was born there was scarcely a town of any consequence in this whole country which could not be reached by train. And "by train", I mean *by passenger train*. You've heard of them? *Passenger* trains?

But in Papa's youth there was no railroad into Melville, and if you needed to get there, you went by steamboat. Melville, if I haven't told you, lies right on the banks of the mighty Atchafalaya River. Well, *on the banks* will paint the wrong picture. It lies behind the high levee that walls off the river and protects the land around from floods. Except on those occasions when it doesn't. Melville could not now be much changed from the peaceful, out-of-the-way, little country town it was when my father was a boy.

But what Melville *did* have was a first-class steamboat landing, and one of the things Papa never forgot was that red-letter day in December when the steamboat would arrive from New Orleans carrying on board the great, wooden barrel that would be loaded with cast-iron toys for every child in town. Those toys were of every size and description and all were packed in sawdust, sawdust being the bubble wrap of the Gay Nineties. One toy from that barrel would be each child's whole Christmas. Well—that toy and an apple. That's what Papa said.

Papa's sense of humor went towards the visual, the kind that lends itself best to live performance. He'd tell me all sorts of stories about his boyhood there in Melville and most of them were probably true. True, at least, in essence, if not in immaculate detail. Most of them I thought were hilarious. Here's one about the first horseless carriage to come to town. It was a Ford, of course. Among the first of the famous Model T Fords, and it was called the Tin Lizzie. Maybe you've heard of it? This may not be so at all, but I think I heard once that Henry Ford's wife may have been named Elizabeth and that Henry himself called her Lizzie, and that's how the Model T came to be called The Tin Lizzie, after Henry's wife. That may be only folk etymology, but it makes for a good story anyhow.

How'd she get there? Well, you can bet nobody drove her there! Only a man on horseback or riding a wagon could manage what passed for roads in those days. The best road anywhere around Melville was a mile stretch of hard, flat ground on top of the levee. But it didn't go anywhere. Just to where you had to turn around.

No, that Model T got there the way most things did—by steamboat. Papa was at the landing the day it arrived. He said that whenever a steamboat was heard coming, everybody in town just naturally went down to the landing to watch. So Papa was there looking on when the crew off-loaded that T Model. But that ended it. They just left her sitting up there on the levee. Nothing else they *could* do. The man who'd bought her couldn't drive her. Drive her? Hell, he couldn't even *start* her. Didn't even know how to turn her engine over! And he was the only man in town who'd ever even *seen* a motorcar.

But she looked mighty pretty, sitting there by the river, up on top of the levee. In fact, she looked so pretty and fine that folks came from every direction for miles around just to take her in. They wouldn't say anything, they'd just walk around her a time or two, then stop and stare. Sometimes, if he thought nobody was looking, some fellow might get up courage enough to reach out and touch her. Give her a little pinch. Wouldn't you want to touch her? Steal a little feel? First motorcar you'd ever seen? Sure you would!

Well, three or four days later, a traveling salesman came to town and even before he got off the boat, he had his eye on that Lizzie. He couldn't help it, him being a traveling salesman and her a sweet little thing sitting up there on the levee, so saucy looking. So pretty and pert and all by her lonesome. So as soon as he walked into the general store—well, it was more like a commissary—but anyhow, that's where he went with his samples, and right off he asked about that brand new Tin Lizzie sitting on the levee out front.

That's when the owner of the commissary came around the corner, and of course it was him who owned her. Mr. Mouton, that's the name I think Papa called him by. Well, Mr. Mouton allowed as how she was his, but then he had to turn right around and admit that he hadn't learned how to get her started as yet, and that's when that salesman said, *Let's go, cause I know how to drive her and I'll show you what to do.* Of course, word of that just flew through town, and right quick a good crowd is gathered around Lizzie—all of them talking and jabbering, and more coming every minute. Come on, let's me and you go watch, too. This is something you don't want to miss!

Not long after we get there, a hush falls over the crowd and we move back a bit to let Mr. Mouton and the salesman come through. The salesman has brought his sample case along, and Mr. Mouton, he's now wearing the new touring car costume he brought back with him from New Orleans. That's where he'd ordered himself that Tin Lizzie, in New Orleans, and now he's looking mighty cool, in a pair of driving gloves with big, rolled cuffs and wearing that long, tan, knee-length duster. But get a load of what he's got on his head! An honest to God, turn-of-the-century, cross-country race driver's cap, complete with a big pair of goggles up over the visor!

For a long moment the salesman stands back, silently assessing the challenge that lies before him. Evaluating that Lizzie as one would a fresh, young, un-broke mare one is about to saddle up for the first time and mount. Not one of us speaks. By and by, satisfied with what he's seen but still without taking his eyes off that Model T, he hands his sample case to a nice looking boy who has worked his way up close, so as not to miss anything. I recognize that boy! He's my own beautiful father, aged fifteen, and, as I told you, it was from him that I first heard the story of this very same traveling salesman and it was him, my own father, who told me just how it's all going to unfold. But we'll have to see about that. We'll just have to wait and see if what Papa told me comes true.

But now the salesman is folding his coat and, just as he did his sample case, he passes it back to my father. There's yet another long moment of this ever growing suspense, tightening even more as that traveling salesman, rubbing the palm of his left hand with his right, begins his slow and courtly advance upon the Lizzie herself.

But first, there are a couple of things you possibly should know about, so let's freeze-frame the action right here for a moment. You're sure you don't mind? You see it in opera quite a lot. The librettist just suspends the action whenever he, or the composer, suddenly takes a mind to walk off from the plot in order to call our attention to something else they've suddenly become more interested in. And they always seem to choose the most inopportune of times to do this. Generally, it's at some moment of greatest suspense, and so, in place of the promised action, what do we get? We get reflection, emotive meditation, that sort of thing. An aria or a duet or quintet—something in which the swords are hung out to dry and revelations are made and character intrudes and vexed emotion carries the burden of the song.

And if they can get away with it, why can't we? Why can't we step aside for a moment and give consideration to some other matter? Some important matter, such as the character of the traveling salesman? Wouldn't you like to know more about him? Sure you would, so here goes.

Well, up until maybe forty years ago, the traveling salesman had long been a stock figure in America's domestic comedy. Most conspicuously—but, mind you, not exclusively—in what were called *dirty jokes*. These were the jokes which, of an evening, men would forgather back in America's kitchens to pass around among themselves, a rite they celebrated with much mirth and many a knowing wink and always to the accompaniment of the cheerful music of the ice tinkling in the highball glass. Its every clink and rattle rich with tradition.

Of course, I'm old now. Rocking chair's got me and I don't get around much anymore. So although I've not heard one in some two generations, it's possible that a traveling salesman story or two is still out there somewhere, lurking about, but if the traveling salesman story does still lurk, then the traveling salesman himself, I mean the *subject* of such a story, certainly must not.

Now, I myself don't see the salesman's passing as, in itself, constituting a national tragedy, but together with the salesman's passing went the passing of the American passenger train, and, in my view, the disappearance from our scene of all those great fleets of trains that people could ride on has clearly been a very great loss indeed. You see, the two once went hand in hand in our culture, the traveling salesman and the trains on which he made his weekly rounds. Or so it seems to me. In any event, I think it certain that pretty soon now in our country, there'll be few indeed of you young people who've ever even *boarded* a train, and there's at least one old man left alive who thinks that that is a very great pity indeed.

But if you don't know them, the salesmen of those old tales were a raffish lot. Like Sinbad, they found themselves forever sailing the seas of high adventure, never failing in their travels to encounter some fetching young damsel, classically some farmer's daughter. And come to think of it, our own traveling salesman *did* arrive by vessel, did he not? Of course he did! And so yes—yes, we might indeed think of him, of our own traveling salesman as a sailor, a latter-day Sinbad the Sailor.

And by the way, those traveling salesmen were no fools. They were practical men of the world, and you can just bet that our salesman in the story would certainly have known how to drive that Tin Lizzie. Why, when I was a young boy, the Model T was still coming off the line, and although I don't remember that I ever drove one myself, I did at least learn how to start one. Learned from an older boy up the street whose father had one he'd let him drive.

Like Sinbad, it was only in the rare case that salesmen like ours would not in the end somehow prevail. Willy Loman was of course that rare case. Oh, yes, Willy! He, too, committed his own itinerant sexual transgression. Had his day in the hay like all the rest of his celebrated breed. But unlike the others, Willy paid for it. Paid a dear price. And it was surely because his acts were followed by their consequences that Willy became one of the great, central figures in all of twentieth century American drama, A figure as close to tragic as our century, unlike Lincoln's, could come.

But in all of those highly romanticized trystings— OK, assignations—but anyway, those *encounters* of his with the intriguing female form, appearing to him as it did in all its various versions of its disparate manifestations, the traveling salesman would always have his way. Wind up on top. Speaking figuratively, of course. And such being the case, basic dramaturgy required that the character of the salesman be rewarded with the curtain speech, the last laugh. And those final words of his, frequently a lascivious double-entendre, were invariably of a frankly sexual nature—a virtual necessity, if he were to remain *in character*—right? And although, in retrospect and under examination, they would be seen to have been painstakingly prepared for by the story teller, those last words of his would somehow always afford one the pleasure of the completely unexpected.

But as I say, the traveling salesman is a creature of our country's distant past, and if one of those stories of him is ever to be heard again in the land, then I suppose it'll be one that I myself, like a latter-day Scheherazade, will have to tell.

Now, rolling up his sleeves as he goes, the salesman reaches over Lizzie's dash to adjust a small lever on her steering column. He's advancing the spark before moving up front to take hold of the crank. He turns the crank to compression and gives it a serious pull, but the engine kicks back on him, the crank handle left spinning wildly around. The crowd stifles a gasp, but I see he's OK. He'd let go of the crank quick enough for his arm to be still in one piece.

We don't move. None of us do. But the salesman does. He returns to the dash, advances the spark a bit more and, his confidence unabated, returns to have another go at it with the crank. But this time, after spitting on his hands, he does something a little different. And not a little strange. This time, as he grasps the crank handle, he also wraps his left arm over and around Lizzie and gently tap-tap-taps on her hood with his hand, and then, strangest of all, he seems to be saying something to her. Whispering something to her, you might say. But what it is he's whispering I can't quite make out. Then he gives the crank an even more determined pull.

And sure enough! This time when he cranks her, the Lizzie doesn't kick back She coughs once and sputters into half-life, her body beginning a gentle rocking motion. Just a bit, side to side. And at this, beckoning to Mr. Mouton to follow, the salesman climbs under the wheel and throttles her up to a roar. A mighty roar of victory floating up over the river and over the heads and the cheers of the crowd. And then, without more adieu, the two of them drive off down the levee.

No one leaves the scene of course. We're all still there on their return, and I'm glad I am, because I am about to have my faith in my father fully justified. I'm about to hear with my own ears what it was that traveling salesman had said to Lizzie. To hear the very words that my father told me so long ago that that salesman had said.

For on their return, and well in my hearing, Mr. Mouton tells the salesman that he'd carefully watched what the salesman had done, and, but for one thing, he's sure he could now get the Lizzie started all by himself. But Mr. Mouton wants to know of the salesman just what it was the salesman had done there at the end, and just what it was he'd said that finally got the Lizzie going.

And I hear the salesman's reply, *Oh, not much, really. I just reached over and put my arm around her, kind of gentle-like, and patted her a bit, and then I just whispered in her ear, Turn over, Lizzie. It's me. Henry.*

NOLA

De mortuis nil nisi bonum.
      Diogenes Laertius
      Lives and Opinions of Eminent Philosophers

Ergo nil.
      Charlton Havard Lyons, Jr.
      Songs I Heard My Mother Sing

    The whole time I was in college——well, even long before that—it had never occurred to me that I would not turn out to be a writer. And so, with that in mind, I began posting in this little book here, material I thought might come in handy later on. You wouldn't call this thing a *diary*, although for a while I did keep a diary, too. No, this is just a bunch of feuilletons, a commonplace book to which I committed various notions as they occurred to me. Most of them were prompted by my reading, but of course, as I never actually became a writer, nothing in here was I ever able to use. I'm not sure why I kept it.

    But I was looking through some of this stuff this morning and, frankly, I found much of it rather embarrassing. The sorriest kind of juvenilia you can imagine. Bore you to death! Of course now, I was very young then, and wholly innocent of the evil spirits that everywhere abound. Literary critics, even overly-critical general readers, who would, had I, in the event, become a writer, have devoured me alive. That is, had I been so venturesome—well, no, so completely *foolish*—as to have actually attempted to write the delusional, idiosyncratic, self-indulgent, contrarian sort book I once thought the world, being itself all of those things, badly needed if it was ever to see itself as it really is.

    But not quite everything in here is juvenescent. I might even have found a use for some of it. That is, had I become a writer.

    You see that sweet little bunny rabbit over there across the yard? Do you see how contentedly she's nibbling away at the lawn? She's utterly oblivious of any threat that might lie in wait, isn't she?

But now, if you'll look a little closer, you'll see that there's a cat over there, too, just to her right, lurking there in the azaleas, ready to do her in. That's Peggy's outside cat. Her name is Snappy, and if you're not aware of it, a female house cat is probably the most casually bloodthirsty killer that ever lived. Critics—literary critics—are a lot like that cat. But that's not really the point I was about to make.

    I've been thinking a lot lately about New Orleans. About Katrina, of course, but more about the city itself. I've been hearing *NOLA* in my head. When I was a boy growing up, that's the piano music I'd hear constantly on my crystal set. A crystal set? That was the minimal kind of radio we boys had beside our bed seventy-five years ago. But no, there's nothing I want to say now about New Orleans, one way of the other. You saw there what Laertius had to tell us and that pretty well sums it up. He just means that, if we feel constrained to speak of the dead at all, then please let it be something favorable, won't you?

    But let me read you something quite to the contrary that I found I'd written down in this little book here. It seems that not always has everyone agreed with Laertius. Nothing unusual about that, of course. I must have had doubts myself when I was in college, because there's something here in this book that interested me enough so that I wrote it down to save it. It's the opinion of Laurence Sterne. I have no idea where I found this quotation, but here's what I've got here.

> *Sterne, in answer to the reprimand—De mortuis nil nisi bonum—which proceeded from a friend of a deceased doctor treated by Sterne in his usual deflatory manner, had this to say: I declare, I have considered the wisdom and foundation of it over and over again as dispassionately and charitably as a good Christian can, and after all, I can find nothing in it, or make more of it, than a nonsensical lullaby of some nurse, put into Latin by some pedant, to be chanted by some hypocrite to the end of the world.*

    Sterne, of course, was himself a born-again contrarian, the ultimate eccentric. Did he not write the strange life of Shandy? Who could ever forgive him for that? A few didn't. It was because of those very flaws, fatal in their eyes, that most of the critics of his day held him in a great disrepute. I'm including Dr. Johnson among those who couldn't suffer him. But in spite of his strange ways, the general readers of his day just loved him to death. They couldn't get enough of their own dear Laurence Sterne, so there you are.

Ride a cock-horse …

The biggest change that occurred during my life? You want to know that, do you? The atomic bomb? Nope. International terrorism? Nope. The Internet? You're getting warm. Look at the statistics. I've read that at the end of the First World War, when I was born, as many as 70 percent of our people lived a rural life. Many of those lived in villages but most out on the countryside, where the mass of people had always lived. So only 30 percent lived in towns and cities. But just imagine that! Seventy percent of us living out there on the land! You know how many of us live out there now? A mere seven percent! Think of it! A migration of that enormous magnitude in just the short span of my lifetime! But that horse has been gone from the barn for a long time, and no one now seems even to notice. Well, no one but me.

Take the horse. In the days of my youth the horse was still everywhere in evidence. Even in the towns. Even here in hometown. Three mornings a week I waked to the sound of a horse-drawn wagon. I could hear it plain as day. Even after its iron-shod wheels were mounted with rubber. It was delivering milk. The milkman gets sick? No problem. Just put some one else up on the seat. Didn't matter who, because that horse knew the route better than the route man.

Wherever she'd halt, the milkman would climb down and load quart bottles of milk and pints of thick cream into a stiff wire basket. A wire handle and compartments for eight bottles and I can still hear those bottles rattling as he carried it up our driveway, past my bedroom window and around to the back, where he'd find the empties we'd left out on the back steps the day before. They'd be crystal clear, of course, and we'd be left with full bottles in place of our empties.

And this was *real* milk! Not that skimmed milk we used to call blue john, hell no! Not even that stuff they knock most of the cream out of nowadays and call *homogenized*. The top third of a quart bottle of milk would be cream. You could see it was cream, too. Thick, yellow cream! You've never seen a real bottle of milk, so you wouldn't know, but cream *does* rise to the top, just like they say. But nobody tells you about the scum. Oh no! You've got to learn about the scum yourself. But the scum acts just like the cream. It rises to the top, too! Did you ever stop to think about that? Well, you ought to. An example? You want an example? *Huey Long.*

Same way with the iceman. He'd come in a wagon, too. Horse-drawn. Well, later on, up in the thirties I guess it was, they got to ride around in trucks. Now, the ice man, he'd be wearing a thick leather jacket and he'd carry that ice on his back, a fifty pound block of it. He'd carry it all the way up from the street onto the back porch, where there was a little door in the wall. Just inside that door was another even smaller door, and that was the door that opened right into the back of the icebox. And that's how our ice got delivered right into our icebox. You've got to admit it, that was really living!

What? Sure he could have come in the kitchen if he'd wanted to. Walk right in, sure could. But why would he do a thing like that, and mess up the whole kitchen with his dirty old boots? That was the whole point of it, not to mess up. *Locked?* The kitchen door wasn't locked! Front door neither. We never locked our doors in those days. Nobody did. What for? *Crime?* Why, we couldn't have spelt it.

Most everybody in town had a cistern beside their house. Ours was right there by our back porch. Our house had rain gutters all around it. At the eaves. Nailed to the fascia board at the front of the soffit. Those gutters were there to collect rain water running off the roof and let gravity deliver it to the cistern. This may surprise you, but we never drank the water out of that cistern. No, we had good artesian well water to drink. That was also the water we cooked with. We bathed in, too—in that well water.

Maybe I told you. I grew up in a little village called South Highlands. We didn't become part of Shreveport until about 1927, but we had wonderful well water long before that. But good as that water was, it wasn't quite good enough for some people. None of the women would wash their hair in it. They had to have *rain* water for washing their hair. They said that well water made their hair smell stump-sour. Can you beat that? Somebody had put it in their heads that if they used well water, it would turn their hair into a—a dirty, stinking old mop—something like that. Oh, never mind.

Talking about horses, when I was a little boy, on Saturdays when my father went downtown to his office, he'd usually take me with him. Used to be that Saturday was the day everybody came to town, so you could see horses down there on Saturdays. Right on Texas Street. Texas was then the main street. Still is. But nowadays, you can shoot a cannon down Texas on Saturday and not hit a living soul. But back then, on Saturdays, you could still see horses downtown. Mules, too. Hitched up to wagons. I don't remember a buggy. A saddle horse would have been rather unusual by then, but it does seem to me I did see one parked down there one time.

Those that came to town in wagons would tie their rig up to a hitching post and go shopping. Or just look for somebody to talk to. During the week country people didn't see much of anybody new, so when they came to town, they came to talk. And don't think they didn't know how! Talk your arm off. Grab you by your shirt, so you couldn't get away. They'd do that out in the country, too. Stop you out there even when you were bird-hunting. Stop you just to talk.

And horse manure in the streets? You better believe it! You just don't know what the streets were like in the great days of the horse. I can see those men now—those street cleaners in overalls shoveling that dung into carts to haul it off.

Horses? In the First World War, the British alone lost 500,000 horses. Why, the livery stable out on Texas Avenue didn't go out of business until in the 1950's. I think there must have been a lot of hitching posts still standing here in hometown when I was a boy. Must have been hitching posts in front of some of those older houses closer to town. Probably even a mounting stone or two. Out front. At the curb where people climbed up into their buggies. A big stone like the one that stood in front of my great grandparents' farmhouse in Wisconsin. I'll show you a picture of it some time. I've got a good one.

I loved horses. Every boy once did. Horses and dogs. One time, when I was about ten years old, I went to a summer camp for boys down at Kerrville. Kerrville, Texas. Camp La Junta. It was a camp just for junior boys, and it was mostly for riding, so that's why I wanted so bad to go. It was a dream I had. A day dream. Riding a horse. Of course now, I'd never been up on a horse. Not in my whole life, but the significance of that was lost on me. That's the way it is with dreams. They leave a lot out, day dreams do. But day dreams are fine, or at least mine are. Night dreams are not. I think being insane must be like living in one of my night dreams. I hope I'm not headed there when I die—into one of my night dreams.

But now, at La Junta we'd go on a trail ride almost every day, and that string of horses they had down there just weren't meant for young boys like us. Not well broken, if you know what I mean. Not all of them anyway, and when we'd head back and get a quarter mile or so from camp, as like as not, four or five of those horses would bolt. Then, all of a sudden, here comes the whole rodeo, heading for the barn hell bent for leather. Horses at full gallop. Counselors trying to head off the stampede, whooping and hollering and waiving their hats in the air. Boys falling off everywhere. We put on quite a show.

Anyway, that's when I began to sober myself up about horses. They'd step on your foot while you were saddling up. Hurt like hell. If you didn't pay close attention when you were cinching up, there were some that would blow their barrels up and pretty quick after you mounted, the saddle was under their belly and you were laying there on the ground. One of the boys wrangling those horses had a cropped ear. Horse bit it off. We think cars are dangerous? Horses killed a hundred times more men per passenger mile than the motor car ever has. Lots of people were afraid of them. It was a horse killed Scarlett's father, don't forget that. And didn't her daughter die from falling off a horse? A horse can hurt you bad.

Maybe it's the same now, I don't know, but when I was a boy, there was no shame worse than that of being called a coward. Or even *thought* a coward. So among all of us then, there was this dreadful, boding fear that we might someday suffer that shame. The shame of being called a coward.

At that camp, we didn't just trail ride, we rode some in a riding ring. We even did a little jumping. I remember like it was yesterday, my first try at jumping a horse. Just a little jump a horse could almost step over. But just a day or two before, when she'd caught the smell of the stables in the air, a surly, scheming, pernicious brute of a horse had taken off with me and run herself up under the limbs of one of those post oaks they've got everywhere down there, and she'd scraped me out of the saddle and off her back. She did it all on purpose, of course. I was plenty scared.

Eight or ten of us—just the boys in my cabin I think—were out there that morning, sitting up on the fence waiting our turn. By that time I was hoping a bell would ring or something would happen and my turn would just disappear. But pretty quick my name did come up, and so I had to get down off that fence and climb aboard that jumper, whether I wanted to or not. It was in that instant that I became fully confirmed in the conviction that I wasn't cut out to be a cowboy after all, a natural cowardice being more in my line.

I lost my seat on the first jump. Fell off. I knew I would. I could hardly breathe when I got up there. Our instructor was no more than a boy himself, and he never moved from his seat on the fence. He just looked down at me to see what I'd do next.

You've got to understand that for me he wasn't just an eighteen year old kid out there with his first class of junior boys, trying to teach us a little bit about riding. In my eyes he was a cowboy. The cowboy I'd been reading and dreaming about. And he looked like a cowboy, too. He wasn't wearing any costume. He was wearing the clothes he lived in, and I knew in my heart that he was the god of the Wild West and that he was there to pass judgment on me.

My horse had stopped dead still when I went over her head. I don't recall when it was that tears began to run down my cheeks but they did. How I did it, I don't know, except maybe I'd gone stark, raving mad. But I managed to climb back up on that horse, and I took her back around and went over that jump, and this time I held on. I did not fall. Not on that jump or on the next three, before I was back in front of that cowboy. Where I got off my horse and took my seat on the fence. But even there at the end, I was still sobbing. But although my head was not down, because I was filled with pride that I hadn't acted the coward, I was still filled with the shame of my tears. The terrible conflict between pride and shame! Nor would that be the last time in my life that I would find myself so conflicted.

I've remembered it so long, my experience that morning in that riding ring, that there ought to be a lesson in it, but I couldn't tell you what it is. I know one thing. In those days that was the way boys learned almost everything— by the ancient process of trial and terror.

But much as I came to distrust and fear horses, they never lost their attraction for me, because, you see, they stood for everything I loved best in my little boy's heart. The Wild West was in my blood. Did you know that a generation before me, when Nabakov was a boy in Russia, he and his friends read everything they could lay their hands on about the nineteenth century American West? That was me, too—everything I could get my hands on. Things you may never have heard of, like *The Sea Of Grass*. And *The Virginian*. I could once quote from *The Virginian*. And Huck Finn, of course. Someday soon, it would be me lighting out for the territory, and as a boy, I was ready.

Nobody remembers the *The Virginian* now, but in its day, it was *Gone with the Wind*. Owen Wister wrote it, a very interesting man who made an old fashioned, cowboy book of a rather romantic vision he had of our West. It was a fiction just made for the silent screen. Nobody even knows Wister nowadays, but fortune casts a long shadow, and only a few years after I'd read his book, I came to learn quite a bit about Mr. Wister from a son of his I served with during the war. But that's not only nostalgia speaking, it's the quite aimless nostalgia of a rather peculiar old man, and we certainly can't have anything like that wandering around loose, can we?

That month I spent down at that boys camp was my first time ever to be away from my parents. I wasn't homesick down there, not at all, and that gave me to believe that I was immune to that dreadful malady. But events were soon to prove how terribly wrong I was!

But yes, there *was* one lesson I learned at that camp. You'd better be pretty careful about what it is you love. Maybe it's a horse. Or a dog. Better yet, a black dog. Well, maybe even a woman. Maybe *especially* a woman. But whatever it is, that's the very thing that's going to hurt you the most, and maybe do you in. But everybody knows that.

There now, that's enough about horses and that still largely pastoral world into which I was born, so let's talk about something else.

Opus 3

The obbligato

There's something I've been meaning to tell you for quite a while now. You see, my children have learned about these evening visits you and I are having here by the pool, and they can't believe I've been telling you all these stories about things as they once were long ago. They ask me, *Pa, why are you telling someone you've only just met, a total stranger, things you've never even told us? What about us? Don't we count?* Don't blame them. Too busy, I guess.

It's only natural, I suppose, that they'd be envious. They want to be here, too, and listen to these old stories themselves. But that's not the worst of it. Two or three of them are now after me to write a book. Oh, no! Don't worry! They get the same answer I give you. Just talking is challenge enough for me these days. They laugh.

One of my five daughters, my daughter Stafford, writes personal essays, and she's written one about me that she wants you to read. In fact, she wrote it just *for* you. She said so. Mailed me a printed copy of it to give you. Made me promise, so here it is. It's all about those letters I wrote Stafford's mother from over there. Stafford's mother was Susybelle, my first wife, and she gave Stafford all those letters I wrote to her from overseas during the war.

It looks like Stafford's got more questions than answers, and that's my fault. There *were a* few things I didn't choose to write home about. Certainly not to my wife. Didn't want her to be worrying about me over there. I was doing enough of that for both of us anyway. Mostly, I just tried to put it out of mind. Look, I know that stories from the war probably fascinate you to death. They do most people. But my war stories are of no interest to anyone, not really. And anyway, I've just never felt much like talking about it.

Now about Stafford. She one of those who wants me to write a book, and if I did, I'd feel myself obliged to put *something* in it about that war. And this piece Stafford's written, I could use that. It might be enough all by itself. But then, maybe an introduction of some sort by me wouldn't hurt. It might clear some things up a bit.

But those letters I wrote Susybelle weren't the *only* letters I wrote home. I've got a scrap book my parents kept that's full of letters I wrote them from over there. Of course, I didn't tell them quite everything either! Held a few things back. But there *is* one letter in that scrap book that's quite a bit more candid. It's one I wrote Fred Ryan as soon as the war ended, while things were fresh on my mind. I knew that Fred would want to know how things over there had really been with me, so writing him was easy. Fred was never much for palliatives anyway. Lost a leg when he was seventeen, playing ice hockey. You should have known him.

You know what? I could put that letter I wrote Fred right there in my book—right alongside this piece here that Stafford wrote. But then maybe I'd do better just to quote parts of it. No—no, no! That letter shouldn't be in the book at all. It's the kind of thing that belongs in an appendix. Yeah, that's what I'd do with it—put the whole damn thing in the appendix, where the people who were interested in that sort of thing could read if they wanted to.

But back to those letters I wrote Stafford's mother. I was only over there some six months or so, and that's when they were all written. About a third of them late in the war and the rest while we were in occupation. I'm talking now about the war in Europe, did I say that? The European Theatre of Operations? The ETO?

No, that's never been something I'm quick to talk about. You can understand that, I'm sure. But now, if it's all that important to you, then maybe right now is as good a time as any to get it out of the way. So, OK, let's do it. Let's go ahead *right now* and get the whole damned thing behind us. Over and done with. Actually, when you come right down to it, compared to most of those war stories you hear, mine are just plain boring. But I didn't write the script. None of us did. We all just went where we were told and did our duty as best we could when we got there. So just consider this the obligatory scene. Because that's all it is—the obligatory scene. I only hope it won't sound too—too *potted*.

Before I begin, let me get something off my chest right here and now. This happened about three years ago, and it still ticks me off every time I think about it. One of my many fine grandsons was trying to draw me out about the war, when right off the bat, out comes that damned expression, *in harm's way*. Politicians use it all the time. If you listen to them, the *last* thing any politician would *ever* want to do—oh, no! God forbid!—would be to put any of *our boys in harm's way*. I'm sick of hearing it! What the goddamn hell is wrong with everybody today? Why can't we say what we mean? In combat, you're not *in harm's way*! Hell no, you're out there where you may get your goddamn ass shot off! But oh, no! It would never do to say a thing like that. We don't want to hear the truth. What we want is *euphemism*. That goddamned, emasculated and fumigated, primped and perfumed, *in harm's way*! In harm's way? Shit you say!

Let me tell you something right now. Every time I start thinking about that war—or about Viet Nam or Iraq, or any of the other ways we kill each other off—I boil over. I get hot as a five dollar pistol. I'll try to hold back, but be prepared for some ill temper and a few bad words. And don't think I don't know a few!

But although hearing about being in harm's way irritated the hell out of me, that wasn't the really terrible thing I heard from my grandson. And he's one of my favorites, too! Like most of his generation, he's never done any military service, so you can't expect too much from them. But he *is* fully grown, and a college graduate with children, so you'd think he'd have learned *something*! I don't mean in school, I mean in *life*. Just knocking around! Now, this is going to astonish you—take your breath away. At least I hope it does. Here's what my fine grandson asked me, *Pa, when you were in the army, they kept people like you out of harm's way, didn't they?*

That's just what he said. Said it to my face! It was so perfectly insane that I thought I must have misunderstood what he said, so I asked him just what the hell he meant by *people like me*. Here's what he said. Without the slightest hesitation. *I mean college graduates—educated people. In the war, they put people like that somewhere safe, didn't they? They wouldn't make them get out there where they might get killed, would they?*

Now, just imagine! My own grandson insulting me like that! And him with no idea of what he'd done! No goddamn idea at all of the enormity of what he'd said! And not just me. In one breath, he'd managed to insult just about every boy I grew up with. Oh, sure, even then we had people looking around for a soft birth, scared to death of being shipped out overseas. But overseas was where the vast majority of us *wanted* to go. So he was insulting a whole generation and he was too ignorant of the relatively recent past even to be aware of it. He knew absolutely *nothing* about the way we were just three generations back. That's why those words of his are another lantern on the levee, another bright red warning that all is far from well with us. That the center just may not hold.

Did I ever tell you I served with the Tenth Armored Division? Oh, I did? Well, actually there were *two* times I served with the Tenth. Two separate occasions. The first time was in the States, at Camp Gordon, Georgia, just outside Augusta. That was for almost seven months in 1944. From about late January till mid-August, I was in Battery B of the 419th Armored Field Artillery Battalion.

Well, hell, if I'm going to go through all this, I might as well begin at Pearl Harbor—when our self-contented little world blew itself all to pieces. On that Sunday, I was almost halfway through my sophomore year at Yale. Ten weeks later, on February 16th, I registered in the draft. But I also volunteered. So did about everybody in my generation. When I volunteered, that's when they placed me in what was called the Enlisted Reserve and told me to wait till I heard something. Fact is, the government didn't seem that much interested in getting us into uniform. It seemed like they *wanted* us to stay in school. At least for a while. I suspect one reason was that the reception centers couldn't induct us any faster than they already were. Right after Pearl Harbor, there were hundreds of thousands of us, probably millions, standing in line waiting to get in. A lot of boys quit school to get in the service. Charlie Higgins did.

Although I couldn't wait to become part of the military, I'm pretty sure that until Pearl Harbor came along, I wouldn't have even given a thought to the ROTC. There were too many other courses I wanted to take. But all that changed when we woke up that Sunday morning to find ourselves at war. And suddenly, there it was! The ROTC! And I hadn't even noticed it. As I said, I was already in the Enlisted Reserve and ordered to sit tight, but there was one step left open that would, you might say, jump-start my military career, and I took it.

At mid-years, in January of 1942, I passed up a wonderful opportunity offered me by my professor of Greek. Skipping the details, I was already signed up for one regular course under him, but he wanted me to go to work for him that semester and do a statistical analysis of a bunch of Homer. Not only would that job give me credit for a whole extra semester of course work, but I would be working with Gene every day. I'd be one-on-one with him, so I'd learn a lot. And I'd get paid for it, too. Hard to pass that up, but I did. I signed up for ROTC instead. Jack Moment did the same. A lot of other fellows in my class did, too. We didn't necessarily expect to get a commission out of it. It was just something we could do to take part, while we hung around waiting to be called up.

You see, at *my* Yale—that is, at the Yale that then was—there was an ROTC unit right there on campus, and although not a part of the quadrivium, or even of the trivium, ROTC was at least an academic discipline honorable enough to be included as one of the courses regularly offered by the University. By the way, the Yale of those days had little or no sense that it was some *elite,* infinitely superior, institution. Not at all! All of us, faculty and students alike, we just regarded ourselves as completely normal, fully participating members of our American civil society and as responsible as anyone else for our country's welfare, including its defense.

But within a generation, all of that was to change. Yale was to loftily eschew any direct, meaningful contribution to our country's military—priding itself instead on its preparation of its people for other, and *higher,* forms of public service. Service rendered not only to the nation's top law firms and financial institutions but, and notably so, even to government itself. This latter service has, of course, been well and truly performed by Yale graduates for generations, but, things having now become what they are, Yale's men and women these days perform that service strictly as civilians, and at entry-levels not lower than that of cabinet rank.

Our armed forces are now all volunteers and that would be well and good but for the fact that not *all* of us are volunteering. But deeply troubling as it is, that is by no means the only ill-boding I see for our country. Not the *only* lantern I see burning brightly up there on the levee, when I lie there, owl-eyed and restless in the night.

Back to the subject. I entered Yale in September of 1940 and managed to graduate in three years. On June 14, 1943, I was inducted into the army at Fort Devens, Massachusetts. About thirty of my classmates from Yale were all inducted together that day. My dear friend, Jack Moment, and I were among them. We would all wind up as artillery Forward Observers. After a week of KP and policing the area, we were again sent as a cadre, all together, to the 704th Combat Military Police, a battalion scattered around Boston. I was one of the eight or ten of us that got assigned to C Company.

Now, this C Company was a very peculiar outfit. Truth is, it wasn't a *company* at all. It was a committee, an ad hoc committee of untrained and undisciplined civilians. The few of us who'd just arrived were wearing brand-new uniforms and the most of us were armed with shotguns. Eight or ten had rifles. The British Enfield from World War One. There were 108 of us enlisted men but only one officer. He was a First Lieutenant. I don't recall his name but he emerged from his quarters so seldom that it might have been Kiji. Kiji was a Baltimore cop, a retread who, like the Enfield, had served in World War One, and who wore his wrinkled age the same way he wore his rumpled uniform—with a classic want of elegance.

Company C was stationed in a former CCC camp in a place called The Blue Hills Reservation just south of Boston. It wasn't far from Mattapan, so getting into town was easy. I heard the Boston Pops two or three times. In those days, the concert hall in which the Pops played was nothing like the one in which you see them play today. We sat at plain, deal tables set about on the floor. It wasn't crowded. Plenty of room around you, so you could order pitchers of claret punch and just rare back and listen. Kind of down-homey.

Soon after my arrival I was made part of a company detail, some forty of us, which went over to Quincy to march in a big Fourth of July parade. We did our best to look—how shall I say this—if not bloodthirsty, then at least fierce? Well, OK—stern. But the crowds lining the streets must have liked our looks, because they cheered and cheered us as we passed. I wouldn't have cheered. You see, our primary mission was to repel invasion—no kidding! and some sure instinct told me that that was a duty for which we were ill prepared. We were just boys, you know. All of us, just boys.

At the end of the parade, I remember standing at attention during the dedication of a large plaque mounted in front of a church there in Quincy. As I recall, it was an historic old church whose churchyard contained the graves of both John Adams and John Quincy Adams. Now that was a Fourth of July to remember!

But then, after a couple of months of playing soldier and a promotion to corporal, I boarded a troop train with all the others for the artillery Officer Candidate School at Sill. That's where Chief Quanah Parker is buried. At Fort Sill, Oklahoma. In December, I was commissioned and sent to a postgraduate school at Ft. Bragg in North Carolina. Here's a mug shot of me taken in my brand new Second Lieutenant's uniform. This shot would have been taken at Fort Sill, at the time I was commissioned.

Then I was sent to Camp Gordon and the Tenth Armored Division where I reported to our division commander, General Newgarden. I can see him now seated at his desk, barrel-chested and ramrod straight. He was carrying his automatic right there on him. In a shoulder holster. That was the closest I ever was to him, or to any other general officer for that matter. But it was instantly clear to me that I was in the presence of a full-time, professional soldier and that the clip in that forty-five he was packing would be fully loaded.

But General Newgarden never made it over there. No, he was tragically killed in a plane crash here in the States in July. That sort of thing, those so-called *operational* accidents, they were quite common during the war. They were happening all the time, both here at home and overseas. By operational, they meant *non-combat*. That is, none of the enemy happened to be around when you died. I've read that on just one day and in just one place in New Guinea, thirty-seven aircraft died in just one storm, killed dead along with all their crews. Most of them were bombers, I believe. So there's no telling how many American airmen, all told, died that way in the war. Ten—twenty thousand? I knew fifteen or more myself who did, so who really knows how many?

When I left General Newgarden's office, it was for duty with the first real combat outfit of which I was ever a part. The 419th Armored Field Artillery Battalion. I reported to its commanding officer of course, Col. McCabe, Lt. Colonel Robert McCabe, but my memory of Col. McCabe as he was when I first saluted him, is now not even a smudge. I suppose that's because I had just come from General Newgarden and Newgarden was, in his immediate affect, everything that Col. McCabe was not. But appearance is notoriously deceiving, because, as I soon came to learn, McCabe was every bit the soldier that Newgarden was. Like Newgarden, McCabe was a West Pointer, but a couple of generations down. Strange to say, though I served with the 419th for seven months, the only two names I can now recall from my time in that battalion are those of Col. McCabe and Sgt. Wister. It was McCabe who could have had me court-martialed in early August, when I went AWOL to New York to get married to Susybelle. Sgt. Wister was our ammo sergeant.

I was assigned to one of the firing batteries, Battery B, as a Forward Observer, where I soon found myself to be a supernumerary. Superfluous on arrival, because that battery already had the two Forward Observers called for by the table of organization and both of them had been serving in that battery for a year or more. They outranked me by date of rank, too, of course. By a lot, but then—who didn't? So it seemed to me that my chances of going overseas with the Tenth were poor at best and, in the event, I didn't get to go along when the division shipped out later. And guess what? Of all the ships in the world, it was on the *SS Brazil* that the Tenth went over there! The same *SS Brazil* as that on which, three years before, I had sailed with the Yale Glee Club on a concert tour of South America. And the same *SS Brazil* as that which, later on, was just ahead of my ship in the convoy when I went over myself.

During the war, Augusta was a very friendly place for all of us stationed out at Camp Gordon. Not every town was, you know. If you were stationed around a few of those towns, you just stayed out on the base. But it was nice going into Augusta on a Sunday, getting away from the barracks. I even joined the Augusta Country Club. I've always loved golf and their country club course was super. It backed up to the Augusta National where The Masters is played. One of the Country Club's tee boxes looked out over The Masters. Just a few strands of barbed wire between me and what had been a gorgeous, manicured fairway of the Augusta National. But this was in early 1944 and that course was then nothing but a pasture. Eighteen holes of pasture, dappled with the cattle I could see grazing over there. Right after Pearl Harbor, the Augusta National ceased life as a golf course and was reincarnated as a Victory Garden. For beef cattle. That exquisite course you see on television every April? In just two years it was gone with the wind. Gone back to nature. All but the azaleas.

But not to worry. Surely it will take nature far longer to reclaim the rest of our high culture. Our graceful parking lots and vaunted shopping malls. Not to forget the highways that lace our countryside, ribbons of concrete long enough to stretch to the moon and back a hundred times or more. And yes, even the dumps for our atomic waste and the sprawl of our other contagion, they'll someday all be returned to nature, too. For she's always lain in silent wait, nature has, to snuff out that little campfire around which we've huddled ourselves for so long and warmed our hands. That little lamp that burns so hopefully, deep in the jungle of chaos and ancient night which still surrounds us and whence, not so long ago, we so mysteriously came. That soft glow we call civilization.

But let's skip ahead six months to the time late in the war when I *did* finally make it over there. Not as an artillery officer—as an engineer, of all things! But once over there, I quite literally talked my way back in—first back into the Tenth Armored Division and then into the artillery. I explain it in that letter I wrote Fred Ryan.

But this time, I went to a different battalion of the Tenth. The 420th, Battery A. I was a Forward Observer, of course. That's all I ever was, a Forward Observer. Doesn't matter. I got over there so late and saw so little fighting that I'd be half-ashamed, but for the fact that, like all of us, I was never given any choice in the matter.

But now about this piece that Stafford wrote. There's something in here about my being sent from Battery A to the 609th Tank Destroyer Battalion before coming home. The 609th had been attached to the Tenth Armored during the whole of the war, and it was being sent home, too. But I have no idea why I was sent there. It wasn't much of a move. The 609th's headquarters was down at the Walchensee, just a few kilometers south of us. About all I remember of my duty with the 609th was taking all our tanks in a convoy to Augsburg, to be turned in at an ordinance depot. I think it was Augsburg. I know that we were on an autobahn and got going too fast and threw track right and left and burned out a lot of idlers.

With the 609th, I bunked-up with the other officers in an alpine chalet on the north side of the lake. It was up above a small hotel on the lakeshore down below us—high enough up the hillside to have a dramatic view of much of the Walkensee itself. Wherever he was then—probably lying in a soldier's grave somewhere, who knows?—the owner of that chalet must have been someone highly literate, because he'd furnished his rather nice little library with some excellent titles. He'd even shelved a few books in English, and since it had been five months since I'd even *seen* a book in English, and since I had no German at all, that library became my retreat.

Oh, yes, and not a hundred yards away, on a rough-hewn rock plinth, stood a handsome head of Goethe. Highly polished, his eyes looking out over that beautiful Walchensee. At that latitude and that time of year, the nights, of course, were dark for only an hour or two, so, late in the evenings, the time when, as you know, I like to sit outdoors, Goethe and I would sometimes be out there together, looking out over the lake. And the two of us would find ourselves discussing how in hell Germany could have possibly submitted to the insane atrocity that Hitler so plainly was. There'd be no such thing, of course, as *that* Germany until fifty years after Goethe was gone. But Hitler's Germans not only spoke Goethe's language, they were his direct cultural descendants, so how to explain it? Goethe told me himself that he couldn't figure it out any better than I could.

Have you ever thought of Hitler as being a very funny man? As a highly comic character, who could make you laugh out loud the way that Chaplin could? Well, before the war for many of us that's what he was, a grand comedy all by himself, and, ironically, absurd in much the same way that Chaplin was. Just to look at them made you laugh. They were both *poseurs*. Hitler for the calculated political effect, Chaplin for the equally calculated comedic.

Until the advent of TV, we depended in great part on the newsreels for our visualization of the historic events taking place in the great world outside. Pathé News. Movietone. March of Time. Others, too, that I forget. In the nineteen-thirties, before the feature film would be run, we would always be shown a newsreel. It might run as long as twenty minutes, and, more and more often, we'd be treated to the spectacle of someone named Hitler. Audience reaction to him in our country was about the same everywhere. The same in theatres here in hometown as it was in that little frame movie palace in Chetek, Wisconsin, that I knew so well growing up. That I attended through all the summers of the first twenty years of my life.

When the house lights dimmed to dark and you heard the projector begin to roll, pretty soon, there he'd be—Adolph Hitler! Flickering away in the dark of the house, up there on the screen, in living tones of gorgeous black and white. We generally saw him haranguing a gigantic crowd. Carrying on like a crazy man. By the way, for the young people of my generation, a movie was not always said to be a *movie*. It seems to me we were just as apt to call one a *flicker*. That was because all of them flickered away like mad in intense shades of black and white. But maybe you already knew that.

I can see him even now. In thrall to his own megalomaniacal vanity, he's all puffed up like a peacock on a cold and blustery day. You can see right off he's strutting his very best stuff. But we're not the audience that matters. What matters is that absolutely enormous crowd he's holding there captive, a crowd that simply adores him! He's already got them in the palm of his hand, and now he's massaging their impulsive little ids—milking them of the very last drop, the last vestige of rationality left in them. They're quite insane.

They've been hypnotized. Hypnotized by all that strutting about on the stage. That drum-drum-drumming on the lek. All of it carefully choreographed to woo the unwary. The crowd's been on its feet for a great long while, standing up through it all, so their heads are now entirely empty—as drained of sense as they are of blood. That's why their faces look so ghostly as they lift them up to this latter-day saint. This Moses! This people's politician, just come down from the mount. His passionate words punctuated by every variety of calculated gesture known to mesmerize the masses into the commission of an insane mayhem on a scale to us unknown. Of a horror, by us sitting in that movie theatre, not even imaginable!

But this Hitler, this deliverer, is by no means empty rhetoric and bombast. Oh, no, he's the real McCoy. He was himself a true believer and so all the more persuasive, as he offers them the promise of land. *Lebensraum*! Forty acres and a mule, so to speak, and every man Jack, a king! Never mind, that, for a very great many of those same men standing there, transfixed, before him, the land he promises will, in the event, be not only an early grave, but, as likely as not, one dug in some foreign and inhospitable soil.

But he's not appealing solely to their avarice. Oh, no, his rhetoric has now risen to an even higher plane. He's urging them to consult their vanity. Are they not a race of super men? Of Aryans? To whom all glory is owed and for whom no glory is ever sought in vain?

But, irrelevant as it was to subsequent events, his effect on us in this country was, of course, entirely different from the effect he was having on his own people over there. When Hitler first began to make his appearance on our newsreels, he would be met with an uneasy silence. No one quite knew what to make of such arrogance. Such strutting pomposity. It was something utterly alien to the quite simple and rather modest souls we were, most of us only one generation removed from the land. We who, all through the depression years of the thirties, filled America's movie houses, all of us desperate for a laugh.

To us, he looked—and yes, he sounded—well, *surreal*. Even his strident voice, so high-pitched and tinny, seemed scarcely human. Remember now, the movie sound tract was then still in its infancy. Many a great star of the silent screen fell from the sky when the sound of *The Jazz Singer* was heard. But in addition to that, Hitler spoke in a language that was so incomprehensible, so strange to our ears, so innately *funny*, that we assumed it must itself be part of the act, of the joke. As I say his gestures often seemed Chaplinesque. Just look at him there! Heiling and goose-stepping about, he looks for all the world like a mechanical man. A wind-up toy. We laughed. A lot.

If I recall, it was the *sight* of this wind-up toy that, most of all, would make us see him as comedic. Before long, a half-stifled titter would be heard in the house, and that titter would encourage a braver guffaw from someone in the back, and then the laughter would break out in earnest and we'd all be splitting our sides, laughing. Laughing at that self-important little man with his ridiculous moustache. He was our Borat—absolutely the funniest man alive!

By mid-August, both the Tenth Armored and the 609th were pretty well broken up and I found myself back in France with a bunch of other officers from the 609th, all of us living in tents in one of those huge redeployment camps around Rheims. Pretty sure it was Rheims. Tens of thousands of us. Hundreds of thousands, for all I know, in four tent cities. Our's was named Camp Atlanta.

As it happened, that was a very exciting time for me because my wife, Susybelle, was pregnant, and our first baby was due sometime early that August. But when I left Bavaria for France to wait ship for the States, I knew from hard experience that I'd never get another letter from home as long as I was overseas. Never get any news from Susybelle that our baby had been born. Not until I got home myself.

You see, there were then millions and millions of people in transit like me. People whom the army mails couldn't possibly reach. Americans in uniform scattered all around the world and all beginning to stir about from place to place on the long road home. I read somewhere that when the war ended, there had been some twelve million American men and women in uniform. And our country was very much smaller then. Sounds incredible, doesn't it? But that's what I read. Twelve million of us!

But I was not altogether without hope of news about the baby. There was a newspaper, the Paris edition of the *Stars and Stripes,* that was published every day by the Army and quick as peace came, we'd get that paper early almost every morning, and in every issue there'd be two or three whole pages containing nothing but very brief, one line announcements of the birth of babies born to fathers who were then over in the ETO. Columns and columns of names. As best I remember, those lists were single-spaced, giving the baby's name and sex and date of birth, and certainly the name and rank of the daddy. We had agreed that as soon as our baby was born, Susybelle would get word to the *Stars and Stripes*, and, if all went according to plan, then there'd come a day when I could read all about it in the army's paper. How was she to get word to the *Stars and Stripes*? How should I know?

So every morning when I went down to the mess tent for chow, the first thing I did was to look in that day's *Stars and Stripes* to see if I was one of those who'd become a daddy. Of course, all the fellows knew that I was expecting and half of them had a bet laid on it. They'd made up a pool on the day the baby would be born. So every morning, even before I came down to the mess tent, half of them were there ahead of me, looking carefully for my name in the paper in hopes they'd win the pool.

This had been going on for ten days or more with no news, when one morning—it was actually August 24th—after looking through those long lists and once more finding nothing, I had no sooner put the paper down and picked up my coffee, than the fellows were pushing that *Stars and Stripes* back in front of me. The announcement of our baby was in there of course and I'd just flat missed it. But they'd seen it and said nothing. They wanted to see my expression when I read it. That's how I learned of the arrival of our first child. She was named Susybelle, after her mother's aunt. When I read about her in that paper, she was already two weeks old.

When we arrived at that Camp Atlanta, it was to wait our turn to go to Le Havre to board ship for home and a forty-five day delay-in-route before leaving again for the Pacific. But we hadn't been waiting there long, when word came of Hiroshima, and suddenly—just like that!—the war was over, and I wasn't going to the CBI after all! I was going home, baby! Home to stay!

Anyhow, during the first three months I was over there, I was on the move almost every day. It took almost a month to catch up with the Tenth Armored. Our combat command had moved into Garmisch around the end of April. Maybe the first of May. The Germans surrendered and we took it without a shot fired. The war was over anyway. Now I can't even remember the last rounds we fired.

While our battery was there in Garmisch, I found out that the house we used for battery headquarters, and where I slept, was right next door to the house in which Richard Strauss was then living. Been meaning to tell you about that. I'd seen Strauss walking around over there across the fence, but I didn't know who he was. Not till the men told me. Never underestimate the American GI. If there's anything of interest going on anywhere around, he'll know about it! Strauss was old then, but he wasn't bent over. He died four years later.

Just before we left Garmisch to go into occupation we put on a full dress parade. Marched right through town. Whole division. Most of it anyway. I don't recall that we had a division review, just a parade, and believe it or not, a big crowd of Germans turned out to watch. I know it doesn't seem right that they'd do that, but I'm sure they did, because I can still see them standing there. Lined up along the street just like those people had done two years before on that Fourth of July we marched in Quincy. A little less than two years had passed but I was not quite the same person I'd been back there in Quincy. I'd become someone else. Someone a little different. And different in ways I couldn't have described, even to myself, but only felt. I just wasn't quite me any more.

Then the occupation began and my battery was ordered to move from Garmisch to the little Bavarian village of Bad Heilbrunn. That was the only place over there where I was ever stationed for any length of time. Stafford writes a lot about Bad Heilbrunn, so I must have done the same in lots of those letters I wrote home to my wife.

Now about Bad Heilbrunn. When I got Stafford's piece here, I went to the Internet and dialed up Bad Heilbrunn. You know, just to see what I could find? You won't believe it, but I found an aerial photo of that beautiful little village and, but for the Technicolor, it looks now just as it did sixty-five years ago. Or at least, it looks much as I remember it. Kind of spooky, seeing that. Have you ever seen a ghost in Technicolor?

Down low, at the right edge of the picture, I could even see the very house where I had my digs. That house was our battery headquarters. And that little open field between that house and the town, it's still lying vacant there. That was where we parked our M-7's, in that field. We had six of them. Two or three tracks and Jeeps and six- by-sixes. Beg pardon? A track was what we sometimes called a half-track and an M-7 was just a regular Sherman tank without a turret. It had an open cockpit for the ammo and a 105 mm howitzer. And a ring-mounted 50 caliber, it had that, too.

You can see that picture of Bad Heilbrunn yourself if you want. Just search Bad Heilbrunn on the Web and click the first entry and then click the word "Gemeinde" and presto! there at the bottom of the photo is the very same Bad Heilbrunn where I lived for a couple of months, right after the war.

No sooner had we got ourselves settled there in Bad Heilbrunn than word came down from Div Arty that the Germans were already operating a brewery in Munich and that we could go up there and get some kegs of beer. We'd been able to get schnapps all along of course. The Germans made it everywhere, right through the war. Made it out of an infusion of stump scum, dirty socks and kitchen midden. That's what it tasted like to me. It tasted simply awful. Worse than castor oil. I couldn't drink the stuff, but the men sure could. They'd fill their water cans with it. Pour out the water to make room for the scum. Can you believe it?

These are a couple of snapshots of me hanging out in Bad Heilbrunn.

Incidentally, a friend from earliest childhood showed up in Bad Heilbrunn and took these before the two of us left for Munich. He was Tom Stagg and right now, Tom lives just over there a ways. He's within easy walking distance.

We hadn't been long in Bad Heilbrunn, when I got a call from Tom. He'd had a rifle company in an infantry division, but he was then with corps somewhere nearby. Bad Tölz, I believe. He knew what outfit I was in and he was calling to see if I could get loose to go up to Munich with him. It was a miracle he got through to me. That call came through *six army field switchboards*! Connected by miles and miles of wire, all spun off a reel mounted on a Jeep and strewed along beside the road! I turned to the Captain and he said I could go. So Tom picked me up the next day and we went up to Munich, where he had some business to do for corps.

But that trip with Tom wasn't my first trip up to Munich. The first trip was for beer. Beer had been awful scarce, so when that word came from Div Arty, our battery commander, Skinny McClain, sent my friend, Ken Machado, and me with a six-by-six up to Munich to get some kegs of it for the battery. Ken was the other Forward Observer and I liked him a lot. He was from California. Portuguese. Silver Star. Wonder if he's still alive?

Munich wasn't far north of us. Fifty kilometers? It was plumb bombed out of course. Leveled to the ground! The whole city. Nothing but a vast pile of broken stone and mortar. The MPs conducted Ken and me through to the brewery. They had to. Mostly one-way traffic through rubble piled up on both sides of the street. It was ten feet high, and higher. The engineers had only just cleared it. Bulldozed a passage through, all the way from the south side of the city to where the brewery was on the north. When we got there, we couldn't have been more than ten or twelve kilometers from Dachau.

That's right, Dachau. Dachau's just outside of Munich, did you know that? I don't think Dachau was quite the first of those Nazi charnel houses to be exposed, but Ken and I would probably have known about it from pictures in the *Stars and Stripes*.

Did you know that it was at Dachau that we committed an horrendous atrocity of our own? Well, we did. We gunned down some hundred and twenty Waffen SS who'd surrendered and were standing with their hands in the air. Some GI just sat on a machine gun, mowing them down before an officer could stop him. That had happened not more than two weeks before Ken and I were there.

I'd had an experience a little like that myself. It was while I was in a replacement depot, waiting on a truck to take me and some GIs the final lap to the Tenth Armored. It seems to me that there were as many as a thousand of us in that center, most of them men who'd been wounded or sick and were headed back to their outfits, but there were a few replacements straight from States, like me. We were inside some town in Germany, I know that, and I'd pulled duty as Officer of the Day, when I was called out to go with an MP Sergeant to investigate a shooting. It was at night, and when we pulled up in front of a little house there in town, it was all over. I went in and there was this old man lying on the floor, his wife just standing there. He was stone dead, had a couple of bullet holes in his chest. One of our GIs had knocked on his door, and when that old man opened it up, that GI killed him. Shot him dead in his own doorway.

That's all I remember about that little episode, but nothing in my previous life had prepared me for anything like it. It was my first inkling that we human beings are simply just animals—and by no means the prize specimens of that otherwise admirable Kingdom.

By the way, my friend Fletcher Thorne-Thomsen was probably the first American to see Dachau. Fletcher was a sergeant in the Eighth Armored Division, in command of a track doing reconnaissance for the artillery when he just happened upon Dachau's main gate. He looked around for a minute at the grim scene in there and got out. Never saw one German soldier. It must have been within hours after that that those SS were machine-gunned. Not by the Eight Armored! Some other outfit did that.

There was a lot of anger in me towards the Germans. There was in all of us who were over there. It's mostly gone now, and I'm glad it is. But anger now, isn't it just another form of perfectly human sentiment? And without sentiment, might we not as well be dead? Might we not as well have not lived at all?

Those Germans, old people and kids, they were out in their fields working right through the war, while the French were sitting on their ass. We laughed about the French. Right today, forty percent of the population of Chippewa County, Wisconsin, claims descent from German immigrants. And it doesn't get any more American than it does in Chippewa County. So you figure it out.

Of course, when the war ended, the enemy was all around us, everywhere I looked. We were in their midst and now and then, on the odd face here and there, I could plainly see that stiff-necked arrogance which their recent political acculturation had taught them was their right. But back then, they had for me become clearly identified as the enemy of mankind. All but the children. With the children, it was different. They weren't to blame for it, and they were everywhere in that village. Hundreds of them, mostly from Hamburg. It's beyond me how they had survived all those years in that maelstrom.

At the end of the war, that whole countryside down there was full of refugees. And not just from all over Germany either. From all over Europe. Even Russians were there. About fifty Russian slave laborers were camped not a quarter of a mile from town. They caused us a lot of trouble. Refused to go back to the Russian Zone.

You don't know me, not really. Not yet. Like most of my generation, I was an innocent. And it was not because I had led a protected life, either, because I hadn't. My parents simply didn't believe in protecting me from the world. And by then, of course, I'd been away from home, and on my own, for almost ten years anyway. No, it was because our country was then, by and large, a nation of innocents. So I could scarcely believe that these people were the same German people that music and reading and a few hours with German expatriates had caused me to so much admire. The same abhorrent people with whom I'd thought, until then, that I had a natural kinship. The same people for whom I had now come to feel a loathing so violent I could hardly bear to look at the hideous face of even one of them, lest I smash it in with the butt of my carbine! But I don't want to get into all that again.

We humans are such destructive animals, I wonder why my parents held the breed in such esteem. Held out such hopes for us. Such aspirations. How could they *possibly* have been so optimistic? And that fascist mentality, it's still around, of course.

I've wondered about them. About those fascists. They're fellow human beings, aren't they? I've certainly been told they are. So how should I regard them? As insane? Certainly not! No, they are quite ordinary people really. That's the problem. They manifest in themselves those same, basic, all too human instincts which in my time organized themselves into the moral and ethical corruption that was Nazi Germany. I'd give anything to know what a man like the Captain of the *Graf Spee* was thinking when he pulled the trigger. Took his own life down there in BA, in Buenos Aires when the war had only just begun. I wonder, did he foresee what was to become of his country in consequence of that catastrophic war of self-aggrandizement that engulfed us all and killed so many of my friends? Or was it simply out of shame that he did it?

Forsan et haec olim meminisse iuvabit. I learned that from Doc Harwood. From Vergil. And I've never forgotten it either. Perchance the day will come when we'll think back and take pleasure even in such a memory as this. Not very elegant, but that's the sense of it. Whenever I find myself thinking black thoughts like that, that's where I suddenly am. Stranded on a hostile beach with Aeneas and his men. Without my memory of my father and my mother, I'd have no hopes for us. None at all! But I shouldn't be thinking like that. Not when I ought to be thinking of my parents. Of them, and of all the hopes and aspirations they had for me when I was small. To turn my back on them now—when they're both gone, leaving only me—for me to count as nothing the hopes they had for us all, for me to abandon them now—wouldn't to do anything like that be at the peril of whatever sorry little soul I've got?

I can't believe I've talked about that war so long. I never do that! Well, not often. But I couldn't seem to stop. It must have been some of the things Stafford wrote in that piece of hers. Seems like the time I spent in the army was in some way radically different from all of the rest of my life. In fact, I don't think it's too much to say that there's some essential part of me—something stored in me that's deeper than memory, some creature that's still alive and crawling around down there—that would never have drawn the full breath of life at all, had it not been for the army and for that war. For the experience of those three years I spent in uniform.

Stafford's surely right about one thing though. It must have been while I was over there that I became so cynical—that my dreams first turned to ashes. That beautiful land of boyhood dreams on which grew the wheat that soon would turn to straw.

But getting back to Stafford's piece, she didn't write it for me. No, it's for you, so I suppose you'll probably want to take it home with you and look it over. You'll see in there that Stafford refers to me as "Pa". It's not only my children who call me that. For more than sixty years, all sorts of people have called me "Pa". Many of my friends, even my own parents, called me "Pa".

There's one more thing I might tell you about before I shut up. The 420th was the artillery battalion for Combat Command B of the Tenth Armored. A battalion of infantry, a battalion of tanks and the artillery of the 420th, plus some Tank Destroyers, that's what made up our combat command. And it was Combat Command B that Patton ordered to Bastogne. In fact, they were the very first troops to arrive in Bastogne. Got there even ahead of the 101st. One of those paratroopers from the 101st told my radio operator that the five foot jump he'd made off the tailgate of a six by six truck in the town of Bastogne turned out to be the longest, toughest and most fearsome jump his division had made in the whole war. But everybody must know all about Bastogne by now.

Our battalion received the Presidential Unit Citation. Not just the battalion, the whole damned combat command did. There were three days there when our M-7s were just two hundred yards back of the infantry's perimeter defense, firing those howitzers point-blank. Firing their fifty calibers the same way. Direct fire, just like the tankers. That's how close the Germans got. That must have been where Jim Ackerman earned his Silver Star. He was our Exec. Earning a Silver Star, that's got to be highly unusual for the Exec of a firing battery. But that's the way it was at Bastogne. All the fellows told me that at Bastogne they were all up front.

I was not at Bastogne, of course, but everybody else in my battery was. But Bastogne was only one of the places they fought. Just one battle. It was a big one, but there were lots and lots of others. As for me, just say that they didn't let me out on the stage until the curtain call, but that I went out there carrying my spear.

When I reported to A Battery, I soon learned that they'd lost nine men. That's an awful lot of men killed for just one firing battery. Even in armor, it was. Anyway, I knew of course that I was likely replacing some Forward Observer who'd been killed, or maybe too shot up to come back. But I never asked the name of that man whose place I was taking or what had happened to him or anything like that. I'd never have asked such a thing as that. No one ever told me either. No one ever seemed to speak his name. That's just the way it was. Things like that just weren't talked about much. Too deep. There are things as deep as that you know. But just last year I myself came to learn who that man was. It was in the process of disinterring the past that I learned the name of that other Forward Observer in the 420th whose place I'd taken.

Do you see this book? It was published in 1994, the fiftieth reunion year for our class at Yale. I ordered a copy, but when it came, I just put it away. Never even opened it! So it was not until last year, not until 2006, when I finally took a good look at it, that I found here at the very beginning, up in the front where they belong, brief biographies of my thirty-six Yale classmates who died in the war. Thirty-six of us killed out of some six hundred or so.

Ah! Here's what I'm looking for. The name of the man I replaced. He's number 32. Van Cortlandt. Augustus Van Cortlandt, III, of Mount Kisco, New York. Gus was one of that little bunch of us who were inducted into the army together at Fort Devens and went together to that Military Police outfit and on to the Field Artillery School at Sill. Let me read you what it says here about Gus.

32. Augustus Van Cortlandt III of Mount Kisco, New York, was a member of Branford College, The Fence Club, and Berzelius. He rowed on the freshman crew, and played college football. A member of the Army ROTC, he was called to active duty in June 1943, and commissioned in the Field Artillery in December. Assigned as a Forward Observer (in a heavy tank) for the 420th Armored Field Artillery Battalion, he won the Silver Star for valor during the Moselle River crossing in November 1944: 'Although wounded by grenade fragments, Lieutenant Van Cortlandt . . . gave continuous and effective observation for his unit, while under enemy *mortar and artillery fire both day and night.'* Trapped in the town of Bastogne on Christmas Eve during the Battle of the Bulge, he won the Bronze Star for evacuating wounded soldiers from an aid station that was on fire from a direct hit. He died a few weeks later in a fierce battle for the town of Nauborn. The citation for Oak Leaf Cluster to the Silver Star said: 'Although mortally wounded during the action, Lieutenant Van Cortlandt continued directing effective fire upon hostile forces, repelling them with heavy losses'.

Dulc'et décor'est pro patria mori? Wilfred Owen and Brecht and countless others thought differently about it. And yes, I've sometimes had doubts myself. But then I ask myself—would Horace have told us this if there were no truth in it? So it's something I've thought about. As a matter of fact, I've been thinking about it a whole lot lately. And what I've decided is, that it's yet one more of those many things about mankind that I'll never know for sure.

But there *is* one thing I *do* know. And it's something I know for *absolute* sure, because I knew him very well. Gus would never have doubted, not even for one moment, what it was *he* was sent over there to do.

Over there, over there …
(Pa's War Letters)

November 17, 2006
Stafford Lyons

There is a picture of my father coming out of a building somewhere in Europe while he was serving in WW II. I look at that picture with curiosity and a bit of regret. I don't know that man, a 23 year old 2nd Lieutenant, dressed in fatigues, and sporting a dapper, blond mustache à la Errol Flynn. He's smiling and seems just about to speak, or just about to laugh. It would be like him to be thinking of a joke. He has an easy, confident posture, almost too comfortable for the time he's living. I wonder at his gaiety. Why does he seem so happy on that particular day? In the picture he doesn't look like any kind of warrior. Skinny as an adolescent boy, he hardly looks old enough to know what he's fighting for, and can't be much of a threat to anyone. I know he had to drag his men out of cat houses in Paris. How was he able to do that? My father is a sensitive man, a gentleman. How could he have brought himself to be involved in that war in the first place?

Like many of his generation my father has never talked much about the war, neither did he talk much about any of his youth, saying that he didn't have a childhood, or there was nothing about his life that would interest me, or that he was too busy planning the future and didn't want to think about the past. I'd come to think I would never learn anything new about him, at least nothing that would help fill all the gaps in my understanding of what led him to become the man I know. Then a wonderful thing happened. My mother sent me a packet of letters he wrote to her in 1945 during those six months from March to the end of August when he was stationed overseas, and suddenly I had the man before me.

As one might expect, the letters from a new husband to his wife are filled with loneliness and longing. But censorship was in full force, so there is scant detail about events or the job he is required to do.

Taken all together, the letters reveal little about the young man who went to war. One of his duties as an officer was to censor letters his men sent home. About them he said: *"I find that in spite of variations in spelling, grammar, and diction, most soldiers are scared to death of combat (especially those who have been wounded), love their wives, their homes and their families, and seem to live a dreaming life."* (April) Was he afraid, too? Was his experience one of a dream-like state so that the days ran together and nothing seemed real? He had wanted to enlist, and his entire class graduated early from Yale so that they might do just that; but once in Europe he seemed to welcome the same kind of ennui as that of his men. Here's what he says:

"It may be no good to live like this, dreaming, but I find I'm a weakling and take it like dope to numb my painful loneliness. It's true that I've learned some things about war and people that I could never learn at home, but they are things no man should know. And I take them rather harder than most." (April 8?)

In his letters he doesn't say anything about the cause for which he was fighting or the value of his commitment. He doesn't mention the reasons that compelled him to want to join the army, though I know most people in those days felt a strong duty to serve their country. Indeed, not long after arriving his thoughts are most often focused on returning home:

"Every fine day hastens the war along, hastens me home again. As far as I can tell I stand about as good a chance of avoiding the army of occupation as the next man. Let's hope for the best, anyhow, and be prepared for the worst." (April 8.)

"The worst" was never explained.
I can assume that he didn't want to worry his family unnecessarily by giving up all his deepest, darkest thoughts. Locations and dates were left out for security reasons, and my father not only censored the letters from the men under his command, but also had to censor his own, so place names were often left out,

as he did in this letter. *"Nimporte quelle place en Belgique."* (April 9?) But there's hardly any hint of all that is not said. I can understand that in his loneliness and with the constant, seemingly arbitrary, shifting of location and conditions mail was of extreme importance. For long stretches he wrote a letter almost every day, yet all of this writing was done without any response.

"Five weeks now and not so much as a postcard . . . The way things are and the way I've been moving, I have no hopes of getting mail for another month." (April 17.)

"No mail still. I feel like a hot-house plant left for months out in the woods with no water." (May 8.)

Finally, on May 11 he dashes off a V MAIL in which he describes getting sixty-one "magnificent" letters but is too emotional to do more than report the event—*"Now I'm so excited and choked up that I don't trust myself to begin . . . My morale breaks all records."*

I remember my first year of college in rural New York State feeling a long way from home and everything else. I checked my mailbox sometimes twice a day for anything at all that would connect me with something familiar, and my deep ache when nothing was there. That was in a sequestered, friendly place—not a foreign land during war. How immensely heartbreaking must have seemed those sixty-one letters when they finally arrived after so long a drought. To weep with gratitude in the presence of them must have been the only possible response.

In but one letter, written April 18 in Germany, does my father allow himself to reflect to my mother on the war. He begins by describing the beautiful gardens cultivated by the hard working Germans, then wonders how their strong love of beauty could coexist with such grotesque hatred of their fellow man.

"I cannot for the life of me understand why these people went to war. With what were they dissatisfied? I cannot see. Perhaps, it was merely the lunatic fringe: the militarists joined with political fanatics

and the malcontents. It's the same in nature. The shape of a lake is determined by the weedy shallows off the bank; the calm clear depths count for nothing."

This stirring passage touches me like no other. The father I know doesn't reside in the "weedy shallows," and is often cynical about human nature. Was that attitude born of the war? Was he exposed just a little too much to those malcontents? Those are some of the things I'd love to know.

In all that I've heard and read about the European theater of WWII I learned of battles and movements and armies engaged in looking for, or fighting with, or retreating from the enemy. I was, perhaps, only faintly aware of anything like a surrounding army of support systems and fresh troops: soldiers waiting, relocating, then waiting some more, marching, repairing gear, writing letters home—while still waiting. This seems to be the kind of army my father was engaged with, one always on the periphery--getting ready to be, but never quite being involved.

"The division is now out of the lines for good and I suppose there's no more real fighting anywhere. I got to see little but I've learned everything I wanted to know." (May 8.)

What "little" he saw he doesn't reveal in any letter. That may be because he can't mention what he's doing or where he's going, so it's possible that he played a greater role in the effort than he can say in letters. Whether or not he ever engaged the enemy in battle, there must have been an ever present dread of what might lie ahead. And surely the arbitrary movement from one place to another and the lack of any satisfactory work must have been frustrating and demoralizing.

In spite of his sense of humor, he probably experienced much more discomfort than he will admit. Of his relocation to Germany he writes *"As you see I have moved to a much safer spot--really. Quite a long, slow, uncomfortable trip by petite boxcars. The ventilation was excellent, there being almost unlimited quantities of it"*. (April ?)

I do know he was moving constantly. By April 26 (about six weeks into his stay in Europe) he wrote that he'd already been to France three times, Belgium twice, and Luxemburg twice. In Germany alone he saw Cologne, Aachen, Worms, Sarreguemines, Stuttgart and Wiesbach:

"One time last week I missed my train in Saarequemines—nothing unusual. There is no schedule of course, the trains stopping for hours and starting off again without warning or apparent reason. . . . The whole of eastern France, Belgium and all of occupied Germany is the most tremendous mass of U. S. Army transportation you ever saw."

Not until May is he able to stay put for a while, but it's apparent that even before then his nourishment came from nature and the pleasures of civilization such as reading and smoking a cigar or finding a bottle of good wine. Nature is always in the forefront:

"All the trees bear the sweet light leaves of spring, and in Belgium particularly does the irregularity of the landscape make more variety than you can imagine in the little sameness of towns, fields, roads and streams that is Belgium." (April 8?)

And this:

"I'm most comfortably located in a good house in the Bavarian Alps, probably the most beautiful part of Germany...There is a grand stream in the valley bottom which I have fished (as yet unsuccessfully) for the trout which really do inhabit it...The valley is settled in little villages with the ubiquitous red tile roofs. And but for buildings and roads the whole floor of the valley would be emerald green, the new leaves of trees exactly matching the grass, this light green broken only by apple blossoms and a few wild flowers."

(May 8.)

I've read elsewhere that people experiencing great upheaval will cling to vestiges of everyday routine. All through my father's letters are strains of normalcy—a search for a good camera, learning to play poker and bridge, making plans for a new house, enjoying a quiet moment reading his letters, and paying special attention to and appreciation for the landscape around him. These are actually the qualities of him with which I'm more familiar. He must have looked hungrily for a fishing spot in every venue because he often writes of rigging up something to fish a beautiful stream and cooking up a batch of fresh caught fish. Those simple pleasures may have brought him hope and a modicum of joy as I know from my own observation of him they have all his life.

But I wonder if he made those moments deliberately, sought out the trout streams and good music; or were they fortuitous moments that emerged out of the chaos like a familiar voice in a crowd? Surely, they are the things that helped him pass the time more sweetly, but does he mention them not only because they happened, but also because he needed to talk of them to stretch the duration of their effect?

In the middle of May he lands in Bad Heilbrunn, Germany, a place that seems to have held special significance. Was that because the European war was over and fear no longer laced the chaos? Was it for the easing of restrictions that he was able to finally express the weight of a place, or was work itself more meaningful and clear? He says, *"We are organizing to control everything. It's a hard job but a pleasant one to me (after so long a stretch of inactivity) and tremendously interesting."* (May 17) Perhaps Bad Heilbrunn represented something else--a settlement, a rest, a reality? I'm sure it was at least more comfortable with *"hot and cold water in most rooms, an excellent bathroom, attractive furniture, two 'kind of' lounge rooms downstairs on the first floor just made for paper and relaxation."* (May 15.)

His work in Bad Heilbrunn seems not only interesting but also significant--running a twenty-four hour guard duty over all the "good road entrances" into the area and covering the entrance to Bad Heilbrunn (a command they set up in just two days.)

"All civilian traffic, mounted and dismounted, is now frozen in place. The purpose of this is principally to gain control of the situation and to prevent the cluttering of roads with straggling refugees and vagrants.

We have dealt with upwards of four hundred people taken off the roads by our guards. We have handled and shipped away by truck twenty odd Italians and forty-two Frenchmen. We have a cargo waiting of Dutchmen and some more French and Italians. We have in our area Poles, Yugoslavians, and Russians. Germany has millions and millions of pressed laborers from other countries who must somehow be got home...

This dealing arbitrarily with hundreds of humans is a great, queer (and to me often disagreeable) thing. One is continually making snap decisions on matters which to you and to military government are of no importance at all but which, it is easy to see, means a great deal to the luckless supplicant.

Our government is strictly fair and sometimes even merciful. But so great is the [hubris] of this sinful race that I know many of them consider themselves hardly dealt with." (May 17.)

Yet, in spite of fourteen to sixteen hour days he found life so interesting and unpredictable that it was actually "enjoyable." One such moment was the following:

"This morning I dropped into a farm where thirty odd ex-French soldiers (slave laborers later) were staying to tell them a truck would pick them up in the morning to take them "chez vous." They broke open the last of their wine and we toasted hot and heavy for about an hour. Then they took me back to a shed and presented me with a two-pointer buck freshly killed last night. So me and the driver eased back into town all wined up with a deer on the hood of the Jeep. We gave the deer to a house full of children because it wasn't enough to feed the battery. I'm just now getting over the wine. Wow!" (May 18.)

The importance of Bad Heilbrunn may be only that he was there long enough for it to grow on him. I don't think he ever went back. I'm sure he didn't.

My father has always put his best effort into anything he attempts. I know he must have done the same in the army even though any bureaucracy and especially the military is rife with inefficiencies. Hierarchical procedures and endless, arbitrary orders must have been grating. Though he got along well with his men, he knew that he wasn't the kind of malleable character that the military needs.

"When I left "A" Battery to come to the 609th, at least half of the battery sought me out personally to say goodbye. Two of the older Sgts. told me that with two exceptions I had been the most popular officer ever in the battery...I think in large part it was the result of talking always in their terms without changing my point of view to conform with theirs. Most important I never stood on rank (which they all hate in an officer and which is the thing in the army I too detest most. ...The truth is that though I know I'm a good officer, I am aware that I never or seldom appear to be one outside of the battery. And that is partly because I don't cut a very military figure and partly because I can never bring myself to act before my superior officers in a way that I do not when they are gone. My Captains appreciate this but not the Majors and Colonels." (July 3.)

Right after that, he did finally get a promotion, and though I'm sure he was pleased, I suspect that it wasn't the great honor to him that some might think. He spent only three sentences on the news: *"So you thought you were married to a 2nd Lt. did you? Well, you're not! You're married to a first lieutenant or more rightly a First Lieutenant."* (August 1.) That's it! Not exactly an ecstatic reaction.

It's easy for me to assume that his time away from home in a foreign land during a tumultuous upheaval was easier than many. He never mentions combat; he was an officer, which improved his living conditions; he came at the end of the war when most of the carnage was over. But he was only twenty-three, and he, like most of the troops, had never experienced anything like what he experienced in that war. When I think of myself at that age, I know he wasn't prepared for it. How does one prepare? Surely the life lessons were hard learned. And yet, his letters must have encouraged his pregnant wife and soothed his parents whose other son was in the Pacific.

On July 20 he learned he'd be coming home but didn't know when. Then those orders were changed, and he was again uncertain about where he was going and what he'd be doing. Most of what he wrote in July and August are responses to letters or questions about home and family, as if the last, long days in the army were still a kind of purgatory with nothing to do but wait. The last months of his duty in Europe were spent thinking more and more of home and less of anything that was happening wherever he was: *"My letters get more and more trite. I've stopped altogether having any life but the one at home..."* (August 1.)

My mother's letters steadied my father. The news of the war encouraged. But what changed him emotionally from that raw boy in the picture to the father he became? Was this a time he grew in leaps? If it was, I don't see it in his letters. I can picture from time to time the man who howls delightedly at the hint of a pun and sings in full throated a cappella at every opportunity; but there is also a calmness and restraint in his letters that hardly seem my father at all.

People change over the years, of course, and I know my father from a later period when his life slowly settled into an ominous predictability and dreams began to sink into a morass of frustration. In his letters I do not see the man who rushes, pushes, obsesses, and works and works and works, the critical man, the impatient man, the absent man.

What I do see, though, is someone I feel I've known all my life, the essence of the man. I don't think it's wishful thinking to have always loved my father for what I imagined him to be under a veil of abrupt and often angry outbursts. My imagination didn't have to work hard. It was there always: a tenderness and sensitivity, an appreciation for beauty and order, a joy of learning and delight in having done something wholly new. If he showed restraint in his war letters, the reason was likely that he didn't want to alarm. But I think there is much that he didn't say about that time that should be said, things that I want to know if only to get the whole picture of the man he was and the time he lived. It's natural, I suppose, to think that we grow so far beyond our early years that the person we were is no longer relevant. But I believe the past is the frame on which we build the present. Without it we crumble to nothing. So I want to know who my father was, to see what made him who he became, the then and now, the all of him.

Traditional: Michael Hall of Wisconsin

    Of my eight great grandparents, all but one predeceased my birth, but I saw a lot of the one I did know. She was my Grandmother Hall's mother, my own Great Grandmother O'Rourke, and since she lived on well into my own life, I remember her rather well. I called her Grandmother O'Rourke. So did everyone else. She was born Florence Ella Stevens on May 30, 1856, at Albany, Vermont, and she married one Andrew Alexander O'Rourke. When they married, Andrew was Road Master of the Wisconsin Central Railroad. By Andrew, Grandmother O'Rourke bore seven children, including my Grandmother Hall. Although she was sometimes called Aunt Laura, she perfectly graced a beautiful Irish name by which she was more often called, and that name was Annie Laurie.
    Not long before I was born, Grandmother O'Rourke fell and broke her pelvis. There was no mending it, not in those days, so you'd think that that would have done her in, but you'd be wrong. She had someone standing by who truly loved her. Loved her in the old way, and if you don't already know the difference, then don't ask me to explain. So she lived the last third of her life in a wheelchair—Annie Laurie with her every hour of the day and night. She finally died in 1953. She was ninety-seven when her daughter closed her eyes.
    I can see her in that wheelchair now, but then, I never once saw her out of it. Sitting there, the picture of patience itself. A patience so stoic, so uncomplaining, so utterly silent that I have no memory of how she spoke. And that causes me some trouble, too, because I'd really prefer to hear a bit of Irish on her lips, but I don't. I knew a great many of my mother's people, and although they were all Irish to the bone, I don't think I ever heard even one of them speak in a way that you or I would hear as *Irish*. Did I fail to notice it? Did I have a tin ear? Have I simply *forgotten* how they spoke. No, I'm sure there was hardly a trace of Ireland in the speech of any of them. Not only nothing of the accents, but nothing of those interesting and peculiar figurations of English we hear as specific to the Irish tongue.

You've seen those pictures I have of Annie Laurie and my Grandfather Hall, but now, just take a good, long look at these photos of Grandfather Hall's parents, Michael and Mary Scally Hall.

Oh, my! Just look there into Michael's face! His eyes! Those cold, penetrating and perfectly level eyes! They'll look you down, won't they! In those eyes you can see just what kind of man it took to break the vast, vacant and primal sod that was once our own Midwest and put something somewhat resembling a civil society in its place.

Well, he *does* look awfully cold and hard in this picture, doesn't he? But you can see how real and basic he was. How tough—tough as that tough, thick coat he's wearing. But my mother always told me that, down under, he was the very kindliest of men. A truly gentle man, she said. Well, except on those days he'd be riding out and find himself challenged by the sight of some farmer in the commission of one of those grievous, back-country sins that made him mad enough to fight. And woe to you if you were the culprit! That's what my mother said and she'd know all about him. Growing up there on her grandparents' farm had made a profound impression on my mother. One she would never forget. And for some reason, the lessons she learned got passed on to me.

Although he was not a very big man, Michael never carried a gun—not even when he was High Sheriff of Chippewa County. But when the need arose, he was ready enough with his fists. That's what my mother told me. You'd never believe what it was that made a peaceful man like Michael mad enough to fight. Mad enough to climb down from his buggy and become the Irish brawler my mother said he became when he got riled up. And now, when I look closer at his face and look into those eyes, I can see the unusual man my mother talked about and why they said he'd get so fighting-mad.

But look here, if you expect me to tell you about Michael and Mary, then you'll need some background first. History. Context. So I'll begin in 1859, when they first arrived in Chippewa Falls, a tiny new settlement in far northwestern Wisconsin. I'd begin earlier than that, were it not for some—shall I say, *disquieting* conflicts between family legend and some other sources I've had a look at. You know, the usual discrepancies between folklore and fact? But I've got a strict rule against self-deception, and here's what I *can* tell you pretty much for sure about how they came to be in Chippewa. Chippewa is what Chippewa Falls is more often called by those of us who know it. As you might guess, it's on the Chippewa River, a headwater of the Mississippi. The word *Chippewa* derives from the Ojibwa Indians. The Atchafalaya, that's also a river with an Indian name, but I don't know how it derives.

But first, where do I fit into this story? If I haven't told you, I am a direct descendant of Michael and Mary. They produced five daughters but only two sons. Their only son to survive into adulthood was Harry Hall, my mother's father. I already told you a bit about him, haven't I? My Grandfather Hall? I'm sure I have.

Now, as for Mary, I know she was née Mary Scally, on November 15, 1838. It's also a fact that she was born in Longford, Ireland. Her 1913 obituary assures us that she was born in Dublin, but there's far better evidence—including her own statement in her own hand—that she was born in Longford, Ireland, and not in Dublin at all. For that and other reasons, I don't too much trust those old obituaries I have of the two of them. So what *should* I trust? Well, not family legend either—not completely. Or, in another context, the sworn testimony of any of the defendant's crooked real estate appraisers. The town of Longford's in the dead center of Ireland, but how Mary got from there to Wisconsin, God only knows!

Let's see, now—about Michael. His obituary recites that he was born in Dublin and I'm satisfied he was. His date of birth was January 20, 1836. But there *is* varying evidence—as fascinating as it is conflicting—as to when and with whom he came to this country. If we are to believe his obituary, then he came with his parents when he was eleven years old and settled with them in Hartford, Connecticut. But there's another altogether different, and far more romantic, story. A story that was always told to me as fact but which I've had to recognize may well be only family legend. However, I've got to admit that it's just as apt to be true as the other one. Nothing in life is harder to find than the true facts about anything.

Do you see this book? It's a compilation of family genealogy. A lot of it is pretty hard, well documented, historical fact, but other parts of it are largely anecdotal. You can expect that. My father put this book together and published it in 1965, not long before he died. See, it says right here, *The Lyons Family*. But the

Michael Hall family, my mother's family, figures in here just as large as his. If I were ever to do anything so ill-advised as to write about those Irish ancestors of mine, I could put Papa's book to very good use. Maybe just select and copy the meatiest parts—the parts about Michael and Mary and their farm—and paste them in my book somewhere. Maybe in the appendix.

There's a family legend in this book to the effect that Michael's father was bitterly opposed to British hegemony, and that, under threat of persecution, he left Ireland in the dark of night by sailing vessel for Australia. He and his ship were lost at sea in a heavy storm. Michael's mother died soon after, and two old maid aunts brought Michael over here as a little orphan boy.

But, as I said, his obituary says he came over with his parents. It was published on October 17, 1911, in the *Daily Independent*, but whoever wrote it would have known nothing about Michael's early life. Not first hand, he wouldn't. And anyway, that obituary, like the one of Mary, is itself highly suspect. It reports that Michael first arrived in Chippewa in *1854*, while, directly to the contrary, we have it from Michael himself that the Fourth of July of *1859* was the first that he and Mary spent in Chippewa. I found that important information in Michael's own lengthy, highly personal and quite interesting account of the two or three days that immediately preceded the Fourth of July of 1859. That's something else that could be pasted in an appendix.

That piece was something Michael wrote himself and it appeared on July 1, 1904 in a Chippewa newspaper. In it, he attempts to describe for the young people of Chippewa the difference between the Chippewa of 1904 and the Chippewa of 1859. His central theme is the extreme difficulty that he and a few other like-minded early settlers had faced in making preparations for their celebration of the Fourth of July of 1859, maybe Chippewa's first. There was no money in town, so it seems to have been almost impossible to obtain whisky in the quantities then deemed essential to the proper celebration of our country's birth. He concludes with an assurance to his *young readers* that the Chippewa of 1904, is a far, far better place than was the Chippewa of 1859. He tells them, that in 1904 Chippewa has not only millions of surplus money but saloons galore! *Saloons galore*! Can you beat it! Hard to find honesty like that in the paper anymore. Or anywhere else. The main point of the story is how Michael and his friends managed to get the necessary whiskey, but in that same piece Michael also mentions that the Fourth of July of 1859 was the first Fourth of July he spent in Chippewa.

Now, it's true that in that piece, Michael is writing long, long after the fact, so, given that his mind was reaching back to the events of July, 1859, he could well have *disremembered* that he had actually first come to Chippewa five years earlier, or in 1854. So I'm not altogether certain that he *did* first arrive in 1859 and not in 1854. But if he *did* arrive in 1854, then he could have met and shook hands with every man in town in half an hour. The jury's still out, but when they come back in, I expect a finding that 1859 was the year.

Where Michael and Mary first met is also shrouded in mystery. Even the two accounts I have of *where* they were married differ wildly. But there *is* agreement that their wedding took place on January 17, 1859 and that their first child, Mary A. Hall, was born on December 13, 1859. Strangely, that daughter seems not to have been born in Chippewa as you'd think, but all the way back in Palmyra, New York. I have that in Mary's own hand.

But there's little doubt that, at least as a couple, Mary and Michael first arrived in Chippewa in very early 1859. It would seem highly probable that, as Papa reports, they'd come from somewhere in the East, traveling by keel boat down the Ohio to Indiana, and, from there, by wagon through Chicago and thence on out west, either to Minnesota for a short while, or directly to Chippewa.

There's evidence, too, that Michael may have gone alone, probably in late 1858, to some place in the vicinity of present-day Minneapolis. So it may have been that it was from there, from Minnesota, that Michael, or conceivably the both of them, journeyed east, some 80 miles back to the County of Chippewa, in the far northwest of Wisconsin. And Chippewa County was not even *organized* until 1854. How about that!

In 1859, Wisconsin had itself become a state only a decade before. But that was not owing to settlement in the north half of the state. Almost all of the population that qualified it for statehood had settled the land that lay along its southern border. This was land that lay ready-made for farming, while most of the rest of the state, being both more remote and less inviting to people intending to farm the land, was, as yet, largely devoid of humanity. Chippewa County itself, when it was first laid out, may have encompassed as much as ten percent of the entire land area of the state and have reached all the way north to the shores of Lake Superior. But for myself, I doubt very much that it was anything like as large as that when Michael became its Sheriff in 1871.

This'll give you some idea of the demographics of the place where Mary and Michael made their home. In 1850, Chippewa County, enormous though it doubtless was in land area, had a total population of a mere 615 souls. Some of those would be already at work as loggers, but certainly at least a few would have still been trappers and Indian traders. That was the 1850 Federal census and Indians wouldn't have been included in that, would they?

Anyway, there's no doubt at all that Mary and Michael were among the very earliest of the pioneers who came into that heavily wooded wilderness to settle. A wilderness of virgin pine timber, broken by breaks of heavy brush and by the lakes scattered at utter random everywhere about. Even to this day, that country is called the Land O'Lakes, and for good reason, too. Lakes in their thousands, and of all shapes and sizes, gouged out, helter-skelter, twelve thousand years ago by the last glaciation—the one geology has appropriately named *The Wisconsin*. And, oh! those magnificent rivers! Look at this.

That's the way the Chippewa River looked around 1890, when my great uncle, Joseph Hall, was drowned in it. And oh my God! but that picture takes me back! That's how I grew up, floating those rivers in a canoe. And not only the Chippewa but the Flambeau, too. Both forks of it. Not to mention the St. Croix. And certainly most often of all, the Red Cedar. Fishing and drifting—fishing and drifting my way through the long, slick-sliding pools, only to pitch over the edge and pour pell-mell down a long stretch of brawling rapids, thence to emerge, through the froth and the spew at the foot of it, out onto the buttery bosom at the head of yet another long reach of any one of those beautiful rivers! Oh, my God!

That's the way those rivers ran—south and west to the Mississippi, alternately flowing gently like Afton, or tumbling their way downhill through the tall pines that rose up on either side. That's right. When I was a boy, the Flambeau still ran through tall stands of Norway pine, broken now and again by the canoe birches, both yellow and white. As recently as seventy years ago, on the South Fork of the Flambeau, on your left as you fished your way downstream, there was one small tract still left untouched. It held not only a stand of virgin timber but a spring of sweet, fresh water. That's right, that timber had never been cut! *Never*! At least, that's what the Hervis brothers said, and the three of them were Finns, so they would know.

However, it was not *all* lakes and rivers and tall timber. Here and there was heavy brush. Sometimes a piece of prairie, too. And it was on one such small swath of long grass prairie, a place called Eagle Prairie in fact, that they would soon settle down to sing their harvest-home. So there! Now you have some idea of that pristine land into which Michael and Mary came as pioneers.

But I think they would not at first have lived out on the prairie. There was nothing out there. No, for a while they'd have lived in town. Although Chippewa was destined to become a great sawmill town, when they arrived there, in 1859, it was only the merest suggestion, the kernel of one. Then, in 1865, only six years after their penniless arrival, they managed to become the record owners of 80 acres of land in Section 28, just north of town. Their title to the other 80 acres came the following year.

I have copies of both deeds and there's no vendor's mortgage in either one. No evidence at all of any loan on it. So it seems that their farm was not bought on credit—no, it was bought for cash! They paid $750.00 for the first eighty and $1,200.00 for the second. But if not bought on credit, then where did all that cash come from? That was an awful lot of money in those days. Ah, look what we have! A great, unsolved mystery! Well, possibly not. Probably not. Almost *certainly* not. No, indeed! No mystery to it at all.

Because Michael went out and earned it. He was then twenty-three and he went straight to work as a mill hand. I think it's more than likely that Mary took work, too, but I don't know that. But that's where that cash came from. They *earned* it and *saved* it, every dollar that it cost them to buy that quarter section of raw land out on Eagle Prairie. In that same newspaper account of Michael's first Fourth of July in Chippewa, he makes it quite clear that, on his arrival in Chippewa, he had immediately found a job as a hand in the saw mill operated by the Chippewa Falls Lumbering Company.

On July 3rd, Michael drove its local manager, a Mr. Jourdan, to Eau Claire to borrow $2,000 in cash for the men at the mill to use to buy the whiskey they needed to properly celebrate the Fourth. That done, Mr. Jourdan gave all that money to Michael and told him to take it back to Chippewa and pass it out at the mill. Thereupon, and without another word, that Mr. Jourdan took the stage from Eau Claire to Sparta—never to be heard from again!

That $2,000.00 was the only cash money that came into town that whole year of 1859, and every dollar of it went for whiskey! Just think of that, sports fans!

Although the men continued to operate the saw mill until late into the fall, finally, in November, the company went bust and no one, not even Michael, was ever paid a dime for their long summer's work. There were three million feet of lumber left floating in the river, and the men were told that if they wanted to float it downriver and try to sell it somewhere on the Mississippi, it was theirs. But there was no market down there either, so no one ever claimed it.

Chippewa Falls in 1859! Try to put yourself there in its earliest beginnings. Here's something that may help you orient yourself a bit in the times in which Michael lived. Mark Twain, was born far downriver in Florida, Missouri, not far from Hannibal. He was born there on November 30, 1835, and less than two months later, Michael Hall was born in Dublin, Ireland. Twain died on April 21, 1910 and Michael Hall died on October 16, 1911. Michael and Mark lived lives that were almost perfectly contemporaneous.

Or this. In 1871-72, a dozen years after coming as a stranger into that huge, almost vacant county called Chippewa, Michael was serving as its Sheriff. The High Sheriff of the whole of Chippewa County, Wisconsin! I've looked and only rarely did any of those early sheriffs succeed himself in office. The term was two years and only a few served longer than that. Which makes it plain that the men of his time and place were not politicians. Serving as sheriff then was not a political plum or a power base. It was a civic duty.

But it would be quite some time after that before the young Ántonia Shimerda would come with *her* family all the way from Bohemia to Krajiek's cave near Squaw Creek. Hanover and Black Hawk! Two small towns that Cather's brand of fiction made truer than historical fact. If your Cather's gotten a little rusty, then Squaw Creek was out on the prairie that lay all round the town of Hanover. Hanover was down there in Nebraska. So was Black Hawk. So we're talking here about the Chippewa Falls as it was a full generation before those two towns of Cather's made their own appearance on the literary map. And as for *Main Street*—well, not for three more full generations would Gopher Prairie come along.

And oh, yes! Here's something else. Just a decade before Mary and Michael arrived in Chippewa, Marx and Engels published their Communist Manifesto. If you know them, that should prove even more helpful.

About Eagle Prairie. In my memory, Eagle Prairie stretches for some six miles or more north of Chippewa. The Hall farm was one of the first three farms out on Eagle Prairie and it eventually became an historic local landmark. That farm, and the solid home they were to build on it, became the hearth around which, for two full generations, the whole Hall family would warm its hands. What the farm meant to them was what the family farm once meant to most everyone in this land of ours. That is, until the time when I was born and the move to town began in earnest.

Not only was my mother born on that farm, that's where she was raised up, and if I'm any judge, she became who she was more by the good example, tutelage and inspiration of her two pioneering grandparents than even by that of her own mother and father. It was right there on that farm, and nowhere else, that my mother became imbued with the optimism and the determination and the very intense, humane sense of personal responsibility for every person and thing around her that defined her all her life.

But here, look at this old photo of my mother when she was a little girl. This is her and her younger sister, Norma, both of them in costume and playing roles the way little girls have always loved to do. Mother looks to me here to be about eight or nine, so I'd guess it was taken in maybe, 1902.

But have you ever seen such a sure sense of the histrionic in anyone so young? And look at the easy, natural perfection with which she poses herself. How could she have known how to do that, a little girl who'd spent her whole life out on her grandparents' farm? Perfect *contrapposto*! Not the mere suggestion of counterpoise that we see in *Kritios Boy*, but the full-blown *contrapposito* of the baroque. And so soignée! I'll bet she'd never even heard of either of those words! Yup, she was the whole enchilada all right! Nature had obviously done something right.

But growing up on that farm was also where she learned to cook and to sew and to raise vegetables and to can them for winter. My mother's need to return to the farm was so great that, just before the end of the war, Papa bought her one. Out eighteen miles west of town, near the Texas line. She immediately named it *ultima Thule*, and for the next ten years or more, that's where she lived, breathed and had her being. At that time, no one thought it possible that raspberries could be raised in the Deep South, but she didn't know that. She just did it.

She had some help out there, of course, but she knew a lot more than the help about what needed doing and how to do it. She kept a fresh Jersey cow and churned her own butter. That would leave us with buttermilk—*real* buttermilk. Real buttermilk is unbelievably delicious, but it's fifty years since I've even seen any. Like the passenger train, it's gone—forever, I suppose. Oh, yes, and she made cottage cheese and two or three kinds of soft cheeses. Oh, well—you get the idea.

She told me that, from the time she was very small, she would ride with her grandmother everywhere her grandmother went—sometimes into town but mostly to visit other emigrant families living out there on Eagle Prairie. Many of them newcomers, trying, as often as not, just to survive. Mary made it her life to visit and care for those poor people out on the prairie. She nursed them when they were sick, took them baskets of food to eat when they had nothing, and showed them what they had to do to survive out there. My mother was always by her side.

And do you know how the two of them got about—my mother and her grandmother? In a goat cart! A *goat* cart! I'll never forget the image of that elderly Irish lady and that little red headed girl, riding up and down that Wisconsin prairie, succoring the hungry and sick, and every mile of it behind a goat!

I don't have a picture of that goat cart, but I can show you where it was sometimes hitched. And you can see for yourself the very mounting stone that my mother would have used to crawl up there on that goat cart beside her grandmother. Up behind a *goat*, of all things! Look at this! It's the Hall farmhouse, taken, maybe in 1890.

Until I was past forty, I could see that farmhouse myself, off to the east as I drove the few miles from Chippewa up to Chetek. There's nothing left there now to mark the place my mother lived. Not that hitching post. Not that mounting stone. Nothing. Just like the Old South, it's gone with the wind. Just open land there now, every bit as bare of signs of human life as it was in 1859.

My mother saw lots and lots of poverty when she was a little girl, riding the prairie in that goat cart. Saw it first hand. *Real* poverty. No safety net back then. Just the neighbors. Poverty is not now at all the same thing that it was then. You're considered impoverished now if your cell phone's been taken away and you find yourself reduced to one TV. In those days, poverty meant something approaching utter destitution. The imminent threat of death. Here's something from a letter my mother wrote my father at the beginning of the great depression.

Poor Aunt Kate, When I think of all of them I'm terrified for us, if we should ever come to such need and it can happen to any of us. Yes, by all means let's do save so that in fifty years from today at this time we can sit back and when we no longer can do for ourselves we can do for others with plenty at hand to provide for those who need it.

I suppose it's fair to say that the Chippewa River is not merely a tributary of the Mississippi but one of its several headwaters, like the St. Croix. The Hall farm was less than a mile from the nearest point on that river. I know I've told you that, like my mother, my father also grew up on the banks of a river. In Melville, a little country town on the banks the Atchafalaya. Well, that word *banks* is misleading. The Atchafalaya is contained, not by banks, such as those that nature makes, but by levees—levees raised up by man on both sides of its course.

Hearing that word, *levee*, that reminds me of something my mother told me once. Whether it's true or not, it *sounds* about right. My mother said that the first production of *Aida* in this country was given in New Orleans. The third act is set on the banks of the Nile. Well, in that New Orleans production, when the curtain rose on that third act, the audience saw before it, not the Nile but the only river they knew anything about, the Mississippi. So there was a fine Mississippi River levee up there on the stage, and to make the transmogrification complete and the audience feel completely at home, what did they see stacked up on top of that levee? Why, nothing but a dozen bales or so of cotton. Isn't that immense!

Incidentally, although levees may have no special significance for you, the levee is actually one of the more interesting features of man's cultural landscape. The word itself derives, of course, from the French word meaning to *raise up* and it's true—the top of a levee is well up over the flood plane, generally the highest ground around. Climb up on top of a levee and from there you can see for miles in every direction. It's just a special kind of wall, that's all it really is. Sometimes, like a prison wall, it's built to keep the undesirables *in*, but generally it's meant to keep something *out* and always something undesirable. Like flood waters. Or rum-runners and drug smugglers. Or even illegal immigrants. Whatever.

But when everybody's got his head down, chopping cotton, the levee tends to be forgotten. Nobody looks up to even notice whether or not there are any lanterns planted there. That's what they used to do, you know. When the high water came and the levee was threatened, that's when you'd see those lanterns on the levee. They were warnings, planted there by people who'd taken the high ground to have a look around. People who had the eyes to see. Lanterns were clear signals that the levee was about to be o'er-topped or breached or compromised and that the people and their way of life were in grave danger. Taken in one sense or another, the levee is all that stands between man and his own primordium.

If you're interested, you might want to talk to Mr. Percy. Not the father, the son. Mr. William Alexander Percy—scion of the Percys of the Mississippi Delta. He was dismissed by some as being merely a decadent, southern aristocrat. Well, he wasn't in the least decadent—that charge is laughable, but he certainly was *southern*, and there's no doubt, either, that he was an aristocrat. But the aristocracy to which he belonged was not at all the one his detractors had in mind. No, his was the aristocracy of the mind.

But as I've said, the Atchafalaya is the mighty stream that, but for man's intervention, would right today be carrying most of the Mississippi to the sea. So, it's fair to say that my parents lived their childhoods at opposite ends of the Mississippi. It would also be on the Mississippi, in New Orleans, that they would meet. That was when he was a student at Tulane and she at the Newcomb College for Women there. They not only met there at the lower end of the great river, at New Orleans—at its *nadir*, as some would say—that was where they fell in love. And it was near the Mississippi's upper end, on the banks of Lake Chetek, that, on August 28, 1917, my two beautiful parents were married. They were married, in fact, on the very piece of land to which Michael Hall had first brought his family by ox cart to camp out for a few summer days, fifty years before.

Beginning maybe as early as 1870, Michael Hall would take his family a day's journey north by ox cart, to pitch tent and camp out on the north shore of Lake Chetek. Later on, family cottages were built on that very same camp site, a grand tradition they'd begun and which would go on for the next hundred years or more. Chetek is a big tourist center now, but when Michael and Mary came there, Indians were the only other tourists on the lake. They'd come every autumn to gather the wild rice that then grew plentiful around the shore. The lake was much smaller and shallower then than now.

Speaking of my parents, they'd be the first to tell you that in most respects they were quite unalike. And that's true—I saw it myself. Everyday. My mother was given to igniting fires, my father to putting them out. Something like that is bound to occasion—how shall I say this?—certain *confusions* and *perturbations* in the relationship of any two people. But even as a boy, I knew that I was safe. Because they were dead ringers in all the important things. All the fundaments. The same optimism. Much the same determination. And their awareness of people, of all that beauty that lies in human voices, that was the same, too.

I'm not suggesting that they were indiscriminate in their affection for humanity. Lord, no! Quite the opposite. They were constantly describing, defining, categorizing everything they experienced. Making distinctions between this and that and ranking everything in various orders of merit. Constantly exercising their judgment and taste, in an effort to discriminate between the more, and the less, desirable. To find the highest ground. Until as recently as forty or fifty years ago, you were flattered if someone said you were a discriminating person. Now discrimination is scowled out of countenance. It's become a *sin*, for God's sake! Discrimination? Where did it go? Who ruined it for us? Why is it that it's now just one more of those sweet old words turned bitter on our tongue?

Anyway, those were some of the values my parents held in common and that's why it was inevitable that, at the end of their two fine, long lives, they were still the same devoted lovers they started out. I look around me, and I see that as something quite remarkable.

Oh, yes, I know what you've been thinking—that I'm a complete romantic about the life my mother lead out there on that farm. And, yes, I've read what Marx and Engles thought about it. Didn't they refer to the rural life as *the idiocy of living out on the land*? Wasn't that about what they thought of the bucolic? The vaunted pastoral of the Roman poets? And that *is* one of the great watersheds of our history as humans. Whether to live out on the land and tend the cattle, or to move to the city and become part of the herd. Well, the vote's in and I'm very much in the minority. But that minority includes the likes of Levin and Shcherbátsky, and I'm just naturally more at home with the likes of them. Just look at Michael's will. I have a copy of it, and prominent among the things he left to Mary were—get this! *The buggies, harnesses and robes.* Those robes were for the horses of course, not for them.

Here's something about life on the farm I want to read to you from Papa's book. I'd be very interested in what you think of it, so let me know.

While living at the farm at Eagle Prairie, Mary found an Indian lying in the snow with a broken leg. She brought him to her home, set his leg and nursed him. The Indian disappeared as soon as he was able to walk. A few years later, the Indian returned, handed Mary a basket filled with beautiful pieces of embroidered bead-work and then left without saying a word.

One winter Michael and Mary traveled by horse and sleigh to St. Paul, Minnesota, to hear Jenny Lind sing.

Fred H. Ryan remembers that his grandmother, Mary Hall, told him that once when alone in her farm home, she sensed that someone was looking at her, and turning her eyes slightly, saw two Indians—in full war paint, peering at her through the window. She knew that Indians were deathly afraid of insane women, so without turning toward the window, acted as though she were insane. The Indians fled.

Well? What do you say? Do you believe that stuff? I mean, do you believe *any* of it?

Damned if *I* do! Not one word of it!

Let's start with that howler about Jenny Lind. It was eighty miles or more from the farm to St. Paul. Do you think—do you *really* think—that Mary and Michael would have left the farm, in a sleigh, in the middle of winter, with six hours of daylight, to drive all the way to St. Paul just to hear Jenny Lind? I suspect that if you collected together all such Jenny Lind folk tales, you'd find that there was not one family who'd lived anywhere east of the Rockies, at any time during the nineteenth century, that did not have at least one member who had traveled some far distance, generally through ice and snow, just to hear Jenny sing. Now, who'd want to be left out of a story as good as that? Would you? I thought not! Me neither.

But there's another small problem with that. Jenny Lind *did* have a great success in this country. She came as a protégée of P. T. Barnum and she drew great crowds wherever she went. I don't know that she ever made it as far west as St. Paul. To me, that seems highly doubtful, but if she did, it would have been sometime around 1850 or 1851, because those were the only years Lind was even in this country, and those were years that fell long, long before Mary and Michael would ever have been in Chippewa

And those Indian stories, they're no more to be believed than the one about Jenny Lind. In pioneer times, no self-respecting family would have been without at least one good Indian story. In that regard, Mary Scally was exceptionally self-respecting—she had *two*. When I was little, I heard one of those Indian stories myself. It was one my Grandfather Lyons told, and I'll never forget it. But the thing is—I *liked* Indians. For boys like me, the Indian was Longfellow's Hiawatha—not Blue Duck.

Did I tell you that Michael Hall could be a fighter? I did? Mother used to quote her grandfather a lot and one of her favorites was this one. *Where Nature has done nothing, you cawn't, I say, you cawn't*! That's how he pronounced it—cawn't. He didn't mean that nurture could do nothing—that man was helpless and everything had to be left to nature. Oh, no! Far from it! He believed utterly in man's ability to improve every living thing, plants and animals, even himself, and all by breeding. What he meant was simply that, without the help of nature, without good stock to breed to, or graft to, he knew himself to be helpless. That nature counts and it counts for a lot. He'd seen that every day of his life—out on the land. Nature and nurture, oh yes! But the power of the individual will, he knew all about that, too.

Mother said that even when he was no longer the Sheriff of Chippewa County, whenever he was driving through the country in his buggy, he would stop when he saw some farmer abusing his draft animals. Or his cows—whatever. He'd get down off his buggy and go straight to that farmer, whip in hand, and he'd berate him unmercifully, just hoping to make that farmer as mad as he was—which is to say, mad enough to fight. At one time he sold farm implements, and he'd do the same when he saw those implements being neglected. Being left out in the weather. Used improperly. He knew what those implements, tools then new to the world, meant to the life of the men who worked the land. Mother said that he came home more than once, beat up from fights he'd had about that.

In another life, I'd prefer to be my Great Grandfather, Michael Hall, but if fortune were to cast me as a woman, why, then I'd want to be Sills, of course. Bevery Sills.

My Grandfather Lyons used to tell me stories about how things were when he was young. The last one he ever told me was about the day he was cutting wood out in the Atchafalaya swamp. Grandfather said he'd felled a tree and had cut it into logs and was just beginning to split one of them, when it happened. He said he had a wedge in it and had it split part way open lengthwise, when two Indian braves in war paint sneaked up out of the bushes and captured him. He told those Indians that he'd go peacefully if they'd just help him finish splitting that log, and they said they would. He told them to stand there by the log, one on each side and stick their hands down in the split in the log and pull hard on it while he drove the wedge on in. So that's just what those Indians did, but instead of taking his axe and driving the wedge deeper into the log, Grandfather knocked that wedge right out of that log, and when it snapped shut on those Indians, it was him who held them captive.

That's the story as my Grandfather Lyons told it. It's a good story, too. I might even have believed him. After all, I'd believed everything else he'd told me. But this was different. Just a few weeks before, I'd read that very same story in a book I had, a book for boys, and it had made a considerable impression on me. In that book, that story was illustrated, and even now I can see in my mind's eye that picture of those Indians and that woodcutter, the three of them standing over that log. It's right at the top of the first page.

I couldn't stand it, so I just told him the truth. I told my grandfather that I'd read that same story in a book. I might even have charged him with lying. It would be just like me to do a thing like that. Anyhow, I stood him down on it. Right to his face. And me just a little boy who loved him so much.

I'd deeply wounded him, of course. He never told me another story. Never read to me again. We never again played chess together. He wanted nothing to do with me. We'd become strangers to each other. Or rather, I had to him. Later on, when he died in the room next to mine, all I could do was lie there with my face in my pillow, crying my heart out in the dark. That was the first profound, crushing, heartbreak and sadness of my life. My Grandfather Lyons my first deeply felt loss.

I didn't intend to burden you with all that. It just came out, I don't know why.

But back to Michael Hall of Wisconsin. Oh, I know, you probably think it's nothing more than nostalgia. A touch of nostalgia for that virginal land of ours I was born too late to see. But every time I think about the Hall farm out there on Eagle Prairie and the closer I look at those pictures of Michael and Mary, the more certain I am that although they've been dead and gone these hundred years, I am their true and direct heir and come of the fruit that fell under their tree.

Try to forgive me if I talk too much, but when I look back down the road I came, I find that at every turn there's more to say.

An early trio

My earliest memory? No problem. It's the memory of Palestine, the first person I ever loved who was not a member of my own family. However her name may have been spelled, it was pronounced "Palace-steen". But first a word about black people and white. In my boyhood in the deep South there was then, as now of course, a pervasive, dark moat of ignorance, fear, hatred and distrust guarding the battlements thrown up by each race against the other, much of it owing to cultural differences and so, in part, inevitable.

But that neither is now, nor was then, the whole of it. If you have some idea of the variety and complexity of the grab bag of racial relationships which existed in the South of eighty years ago, of the close, mutually respectful, and sometimes even affectionate intimacy which, known to my own experience, then could, and did exist, primarily in the domestic situation but elsewhere as well, then you are likely to suspect who that woman might have been—that woman who was the first love of my life. Who, in those days, she almost *had* to be. She was my beloved nurse of course and of course she was black.

Well, now she's black, but in those days, she was colored. Even as recently as fifty years ago, a large majority of African-Americans didn't much care to be thought of as black. They preferred to be colored. Or Negro. They felt either one to be the address of greater respect. How do I know that? I read it in a periodical devoted to sociology, a magazine to which for several years I subscribed in order to teach myself—that is to say, to *learn* something of what that soft science we call "sociology" had to tell us about ourselves. That was the finding in the report of a careful study made not so long after *black*, in its specifically, and inaccurately, racial sense, first came into the language.

But you say that *colored* is not only an old fashioned expression gone completely out of style, it's worse than that. It's a pejorative, and I shouldn't be using it if I want to be PC. Right? Why, of course it's old fashioned! That's what I am myself, for God's sake! And I didn't come all this way to talk like somebody

I'm not. All us old people are old fashioned! Sometime more than a bit cantankerous, too, you're damned right! Anyhow, that term *colored* was *never* a pejorative for me or for anyone of my generation. My father used it and my mother used it and both of them had the utmost respect for colored people and so do I! So why don't we just change the subject?

Here's is an old snapshot, taken in the spring of 1924.

That fine looking woman you see there, that's Palestine. She nursed us both, my little brother Hall and me. Hall was two years younger than me. That's Hall, that little baby in her arms, and I'm that little boy you see down there at the bottom, squatting at Palestine's knee. You can get a pretty good look at me, there. Well, at the little boy I used to be. Looking now into that little boy's face, congealed in the light of that old bit of film, I feel that I'm looking back in time. And I am—back through a scrim of more than eighty years of it.

That little boy in this picture, he's filled with curiosity, I can see that. Oh, yes, he's *profoundly* curious. He looks so familiar that I wonder, is that him? or is it me? and it makes me dizzy. But looking at me the way I was, I feel that back then, at the beginning, I must have been all right. That there was nothing very much wrong with me, nothing bent or broken. Nothing missing, either. At least, not then, there wasn't.

See how intently I'm looking at us! I look as though I might even be trying to see out into my own future, don't I? See it there in that camera's eye? And here I am now, here in that very future, looking back into my own past. It occurs to me that looking at an old photo like this is like looking through a telescope, where the light you see is the light that comes from far back in time—from deep in the past. Even now I can feel something of him, of that boy I was, that little fellow who loved that woman so much. But there are limits of course, and I know that, even though he did become me, I could never become him again. No—no matter how hard I might try.

I loved Palestine with a devotion so constant, so intense, so complete that my parents were torn between smiles and awe. Although I suppose there was then no name as yet for such a creature, I was in every way a Tinbergen gosling, and growing up, I heard as much from my parents. You'd never guess it now, but I was quite late to talk. About a year late. It went seemingly on forever that I never uttered a word. Not even a mumbled, *Mama* or *Papa*. My mother told me so. Repeatedly! So you can imagine the enormity of her relief, when, one day gazing out an open window—in the South of those days, before air conditioning, windows were open most of the year—I pointed outside and said, very distinctly, *See the birds?*

But anyway, Palestine was my queen and there was nothing I wouldn't have done for her. She looks like a queen, too, doesn't she? This may be the only picture of her left in existence, and it's a near certainty that I'm the only person left alive who ever speaks her name or even gives a thought to her. To me, she's got a rather regal look. The same regal look that Leontyne Price brought with her when she would come out on the stage to sing.

Leontyne Price sang at least twice here in hometown. The second time was when she was about to retire, so that must have been among the last appearances she made anywhere, and naturally, her entrance was that of the royalty she was. The instant she took the stage that whole packed house came to its feet and we roared our approval of her great art and of the majestic lady she was. We raised our voices over and over again. At the end of every song she sang. I may be mistaken about this, but it seems to me that we made her sing one of those songs twice. That's the greatest honor a singer can receive, you know that? When the audience insists—absolutely *insists*—that you sing something over again. Won't let you go on until you do. I've had that experience myself, long ago in South America, and believe me, it's one a singer never forgets.

Miss Price was what my mother called a *volunteer*. My mother loved everything that volunteered itself into her life. And not only people but plants, too. Maybe even especially plants. The ones that rose up, uninvited, right out there in what was her garden, all of them beautiful to her and sprung from nature by their own volition.

Years ago, in the early forties I suppose it was, my mother and father were house guests of old friends over in Laurel, Mississippi—the Gardner Greens—and one evening they were honored by a dinner party given for them by Gardner's cousins, the Chisholms, who lived almost next door. After supper, a young colored girl came in and sang a while for the guests. That girl's aunt was the cook or something, I'm not sure, but that's who introduced her. Now, not only was my mother an artist in her own right, but she could instantly recognize the true artist in others. For weeks after that trip, my mother could talk of nothing else but of that young girl who'd sung for them that night in Laurel. Not only of her great voice but of the instinctive art which that young person had brought to the performance of everything she sang. That young girl was Leontyne Price. Mary Violet Leontyne Price.

On a dirt road that ran along just behind our house was a colored quarters and Palestine and I used to walk around over there a lot. She liked to go over and visit with friends who lived there, but mainly she went to buy that snuff she dipped. Palestine kept hers in her lip. Right in front. It came in a little round tin can and was called Garrett's Snuff. There was a real old, colored lady lived in one of those shotgun houses lined up alongside one another back there, and she kept a few things for sale in her front room. That old lady must surely have once been a slave herself, she was plenty old enough. And there must have been other old people living back there then who'd lived all their early lives as slaves. It's sobering to think how large is the swatch of history, almost two centuries of it, that can be lived by just two long lives when laid end to end. You see, back then, when I was small, the end of the Civil War, eighteen sixty-five, that was only sixty years ago, so that tragic war and the tragic era that followed were well within the memory of many then still living. That's how I heard it talked about by the grown-ups, as an experience that with them was still very much alive. The same way some people of my own generation now talk about our war, except that their war was fought on their home ground. Anyhow, that old lady kept a few things in her house for sale to her neighbors—things everybody needed, like lard and cornmeal and snuff—and Palestine and I were among her most regular and valued customers.

But there was another reason we took that walk. Palestine just loved baseball, and those young men and boys had made a clearing in those piney woods back there where they could play baseball, and people like Palestine and me, we could go there and stand around, right up close, and watch. Only two players had a mitt. The catcher and the man who played first base, they had mitts. The rest played with their bare hands, and they played with a hard ball, too, so it was something to see. That place I watched them playing ball is now the athletic field of a private school. The Southfield School. It was founded in 1934 as Shreveport Progressive School. At that time the new theory called *Progressive Education* had come into full bloom. His first year, the new Headmaster stayed with us.

And that brings me to the third person you see in that picture, my brother, Hall. My only brother, as I was not to have another, nor any sister at all. After Palestine, I think my earliest memory is of Brother. In that memory, he's just a little bit of a fellow, standing up in his baby bed, and I'm standing beside it, looking up at him through the bars. He was such a pudgy little duck, and although later on we did sometimes scrap a bit, being close came very natural, so I'd say we were pretty good brothers all those fine years we were growing up.

There's a lovely old story about Brother when he was about five. It's perfectly true, too, even though it does involve my Grandfather Hall. You remember him? Harry Hall? Sure you do.

This happened along about 1927, when America's grand romance with the airplane had just caught fire. Lindberg's historic flight had ignited it, and aviation was, if I'm allowed, much in the air. This will be hard for you to believe, but in the twenties, when an airplane was heard in the vicinity, people would drop whatever they were doing and run outside to see it. They'd run right outdoors and stand in the middle of the street, looking up in the sky like a flock of sun-gazers, hoping to catch sight of it. And if they did, they'd keep their eyes fastened on it until it had passed out of sight. The planes of that day were not only rare, they were very, very slow, so you could be pretty sure of a good, long look.

Late one afternoon over on Erie Street, Hall heard a plane coming and ran out into our back yard in hopes of catching sight of it. And sure enough, there it was. So Brother took a chance and cupped his hands around his mouth and called up to the pilot of that airplane, hollering out as loud as he could, *Come on down here and give me a ride!*

Our house had an upstairs screen porch that looked out over our back yard, and my Grandfather Hall happened to be standing up there on that porch. Grandfather had heard that plane, too, you see, and he saw Brother down below him there in the back yard. And he heard him call up to that plane to come down and give him a ride.

If you remember him at all, Grandfather Hall wouldn't have had to think about what to do—he'd have already done it. There was his little grandson down there in bad need of an airplane ride, so Grandfather cupped his hands just like Hall had done and called down to Brother. *All right there, little boy, I'll come down and get you and take you for a ride, but you'll have to get your mother's permission. And don't take all day about it, because my mama told me not to be late for supper.* That was all Brother needed to hear. He ran into the house, lickety-split, to tell Mother what wonderful thing had happened and ask her permission to go for that promised ride.

Of course, when Hall was finally able to drag Mother with him out to see for herself, the sky was empty and not a sound was heard. This was hard, irrefutable evidence that, even in the face of Brother's mounting protestations of innocence, was about to badly sully his credibility with my mother. You know, my brother's reputation for truth and veracity?

Well, around our house, a lie was not a thing blithely let pass. It wasn't countenanced at all, so the hammer was about to fall and Brother about to be found guilty and sentenced to do time in our bedroom upstairs, when, having seen that the true perpetrator of this heinous affair had slunk cravenly out of sight upstairs, leaving me there alone, the sole remaining witness to it, and faced suddenly with the impendency of a most grave miscarriage of justice, I stepped smartly forward and did what conscience said was right. Yes, I did! I ratted on my grandfather and my brother walked.

But I'll never forget how neat it was, what my grandfather said. The sheer, breath-taking *genius* of it. And so I've been asking myself lately, *Lyons—why can't you be more like your Grandfather Hall? Why, for a change, can't you do something, or even just say something, or play some role that's at least just a little memorable, even if it's only fifth business? Just look at what you've done! Let your whole life wilt and wither away with nothing to show for it. Nothing at all to show!*

As for Brother, that was only the first of many voices he was to hear. Voices coming, if not in any strict sense, from on high, then certainly from strange parts and latitudes equally unknown, and, far the worst of it, from peoples whose intent would be far less innocuous than that of our really rather innocent grandfather.

But I know this much—no voice ever spoke to me from *on high*. Not from up there, nor yet from *down below* either, and that was a rather fundamental difference between us. But remembering the kinds of voices Brother heard, I'm sure that's just as well.

Seeing myself as perhaps a bit of a wraith from Enlightenment times, I've no right to complain that miracles of the sort experienced by my brother have passed me by without a word. But that doesn't mean I haven't seen miracles of another sort, of my own sort, because I have. I've seen them all my life. Still see them every day. But being only every-day miracles, mine are rather different from Brother's.

First off, mine come in natural colors. Do you see that azalea there across the pool? My mother planted that more than fifty years ago. About everything you see out there, she planted. This is her garden we're sitting in, and it wasn't the first one she made either. No, she made her first flower garden where I grew up, over on Erie Street, so this was the second of the green mansions my mother made. Of course, what you see now, lovely as it is, it's just a memory, a green ghost of what it was when she could tend it. But even now, in the spring of the year, it's still lit by the flames of some of the same azaleas she planted here. You see that one over there? That one's called a *Pride of Mobile,* and at the end of March, when it sets itself on fire—well, it makes me feel like I'm already on hallowed ground, so it's all the burning bush I'll ever need to see.

Oh, oh! I see I'd better tread careful here, lest it be on someone's toes. Maybe even on yours. You might have noticed that you and I have been mercifully spared the potential friction of two highly controversial subjects. *Issues* is the word I hear now. And it hasn't been by oversight that we've been spared, oh, no! It's because I've carefully avoided them both. They're soul mates and always, it seems to me, found traveling together, bloody hand in bloody hand. Together, they're the embodiment of what you might think of as *militant enthusiasm* and sooner or later those enthusiasts, acting in the name of those indwelling gods of their fathers, will do their best to behead and draw and quarter all the rest of us. Oh, yes! Religion and politics. Faith and force. Natural allies, traveling arm in arm.

While I'm on it, I might as well tell you that I can see in your eyes just what you're thinking right now. You're wondering to yourself, *What's this guy's politics? Is he at all religious, I wonder?* Isn't that right? Come on now, you know you are. And the reason you're wondering is because I haven't let on about either one of those two little things. The two *issues* that, as the man says on public radio, are the two things America cares about most. Well, now that we've become friends, maybe there *is* something I can trust you with. Something very personal and private I can reveal to you about my politics. And my religion, too, for that matter.

But before I begin, it will be a source of great comfort to you to hear me say that I always vote the very same way you do. Yes, I do—by secret ballot. But first off, I've got a confession to make. I am, by nature, highly partisan. Some say it's very wrong of me—that I should even hate myself for it. But like most folks, yellow dog that I am, I always vote the straight party ticket. No matter if I have to hold my nose. That's only human, right? Yes, and I'll reveal a further detail and this is one you might see as even more damning.

Politically, I am a registered Episcopalian. Yes, I am! And I'm not ashamed of it either! But I'm a true Episcopalian. One of only a few left alive. An antique of the *old* school. And among us old-school Episcopalians, it's an article of faith that there are two subjects which, in our belief, both simple politeness and common sense require be left entirely alone. Never touched. Never, *ever* be discussed. Even mentioned! And it just happens that those two subjects are the same two as those about which I'm told America cares about most. Religion and politics!

Although it is a first principal among us old-school, battle-scarred Episcopalians that we and our church remain aloof from those two common frays, there is an alternative view taken of us, and one widely held, too, and that's the view that the *real* reason we few, we happy few, we band of brothers, refuse to participate in the discussion of either religion or politics is that we are so unacquainted with both as to be without interest in either. There now! That clears all that up!

Before going on, let me say that I hope you don't find these long, irrelevant riffs of mine too objectionable, but that's just the way my mouth seems to run on these days. It takes the bit in its teeth, my mouth does, and I can't seem to stop it. And not only does it run on, it wants to meander, too—flowing on and on, forever, like an endless stream, coiling and snaking its way to some predestined, wine-dark sea. I suppose that's well enough for writers. I understand that there are some modern writers who do it all the time. Especially in narrative. Nothing wrong with that sort of narrative either, because a reader can always look back and forth when confused. Or if all else fails, then do the unthinkable, and stop and think.

But of course I'm not writing, I'm just talking, so the next time I go into my post-modern routine and wander off down some byway, it might help if you were to think of me as—well, perhaps as just a boy. A schoolboy, cap in hand, out for a romp with his dog. And my dog has just grabbed my cap out of my hand and he's run off with it, and I've got no choice but to chase after. You get the picture? After all, I've got to catch up with my hat, don't I? And I'm so sorry if that leaves you with little option but to do the same.

But now, back to my brother. He was in the Navy during the war. Commanded an LCT out in the Pacific, at Okinawa. I'm told that the Landing Craft Tank was the smallest Navy ship afloat. About ten sailors and one officer. Here's Hall and an old friend of mine at Okinawa.

This picture's not too clear but Brother's that fellow on the left, that Ensign, and in the background is his command, US LCT 1326. After he'd been commissioned at some Navy school up around Chicago, the Navy had flown him out to Leyte for fleet duty. But not until he reached Leyte had Hall ever even *smelt* salt water. And in that, Hall was far from being alone. There were lots and lots of Navy boys in that war whose first sight of the sea was from the deck of their first ship.

That Marine you see standing there next to Brother, that's Buddy Johnson. Buddy was an old friend who lived right across the street from us when Hall and I were growing up. Bud died this spring, but in the war he was a fighter pilot over there. Flew a Corsair. Talking with him not long before he died, he told me that the typical fighter pilot in the war never had but one objective—one thing they just *had* to do—and that was to become an ace. Bud said that, as a matter of fact, he never even once *saw* an enemy airplane. Not one! Not in the sky. He did manage to get a two-foot hole shot in one wing. But that wasn't the work of a Zero, that was Jap AA.

Bud said that more than once he'd had to take off in some type of aircraft that was strange to him. Something in which he'd had no instruction. I think he said that one time it wasn't even a fighter! He said that was not all that uncommon. They were just told to climb in and take off. I was a pilot myself, for about fourteen years after the war, and I can just imagine the feeling those boys must have had as they headed down the runway in the cockpit of a plane they didn't really know how to fly. Bud said that, thinking back on it, he realizes now that he had a lot better chance of cracking up and killing himself than he ever had of shooting down some Jap. Become an ace? *Hell, we hardly knew ourselves what we were doing over there.* Anyhow, that's what Bud told me.

Bud thought that what happened to you during the war was just the luck of the draw, and there's a lot of truth in that. That's sure what the war in large part came down to for most of us—just the luck of the draw. You played the hand you were dealt. Which, in my opinion, was entirely as it should have been.

But inherent in *the luck of the draw* is the promise of an even broader relationship than the one between luck and war. That's the one that exists between luck and life itself. By life itself, I mean the whole of evident, discernable reality. If you can think of *the luck of the draw* as being a fractal of accessible reality, then the reality that's immanent in that fractal becomes one that is itself highly problematical. Aberrant and indeterminate. Composed of quanta of uncertain location, direction and velocity. Reality then, is, for lack of a better word, the realm of *chaos*. Absolute chaos. Reality is where you're obliged to live if you're not up to doing drugs and alcohol.

And certainly we can sense the chaos that lies all around us. Every day. But chaos is by no means *all* there *seems* to be *out there*. Hand in hand with that evident chaos, there seems to be—order. And a considerable lot of it, too. So that gives us two *fields* of reality. Two mutually exclusive fields, giving rise to paradox. There is, for instance, within one field, the possibility of some relationship between cause and effect, while in the other there is none.

How to unify these two exclusive, competing, mutually inconsistent fields of reality, each, if common knowledge and judicial notice be held insufficient, being verifiable by repeatable experiment, that is the real question. And it's a question to which we've already received what may be the best answer we're ever likely to get. The answer which seems to have satisfied the ancient Greeks, that being their myth of the Fates. The three Fates who, in each case, decide among them between reason and madness.

Do I understand that stuff? Oh, hell no! I know exactly what the words *mean*. I said it, didn't I? But I certainly don't *understand* it. They're not quite the same thing, you know—knowing and understanding aren't. Anyway, you ought to be ashamed of yourself, getting me off track like that! Now let's get back to Hall and Bud. If I didn't tell you, Bud passed away about three months ago.

I'm not just sure exactly when, but both of them told me this picture was taken pretty soon after the end of the Battle of Okinawa. That was about the end of June, wasn't it? I had another friend who was also somewhere around there at that time. His name was Jake Landsberg, and like Bud, he was a Marine fighter pilot. Jake and I were friends and classmates at Lawrenceville the whole of the five years we were there. Jake's older brother, Mort, was a Navy pilot and he survived the war, but Jake wasn't so lucky. No, he drew a deuce and was shot down. About all I know is that he was killed in combat over Ryukyu Island—wherever that is. It happened on June 29th, I know that much, so he came awful close to making it home.

You were wondering how Hall and Buddy happened to meet up like that over there? Bud said he was just driving along one day and he looked up and there was Hall—standing there on the dock. Coincidences of that sort were commonplace in the war. In both theatres. You ask anybody who was over there, they'll tell you.

In this photo, Hall and Bud would look to be just hanging out, but what they're *actually* doing is trying to catch one more deep breath before taking that next long step into the void—the invasion of the Japanese mainland. That's what everybody in the Pacific was doing about then—waiting for the axe to fall.

That brings to mind those bombs. Those two bombs of August that ended the war. Those people who faulted our country for dropping those bombs must have spent their lives down in some rabbit hole. How could they have not known what it was our boys were faced with out there? That generation of Japanese? On Iwo? On every one of those islands! And bloody Okinawa was just the last! Leaving their own national brand on atrocities scattered all over the far Pacific.

You'd think people would have learned by now just who and what those Japs *were* back then. Even people who can't read English should know. There've been pictures enough in the last few years of those brutal island battles. The Japanese leaping to their deaths off the cliffs of Okinawa! What in hell's wrong with those people who even now still fault Truman for dropping those bombs? Why can't they get it! Their utter ignorance of reality is inexcusable! It doesn't take much imagination to picture what trying to whip those Jap's on their own home ground would have meant for our boys out there! In fact, it doesn't take any. Just look at Iwo, for God's sake!

As I say, I sometimes still hear criticism of President Truman, and to this day my blood boils when I hear it. If our President hadn't made that merciful decision and sent that Little Boy to do the work of two million American men, then an assault on the Japanese homeland would have been unavoidable, and hundreds of thousands of us and millions of Japs would have surely died as the result. Also in that case, this picture I have of my brother and of my friend would likely be the last that anyone would ever see of either of them again. As I say, that damned stupidity makes my blood boil!

This Okinawa picture brings something else to mind. Back in college, I had a friend who lived in Dallas by the name of Constantin. Gene Constantin. Our fathers were acquainted in the oil business, but we had a lot more in common than that. But before telling you about Gene, maybe I ought to tell you first, a little bit about this old diary I've got here. Oh, yes, I know! I'm not the diary type, but I did keep this one for a couple of years. That was in 1942 and 1943, my last seventeen months at Yale and first seven months in the army. I'd forgotten all about it, but it's turned up now and here it is. As you can see, it's exactly like me—it's coming apart at the seams.

One day a year or so ago—it was one cold, rainy morning—I woke up and if you can believe it, I'd suddenly grown old. No kidding, it had happened over night! Literally! I remind myself of something Pierre said. If you're not familiar with South Louisiana, every fifth Cajun down there is supposed to be named Pierre. One morning, Pierre woke up and went out to the barn to find his old horse laying there, keeled over dead. He just couldn't understand it. He told everybody, *My old gray mare, she die las night. I don't know why she do dat. She neva do dat befo!*

Anyway, that fateful morning when, for the first time, I woke up *old*, that was the same morning I did something else I'd never done before. I began to think about—oh, you know, I hate to bring up something like this, but—well, Hell! I'll just go ahead and say it! That morning was the morning I began to think about—about, *final things*. To think hard about my own life. And about death. My own death. Just waking up in the morning is tough enough by itself, but I'm here to tell you that there's nothing worse than starting out the day looking up at the bedroom ceiling and thinking about *final things*. It's like a sinking at sea—it can ruin your whole damn day!

But then I remembered reading something that had made a strong impression on me at the time. Something written by one of those personal advice people. Dear Abby, or maybe Socrates—one of them. It seems that the unexamined life isn't worth living. Did you know that? Well, it's not! All the experts agree on it. So when I read that, it hit me real hard, because I'd never done anything like that. No, sir! In fact, I'd never *examined* anything. Not really. Certainly not *final things*. Leastways, not until a year or two ago.

Look at it this way. Can you imagine anything more sobering, after a long lifetime of endless, languorous license, following hard upon a completely wasted and misspent youth, than to wake up one day to find yourself suddenly *an old man*? No, I thought not. And should that not prove sufficiently daunting, not an ordinary, everyday old man either, but an old man faced with having to examine his *whole, entire life.*

So I was suddenly numbed that morning by the realization that I was actually about to pass on and be forgotten like everybody else. That the great day was coming, and not far off, when, no sooner would I have gotten myself comfortably settled down in there and my coffin nailed tidy-shut and lowered away, then, for the first time in my life, it would be *me* hearing voices. Voices coming from *up there.* No, not voices of the kind that Brother heard. These voices were going to be the voices of grave diggers! And who would those grave diggers be talking about? That's right—about *me!*

That's when it struck me like a cold cod in the face that the last thing I wanted to hear one of those grave diggers say was, *That old buzzard down there, do you think his life could have been much worth living?* And then a different voice comes chiming in. That second voice, that's got to be the voice of that *old* grave digger—the one who'd been leaning on his shovel while the young one did all the work. And that old one says, *Nope. Not when he never took the trouble to examine it.* Would you like to hear that said about you? That your life hadn't been worth living after all? And said by total strangers, too! No? Well, me neither. Especially not after I'd put all that effort into it.

Tell you something else about me, I don't put things off. Even when I was a boy, first thing I got home from school, I'd do my homework. Before I went out to play. Don't put it off. Get it done. That was my mother's law. The law she laid down and the law I've always lived by.

There's always a contrary view of course, and if I'm any judge, the main contrarian view here is the one held by the vast majority of people everywhere and throughout all history. That was for sure the view expressed by Tom Robinson just before he died. That's Old Tom, understand, not Young Tom. Like me now, Tom was then well up in his eighties and living out the tag end of his life when he said it. Tom had worked for my life-long friend, B. F. O'Neal, on the old Johns Place, Forest Home Plantation, down in the southwest corner of the parish. B. F. thought the world and all of

Tom. Not only was he fond of Tom, he had a lot of respect for him. There's a difference you know. An important difference.

A short while back, maybe fifty years, B. F. and I were kenneling our bird dogs down there on the Johns Place, and early one cold January morning, we drove down to pick up the dogs to go hunting. It was a little after dark-thirty and just getting light when we drove past Old Tom's house. But cold as it was, and fixing to get even colder—you know how mortal cold it gets at sunup when the really cold winter air falls down around your ears—well, there should have been smoke coming out of Tom's chimney, but there wasn't. So we pulled off and got out, expecting the worst. We both thought he might be lying in there stone dead, he was that old.

But it turned out Tom was perfectly all right. In fact, he was out in the back, splitting fire wood. That's when B. F. asked him, asked him straight out, why he hadn't split that wood for his morning fire the evening before, because if he had, he wouldn't have had to crawl out of a warm bed and get out in the cold dark to split it, the way he was.

Now, listen to this. Here's what Tom said, *"Mr. Neal, sposen I done like you say and split all this here wood yes-tiddy evening? Then just spose that durin the night, I was to pass? After I done did all that work? Ida done it all for nothing, now wouldn't I? Split all that wood for nothing at all! You ever thought about that, Mr. Neal?*

B. F. scuffed his feet around in the dirt a bit, but I could see Tom had him stumped. There was nothing he could say, not a word. Me neither, so we just up and left. Got the dogs and went bird hunting. There were plenty of quail around then. Not any more.

Now that I've gotten real old myself, I can see that Tom had the right of it. For instance, just suppose that at my age I were to act the fool and begin to do what you say and start to write that book about the misadventures of my misspent life. You know yourself I'd never live long enough to finish it. Why, I'd be a year or more just making notes before I could even begin! Then one day, something would come along and carry me off. After I'd made all those notes. So I'd have done all that work for nothing, now wouldn't I? That's the very kind of thing you've got to keep in mind every day when you get old.

Anyway, I didn't put it off. I immediately undertook a full-scale, all-out examination of my whole life. I went scurrying about all over everywhere, trying to find some little something—anything at all—that would demonstrate that, no matter what that grave digger said, my life *had* been worth living. Well worth living as a matter of fact, and that it was him ought to be down there in that box instead of me, because, if I was dead, then at least I was dead right, and not dead wrong, like him. You can get pretty defensive when you're looking up at a grave digger.

And then, just when I was about to give up finding any evidence that I'd lived at all, that I'd ever drawn a breath of life let alone lived a good one, this old diary of mine turns up. I haven't read but just a bit of it and already I see some things I don't remember. But there's much I do remember. Some of it very well. Some of it like it happened yesterday. So I'm going to keep it with me here at the pool for a while. It might not interest you much, but for me it's going to be a real page-turner. A book I can't put down. I'm not likely to ever write a book of course, but if I did, I couldn't ask for a better *aide-mémoire* than this tattered old diary right here.

That's why I'm mighty glad now that I went to all that trouble writing it. Mind you, I don't recommend you keep a diary, sure don't. This diary wasn't even my idea. It was my Aunt Sally's. She gave it to me for Christmas. The Christmas right after Pearl Harbor, and since I thought at first there'd be little trouble to it, I began to fill up those four little lines every day. Didn't much matter what it was. Just write something down. Anything. Couldn't be much trouble? Ha! I was never more wrong in my life!

Keeping a diary is like keeping a fresh milk cow—you've got to milk her every day. A mustache is about as bad. Even a little old pencil mustache will nag the life out of you. Every damned morning, there she is, looking back at you in the mirror. She doesn't say anything but you know perfectly well what she's thinking. *You don't suppose he's going to put off trimming me again today, do you? It'd be just like him! And after all we've been to each other!*

So just take my word for it and don't ever grow a mustache! And don't even *think* about starting a diary. Come right down to it, I'd even think twice before I kept a cow, but that's up to you.

Fortunately, these entries had to be very brief. Just four short lines to fill out every day. They're nothing at all like those note books, those conversation books that Beethoven kept, but then again, some of it's interesting enough. Here's an example. Listen to this.

> *April 7, 1942*
> *Had dinner with the von Trapp family before they gave their concert in Calhoun. The girls all possessed a pure virtue & chaste & noble bearing. That I am sure no American girl could boast of. And they made excellent music.*

And here's the entry for the following day.

> *April 8, 1942*
> *Glee Club sang a concert in Bridgeport tonight with Oscar Levant playing the piano & talking—a rather droll fellow who plays technically very well but with no expression.*

In 1942, those two dates fell on a Tuesday and a Wednesday. The diary says so. Two consecutive entries in which I briefly describe two rather unusual evenings. I can't say I remember everything in here, but I very clearly remember both those days.

Right now, I could take you to Calhoun—that's a residential college there at Yale—and I could walk right to where we sat at dinner that evening. I and the whole Trapp family. All of them, including Maria and the Captain. There were three or four of us invited to have dinner with the girls. I have no idea why I was asked. Maybe it was because I was doing a lot of singing myself then and might actually have something interesting to say. But who knows why. As someone wisely said, *there is no why*. And whatever it was that wise person may in fact have meant by it, I myself understand it to mean that it was not *intended* that mankind be given the *why* of *anything*. Mankind was meant simply to stupidly lower its head and charge forward with all the bravado and abandon of the brave bull as he enters the ring or the Light Brigade at the Battle of Balaclava.

If you can believe it, the von Trapps were not at that time very well known. In fact, they were almost completely *unknown*. After supper, they sang and played in the common room where we'd just dined. The photo in my head reveals an audience of no more than twenty. Just think what the size of that audience would have been had that concert taken place just twenty years later. Just imagine the announcement in *The Yale Daily News* that there would be a live performance of *The Sound Of Music* with the ur-original cast, and open to the public. That's right, for free you could see and hear the von Trapp Family Singers themselves. And all dressed in their native costumes, too. The very same cast which, following close on the heels of its narrow escape from Austria, and its dangerous passage through Switzerland, had only just landed on our shores! The venue would, of course, have been Woolsey Hall and not Calhoun, and even Woolsey would have been SRO.

I also remember the Glee Club's appearance in Bridgeport the very next night. That event was most likely one to sell war bonds. Although he was well known and could draw a crowd, Oscar Levant was then not at all what you'd think of today as a celebrity. Think, rather, in terms of him as a personality, a major personality in the performing arts. The difference being, that he was not at all the air-brushed, air-headed nonentity, the empty costume making the manufactured gesture that is the celebrity of today. He didn't need a script or a Teleprompter and he brought a bit of talent with him.

The house was packed of course, but perhaps, as is sometimes the case in show business, the best show was the one that took place in the wings. Before the show began and whenever neither he nor we were onstage, Levant was all too happy to stand about in the wings with a little group of us who had made bold to engage him in the banter which we sensed immediately was his native tongue. And when offstage like that, he was as amusingly offbeat as he was when on it. But we were not defenseless. To even things up, there was one tall bass among us, Bob Some-body-or-other—Fitzwilliam, wasn't that it?—who was every bit as quick and tart and saucy as he was. So the badinage and repartee that was exchanged offstage, had it been performed out there before the crowd, would have brought down the house.

If you think I'm telling you these things out of some vanity or pretentiousness, then you're quite mistaken, because, beginning with our very first evening together, I've hard-wired my tongue straight to my memory bank, and memories just don't come from the memory bank burdened with any such baggage as that. No indeed! Memories come to us just as ghosts do. Unbidden and unmediated and just as they are.

In this entry here about Levant, I see that I unburdened myself of an opinion as to his virtuosity, and that brings to mind another performer of whose talent I also had an opinion. He was one Elvis Pressly, So before you hear it from someone else, let me tell you about Elvis and me. As you know, Elvis began his career right here in River City, down at the Louisiana Hayride. There's a big statue of him down there now, downtown in front of the auditorium, holding his guitar. I only went to the Hayride once or twice myself, but my wife and I had friends who were regulars, and one night we went with them and Elvis was on the program.

Later that evening, there was a general discussion of the program and Elvis received most of the attention. Most of the applause, too. The ladies made it immediately—and pellucidly—clear that they had been much taken with Elvis. I hadn't myself been so taken with him, but, being by nature loath to express dissatisfaction with any other human being, least of all with a singer, I withheld my opinion. That is, until those ladies goaded and pushed me more than I could stand. That's when, still with some reluctance, I gave it as my judgment that Elvis would be no more than a flash in the pan, uttering, as my final appraisal, the immortal words that would be destined to sink his ship and spell his doom. *I've listened to him, ladies—listened close—and take it from me, in six months time, not one of you will even remember his name.*

But with Leadbelly, it was a different matter. Huddie Ledbetter, after all, came from right here in hometown. In fact, if I'm not mistaken, he got his name from a local family, the Ledbetters. When I was little, there were some of those Ledbetters living right in our neighborhood. In the early thirties, I'd been around Huddie's wife some—over at the Moodys, so I knew Martha. Huddie might have been there around the kitchen, too, but maybe not. But I'd heard him on records. Maybe on the radio. But the first time I heard him sing in person was there in New York, in 1942. But long before that, I was well aware of what he could do. He could sing.

In the early thirties, Martha was cooking for the Moodys. The Moodys had two boys just a little older than me. One was Bobby and the other was—well, I can't remember the other one's name. It may have been John. Anyway, the Moodys lived over there on Oneonta, just a few houses from where Grandmother Hall and my Great Grandmother O'Rourke were living then. So I was in and out of Bobby's house from time to time, and that's why, in 1942, when I went to a place I knew down in the Village to hear him sing, and sent a message backstage, Martha remembered me and she and Ledbelly came out for a visit. Listen to this.

> *Friday, January 39, 1942.*
> *Hank Woods drove down with me.* [To NYC.] *Daddy flew up as a surprise. Date with Florence. Saw <u>Solitude</u>. Heard and met Leadbelly & Martha at Village Vanguard.*

We had highballs together, the three of us, sitting there at a little table about the size of a postage stamp, talking about back home.

But now, about my diary. As much as I came to hate the daily chore of making those entries, this diary is now providing me with one nostalgic, fluttering glimpse after another of old times and old friends—pictures of a past resurrected in these pages like some long lost, black and white, silent movie that's just been found in a garage in Topeka, Kansas. Pictures that might—just *might*—provide the much needed hard, documented proof that my life *was* worth living after all. So I see it as a cache of long forgotten nuggets, found treasure from those golden times of our generation, when we were all still young. When most of us were still alive and hope was in the air. Don't worry, you'll be hearing from me about some of the fascinating stuff I've found here in this old diary.

Now what was it I was going to tell you? Oh, yes, about Gene Constantin, my Yale friend and classmate from Dallas. First, in what I'll read you here, we were returning to New Haven together after Christmas. Then, the next day, we drove together back down to New York to visit the Metropolitan Museum of Art.

> *January 5, 1943*
> > *Lots of Princeton and Yale people on the train. Talked to Gene Constantin about Catholicism.*
>
> *January 6, 1943*
> > *Gene Constantin and I spent several hours at the Met. Museum of Art, returning to Rodin's <u>Hand of God</u> & <u>Pygmalion & Galatea</u>.*

So when I began to look back on my life, to examine it to see if it had really been worth living, Gene was naturally one of those old friends I thought about, wondering what had happened to him since the war, why I hadn't heard anything from him in all these years. Especially if he was still living over in Dallas. That's odd, I thought, that's *very* odd! Didn't seem right. I've told you about this book I have here, commemorating our class at Yale. Well, I looked him up and it turns out that the Japs killed him. Right there on Okinawa, too, and just a few weeks before that picture of my brother was taken. Here's what it says in our class book about Gene.

> *5. Eugene Pierre Cyprien Constantin III of Dallas, Texas, was a member of Jonathan Edwards College, Delta Kappa Epsilon, Aurelian Honor Society, and Scroll and Key. He played junior varsity football and was a leading light in college productions of Gilbert and Sullivan. A member of the Marine V-12 Program during the summer of 1943, he left Yale in October for boot training and OCS. Commissioned in August of 1944, he was assigned to the 4th Regiment of the Sixth Marine Division. In the fierce fight to capture Okinawa, the final battle of the Pacific War, Second Lieutenant Constantin was killed by a rifle bullet on April 16, 1945, while leading his platoon in an attack against Japanese positions on Mount Yaetake. He was posthumously awarded the Bronze Star with Combat 'V', and Mount Yaetake was renamed Constantin Hill.*

I wonder how long it's been since anyone has remembered Gene. Do you think there's someone out there even now, thinking of him, or am I the only one left around who'd do a useless thing like that?

Getting back to my brother Hall, he and I were once very close, and it was a long, long time before that changed. Not until well after the war in fact. But then we began to drift apart. At first, so little I hardly noticed, but then a little became a lot. How did that happen? That's what I've been asking myself ever since this old snapshot of him at Okinawa turned up, and I got to thinking again about my brother. Oh, yes, some pretty fundamental differences did gradually make their appearance, but despite that—despite anything and everything—how could I have possibly permitted such a thing to happen? Especially since almost the last thing my father said to me before he went into that final coma was, *Pa, look after your brother.*

Brother's dead now. He died in ninety-eight, but sometimes, back there in the far reaches of memory, he's still very much alive. And if I'm careful to think about the two of us as we were in our boyhood, and not as we later became, then I can smile and smile and then smile some more, at the very thought of us back then, all those summers ago in Wisconsin, when we were very young. Those were the long years of our boyhood, and we spent most of them together, Brother and I did, and, for the most part, we spent them fishing and hunting. Taking it all in all, those long ago days I spent with my brother were some of the very best days of my life.

But even in those days we'd start out with different things in mind. I suppose the last time we found ourselves satisfied to be going in the same direction was the night we had to use a compass to find our way back to the fire lane where I'd left the car. We were fishing on Lost Creek. Excuse me, *Crick*. Back then, there was not even one *creek* in the whole state of Wisconsin. Every little brook or streamlet you'd naturally want to call a *creek* was in fact something called a *crick*. It was in Lost Crick that I hooked the fish of a lifetime—a German brown of absolutely super-heroic proportions. Biggest trout either of us had ever seen. Well, we actually never set eyes on him. We finally had to break him off. That'll give you some idea how big he was. But that's a story for another day.

Starting when I was fourteen or so and had learned to drive, Brother and I would go bird hunting together when I was home for Christmas. We were perfect companions until we left the car and began to hunt. That's when the problem would always present itself. Our ideas of which way to go always differed, and we'd invariably want to hunt off in opposite directions.

In those days Papa kept only one bird dog, a pointer bitch named Bobbie. Bobbie was the kind of dog whose nature it was to hunt for *you* and not for herself. She'd always be keeping her eye on you, taking notice of the way you wanted to go, and then she'd make her casts out in front of you, you know what I mean? Fine nose, good bird sense, everything you'd want in a dog. It pains me now to think how Bobbie must have suffered when Brother would walk off in one direction and I'd take off in another. And all the while, the distance between us would be growing ever greater, as we went our separate ways.

And so I suppose it was only natural—entirely to be expected, really—that, as we grew into young men, the difference between Brother's ways and mine would only become ever greater, and with that, so would the distance that lay between us. I suppose our drifting apart was as simple as that. And perhaps inevitable. Much of life seems to be.

Der Wanderer

It was after we'd had our last supper together, down at the old Columbia Restaurant on Market Street, that my parents took me over to the Union Station and put me on the train for boarding school in the East. To a school called Lawrenceville. It's in New Jersey, just some eight miles soft of Princeton. Around about 10:30 that night, I hugged and kissed my folks for the last time and turned my back on them to climb up into that Pullman all by myself. I can still see them now, as I take one last look over my shoulder, standing there on the platform, waving me goodbye. The porter had already taken my suitcase and put it up in my berth. Oh, sure, I was awful young, but I can remember all that just as clear as yesterday.

I can even tell you the exact date. Sunday, September 8th, 1935. And I know the number of that Pullman car, too. There was a placard in the window that said it was car number *M 10*. It was just sitting there on the track by itself—all by its lonesome, with no engine, no mail car. Nothing at all hooked on. You wouldn't think it would be going anywhere. At least, not any time soon. But you'd be wrong. About thirty minutes later, while I was lying there in my pajamas, on my back in that upper berth, owl-eyed, I could hear a steam engine come puffing up. Then I could hear the brakeman out there, coupling us up, and then, *chug-chug-chug*, off we went for Texarkana.

Texarkana was where Papa had told me that M 10 would be made up into a big, long passenger train, passing through Texarkana on its way from Dallas to St. Louis. Even though that happened in the wee, small hours of the morning, I was most likely still wide awake when it did. I'd just be lying up there in the gloom, listening to all the clanging and banging around going on outside. In an upper berth, you couldn't see outside. No window, like there was in the old lower.

Saving one summer when I was away at a boy's camp, this was my first time ever to be away from home. Well—away from my parents. I'd spent almost every summer up in Wisconsin, but I'd be with my mother, so that didn't count. I was thirteen years old when I left home and nothing would ever be the same again for me. I didn't know it then, but thirteen more long years were to pass before I'd come home again—home again to stay. You can, you know. I did.

Now, before you ask me how I could possibly remember all that stuff—all those little details, I'm going to go ahead and tell you.

No, I couldn't possibly have remembered that date. After the passage of more than seventy years? Of course not! But I certainly could remember the year, 1935. And that it was in early September, because that's when the schools always opened then. No, just this morning, I went to the Internet and looked it up. You don't believe me? Shame on you! You don't believe that there'd be such a thing as that on the Internet? The exact date I left home for Lawrenceville? Well, you'd be quite wrong.

My Uncle Semmes—he was my great uncle, married to Aunt Julia. Julia Havard, my father's aunt. Aunt Julia had a sister, Aunt Katharine. She never did marry, I don't know why. She was one of the loveliest women you'd ever meet. She was a doctor, too. I was told that she was the first woman gynecologist in Louisiana. Right after the war, while I was in law school at Tulane, Susybelle and I were living down in New Orleans, and Aunt Katharine came out of retirement just to deliver two of our children. We had two born when I was in law school. First, Stafford, and then, eighteen months later, she delivered our son, Charlton, III.

Let's see, where was I? Oh, yes, Uncle Semmes! He happened to be here in town right then. He'd come up from New Orleans, and he was having supper with us that night at the Columbia. We weren't but half way through, when two reporters showed up, one from the *Shreveport Times* and the other from *The Journal*. They knew my uncle was in town and they must have called around and found out that he was there at the Columbia with us. They said that news had come in over the wire from Baton Rouge that Huey Long had just been shot. Who'd ever forget a thing like that?

It doesn't mean anything now, but my Uncle Semmes was then the mayor of New Orleans, T. Semmes Walmsley. Not only that, he was the bitterest enemy Huey had in the whole state. Huey hated him, those reporters knew that. Called him *Turkey-head*

Walmsley. Or was it Turkey-*neck*? The funny thing is, calling him Turkey-head did make you want to laugh, because Uncle Semmes *did* look kind of like a turkey. He even had the wattles. But anyway, all I had to do was Google up *Huey Long* and Bingo! *Sunday! September 8, 1935!*

But that personal insult, that turkey-head business, that was Huey's style, his political rhetoric. It was more than ad hominem, it was ad personam! That and promises. Huey would promise them anything. Forty acres? You got it. A mule? Elect me and I'll see that you're sitting up on the seat of a brand new wagon, driving a team. He was a man utterly devoid of any principle—save, of course, that of the further aggrandizement of his own personal power. Huey, he and his regime, represented brutal force and infinite corruption. His henchmen were all just like him. Corrupt, even for politicians. Even for *Louisiana* politicians! With Huey gone, a number of them served time. And those are by no means the *worst* things that could be said of Huey Long. Think of him as the last Kingfish of Scotland.

Anyway, Uncle Semmes didn't go with us to the station. Didn't even finish his dinner. He left with those reporters and went over to the newspaper office to get the latest about the shooting. That's how I can be so certain about the date I left home for Lawrenceville. Because it was on the same Sunday night that Huey Long was shot. And I found it on the Internet, just like I told you!

But now, how can I be so sure that the number in the window of that Pullman was actually M 10 and not something else? Well, for the next eight years, several times a year I'd be leaving hometown to go back to school in the East, and every time I'd be pulling out of Union Station. And it was always at eleven o'clock at night and always on that same sleeping car. And before I'd climb aboard, I would always see that same number, M 10, there in the window by the steps leading up into the vestibule. It was right there on my ticket, too, of course. M 10. Forget? You don't forget important things like that when you're young.

It was the same way coming home. Same thing, but only different. Taking the train out of New York, when I'd reach the station in St. Louis, I'd have to walk around to get on the train I was to ride home on, and that same Pullman car would be there waiting for me. She just bounced back and forth, back and forth, between St. Louis and home. But when I'd board her there in St. Louis, she'd no longer be M 10. No, she'd be *L 5*. Exact same car, just a different number for the return trip. The porter would just exchange the signs in the window—M 10 for L 5, that's all it took.

Here's something else about Pullman car numbers that might interest you. Something from my boyhood that I've never forgotten. It was during those same years, in the late thirties, that I was reading Thomas Wolfe. Just about everything he ever wrote. Well, all the novels, anyway. I could understand Wolfe right off. Even if he did go to Harvard. He wrote Southern and he was talking to me.

As I remember, when Wolfe was at Harvard, he'd ride the train back and forth between Cambridge and his home in Asheville, and that's when he had the same experience with Pullman car numbers that I had. In one of his books, *Look Homeward, Angel* or maybe *You Can't Go Home Again*, one of Wolfe's characters, maybe Eugene himself, becomes obsessed, it seems to me, with the numbers on the railway car that took him to and fro from college. And like me, that car always bore one number going away and the other number coming home. What's more, he could even tell you, solely from memory, exactly what those two numbers were!

All that was nothing more than pure nostalgia on his part. Nothing but Wolfe's nostalgic attempt, through his writing, to live once more in the olden, golden, sweet sequestered yesterdays. I sincerely hope that I may never fall prey myself to anything so bathetic as that—so *unforgivably self-indulgent* as, God forbid! to burden you with a bunch of trashy tales of my own boyhood. As if they could be stories in which you'd take the slightest interest. But I do recognize that's a weakness I've got to watch out for, and that's the only reason I mention it. But I've got to confess to you—I can remember even now how warm I felt when I realized that the great Thomas Wolfe and I had lived at least that little bit of life in common.

So now you know how I entered upon the second of the only two real adventures that life has to offer—the first great adventure being, of course, the discovery of home, and the other, that of quitting the nest, when, like the great birds, we spread our wings and fly. When I myself left home that night, I had no idea what I would be getting into, but I was absolutely determined that, come what may, I would never fail the hopes and expectations my parents had placed in me. My God! how they must have loved me to have been willing to send me off to school so young—to part with me like that. I think of the two of them a lot these days. Off and on, every day, in fact.

The next morning, when the train pulled into St. Louis, I picked up my suitcase and somehow found my way through that enormous railway station to the train that would take me on east the rest of the way to Jersey. And the morning after that, too, I again comported myself with dignity and honor. I had the porter wake me up very early, so I'd be ready when the train reached Trenton. That's where the train was to make a rolling stop, so I could jump off, and that's what I did—the porter throwing my bag out to me as the train pulled away. I don't remember everything, but I do know that I took a bus from Trenton out to school, because I can see myself getting off that bus when it pulled over to the curb across the street from the Jigger Shop.

I must have walked the rest of the way with my bag through the Circle to Lower School, where I was to report for duty. It was still early—eight o'clock in the morning. There didn't seem to be any other boys around, but I wasn't worried. I was feeling pretty proud of myself about that time, just for getting there. When I got to Lower and opened the door, I expected the place to be full of kids, but I was met with total silence. There was hardly a soul around.

Bottom line is, I'd arrived a day ahead of the date set for the opening of school, and that's why the silence. But it turned out I was not quite alone. Two other boys had arrived in Lower School even ahead of me. Got there the day before. They'd come all the way from Cuba. From Havana. The Brothers Benitoa, Joseph Pérez and Anthony Pérez. They weren't twins, just brothers, but both were entering the First Form, the same as me. Neither one arrived encumbered with English. Spanish? Me? You got to be kidding! So I don't need to tell you, our communication was as much by gesture as speech. I soon gave up trying to talk, but Joe and Tony, they didn't. They had each other to talk to. In Spanish. They took one long, incredulous look at me, standing there in my short pants like a jackstraw *en papillote*, and that's when they really commenced to jabber. I can still see that scene clear as day, but how can I make you see it? Well, try to see them as a couple of matadors just come up from Granada—both of them obviously prepared to meet death in the afternoon, only to be faced, not with a raging bull, but with a Brown Swiss in a tutu, chewing his cud and lowing in a foreign tongue.

It was obvious that they'd never seen anything like me before, but then, I'd never seen anything like them either, so you could call it a draw. If I had to guess, I'd say I was wearing a short jacket of some kind. Not a suit coat, because I didn't have a suit. I wouldn't get my first real suit, one with long pants and a vest, until that Christmas. But I *was* wearing a hat, I know that. My mother called it a *pork pie*. I'd felt strong reservations about that pork pie from the very first day she'd put it on my head. The fact is, I hated it. And that was notwithstanding her assurances that the *pork pie* was the total rage all up and down the eastern seaboard. I don't know the source of my mother's sartorial intelligences, but her faith in them was absolute. But then, her faith in *all* her beliefs was absolute. The whole of that fall, I kept looking everywhere, for just one more pork pie hat like mine. Total waste of time. Mine was the only pork pie hat then in existence. More likely, it was the only one ever made!

But I think it was probably my shorts that drew the most attention from Tony and Joe. Their mother hadn't warned them about anything like me in my short pants. They were both of only average height, while I was quite tall for my age—a string bean well on the way to the six feet I'd be reaching before long—so in my short shorts, I must have looked awful peculiar to them. With those long, skinny legs sticking out of those short, short pants, you'd have thought I was some exotic shore bird wading around in shallow water on stilts. And to think that my mother had been so proud of those short pants! She thought they'd be just the proper thing for a prep school boy in the East. So, for those first few weeks, shorts were all I wore, and not by choice. They were all I had. It must have been a month or more before I could get some long trousers sent from home.

All that was embarrassing enough, me being the only boy in the whole school not in long trousers, but I was to suffer an even greater embarrassment the first day it rained. That's when I had to parade in front of the whole school, docked out in my little short pants and wearing a strange type of footwear wholly unknown to the far more civilized South. *Galoshes*! No wonder everybody turned around to look when I went by. How would you feel if you'd been me, a stranger in a strange land, having to walk my long, bare legs across the campus, wearing those galoshes, and knowing all the time what they'd all say. *Hey, just look at the socks on that rooster!*

But Joe and Tony, they looked as strange to me as I did to them. They didn't even look like boys—not like the boys I was accustomed to. In fact, to my eyes, they *weren't* boys at all, they were little men. They made a strong and favorable impression on me that first day, they were so stalwart and handsome. They were of a healthy summer hue—something between walnut and sienna, as best I can describe it. Think of Omar Sharif as a boy of thirteen, and you've got Tony down cold. Joe wasn't quite so handsome. That's about all I can remember—my general impression of them. I know that their manner would have been extremely courteous. And that they would have been beautifully turned out in suits that fit them perfectly. Very stylish, too, you can bet on that. Probably in a pinstripe. And since those suits were likely bespoke from J. Press, they probably also wore fine, white linen shirts as well. With starched collars, of course, not button-down. And all topped off with silken cravats, in some Burgundy or puce that would have picked up the subtle thread in their suits. You get the idea.

I was instantly aware that, up beside the two of them, I didn't count for much. I can't speak for Joe and Tony, but I can speak for myself. At that moment and for many, many months to come, I was the most completely disoriented, and culturally displaced, skinny little country boy from the Deep South you could possibly imagine.

For the next two years, Joe and I would live together, and become the close friends we would remain. The two of us were placed in Davidson, one of the four houses which then constituted the Lower School. Tony was in some other house. There were two other boys in Davidson that first year who became even closer friends than Joe. They were Fellner and Harbach. Although that was their first year there, too, they were both of them a year ahead of Joe and me in school. They were in the Second Form. That was the ninth grade. Joe and I were in the eighth grade, or First Form. Nick Fellner and I were to be housemates once again in Dawes a couple of years later and we'd remain in close touch through college and into the service. Not until then, till the war parted us, did Nick and I drift apart for a period of years. A period of years? How about sixty-three? That's right, it was sixty-three years before Nick popped up again. This time on television.

But that's how it happened that I became the first member of our class to set eyes on Joe and Tony. Five years later, the three of us would graduate and go off on our separate ways, but I'll never forget the strangeness of that first day the three of us spent there, alone together, in that strange, and, at first, forbidding place.

After our graduation in 1940, I saw Joe and Tony only once more. That was fairly late in the nineteen-fifties, I think. My first wife, Susybelle, and I took B. F. and Nancy O'Neal with us down to Havana for a few days. As soon as I checked into our hotel, I looked in the phone book, but neither Joe nor Tony Benitoa could I find. So I began making inquiries, but all I could get out of the concierge was, *Oh, yes indeed, we know who they are*, and then he clammed right up. I finally went to the hotel manager. At first, he wouldn't say much either—just looked at me, sizing me up. Very, very suspicious. Didn't trust me. Wanted to know just who I was. What business could I possibly have with the Benitoas. These were trying times down there. Anyone connected with Batista, as the Benitoas certainly were, had to be on guard. But he did eventually allow as how he'd see what might be done. He said he'd call me in my room.

Thirty minutes later, the phone rang. It wasn't the manager, it was Joe. Another thirty minutes and Joe and his wife, Helen—she was his first wife, an American—they picked up the four of us at the hotel and showed us the town. Took us everywhere. For two days. We met Joe's dad at the Benitoa family compound. That's where I saw Tony, but only for a moment. He was still doubling for Omar Sharif. I never did meet Tony's wife. She was Batista's daughter. Then it came time to head for home.

There's a letter somewhere around that Susybelle and I wrote the children from down there in Havana. I think it may be in one of those albums over at Laurie's, she's got almost thirty of them. If I can ever find it, I'll show it to you. It's worth a look.

Long ago, I got worried that Joe and Tony might have been killed in that revolution they'd had down there not long after we left, so I tried to find out about them. It took me a while, but finally, through some connections I had with people in Miami, I found out that the whole Benitoa family had somehow got out alive. Then, last year, being the necrologist I've become, I inquired of the Alumni Office at Lawrenceville, but their records just showed both of them as missing. That's when I set about trying to find Joe. I didn't locate Joe, himself, but I did finally locate a son of his—a child of *le deuxième lit*, as he promptly made clear, who was living there in Miami. He told me his dad died some years ago, playing tennis right up to the end. His uncle Tony, he said, was dead, too. Died in the Philippines, quite a while ago.

It was on that trip down to Havana that I made the only forced landing I ever had to make in fifteen years of private flying. If I haven't told you, pretty quick after I got out of law school, I got my private pilot's license. I flew quite a lot those first ten or twelve years, but when my hours started falling off, I finally gave it up. If you're not flying a lot, then it's best if you not fly at all.

Right after the war, there were a lot of insane notions floating around about what the future might hold. One was about the Second Renaissance that was sure to come, and as insane as any, was the notion that, within a very few years—well, right away, in fact—the family automobile would become a thing of the past. There'd just be the family airplane. That's right, the family flying flivver would be parked in every garage! Some thought it would be just like when the automobile replaced the horse. It didn't happen of course. But we did get the two-car garage and the concrete slab out of it. The closest we came, I suppose, was the window fan.

I didn't believe the motor car was about to disappear, but I *was* interested in flying. At first, it was the flying itself that intrigued me. The handling of the aircraft, but that soon passed, and I became more interested in navigation. I'm *still* interested in navigation.

Visual navigation and the use of maps. Radio aids, too. At least, the rudimentary ones we had then. But now here lately, this GPS business, it's taken all the adventure out of it. It's always been important to me to have some sense of where I am—where I'm located. And not only in space, but in time, too. But it's always seemed to me that most people aren't really that much interested in either one. They can't point north and they can't look back.

I was interested in weather, too. I'm still interested in that. You learn a lot about weather, flying. You study over those weather sequences before you take off, and then you get up there and you can see those sequences all laid out there before you, written in the sky. Fifty years ago and more, that was pretty cool stuff.

When I first started out, other than contact flying with maps and dead reckoning, we had only the old low frequency ranges to fly by. And the ADF, of course. It was crude. Crude but useful. But omni was only just then coming in. I can remember how wonderful it was the first time I could fly all the way to Minneapolis with never any need to look down at the ground—just flying from one omni station to the next. Now, *that* was really living!

About a year after I got my license and had some hours, I bought a Navion, and for the next several years that's the plane I mainly flew. My brother Hall had a Bonanza and a Cessna on wheeled floats, and I got myself checked out in them. And there was a long time there when Papa was flying all over the country and he had a DeHavilland Dove. He had a full-time pilot to fly it, a grand guy named Evan Davis. But I was never checked out in the Dove. Well, I did log a lot of hours in the right seat, flying with Evan. I mainly wanted to be sure I could get us down OK if something happened to him. But I never was a multi-engine man, not by a long shot. Later on, I sold my Navion and for the last few years I just flew Hall's Bonanza. If you've ever flown one, the Bonanza is a lot slicker airplane than the old Navion ever was. I flew Hall's Bonanza a lot. I flew Hall's float plane, too. Especially down in the marsh.

But when we took off for Havana that morning, we were in the Navion. B. F. was in the right seat, Susybelle and Nancy in back. B. F. had been a pilot in the Air Corps during the war and we used to fly a lot of places together back in those days. We planned to fly down to Key West, get altitude and then cross over to Cuba. That way, we wouldn't be over water for long. We figured there'd be only thirty minutes when we couldn't reach land, one way or the other. We were off the airways at about eight thousand feet. Not a cloud in the sky. Everything CAVU and we'd just crossed the Mississippi, heading for Tallahassee, Florida, when all of a sudden it happened.

I smelled something, that was the first thing. It was the kind of smell you especially don't like to experience in an airplane at eight thousand feet. The smell of something burning. As quick as I smelled it, I knew what it was. What it *had* to be. Because, not a month before, I'd read a NOTAM about a problem that someone had recently had with their Navion, and that fellow's problem looked just like the one I was having.

On the old Navion—I doubt if there's even one still flying—the pitch of the prop was controlled by the pressure of engine oil on a black rubber diaphragm. I think it was black, but it was mounted at the hub of the prop, just under the spinner. There was a push rod, a plunger on the firewall, and the pilot could adjust his prop pitch by moving that plunger in or out. That would increase or decrease the pressure of the oil inside that rubber diaphragm and that would either flatten the blades out or cause them to dig in deeper. I don't know whether the guy responsible for that NOTAM was killed or walked away or what. That was probably just an inconsequential detail those old NOTAMS didn't think really worth mentioning.

I can see you're simply fascinated by all this, but when I smelled that first little stink of burning rubber, I remembered that NOTAM. It was a report that that rubber diaphragm had recently given way, ruptured, on *some* Navion, *some* where, and engine oil had been let loose under the hood and everything there under the spinner had turned to metallic shit. *Not* good! I slowly throttled back a bit and—oh, oh! sure enough! As I did, tiny bits of metal began spitting themselves out from under the cowling and rat-a-tat-tatting against my windshield just like that NOTAM had said they would.

Fortunately, because of that NOTAM, I knew just what I had to do to have any chance at all of saving the prop and not have it flying off into space. Hoping for the best, I put her nose down, throttled the engine all the way back to full idle and left the prop just slowly wind-milling out there. Then came the silence. You can't believe how quiet it gets up there, with the engine just barely turning over. Just that deadly *click, click, click.*

My next problem was getting her down on the ground, preferably with the wheels down. That wasn't too big a problem though. McComb was on my nose, only six or eight miles ahead and McComb had an airport. Not a real airport, just a grass field with a barbed wire fence around it. No runways, of course, but who cared!

Susybelle had never been much taken with flying. Especially not in a small, four-place, single engine aircraft like mine. The fact is, it terrified the living hell out of her. I couldn't blame her either, not after we were safely on the ground and she confessed that she'd always thought that without the engine running, we'd fall out of the sky like a rock. Anyway, I wasn't too surprised when I heard some heavy duty hyperventilation coming from just behind me. I knew Susybelle was sitting back there, petrified. For some reason, probably because I'd just read that NOTAM, it never occurred to me to panic. Sheer stupidity, I guess. I doubt I even gave a thought to the ten little children we'd just left back home. Nancy and B. F., they had four.

I knew I had to say *something* to Susybelle, so I turned around and told her that I'd felt a sudden urge to go to the bathroom, that I just couldn't wait till we got to Tallahassee, so I was going to set her down at McComb. With that, Susybelle ups and says, *If you say another word I'll kill you*! It doesn't make sense that she'd get mad at me like that. Besides, thinking back on it, what I'd told her could very well have been pretty much the truth.

Well, when I got to that little grass airfield, we still had a thousand feet or so of altitude. I put her wheels down. I lowered the gear and got us safe to the ground. I never once touched that throttle. It was the last thing I wanted to do and it was a good thing I didn't have to. Once on the ground, I went around to have a look and sure enough, the spinner was drooping down like a snotty nose. You could see it yourself! That confirmed what I already knew—that had I needed a little lift at the end to get her over the wire and into the field, that prop would have flown right off. The next morning, I met the mechanic who'd flown himself in from Dallas with the parts he'd need to get us back in the air, and when he started to work on it, the prop just fell off in his hands.

But now, getting back to Joe and Tony, I know without any doubt that I was the first of our classmates at Lawrenceville to lay eyes on them, and from what I've just told you, I'm also pretty sure that I would have been the last. If you're ever down in Miami, you might want to drive out for a close look at Miami's major landmark. It's *La Ermita*, a 120-foot tall simulation of the Virgin Mary's mantel, constructed in the late nineteen-sixties. I read somewhere that it's very important to that whole expatriated Cuban community. It's where they gather in times of crisis. A friend who once lived there confirmed it. He said *La Ermita* is very well known to everyone in Miami. Well, *La Ermita* was designed by one Jose Perez Benitoa, and Jose Perez was Joe and Tony's father. I'm sure I would have met him several times at school. I know I did on that trip to Havana. I can remember Joe taking us into his office. But I have no impression of him at all. No recollection even of what he might have looked like. It's gradually coming through to me how selective my memory is. Why is it that memory saves so much of the past in elaborate detail but turns around and arbitrarily deletes all the rest?

Speaking of going off to Lawrenceville, I've got something sad to tell you. Something I didn't learn about till today. One more very old, very close friend of mine has died. Moment. Jack Moment. Have I ever mentioned Jack to you? I can't remember.

John was his real name, but nobody used to call him that. I hadn't seen him since 1980, when we both returned to Lawrenceville for our fortieth reunion. I can tell you exactly when Jack and I first met. It was on Wednesday, September 11, 1935. That was again in Lower School, and both of us were Rhinies in the First Form. Not only were we close all the way through those five years at school, we went on to Yale together. There were five of us who did that, a quintet. Charlie Higgins, Bill Flemer and Johnny Green were the other three. Our Freshman year, Jack and John Green and I had our digs in a triple in Vanderbilt. Charlie Higgins and Bill Flemer were in a double just across the courtyard. But the five of us were so close it didn't matter which way we roomed. Then, in the fall of 1941, all five of us went on to live together in Davenport. That was for the next year and a half, until every one of us was finally in uniform. Johnny Green went into the Navy, and the rest of us signed up with the Army.

In fact, Jack Moment and I were inducted into the Army together. That was on June 14, 1943 at Fort Devens, Massachusetts. First, we served together as privates with the 704th Combat MP Battalion for a few months and then we both went to the Artillery OCS at Ft. Sill, Oklahoma. We were even commissioned together there in early December, 1943. Jack wound up overseas as a paratrooper with the Seventeenth Airborne Division. I guess that reunion was the only time we were together since that day we got our bars. That was at Fort Sill, at the end of 1943. Haven't I told you that already? I believe I have, but I may not have told you that Jack and I were together through all of that.

Starting a couple of years ago, Jack and I began flying e-mails back and forth, talking together like old times. He'd been living on an oxygen tank for the last year, so he couldn't have had much of a life. But for those eight years beginning in 1935, we were very, very close. Every day. He was a born artist, but more than that, he was a damn good man and good company and I liked him a lot.

All day now, I've been thinking that maybe I ought to reconsider writing that book. Now with Jack gone, and Flemer breathing oxygen and on the ropes, it looks like I'm about the only one of us who's left around that could. Oh, I know—that book's just an idle dream I keep having, so who do I think I'm kidding?

I told you about that day I met Joe and Tony. It would have been just the day after that, I suppose, that I met Moment. I guess I said that, but I can't get him off my mind. All that time we had together, and there were still a few things I never quite got around to telling him. Personal things I wanted him to know but was too embarrassed to say. You know—too sentimental? Too late now.

Here! Look at these line drawings I brought out to show you. These are some—*momentous* impressions of the Yale he and I knew. Sorry about that, but Jack would have loved it. Jack knocked these drawings out for a book that commemorated the fortieth anniversary of the graduation of our class. This'll give you some feel for how it was with us back in New Haven in the early forties.

"... The shortest, gladdest years of life..."

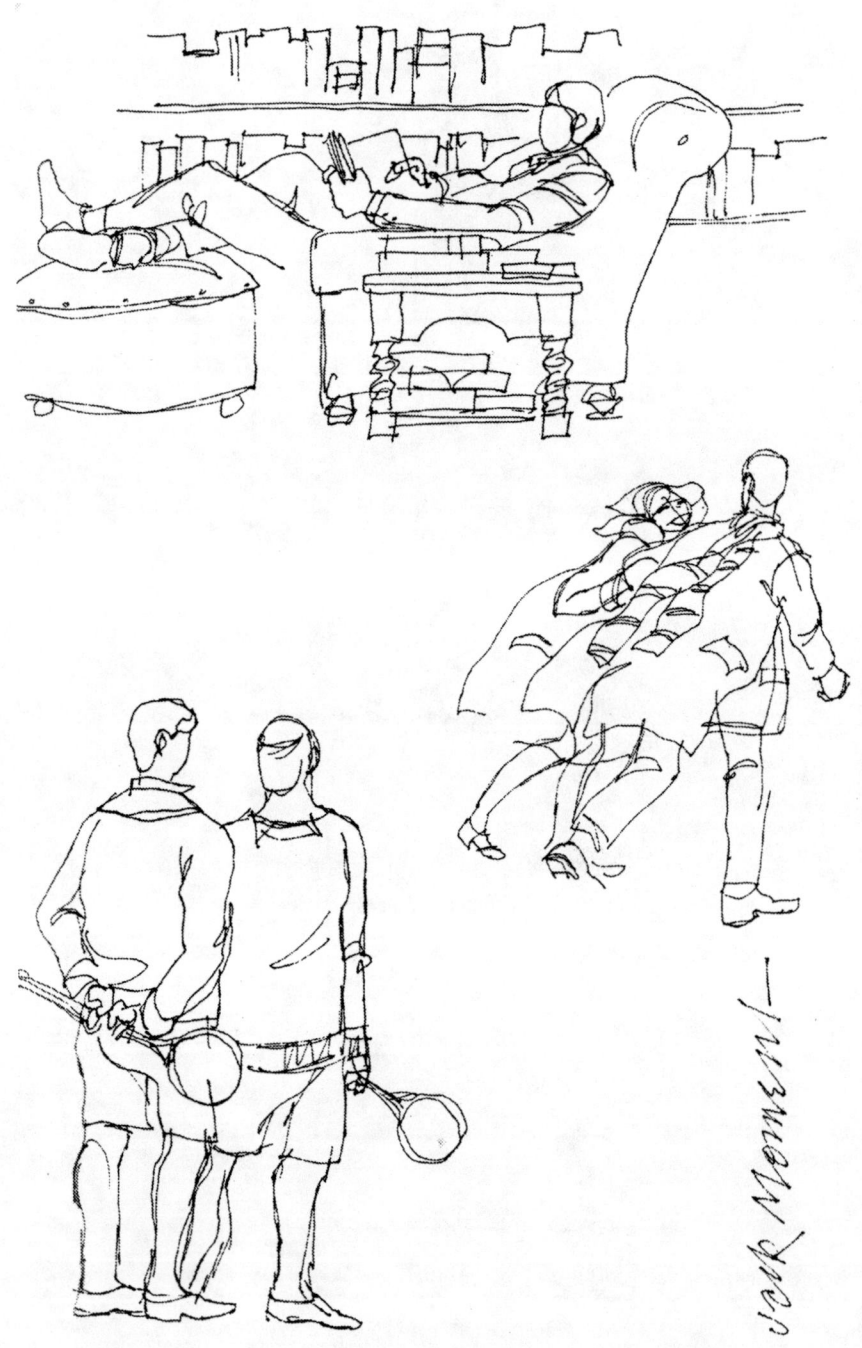

Die Forelle

    Some two hundred miles southwest of Anchorage, the Iliamna River flows south out of Lake Clark to empty into Lake Iliamna, one of the largest lakes in our whole country. Part way down the Iliamna from Lake Clark to Lake Iliamna, there's a busy little, boulder-strewn stream that enters the Iliamna to your left. By that, I mean, from the east. As I remember it, that little stream's only a couple of miles long. I know it was all white water and I know they called it a river, the American River. Its source was a little lake, what you might call a mountain tarn, that nestled high up above the Iliamna. It seems to me there was another river somewhere in Alaska that was also called the American, but that other American River, that was a *real* river, a big, important river. The river I'm talking about now, *my* American River, it's of no importance whatsoever.

    About thirty years or so ago, there were two of us on that little river fishing for rainbow trout. We'd been told that rainbows were the only fish we'd catch in there, but that was fine with us. Since we planned to release everything, we were using barb-less hooks and there was no need for a creel. We did take fly rods and hip boots but that's about all. The current was so heavy in that little stream that even when I was standing in it only knee-deep, I had to be awful, awful careful, lest it tump me over.

    Peggy and I had gone with about ten of our friends up to Alaska to spend a week in a fishing lodge on Lake Clark. It was a week in paradise. Every morning, we'd fly out in one direction or another. Usually we went four to a float plane. Plus the pilot, of course. He'd double as the guide. We'd fly sometimes two- three hundred miles to fish. Mostly rivers, but sometimes we'd drop in on a lake somewhere. There's beautiful water scattered all over southern Alaska. And oh, the salmon! The silvers were running then. And char, arctic char and grayling. All sorts of beautiful fish like that. But that morning, because the American was such a short, stubby little thing, only two of us had flown down there to fish. Me and my young friend, Don Wiener. It was a tight fit getting into that lake, but our pilot knew what he was doing, so we skidded in OK.

After we'd tied the plane up to some rocks and unloaded and strung up our rods, Don right off insisted that I head down-stream first—ahead of him. He wanted me to believe that it was his *personal preference* to start fishing right there where we were, where the river let out of that little lake. But I knew he was lying. He was lying through his teeth, and he knew I knew it. What that nice young man was *actually* doing was trying to arrange matters so that he'd be fishing down the river *behind* me, and if anybody wound up having to fish over water that had already been fished, it would be him who'd have to do it and not me. What can you do with someone who wants to take advantage of you like that? I did the only thing I could do. I walked a good long ways downstream before I ever wet a line. That way, I'd start so far ahead that, with the limited time we had, he'd never catch up.

That's why I was almost out of sight of Don when it happened. I'd been catching rainbows right along. Nothing to tell about. They seemed to be all of a size, around fifteen inches. I remember that. But there was enough action to where I had my eyes focused on what I was doing and not on what was around me. That's when I heard it. It was something huge. Something to my left. Downstream. It sounded like—well, I can't tell you exactly *what* it sounded like, because that was the only time I ever heard such a sound as that. It just sounded—enormous! A*bsolutely enormous*! Like a water buffalo had jumped in down there. Or a big boulder had come loose from the moon and landed in the river. Something perfectly huge like—like I don't know what. And threatening!

And it was close. Awful close, that was the worst part. How close was it? Fifty yards? Isn't that about right? But let me just say right here that fifty yards is by no means a measure absolutely fixed and certain. For instance, when you're looking at a great big grizzly bear, perception becomes everything, and perception is mostly about how we *feel*. Anyway, he *seemed* much closer than fifty yards when I looked up and saw that perfectly huge Alaskan brown bear, wallowing about in the river down there. He wasn't a tourist like me. He was a native. A local who'd come out to try his luck, and I'd encroached on *his* water! A stranger was fishing his beat! He was up to his belly button in what had only moments before been *my* river but had now become all his, and already he was pawing out a rainbow. That's when it came over me that I had no further need of rainbows, so I reeled in my line and quit.

Brown bears are wonderful fishermen, everybody knows that. Not that there's any subtlety or guile in the way they do it, because there isn't. They're very direct. They spot a fish, they dive right in. It's surprising how effective that is when you see it done.

But un-subtle as this one was, I'm not sure that he was the *most* un-subtle fisherman I ever found myself around. Or the most effective either. For a couple of months right after the war, my battery was in occupation in that little German village of Bad Heilbrunn I told you about. It was perfectly beautiful country, not far from Austria. There was a little trout stream close by and it was plumb full of trout. Small German browns—fourteen inches was a big one. Somewhere in the house I was living in, I'd found a fly rod and a book of flies and that was all I needed. I was catching enough to think that one day I'd catch enough to feed the whole battery, but I never did. The best I could do was sometimes feed the ten or twelve of us who were living there in battery headquarters.

Then, one Sunday evening, I went into the battery mess to go through the line and what did I see but I great pile of fried fish and every one of them was a trout! There must have been two hundred of those delicious little buggers, enough for everybody. I soon found out they'd all been caught that morning and all in that same little stream I'd been fishing myself. And it only took four of the fellows in the battery to catch the whole mess. How'd they do that? Here's how.

They already knew there were trout down there. Everybody in the battery knew I'd been catching some. What they did was the very essence of un-subtlety. Their fishing tackle, I found out, consisted of two or three bed sheets and about twenty hand grenades. They fished nothing but the pools. No rapids. How many, I don't know, but they must have cleaned out every pool they fished. They'd pull the pins on two or three hand grenades and toss them out into a pool. When those grenades went off, every trout in there would be so stunned by the concussion that they'd all come to the top, swimming around in circles, laying on their sides and barely flipping their tails. In fact, they were scarcely moving as the current floated them down to the race of shallow water running out of the lower end of the pool. And sure enough, those intrepid anglers were there waiting for them. Those bed sheets strung out between them, they skimmed those German browns up out of the water the way we used to skim up ripe mayhaws down at Black Lake in the spring.

Do you remember that old fish picture I told you about? That picture of the fish my Grandfather Hall caught in Lake Chetek? Well, I found it. Just look at these. Just like those trout, these were all caught the same day. You can see that for yourself. I think he told me that he and two friends of his caught every fish you see there. But aren't they lovely! Bass, pickerel and pike. Excuse me. *Great northern* pike! When I was a boy, we never called them just *pike*. They were always called *great northern pike*! Brown trout were always *German* brown trout. That's if they were plural, but, if singular, as they most often were in my part of Wisconsin—that's because they were terrible cannibals and ate up their own kind—then he was just *a German brown*. Like a blue heron. With us, he was always a *great* blue heron. That's just the way it was.

The longest and heaviest of those long, skinny fish you see there, that's what's called *the great northern pike*. They'll hit a top-water just as quick as a bass, but their strike is twice as vicious. Make that four times. In the fifties, there were a couple of summers in a row that my partners in Lyons Petroleum and I would fly up to Canada to camp for three or four days in a remote cabin on the English River. That's a river in Ontario that runs east-west, up north of Kenora. Today, you can probably drive a fancy motor home anywhere you want to go up there. I mean, one of those million dollar babies, fifty feet long and hinged in the middle. Drive that sucker right up to every concrete launching ramp on the whole river. But in those days, the best way to get in there was by float plane. Hall would take his float plane all the way, but most of us flew up in Papa's Dove. We'd go up as far as Kenora in the Dove and go by Beaver from there on in.

Up there you could catch all the walleye and smallmouth you could use. This was the *true* smallmouth, the one with the red eyes. But what I was going to tell you about was all those perfectly huge great northern pike we caught up there. I'd caught a lot of great northerns down in Wisconsin. Some of them were all right, but they were nothing compared with those we caught in the English River. Up there in Canada, we always fished two-to-the-boat and every day every boat was releasing four or five of those great northerns that would weigh from fifteen to twenty pounds. Some maybe bigger. Lots of little ones, too, of course. Ten pounders.

I was casting an old fashioned chunk of wood with three big, strong triple gang hooks on it called a Lucky Thirteen. Sometimes, just for old times' sake, I'd call it my Dowagiac. That's right, *Dowagiac*! It's pronounced *dow-wa-jack*, and when I was a little fellow on Lake Chetek, that's what all the grown men called those early artificial baits they threw back then. It was a generic. And the line they used was made out of linen, believe it was. Anyway, it would rot real quick if you came in off the lake and let it dry on the reel. So what they'd do every evening when they came in, they'd hook a bait on one of those white birches and walk around, hanging their lines around the trunks of the trees so the line was up in the air where it would dry. Then after supper, they'd come out, grab their rods and walk back around, reeling their line in as they went. That was a ritual that absolutely fascinated me when I was a little boy.

Let's see, now—oh, yes! Those great northerns on the English River. With them, you had to use a six inch wire leader. If you didn't, their teeth would cut the line and there went your Dowagiac. We took turns, one rowing and the other casting in to the shoreline. That's where those big brutes would be laying up. Waiting there in ambush in water often as little as two or three feet deep. Hiding in the weeds that grew over those rocky ledges along the bank. OK, go ahead. Throw that Lucky Thirteen in there. Now give it a jerk. Better grab hold of the side of the boat, because like as not, only a few yards away, and right in your face, you're going to see some ugly old predator, a real monster, come charging up out of the water, and there he'll be, three feet in the air, twisting and turning, with that plug in his jaw, its hooks rattling away like mad.

I've caught bonefish on the flats and bull reds in a saltwater marsh and as recently as fifty years ago, when the sea at Acapulco would be alive with sails, I've released two nine foot sailfish on the same day. Of course now, a musky will hit a top-water, too, and I've caught a number of keepers but nothing of any great size. But when it comes to the strike itself, to the sheer, gluttonous ferocity of the attack, not one of them is even in the same league with a really big great northern. Not when he takes a top-water plug twenty feet from the boat. And it doesn't end there either. Once you've got a truly large great northern pike on that five-foot, True Temper, solid steel rod, mounted with a trusty Pflueger Supreme—for years, that's all I ever used—you've got a tough fight on your hands, because that ugly brute of a fish will fight you, fight you hard right to the end.

But strange to say, the one fish that made the deepest impression on me in a lifetime of fishing was not a great northern pike at all, it was a trout. I was twelve or thirteen years old, when the wily trout first swam into my ken. That's when Cap Hagen began to take me out trout fishing with him. I learned how to fish trout from him. Cap was *Casper* Hagen and he was a flush-faced, ever-smiling Norwegian who, when he was fishing, would be so happy he'd sometimes just break out into song. It was always the same song, so I guess it was the only song he knew. There must have been more to it, but these are the words I remember. *A thousand Swedes ran through the weeds, pursued by one Norwegian.*

He must have recognized in me a boy who was just born to fish. Why else would he drive all the way from Rice Lake down to Chetek, just to take me with him out to some little hard-scrabble crick, hidden away back in the woods? It was always someplace we could catch brookies. It seems to me some people called them speckled trout—*specs*. But anyway, the brook trout was the trout native to that country and he was the one Cap was most after.

Rainbows were what the hatchery raised. Trucks from the hatchery would plant those rainbow fingerlings by the barrel-full. They'd drive around and dump them in every creek the road would cross. They didn't even have to leave the road to do it. So as you can imagine, you were knee deep in little rainbows every place those hatchery trucks pulled over to dump them out. Cap knew just where all those places was. But you couldn't get him to fish within a mile of any one of them. Cap said that at the hatchery they came from those rainbows were fed nothing but liver and that's what they tasted like. Liver. He wouldn't eat them. I couldn't tell the difference, myself, but I knew better than to tell Cap a thing like that.

As you know, fly line is made strong enough to hold a horse, and Cap always had me tie on a tippet to match. Three foot of gut leader, that gut almost as strong as the line. Light-wire hook, size 4. Rigged like that, when your hook got hung-up on something under a pile of trash downstream a ways, you could always get it lose by pulling on the line till the hook straightened itself out. We always used hooks made out of very light wire for just that reason.

I learned all sorts of stuff like that, watching Cap. There were a couple of cricks where you could dap a fly. Cap kept some black gnats to dap with. But on most of the cricks we fished you couldn't cast a line. The cover was too heavy. That's why we always dressed our hooks with garden hackle. You can never go wrong with a worm. Didn't I read that somewhere in Walton? I don't think Isaac would have approved of hand grenades however.

We always walked along fishing downstream, letting that worm drift wherever the current took her. Under downed tops and up under cut banks. And of course, one of the first tactics I learned from

Cap was to muddy-up the water with your feet. That's basic. Never mind that that was precisely the evil trick played upon trout by that horrid fisherman in that poem Schubert set to song. Forget that song and just take it from me. If you'll stir up some sediment and let a bit of cloudy water drift down ahead of you, good things can happen to your hook.

But the trout that left such a strong impression on me was not a brook trout, it was a German brown. A huge German brown. He had to be at least twenty-four inches long. I had him hooked solid and on my line for what seemed forever. I never actually saw him, and neither did my brother Hall, but that's what Casper Hagen said he was. Two feet! He said that's what he *had* to be, when I asked Cap about it later on. A very ancient, voracious, cantankerous, carnivorous, hook-jawed German brown, who'd been living for years in that deep, S-shaped pool in Lost Crick, when I happened along. His home was a double pool, maybe twenty feet long but only about eight feet wide. It was five feet deep all over. I know that because Hall jumped in it twice, trying to grab him or get him cornered somehow, but all to no avail. We could hardly believe what was going on.

We'd gotten in there rather late in the afternoon, as I remember. We'd already caught a few and I know it was overcast and threatening rain, and Hall had just leap-frogged to a couple of holes ahead of me, when I got him on. He had a deep hole back up under one bank and he'd swim back in there in his hole for a while. And then he'd come out again and swim slowly down to the end of the pool before making his way slowly back again. I couldn't put too much pressure on him, else the hook would straighten out, he was that heavy. When I saw what I had on, I'd hollered to Hall and he came back to help. Finally, with darkness gathering and a light rain just beginning to fall, we knew we had no choice but to give up. One of us either broke the leader or cut it, I don't remember which. Or maybe I tight-lined him till the hook straightened out and he was off.

Then we had to find our way back out to the fire tower where I'd left the car. We could never have found it without a compass. There was just enough light left to read it, and Hall would walk out forty yards or so ahead of me, on the right heading. He'd be calling out to me as he went, so I would know where he was and could keep him on the right line. Then he'd stop and I'd catch up with him, and we'd do it all again. It took a while, since we were going through trees and heavy brush and were nearly a mile from the car.

So that's the sad story of that great, heroic German brown. Have you ever had the biggest trout of your life, an historic trout, a fish bigger than myth, hooked solid on your fly line, with a short, stout leader, in a hole right under your feet, and couldn't catch him? Couldn't ever even get a good look at him and had to let him go? No? Well, it's the kind of thing you never forget. *Never*!

But we did find the car on the fire lane where I'd left it and we did make it back to gravel without getting stuck, so things could have been worse.

As I've always said, on most days of a man's life, the fish don't bite, the ducks don't fly, reason sleeps and even an all-powerful God finds Herself quite incapable of tempering the harsh wind to the shorn lamb. So my advice to you is to go fishing every chance you get.

By the way, before you leave. If you should ever hear me start to tell one of these stories and it sounds like it's going to be one you've already heard, please don't get the idea that I've lost my mind. That I've gotten too old to tell the difference. No, no! I don't want you worrying your head one little minute about a thing like that. And whatever you do, don't stop me! Because there are some of these stories I just never get tired of hearing, no matter how many times I have to tell them.

Away to Rio!

Too bad you arrived in time to hear only the end of it. *So fare ye well, my bonnie young girl, we are bound for Rio Grande!* You should have heard the whole song. We recorded it in the very late autumn of the world into which I was born. That was the autumn of 1941, just before Pearl Harbor when the long winter of the war set in. By we, I mean the all-male chorus with which I sang nearly the whole of the time I was at Yale. The Yale Glee Club.

About thirty or thirty-five of us went down to New York and recorded it in the most famous recording studio of the day, Liederkranz Hall. Liederkranz? Well, Liederkranz *is* the name of that cheese, of course, the one with its own distinctive, shall we say, "nose"? But in German, Liederkranz means something like a garland of songs. I'd be pretty sure that it's in that sense that Liederkranz Hall was named. But there's another sense in which the German uses their word Liederkranz, another meaning for it, and that's to mean a men's singing society. And that was just what we were when we went there and made that album, a men's singing society.

That was a sea chantey, that song you heard only the end of. Sea chanteys were the songs sailors sang as they worked. You may know this one as *Away Rio!*, but some years before that summer of 1941, when we ourselves set sail for Rio, Barty made his own arrangement of it, and the title he gave it was slightly different. *Away to Rio!*

Who was Barty? Barty was Marshall Bartholomew and he was our music director and he was our conductor and he was the arranger of many of the things we sang, including that song you heard on that disk. We recorded some dozen or more songs for Columbia Records, but only two or three were chanteys. That one, *Away Rio!,* is one of the more popular of those work songs that seamen sang in the days when iron men sailed wooden ships flying canvass sails. It's an old standard, and every time I hear it, the memories of that long ago summer come crashing over me in wave-after-emotional-wave, and I'm taken right back again into the midst of all that intense excitement, that taut sense of expectation followed by the relaxed joy of fulfillment that came to us from singing to all those tens of thousands of people down there in South America. Most of them had never heard a good male chorus sing and they were stunned but it. That summer may have been the greatest, the most wonderful summer of my life. The summer of 1941. The last summer before the war.

The Yale Glee Club had sung its way through Europe many times, but ours was its first-ever concert tour of South America. We went at the behest of the State Department, as part of our South American foreign policy. Something called The Good Neighbor Policy. That's why it was not only sponsored by our government, it was strongly supported by all our embassies everywhere we went. Best of all, the government picked up the tab, so that whole trip cost me almost nothing. Well, not me, my parents.

It was in the fall following that tour that those of us who hadn't graduated went down to New York and recorded those songs for Columbia. It was just last year that my own old copy of that four-record album turned up at the bottom of the stack, but I couldn't listen to it. I found a turntable but I could never locate a needle of the right size, so I sent it off and had those four records transferred to a disk. It was just last month that I discovered in some of my father's old files two letters I'd written my parents from shipboard on our way down to Rio. On our way to Rio de Janeiro, Brazil, where we arrived barely in time to sing our opening concert.

The liner we sailed on from New York was named, appropriately enough, the S.S. Brazil. I remember that I used the typewriter in the purser's office to write this first letter I'll read to you. It was posted home when we reached Barbados. That was our only port of call before Rio. Remember now, this is 1941.

Via Air Mail
On Board
S. S. Brazil

(Barbados-June 25) The Yale Glee Club has completed the first stage of its combined good-will mission and concert tour of South America. We have called at Barbados, a small British island

in the eastern Caribbean, and it is from there that I airmail this account of the first 1836 miles of a seven weeks' trek that will carry us some 13,000 miles before we arrive back in New York on August 11.

Ours is a big job: we must sing to the America "down under," learn their ways, and show them ours in an attempt to strengthen Pan-American unity through the medium of music. I have heard and read that South Americans are an emotional people. Music might well be a better way to impress our kindred, free, singing spirits than much talk or a distant declaration of friendship. Anyhow, we mean to have a try at it, and in the process we shall certainly experience enough to keep this typewriter clicking for a long time.

We sailed on the S.S. Brazil from New York at midnight June 20th. A sailing for South America is something a little different from ordinary sailings, and because of the then recent sinking of the Robin Moor, *there was a high excitement which touched the voice of the crowd with a tense tone of possible danger. We were to be twelve days at sea. Much can happen in twelve days these swift times.*

Let me interrupt myself here to say something about that ominous sense I was trying to convey of the danger of those times. There *was* a dark foreboding hanging over our country then and the danger was real. But as you know, danger can also be not a little exciting. What's more, we'd hardly put out to sea, when news came that Hitler had launched his great eastern army against the Soviets, and that further confirmed our fear that war was imminent. That we might not ever see safe harbor in Rio but might fall off the edge of the world instead.

There could never have been such a ship as this for good will. Just as "National Defense" has become in the United States a slogan for the sale of everything from hair pins to yachts, just so has "good will" become the cry of many who are interested rather in the satisfaction of their stomachs. But you could hardly find a more interesting passenger list. Traveling Tourist Class with us there are seven ballet dancers, each with lines decidedly Zorinesque — only more so. It is therefore clear that we have already set about the business of being Yale-fellows-well-met. I might say that these graceful creatures are somewhat disappointing as partners in the dance; it is too much like driving a high-powered automobile down a dirt road. One of them, Vela Ceres, is a New Orleans girl.

There are also two West Pointers on a semi-official visit to Brazil, Uruguay, Argentina, and Chile. It seems that their chief occupation will be to bestow wreaths on the tombs of the heroic dead and to kiss the either cheek of the less heroic but more appreciative living.

I've got to stop again for a word or two about those West Pointers. Let me read you this diary entry for April 12, 1942. *Shot West Point in skeet today at Lordship. Saw Lee Hamerly. Met two cows: Conrad Koerper & Ed Bennet. They said Bill Knowlton (sp?) West Pointer I met on S. American trip sent me his best & I returned it.* Even now, I can picture Bill Knowlton. Tall, nice looking, gentlemanly fellow. Just the man for The Point to pick for a good will mission by our military to South America. I was on Yale's skeet team all the while I was in college and we went a number of times to West Point to shoot against their teams. In fact, we were quick to go there because at every post there were unlimited shells and we could shoot as many practice rounds as we liked, and all of it was free.

There was another attraction. We'd go there on weekends, shoot skeet all afternoon down under the bluff by the Hudson, have supper with them at the visitors' mess table and then go to a movie or a dance. And there were girls there, too, those weekends, and those girls would all have to be off the base by midnight and they'd all be staying at the Thayer Hotel, just outside the gate. That's where our skeet team always just happened to stay, too, at the Thayer. I mention Lee Hamerly, Conrad Koerper and Ed Bennet. Their names all find a resonance in my head but I can't find their faces.

There is a group of Experimenters in International Living which includes two sisters from Smith and a boy from Harvard. There is a large number of assorted South Americans from whom I have learned a little of what to expect. One Brazilian lady who had gone to college at Penn State told me that we would be very well received in her country, probably better than in Chile and Argentina."

She was right about our reception in Brazil, but not about the reception we'd receive elsewhere in South America. As it turned out, they loved us everywhere we went. Oh, my God! how they did love us down there! But let me read you some more of what I told my parents.

There are a great many professional entertainers on board, including a trick bicyclist and three dance teams in addition to our glee club and the ballet dancers. It would seem that American entertainers are in great demand by the casinos and bistros of Rio and B.A. (an American simplification of the mysteries of Buenos Aires) just as the Carmen Miranda and the Bidu Sayaos are at present among the brightest stars in our country.

Last and least there are six or eight Powers models traveling First Class, passive creatures who spend their conscious hours demonstrating an interminable wardrobe. And at night they usually come back to our [Tourist Class] bar room where they sit like tall, cool drinks of vinegar and long for the days when they were human.

As for the routine on board we have breakfast about nine, then rehearse from ten until eleven thirty. An hour in the sun on deck, swimming and playing games or chewing the rag, and then lunch followed by a half hour part rehearsal. More sun bathing and an hour's rehearsal again at four. We have the rest of the day and night for bridge, dancing to the ship's orchestra, star gazing, or just bending an elbow with the boys.

It might at first sight seem strange that we are spending so much time rehearsing; but there was not much time during May and June at college to spend learning the many new songs we are going to use on this trip, so we have been forced to do a lot of hard labor on the way down. We have two complete programs of thirty songs each, all of which were selected especially for South American audiences by Marshall Bartholomew. When we arrive at Rio de Janeiro we will have ten or twelve Spanish and Portuguese numbers which we will be able to use in addition to over fifty English, Latin, and Italian songs. This does not include quite a few Yale Songs. The Portuguese compositions, most of which are the work of South America's greatest composer, Villa-Lobos, and the Spanish things are to constitute a program early next fall by the Yale Glee Club in New York. They are top-notch. We are very anxious to know what Rio, where we give our first concert on the night of July fourth, will think of us, but we are not worried. Anyway, we shall soon know.

That's the end of that first letter. Did you hear that reference to a ship named the *Robin Moor*? You didn't notice? Well then, I'd better explain. Exactly one month before our ship departed New York, a German U-boat operating in the Atlantic had stopped an unarmed American freighter some 900 miles of the coast of Brazil and sent her to the bottom. We weren't yet in the war, you know, and she had American flags painted all over her, but that didn't save her. She was the *Robin Moor*, the first American merchantman sunk by the German Navy. In Homer's war, we're told that Helen launched a thousand ships, but how many were sunk, I don't think Homer says. Virgil doesn't either, as I recall. In Hitler's war, to the contrary, I have no idea how many were launched, but I do know how many were sunk—50,000. Can you even *imagine* such a number? But it's true. 50,000 ships were sunk during the war!

And then on June 20, 1941—the very same day we sailed for Rio on the *Brazil*—President Roosevelt addressed a message to Congress in which he said that the sinking of the *Robin Moor* was a warning to us from the Germans that our country's ships could henceforth use the high seas only with the leave of the Nazis. Sinking the *Robin Moor* was Hitler's proclamation to the world that the high seas would now belong to him.

And in addition to all that, we knew that very soon we'd be putting in at Montevideo, and that we'd be sailing past the visible remains of the *Graf Spee*. The *Graf Spee* was the German pocket battleship scuttled in shallow water just outside Montevideo only eighteen months before. Only one life was lost, and that, the life of her Captain. It seems only yesterday that we steamed past the *Graff Spee*. Only her superstructure was out of the water, sticking up like a grave stone set in the sea. I can see myself now, standing there at the starboard rail when we passed her by. But of the *Robin Moor*, I could remember nothing. I had to go to the Web to find out why I'd even mentioned her. So it was no wonder that as we prepared to cast off, the excitement lit up the sky all around us the way heat lightening does on a heavy summer night.

Here now, take a closer look at the paper these letters are written on. This is the *Brazil's* own letterhead. The purser gave it to me. And look! That stationary is marked specifically for delivery by air mail. *Par avion!* Wow! Air mail, you see, was something then still rather new in our small world. You see how small these sheets of paper are? They're less than five inches wide, really only note paper. And you see there? I've written on both sides of every sheet. That was common practice then. Saved a lot of money.

In that letter I've just read, I've described only a few of the ship's passengers, but there were others I could have written home about. There was one gentleman on board, one gentleman in particular whom I completely left out of that letter. And although he's left out, I remember that gentleman very, very well indeed. I can see him now, clear as a bell. He's on the promenade deck, amidships the port side, stretched out in his First Class deck chair. He's had the deck steward place it so he'd have the afternoon shade. He's reading. There's a young girl, ten or twelve years old, in the chair beside him. I've seen them together before. I'm guessing she's his daughter, maybe his niece. They're definitely related.

But it's him I'm interested in. And I'm interested in him because of who he is. Because gossip about him has already spread instantly among the passengers. I would use that old, thread-bare expression—the news spread like wild fire—but in this case, there's a more apposite simile, so I'll use it. The news of his identity spread among the passengers like food poisoning on a cruise ship.

People nowadays would say he was a celebrity, but I'm not at all sure that in those days the word *celebrity* carried with it the sense it does now. I think that people then were more apt to have said only that he was a famous writer. But writers just don't count as celebrities. That's because writers are actually required to *write* something, while celebrities aren't required to actually *do* anything at all. In fact, I've been told that the official oath of office required of celebrities before their ascension specifically prohibits them from producing anything other than an inane, photo-op smile. So it's not the celebrity's glitz and glitter but the celebrity's complete uselessness, his utter nullity as a human being, that's at the very core of his celebration. Everybody knows that. That's why nowadays every couch potato would give anything to be one. Wouldn't you?

You might already have guessed that I'm not much impressed with celebrities. My parents weren't either. It stands to reason, doesn't it, that, under the pancake and wig, celebrities are extraordinarily ordinary people? Of course it does, and if you don't believe it, you just ask one, they'll tell you. That's right! Just go out anywhere, right now, and walk up to a bunch of celebrities and ask them straight out, whether or not they're just ordinary people. I guarantee you that every one of them will tell you the same damned thing. They'll all tell you—*Sure thing, Buster! We're just regular folks. We're no different at all from you.* I've been told that some of them actually believe it.

But now about this Marquand fellow. I'm standing there on deck looking at him. That was his name, J. P. Marquand, and you won't believe what it is he's just about to do. In 1937, I think it was, he'd published a book with which at the time I had some familiarity. It was a book about proper Bostonians and I'd read even it. Not because it was a popular fiction, but because I'd long before fallen under the spell of the Forsytes and was interested in what I took to be their Bostonian equivalents. People whose calling it was to be proper. I hadn't known any such myself. Propriety meant something quite a bit different in the South in which I grew up.

The only Bostonians I'd ever known were members of a men's club on Canal Street in New Orleans. Although that club was called the *Boston Club*, I knew the Bostonians one found there were somehow not quite the same animal as those in Marquand's book. In my young mind, true, proper Bostonians were all Harvard men. They *had* to be, I knew that much. But I didn't know any Harvard men. In fact, to this day the only Harvard man I can recall knowing well is Buddy. Buddy's my only son, Charlton, III. He graduated from Harvard way back there in 1970.

Mr. Marquand's book was called *The Late George Apley*. Two years earlier it had won the Pulitzer. And here I am, not forty feet from its author. I'm that young man you see standing there at the ship's rail on this late June afternoon in 1941. You don't know that young man but I do. Because he's me. Or, he *was* me. I seem to remember hearing someone say that as we grow older, when we age, we don't really change, we just become more ourselves. But if that's true, then am I not now more *him* than at that time he was him, himself? I wouldn't lose too much sleep over that, if I were you.

I can say with some confidence that, as I stand there, I am quite presentable, rather mannerly, not forward or familiar in the least, certainly not abrasive or even brash. In a word, I'm just a young fellow who's not a threat to anybody. I also happen to be a very serious and sincere young student, not only of language and literature but of human behavior and culture, and there is certainly *something* about *The Late George Apley* that I very much want to discuss with its author, and its author is sitting just over there. I have no idea now what it is I feel the need to talk with him about. It could be a matter of form or of substance. Even then, one was as important to me as the other. It may possibly be some ideas I've been having about *Apley* in the light of *The Forsyte Saga*. Anyway, those are the sorts of things that interest me. Literary matters. That's the reason I want to speak with Mr. Marquand, and I'm waiting to approach him when I feel that he is most approachable.

Mr. Marquand closes the book he's been reading and lays it aside before rising from his chair. He stands there for a long moment, stretching himself and straightening his tie. He's dressed in a suit, you see. Never mind that it's quite warm. He then strolls over to the rail and stands there, looking out over the sea. He's not ten feet from me. The moment has arrived. I walk over at my most casual to stand beside him. When I speak to him, it's the moment I've been waiting for, and I'm completely at ease. I can't remember any details, of course, but I'm sure this is about how it must have gone.

I introduce myself, tell him I've read his book about George Apley and liked it very much. I must certainly then have told him that I would very much appreciate an opportunity to—but then I'm suddenly left with nothing more to say—left suddenly speechless, because Mr. Marquand, even as I'm talking to him, has looked me directly in the eye, registered his complete distaste, and abruptly turned his back on me and walked away. An unspeakable, fully intended, carefully choreographed, affront!

I have no idea what could have got into that man—what could *possibly* have prompted such inexplicable behavior on the part of someone represented to be a gentleman of Boston and a Harvard man. For his was the very sort of calculated, personal insult which, a hundred years earlier, would have guaranteed the firing off of pistols at dawn the next day. At least, in the Deep South it would.

But there were to be better days. There would be another writer whose path would cross with mine on that concert tour. An ambassador who entertained us in his home, and that writer's reception of me and another Southerner, my friend from Savannah, Sam Ross, would be an entirely different affair. I'll try to remember to tell you about that some time.

But here, let me read you the other letter.

Via Air Mail
On Board
S. S. Brazil

(Rio de Janeiro – July 3, 1941) The first section of this letter concerns the seven day trip from Barbados to Rio, and I am writing it in the afternoon of July 2 as we make our way down the Brazilian coast, watching a heavy ground-swell break and toss itself up in tall, white towers against the rocks three miles away. We have had near-perfect weather during the twelve days of our trip down. Although Rio is usually uncomfortably warm at this time of year, the report has spread around that our concert there tonight will be blessed with cool weather.

Barbados was a pleasant surprise to me. It is more heavily populated than any region on the earth with the exception of China. We hired a cab (an old Dodge made in Canada and with its steering wheel on the right) and went on a twenty mile drive around the island. By far its chief source of income is sugar cane, and the population is something over ninety per cent Negroid. Even in this out-of-the-way bump in the road they are feeling the effects of Europe's war and our own National Defense effort. On the door of a dilapidated stone shed near one of the churches we visited there was fixed a proclamation announcing the registration of all aliens. The girl who waited on us at the "Tip Top Tea Shop", where we had tea and crumpets in the tradition, told us that the defense work being done by our government on Trinidad had caused a great many people to leave Barbados and make the night's trip over to Trinidad, where they could expect an answer to the universal cry of shorter hours and more pay.

When we crossed the equator, the ship was cursed, as usual, with the presence of Neptunus Rex, who held court just aft of our swimming pool. We four who had been freshmen, "than which there can be nothing more contemptible on the face of the earth", were given the dubious honor of heading the list of eighteen selected from the ship's company to go through the rigors of initiation. Everyone else received a diploma without the discomfort of the "royal works", which included the "royal doctor"", the "royal barber" and the "royal bath". The charges trumped up against us were a disgrace to the intelligence of man, but as we finally threw King Neptune (Marshall Bartholomew, our director) and all his court into the swimming pool, the party ended on a brighter note.

Ship life had continued much as it was begun. We have had parties and women and dances and women and bridge and women and drinks and women. The only unpleasant part of the trip has been the service on the boat. The waiters in the dining room seem not so intent on serving the meal as on preserving their explicit equality with the passengers, and the same holds true for stewards and everybody else. It is unfortunate that they do not yet realize that the performance of their jobs has little to do with their personal pretensions. We must all be forever serving someone else, and the one of us who can do that most competently has the best claim to equality if not superiority. The service on the American ships has always been very poor, I understand, but I think probably the present labor shortage has made the situation more acute. I cannot help but feel, however, that it were better for these people to be too aware of our equality, even to confusing it with the performance of their job, than to be too careless of it – to trust its safekeeping to a man who would make the image of the state more sacred than the precious identity of the single human being. You must excuse me if I stray from the matter at hand. From here on I will tell you about our first twelve hours in Rio.

****

I am afraid that yesterday, when I said that I would tell you about Rio, I set a task for myself which could be done only in part. I cannot tell you about Rio. It is a feeling that I have. It is a song without words.

The boat was rather late making port so we came into Rio harbor, the most beautiful in the world, after dark. Coming slowly in past Sugar Loaf, a high dark mound guarding the entrance to the bay, we were suddenly surrounded by a sparkling horseshoe which revealed only dimly the white buildings of a clean, new city. And standing alone in the sky was a pure white figure of Christ, looking down with open arms to welcome the visitor to a place of refuge. There was a thin mist that completely obscured the soaring pinnacle of rock on which the statue is placed; and the lights focused from below on the monument gave it a mystic aspect. But we knew that it was real

Our concert at the Rio Opera House was scheduled to begin at 9:00, and it was not expected that the boat would dock before 10:30. However, we had arranged to be taken off the boat in launches at the quarantine station. We were half an hour late for the concert after a five thousand mile voyage, and if the Brazil had not been late in leaving New York we would have been right on time.

We sang to a full house, and they received us wonderfully. I have not had time to read the reviews in the Rio papers, but while I was standing out front after the concert waiting for a friend of mine, at least fifteen people came up to me and in everything from perfect English to pure Portuguese poured out their praises. I think that Rio was a little dubious of a university glee club as a top-notch musical organ. But we gave them what they wanted to hear, I suppose.

After the concert we all went to a party at the Copacabana Palace, Rio's best night spot. My companion for the evening was rare. She spoke excellent English, much better French than I do, and a little German in addition to Portuguese and some Spanish. She had been to the United States, and most rare, she had the imagination and a feeling about things. Her imagination and feelings were both well trained and suited to a certain modesty that would grant her precedence anywhere. She was the best part of the evening for me. I regret that I have not the time to pound out a more detailed account of my impressions of Rio. As I have said, this is a city whose soul you are only aware of. Its secret does not lie about in the gutters nor in the casinos nor anywhere, but only appears half veiled and mysterious like the figure of Christ in the sky, just beyond us, promising to whisper a secret to our hearts delight.

I see now that I say here that our opening concert was given in the *Rio Opera House*. I could hardly have been mistaken about that since I'm writing that letter right after the concert. The day following, in fact. But there's an itinerary I saw somewhere in one of my files that gives the basic data for the whole trip, and according to that itinerary, the venue for that opening concert in Rio was to be the *Teatro Municipal*. Something seems wrong. That itinerary was printed sometime in the spring, before final arrangements were made, and maybe our opener was changed from the *Teatro Municipal* to the opera house. Or maybe those are only different names for the same theatre. Small matter.

There's something else a bit strange. I just noticed that in neither of these letters do I even mention the two concerts we gave on board ship. One, I know, to all the ship's passengers, probably before dinner one night. That would have been the first time we were able to sing all our new Portuguese and Spanish repertoire to an audience before launching it upon Rio. I seem to see everyone assembled in the First Class lounge to hear us, but that's all I remember.

The other concert was to the ship's crew, down in the hold. That one to the crew was rather perfunctory, as I recall. More of a brief recital than a concert because there weren't a great many gathered down there in their lounge to hear us. Most of them had better things to do, I'm sure.

That brings to mind another thing I remember well. That was climbing even further down into the very bowels of the ship, into the belly of the whale if you like, and how impressed I was. As you know, it's only far down below, there in the engine room with the hairy apes, that you can fully appreciate the power it takes to push an ocean liner through the sea. All that heavy thumping and booming and knocking of those enormous engines. And all the hissing and whu-ush-ing of those slick and ponderous pistons, as they pulse and plunge themselves back and forth, back and forth, in their incessant to and fro.

One other thing. I misspelled the word *contemptible*. But that's not unforgivable in someone with just year of college. I'll bet a lot of people would make that mistake. I was all of nineteen years old when I wrote those letters home, and now, when I read them aloud, it gives me an eerie feeling. A feeling that someone's walking around in the graveyard where I'm to be buried. And then, when I take a closer look, I recognize that someone, and that someone is *me*. Not me as I am now, but me when I was nineteen. Imagine it! The warp of space is of course the warp of time, and so, as I hear my voice reading those letters, I'm listening to the boy I was sixty-five years ago. I'm hearing myself talking to my parents. But not to worry too much. Just another short flight of fancy.

There was one final thing that caught my eye as I was reading. I do not remember myself as being at that time much interested in government or politics, so I can hardly believe that I would offer my parents a definition of Fascism. But see here, I've personified the Third Reich as a man who would make the image of the state more sacred than the precious identity of the single human being. That's what I say, isn't it? And all these years I've thought of myself as having been a boy who would have been largely oblivious of what it was that lead all those German people to do what they did.

Let me tell you this much about that first concert in Rio. Villa-Lobos—*Heitor* Villa-Lobos—was, of course, himself in the opera house at that opening concert, but that was not all. When we first walked out, Villa-Lobos left his box to come up on stage with us and stand there beside Barty. This had all been prearranged, and it was not Barty but Villa-Lobos who conducted us in the first thing we sang that night. Naturally, it was the Brazilian national anthem. And fortunately, it didn't much matter how our new friend Heitor conducted it. We could have sung it at any tempo he set and done so in our sleep if he'd asked!

But then, after hearing a few bars from us and being pleased with what he'd heard, Villa-Lobos turned away from the stage to conduct the house full of Brazilians sitting out there. And guess what? There was almost no response from the audience. From his own countrymen came almost total silence. They didn't know it! They couldn't sing their own national anthem!

Except for the reviews of the concerts we gave in Rio, I have a copy of all the reviews of all of our formal concerts down there. Those reviews in the Rio papers have mostly disappeared, but I do have a fragment of one writer's review of our opening concert the evening we arrived. It's in the second paragraph that he describes what happened when Villa-Lobos came up onstage with us. I've got it right here with me, so I can quote you the end of what that reviewer had to say. This is all I have of it, the last two paragraphs.

The propaganda by these students is of the very best: artistic, a perfect performance in the field of choral singing, because it was a most edifying example which might be followed by our university students who choose much less interesting pastimes.

The truth is that in spite of the titanic efforts of Villa-Lobos, we still do not know how to sing in Brazil. And the proof of this, sad as it is, was when the Maestro directed the Brazilian National Anthem and turned toward the audience to lead them, but could find only a half a dozen who could sing it.

Those reviews might make interesting reading for anyone with a personal interest in such things. One encomium after another, everywhere we sang. They're something else for an appendix. That is, if ever I do knuckle down and bite the bullet.

I'm sorry you can't stay to hear more about that tour but maybe another time? As it happened, those two letters I just read to you were the *only* letters I wrote home on the whole trip. My parents never heard another word from me. Not until they met me at the boat on our arrival back in New York. I *couldn't* write another letter. No time. Too busy. Something going on every minute of every eighteen hour day for the rest of the tour.

After our opening that night in Rio, it was only about five days later that the *Brazil* was steaming past the *Graf Spee,* and then, less than six months later, the elegant *S.S. Brazil* was having her own insides scoured out to be refitted for service as a troop ship in the war. That's how fast things everything moved along after Pearl Harbor.

Before I let you go, I want you to hear something that Peggy said in Southern at lunch the other day. When I'd described to her how Mr. Marquand had snubbed me that day on the way to Rio, Peggy said, *Well, now! Wasn't he the tacky one!*

Introduction, Two-Step and Galop for the End of Time: Harbach and Fellner

Time is ill understood. The past is never so. *Le temps perdu* will insist that it be found again. The revenant just come back from borrowed time will do the same.

Two years ago at Christmas time two separate miracles came to pass. Although one was directly the cause of the other, they happened almost simultaneously. The Christmas eve of 2005 fell on a Saturday, and I was visiting my daughter, Laurie. She and her family live just over there, not three blocks away. That was the first Christmas after Katrina, and Laurie and her husband, Henry Walker, had opened their home to sundry friends and relations who'd fled New Orleans at the end of August for higher ground. Henry's sister, Elizabeth and her husband, George—George Frazier, to be exact— were among the many who'd been living there with Henry and Laurie since their escape from the flood almost four months before.

I'd known Elizabeth most of her life. She grew up very close to some of my own children and was around our house a lot. But Elizabeth's husband, I can't say I really knew George at all. Other than that he came from *back East* somewhere. He didn't talk much, I'd notice that, too. But for me, George was just an acquaintance who was practicing law down in New Orleans. I could not imagine that there was something in the past that had touched us both.

I need to tell you that just the night before, the night of December 23rd, Peggy and I had been watching the History Channel on TV. The program was on the historic air and naval battle that was fought around Leyte Gulf in October of 1944, and suddenly, who should appear on the screen but a very old and very close friend going back to the fall of 1935 at Lawrenceville. He was describing how he'd dive-bombed history's mightiest battleship, the *Yamato*.

While I was telling them about the miracle of seeing the appearance of Nick's ghost—the ghost of someone I'd thought must surely now be long dead—only Elizabeth and Laurie were in the room with me. Well, my grandson, Alston Walker, he may have been there with us, too. But I know George was not. George and Henry were watching TV over in another room.

Nick was Nick Fellner. Haven't I told you something about Nick? Seems to me I have, but anyway we became good friends almost the day we entered Lawrenceville in 1935. There'd been another Second Form boy in Davidson that first year that I'd also liked a lot and who also became a good friend. That was Bob Harbach. So I was thinking about Lawrenceville and, just thinking out loud, I casually remarked to Laurie and Elizabeth that, if Nick Fellner was still alive, then maybe Bob Harbach was, too.

Quick as I mentioned Bob Harbach, Elizabeth sat bolt upright. *What did you just say, Pa? Did I hear you say Robert Harbach?* I couldn't very well deny it, and that's when Elizabeth asked me, *Did he go to Princeton?* Well, as a matter of fact, Bob *had* gone on to Princeton, so I had to fess up to that one, too.

And with that, Elizabeth jumps up and comes straight over to me. *Stop right there, Pa! Don't you say one more word! George has got to hear this!* Then she marches herself to the door and calls out to George. *George! George! Come here, George! Pa just said something that you're not going to believe!*

Now, I've always said things people don't believe. Most of them are even true, but I just couldn't imagine what all that could be about. What could *possibly* be so earth-shattering about some boy I once knew who went to Princeton seventy years ago, that George just *had* to hear about it? And a boy from Lawrenceville of all places. Back before the war, two-thirds of every graduating class went just up the road to Princeton. Princeton wasn't but seven or eight miles from Lawrenceville, so they could have all just walked up there, singing school songs and waving their diplomas in the air.

I remember Bob Harbach pretty well, but the thing I remember most clearly about him was that he was as interested in music and books as I was. That's what drew us together, I suppose. But let me read you something here in my diary about Bob. It's about his dad, too. That is, if I can find it. Ah, yes! Here we are!

Saturday, January 31, 1942.
   Saw Robert Weede in <u>Rigoletto</u> this afternoon. Ran into Bob Harbach. Florence etc. saw "Junior Miss". Met Hank and Nancy. Cafe Society, afterwards.

Hank and Nancy? Hank Buehner, maybe. I'm not sure. But that Saturday afternoon I ran into Harbach at the old Metropolitan Opera House, that would have been the last time I ever saw him.

But now, about Bob's father, I know I would have met him there at Lawrenceville many times, close as Bob and I were, but I don't remember that for sure. And to be honest, I have only the vaguest of memories of being in the chorus of *Hayfoot, Strawfoot*, later on at Yale in the fall of forty-two. That was a new musical that Bob's father and Jerome Kern had written together and were trying out at the Yale Dramat. No, I don't remember, but my diary does.

> *Tuesday, October 6, 1942.*
> *Glee Club (or 30 of us) are to provide the vocal orchestra for a new Otto Harbach-Jerome Kern musical—Hayfoot-Strawfoot—which the Dramat presents for its premier at end of this month.*

> *Sunday, October 11, 1942.*
> *Charlie Higgins is here for the week-end; he goes into the Army Nov.11. Bill Flemer has applied for a camouflage unit; if accepted, he will leave within two months.*

Yes, I know. That doesn't have one damn thing to do with Bob Harbach or his dad, but it *does* have to do with Flemer and Higgins, and I just couldn't pass up a chance to say their names out loud again. They both quit school that fall to go into the Army. So did Nick Fellner. I think I was actually with Charlie Higgins only one other time after that.

Here, I'll just read you a few more of the entries I made about that show.

> *Wednesday, October 14, 1942.*
> *Glee Club rehearsing hard for Kern-Harbach show. I'm now taking three English courses: 17th, 18th Centuries in England and 19th Century American Lit. The spans of time thus come alive.*

Monday, October 19, 1942.
> *Had a conversation with Mr. Harbach, who wrote the show and some of Kern's lyrics. He said Bob is in the F.A. R.O.T.C. at Princeton and leaves for Sill in Feb. He is assisting in direction.*

Mr. Kern wasn't always there for rehearsal, but I don't think that Bob's father missed a one. Thinking about Mr. Harbach, what I *do* remember is that he was exceptionally literate. Even for a theatre person, most of whom I've found to be exceptionally intelligent and well informed.

Tuesday, October 20, 1942.
> *Rehearsed from 7 to 11:30; tough on the voice. Show as yet amorphous, though we give the world premiere on Thursday. Evelyn Wykoff, leading lady, is expert.*

Wednesday, October 21, 1942.
> *Final dress rehearsal & it was so ridiculously hocky as to be hilarious. . . .*

Thursday, October 22, 1942.
> *The show went off very well. The songs, esp. <u>When A New Star</u>, are fine and universally commended. . . .*

Friday, October 23, 1942.
> *Show excellent tonight. . . .*

It's hard to believe that I could remember so vividly so much else that's in this diary and remember so little about that one show. That's likely because there wasn't much in it that was actually *worth* remembering. And that, in turn, is likely why it never made it past New Haven.

You may know this, but in the Twenties and Thirties, New Haven was *the* most favorite place to try out plays before they went up on Broadway. In those days, a new work wasn't pawed over like a whore, the way one is now. It was the expression solely of its authors and not a common clay on which a hundred hands have left their prints as it made its way through work-shops and trial productions in theatres on college campuses and in other testing laboratories all over the country. No, a new work would get to make one lap around the pool, sink or swim. More often than not, the producer would choose to swim that lap in the Shubert Theatre in New Haven. The Shubert was next to the Taft Hotel, as I remember, and in those days it was a thing of beauty and almost brand new.

More importantly, the Shubert was only a block from Vanderbilt Hall, where the five of us lived our Freshman year. Jack Moment and Johnny Green and I were in a triple, with Higgins and Flemer in a double directly across the courtyard. But we could as well have bunked up together any other way, we were that close. The next year we all five moved on to a residential college called Davenport. One long generation before the year we five lived in Vanderbilt, none other than Cole Porter himself lived there. He had his digs in that big, swanky suite in an arcade that led out from Vanderbilt's courtyard and into the Old Campus.

Connecticut Hall was the oldest building at Yale, and it was located out on the Old Campus, just outside that arcade and only a few steps from the entries where we five lived. Every day, we had to walk right past Connecticut ten or fifteen times to get to classes or to anywhere else. Connecticut Hall was where Nathan Hale lived when he was a student, and in front of it there's a statue of Hale, life-size as I remember. If you're not familiar with Nathan Hale, he was hanged by the British as a spy during the Revolutionary War. His last words are said to have been that his only regret was that he had but one life to give to his country. You've heard it a hundred times. Higgins and I must have walked together past that statue more times than that, but I'm sure we never pay it much attention.

But as I say, the Shubert was a lovely theatre. Watching a show in there, you felt you were on Broadway. Because that's what the Shubert *was*—a very handsome Broadway theatre. I saw lots of new plays open and close right there. I happened across this entry in my diary for April 17, 1942. *Saw Ruth Chatterton in <u>Private</u> <u>Lives</u> at the Shubert; she speaks well but was too old for the part.*

I was living in Davenport when I saw that show and I have no memory of it at all. Nothing unusual there, I've forgotten most of the shows I saw at the Shubert. But not all of them. There was one show that tried out there that I certainly *do* remember. It was *Oklahoma*. Or rather, it came to be known as *Oklahoma*. It wasn't called *Oklahoma* when I saw it. It was billed under some other name, but before it reached Broadway, it had become *Oklahoma*. The Shubert! I wonder if she's still there?

About this journal of mine. Most diaries of my acquaintance range from the innocuously quotidian all the way up to some of perfectly stunning banality. But that's not *my* diary. My brand of banality is far more subtle than that. Or that's what I prefer to believe, and I would ask that you please not interrupt me with the truth.

I've read you some of the stuff about Bob Harbach and his dad, so now, while I've got it open, let me read you a few of the entries I made about Fellner. In those days, we were about as apt to call a good friend by his last name as by his first. It was that way in the Army, too. But *Nick* wasn't Fellner's real name. No, Nick was his—oh, well, what the heck, why not? his *nickname*. His real name was Irving Stanislaus Fellner. There was a time when he was either Stan or Nick, take your pick. But then he became exclusively, Nick.

Nick graduated from Lawrenceville in May of 1939, a year ahead of me. He went on to college at Williams, but we still kept in pretty close touch. At least, until the war came along. That's when we all left the old world we knew so well for the new one we knew not at all. Then I lost Nick completely, and, for the next sixty-five years, not one single word would pass between us. Until I saw him that night on television.

Nick and I had kept in touch ever since his graduation from Lawrenceville in 1939. Here are some of the entries I made in 1942, my second year at Yale and Nick's third year at Williams.

> *Thursday, February 5, 1942.*
> *Plan to go skiing with Stan Fellner Saturday and Sunday. Dates with a couple of girls from Smith. O&Bs to sing at York dance after main prom.*

> *Friday, February 6, 1942.*
> *Had dinner with Fellners. Lila home from St. Margarets; has turned attractive. Wonderfully brilliant smile. Saw <u>How Green Is My Valley</u>. Material theme spiritual."*

Lila was Nick's sister and my diary has reminded me here of an invitation from her which, to my profound regret, I was unable to accept.

> *Wednesday, May 13, 1942.*
> *Got an invitation from Leila Fellner to a dance at St. Margarets May 30; but I'll be in Wisconsin then. Heard a Davenport recital by Bruce & Mrs. Simonds tonight. Seniors exulting over completion of Comprehensives.*

Although I'd never skied in my whole, entire life, for some reason Nick had been after me to come up to Williams for a weekend and go skiing with him. He'd made all the plans, including a date for me that I was instructed to pick up at Smith. He even had a bed for me in a fraternity house, and there were tickets for all of us to a Williams basketball game that night.

> *Saturday, February 7, 1942.*
> *Drove to Smith early, picked up my skiing date, Meg Herron, drove to Williams and skied there in the afternoon. Saw basketball game, drank hot buttered rum; Meg superb dancer.*

When I say here that we skied that afternoon at Williams, I'm sure I meant only that Nick handed me a pair of his old Wellingtons, strapped me in a pair of wooden skis ten feet long and told me to walk around in the snow for a while. Nick was himself a old hand at it and would have thought that more than sufficient training. Everything was simpler in those days. Or so my memory makes it seem.

> *Sunday, February 8, 1942.*
> *Drove to Manchester, VT., Mt. Bromley. First thing I saw was a body they were bringing down the mountain on a sled. Fell off ski tow, ran into tremendous boulder, off to practice slope."*

At Bromley, when I was finally able to get my skis tied to my feet, Nick told me to follow him up a trail to the foot of something called *the tow*. This was a rope tow and it was Bromley's pride. Right at the cutting edge—the state of the art of skiing in this whole country. So I was told. You held on to the rope with both hands. Tight! For dear life! Nick must have quit school right after that, because here's what I wrote only eleven months later.

> *January 15, 1943.*
> *Had dinner with Fellners at Branford: Nick is a Naval dive-bomber pilot, assigned to carrier duty; Mrs. F. thinks he is pilot of a large bomber; he said (and not for its effect) that none of them expected to live: horrible, at first.*

> *January 16, 1943.*
> *Nick left for Norfolk, but gets two weeks leave before he goes to west coast for duty. . . .*

> *February 7, 1943.*
> *The week-end noted above was wonderful beyond what a few words say; to think that Nick will likely be killed. Had a buffet dinner at Rev. Sid Lovett's, Univ. Chaplain, who is magnificent of his type & has a very discerning wife.*

If you'll look at my diary, here, you can see that it's one of those typical five year journals in which, on any one page, there are lines for every entry that's to be made on that one date for each of the five years. In other words, the same month and day appears five times on every page, so that entry I made on February 7, 1943 appears directly under my entry for February 7, 1942. As you can see when I refer here to *the week-end noted above*, I'm referring to the week-end I spent the year before that with Nick, the week-end he invited me up to Williams and we went skiing at Mt. Bromley.

I may have overlooked some entries I made about Nick, but here's the last one I've got marked.

> *April 26, 1943.*
> *Letter from B. F. It will be some time before he encounters the full hazard of war flying. I wonder where Nick F. is. He must be on one of the new carriers—maybe in the Atlantic.*

Well, it turns out that he wasn't in the Atlantic after all. He was out in the Pacific, sailing under Halsey, so you know that pretty soon he was right in the thick of it. But he got lucky on the draw. The Fates were kind and he made it back OK. Nick's carrier was the *Franklin*, and in October of 1943, the *Franklin* was right in the middle of the battle of Leyte Gulf. Leyte was the great naval battle fought over the course of three or four days at the beginning of our invasion of the Philippines. Just last year, Evan Thomas published the authoritative history of that battle, *Sea of Thunder*. I've got a copy of it right here, so let me read you the account Mr. Thomas gives of the part Nick played in it. Just listen to this.

> *"Lt. Nick Fellner, a young American navy pilot, was captivated by tension, fear, anticipation, and, oddly, by beauty, as he pushed his dive-bomber along at 12,000 feet above the green islands and deep blue water of the Sibuyan Sea—the snaking inland sea that confined Kurita's ships as they struggled eastward toward the elusive Decisive Battle. A pilot in a bomber squadron off the carrier* Franklin, *Fellner was flying in a wave of thirty planes, the fourth attack to hit Kurita's force that day, and the second in less than an hour.*
>
> *The surrounding scene was peaceful. Fellner could hear nothing but the sleepy drone of his engine. Then, ahead, beyond a few fleecy white clouds, he could see a strange, almost festive sight:*

thousands of tiny puffs of colored smoke—red, blue, green—and yellow and red streaks and sparks. He was looking at the Japanese fleet's antiaircraft barrage, lofted by more than a score of ships, each with about a hundred guns pointed skyward. "A rainbow rain of death," he thought to himself, and pointed his nose down for the 70 degree dive into the maelstrom. The time was 1426, 2:26 in the afternoon.

Below was a magnificent, dramatic sight. The white wakes of great gray warships swirled and twisted as the ships maneuvered to evade the American bombs and torpedoes. Fellner fastened on the biggest ship, a ship he had never seen before, not even in a photograph. Few Americans had. The Office of Naval Intelligence had printed "artist renderings" of the superbattleships, which the pilots used to practice ship identification. Dive-bomber pilots are supposed to fly straight down, but Fellner spiraled and twisted to keep the massive ship in his gunsight as she made a tight turn. As his altitude gauge passed 1,000 feet and colorful blossoms violently exploded all around him, he "pickled" his bomb, releasing it. Almost as an afterthought, he fired his machine guns and 20-millimeter cannon, not really to do any damage, he later recalled, but for "the sheer sense of elation." Then he pulled back on his joystick, and like all dive-bomber pilots, passed out for several seconds from the intense g-forces as his plane clawed above the antiaircraft fire and leveled off. When the Helldiver pilots returned to their carriers, the wings of their planes were smoldering from bits of the phosphorus used in Japanese shells.

Fellner's 1,000-pound bomb pierced the deck of the Yamato *near the bow and penetrated through five decks. When it exploded, it blew two holes below the waterline in the side of the ship, six square feet on one side, twenty-four square feet on the other. The great ship shuddered and began to heel slightly but did not slow. As one of the bow compartments filled with water, a damage control officer opened valves to flood a compartment on the other side with 3,000 tons of water. The* Yamato *righted and plowed on."*

Here's a short bit from something Nick wrote me last year about the immediate aftermath of Leyte Gulf. *Post battle—we, from the* Franklin, *searched for survivors in the waters off the Philippines until the 30th—we were subject to sporadic Japanese attacks by land-based planes. On the 30th (anniversary of my own father's death) we were hit by a Japanese kamikaze—end of the war for us.*

That Christmas eve, when I told Laurie and Elizabeth about having seen Nick on TV just the night before, Laurie wanted to know how long it had been since I'd seen him. I had to tell her that we'd been out of touch since early in the war, but that I was going to change that, now that I knew he was still alive. And that very afternoon, I did. I knew Nick's day and year of birth, so I was able to smuggle myself into his class on Lawrenceville's Web site and get his E-mail address. At 5:22 that Christmas eve, I sent him greetings and at 8:26 Christmas morning I had a great, long reply from him. That was in 2005 and we've been talking back and forth ever since.

Oh, yeah, George Frazier—you wanted to know what about him. When George came into the room to hear what it was Elizabeth was shouting to him about, she was so excited she could hardly tell him. But finally, she did get it out.

George, Pa says he was in school with Robert. Robert Harbach, George! Did you hear that? Pa actually knew Robert. Pa knew him pretty well, George! Pa knew him for eight years, and he knew Otto, too.

George listened, but he didn't seem to be too excited about it. It was a long time, in fact, before he said anything. Even then, he didn't say much. George is rather different from me. No one has ever had to caution *George* to get to the point. But now, me! There are days when that's all I hear. *Lyons! For God's sake, get to the point!* But to get to the whole point of the story, here's what it was that George had finally to say. *I'm glad to hear you knew Robert. I knew him, too. I knew him pretty well as a matter of fact. He was a fine man—just like you say. He died in 1981. Robert raised me. He was my stepfather.*

And in just such wise as that did it come to pass that after a silence of more than sixty years and within a span of less than twenty-four little hours, not one but two old friends stepped out of the mists of borrowed time and remembered themselves to me.

Opus 6

Variations on a Theme by Chaucer.

For years now, people have been telling me that I should have been a teacher. My big mouth, probably. But I'm also hypercritical, and that fits the picture, too. But, no—I could never have been a teacher. I don't have the kind of faith that teachers need in order to teach. The pure and simple faith that, when a student actually learns something, it was the teacher's doing. Teaching being one enterprise and learning quite another, it must require an act of raw will to come to the conclusion that anybody can be *made* to learn anything. Almost anything can be *learnt*, of course, but there's almost nothing that can be *taught*. Or at least, that's been my experience.

Oh, my God! You're not by any chance a teacher yourself, I hope! On second thought, don't answer that question! Don't even *think* about it! You have the right to remain silent, you know, and, as your lawyer, that's what I'd recommend. Ah! Very good! But now, if you *are* a teacher, then you'll want to listen close because I have some very nice things to say about you. Very nice things indeed!

First, I have a very deep and very personal belief in the value of learning. Maybe it's only because the process—the experience itself of learning is so infinitely pleasurable. And it's through learning, isn't it, that we become possessed of knowledge? Now, I'm probably quite wrong in this, but I suspect that at least a *little* knowledge may be essential to the very thing we're all supposed to be naturally in search of. To be wishing for ourselves. The good life.

And I'm pretty certain—well, I'd like to *think* that this thing that we have in the mind and we call wisdom is—whoa there, now! Is wisdom in the mind or is it in the brain? One day soon, science will have to make up its mind about that. You notice that I said, make up its *mind*. I couldn't very well say, make up its *brain*, could I? That wouldn't make sense. Because a man just can't make up his brain, can he? I mean, not like he makes up his bed. You know—like, change the sheets? Maybe a woman could. A woman can do anything. Everybody knows that. A woman may have a hard time making up her mind, but once she's finally got it well made up, then it's no trouble at all for her to change it. Fact is, she can change her mind quicker than you can change the sheets. And just because that's a platitude doesn't mean it's not so. Of course, that doesn't mean it *is* so, either. That's the nature of platitudes.

Now, if you're suddenly seeing me as a misogynist, then you might want to make an appointment with a good optometrist, because I'm not. In fact, I'm located clear at the other end of that spectrum. I adore women. My problem all my life has been that I've wanted to put them up on a pedestal. A low pedestal, mind you, one more like a stage. Not one way high up there, where they'd be out of reach. No, a woman's place is *at* the altar, not up on it.

Now, it *is* true that half of my formative years were spent in a society consisting exclusively of males. From my departure from grammar school in 1935 until I finished law school in 1948, I suffered through the most intense kind of segregation imaginable. No girls allowed! Men only! First, in a segregated prep school, then in a segregated college, followed hard by a segregated army, and concluding with an almost exclusively male law school. Well, there *were* three bright young women in my class at Tulane Law School after the war, but they made their own huddle. They even elected to sit together in class. Up at the front of the bus, so to speak. But despite that curious upbringing, I'm nothing of the male chauvinist pig you might expect. How could I be, when, of my five daughters, every one of them has miraculously turned into a princess.

But now, about this business of knowledge. I'd like to think that this thing we call *wisdom*, however defined, is scarcely possible without at least a little knowledge. No, I'm not referring to what's called *common knowledge*, because there's no such thing. It doesn't exist. Knowledge is never common. It's always uncommon. And always very difficult to come by.

Speaking of knowledge, people are forever assuring you that a little knowledge is a dangerous thing. That's the folk wisdom of the mentally lazy. Because it's always seemed to me that a little knowledge, properly understood of course, is a damn sight better than none at all!

And take that old saw, *what's everybody's business is nobody's business*. You've heard that one a thousand times, too. Well, it's simply not true! Consider government. You'd think that government, of all things, would qualify as everybody's business, wouldn't you? And there's some truth in it, too Many people do leave politics utterly alone. Leave it to somebody else to worry with. But politics is never, ever, *nobody's* business. Not by a mile!

First, there are always a few selfless people around, people who make their government their business, their calling. Their religion is not too much. Thoughtful, feeling, caring people who feel they might somehow make a difference. Although always in short supply, I've known a fair number of the breed. And then you've got those on the sideline. The pundits, the critics.

I might as well tell you right here and now that in my whole life it has never once occurred to me that I myself might make a difference. That it lay within my power to change anything for the better. Certainly not anything that lay beyond easy walking distance.

But for every man or woman of that altruistic bent, there are *thousand*s who enter into politics for altogether different reasons. A few even enter without thought and for no apparent reason at all. They simply seem to have nothing better to do. But by far the majority enter in the hope of making their own political and/or financial fortunes. That, plus the opportunity for easy gratification of that taste for recognition, that little personal vanity which all of us have in common with the peacock. A mere mention in the press, no matter how passing. One's moment on stage. That sort of thing.

And then, skipping over those who are far too obviously brutish or insane to become a factor, and those who go about it in workaday fashion and just to earn their living, we arrive at the deadly poison that rises up from the bottom of the barrel and too often presides over the top—the charismatics of various stripes. Some of them full-blown enthusiasts whose insanity it is to believe that God himself has taken up residence in them and directs them in all that they do. And by the way, but not in the least incidentally, that's the basic sense of the word *enthusiast*. Just pry it apart and you can see yourself how megalomaniacally insane a notion it really is. Theion! The Deity Himself! That's who's in me!

Others are simply visionaries on a mission. But, although all of them are politicians, some few are possessed of a special madness whose property it is to mesmerize. And not merely the masses but many of us who should know better. The self-avowed messiah, the skewed personality seized by a vision of greatness to come—that in itself being a sure sign of madness. And every one of them, camouflaged from head to toe by that damned *charisma*, is a personality with an insatiable lust for power over the lives of other human beings, their charisma being, at bottom, merely so much special avarice and chicane.

Now, if you feel that I have a rather low opinion of most of those in the business of politics, my opinion of the people who elect them, should you care to hear it, would be no higher. So it's a great national problem, our politics is. Not a problem so much as a tragedy, a minor, modern tragedy. The story of the consequences of being the people we've in such large part become. At best, we're a scruffy, ignorant, lot, careless and lazy. And I'm no exception. As I told you, I haven't lifted my hand to help. Well, that's not really quite true, either. I did try twice. But it must certainly be a major miracle that we've got this far together. That we've come all this way and we're still a nation. And still a free one at that. Who would have thought it possible? Many didn't, but so far they were wrong.

For starters, where do you find the able, personable and gutsy people willing to demean themselves by stooping to the traditional posturing gestures of the campaign trail? The stupefying blather that oscillates between the vacuous and the fabulous. Just listen to them! What's not pap is profoundly irresponsible. The straw men they stand up, only to valiantly strike them down. The persistent, gross and shameless misrepresentation, both of plain fact and of the positions plainly taken by their opponents. In place of reasoned engagement from our politicians, we get low blows and cheap shots. And only rarely the admission that solutions to political problems are almost never simple. The consequences of political acts almost never certain. And the willing performance of this mindless, childish spectacle is the price that anyone with pretensions to public office must expect to pay. If you've failed to catch my drift, politics, as I see it practiced everywhere, annoys the living hell out of me!

Returning now to the truth or falsity of bromides, here's a fine finale. *Plus ça change* ... That's a pretty sexy notion. Intellectually seductive, isn't it? The idea that the more things change, the more they remain the same. It seems so sage! But if we agree that the purpose of words is to bear meaning, then the truth is just the opposite. The more things change, the more, by semantic necessity, they are *not* the same! And haven't you been hearing confirmation of that from me all along? Isn't it the universal, timeless complaint of those fortunate enough to have grown old and irascible—namely, people just like me—that things are not only not at all the same as in the good old days, they're far worse? Quod erat demonstrandum.

Now, that makes a nice, logical argument, but I like the contrarian view of it every bit as well. And so what if I'm inconsistent? The real hobgoblin is not consistency, remember, but a *foolish* consistency. So now I'll throw in with the other side and argue its case on appeal. And not only will I argue that there's nothing new under the sun, I'll even offer myself as living proof of it. Follow me now, while I indulge myself in a bit of legerdemain.

I've just now stipulated that there is a complaint that is universal among those of us who have become, like me, if not national treasures, then at least living fossils. And that is the complaint that everything has changed since the days when we were young. And that those changes, most of them, have not been for the better. Let me interrupt here to confess that I have recently been approached by the folks at Antiques Roadshow to appear on TV. I wouldn't have to say or do anything, I'd just appear as an artifact. But I will further stipulate that this complaint is not merely universal among my own peculiar generation but among *all* old peoples everywhere and throughout all history. So, although things may be evermore in a ceaseless flux, we old folks, we remain *evermore* complaining. Which is to say—the same! So there! It turns out that it's *not* just a bromide after all! It's an underlying fact of life, known to the wisdom of our elders, that though things *seem* to change, they actually don't. *Plus c'est la même chose. C'est vrai, n'est-ce pas?*

There now! After a serious venting of frustration like that, a man's entitled to indulge himself in a little sleight of hand, don't you think? And let's face it—there's no indulgence quite so satisfying as self-indulgence, is there? Besides, if the papacy is to be excused for all those centuries of selling it out the back door, there can't be too much wrong if I reward myself with just a wee bit of it. That's another thing I'll have to keep in mind when I write that book—if, and when, I ever do write it. Self-indulgence! That's the ticket!

Oh, yes, I know. There *are* a number of ways in which life for many in our country is better today than yesterday, so if I seem to complain too much, it's at least in part because I've loved my yesterdays so well. All those hallowed yesterdays through which I lived. And not just lived. Lived as a very happy person indeed. So I don't see that there's much wrong with a little bout of old fashioned, irascible nostalgia now and then, do you?

Anyhow, I'm luckier than many because there are lots of the other kind around. The unhappy kind. Those unlucky people who can't abide the times or the place or the circumstances in which they've found themselves. For it has been written—well, maybe it *hasn't* been written, but it *should* have been—that a man whose only wish is to live in another age can be happy in none. That's something Dr. Johnson might have said. Or Horace. But, no, the fellow who's unhappy here, will be unhappy anywhere because that poor devil's got an itch he can't reach far enough around to scratch.

But moving away from blarney and back to learning, you will certainly have understood that I was speaking of learning in the broadest possible sense. As the life-long effort to accumulate a mass of *felt facts* sufficient to form the basis for some sense of human culture. Of the human condition. To which nothing is alien. Nothing high, nothing low. Felt facts of which we are conscious in somewhat the same way as we come by that first essential act of pure faith—the act of consciousness. The faith that we ourselves indeed *are*. I'd best stop right here because I'm not in the least sure what it is I'm talking about. Especially not, when I'm trying to describe my own self-consciousness in the very act of attempting to describe itself.

Aw, shoot! What the Hell! Here goes. When I was little, I not only knew *that* I was, I knew *who* I was, and I knew exactly where to find me. I was a little boy, I had no doubts about that, and I knew that I was right here, right behind these two eyes, looking out the window at what was, when I was a boy but is no longer, a brave new world. Miranda's world, of course, not Huxley's. The question of who and where I was, seemed so obvious. What else was I to think?

So I'm having a bit of a hard go these days getting used to the notion that there's no one home here behind my eyes. Not any more. I've moved out. The little boy I was, has left town, and in his place remains—what? Why, nothing at all! You see, I'm not even a *person*. Not any more. That's all changed now, and probably for the better because now I'm no one. And that's a relief because now I'm responsible for nothing at all. What I am now is a process. An electro-chemical process, and I'm a process that's taking place right here before your eyes, moment by scientific moment. I'm in an as yet not precisely determined location, but most likely I'm somewhere here in the spongy forefront of this mush melon I call my brain. The prefrontal lobe? Isn't that what it's called? All of which would have me to believe that human life promises no more meaning or purpose or order than does a spill of mercury. And, of course, I can see that for myself. See it plain as day. And it makes a lot of sense, sure does. In fact, it explains everything there is, and very neatly, too.

Well, no—no, not quite everything. I'm still left wondering a bit. Wondering why it is that I hold so fast to so many memories of so many of the people I've known, so many perfectly beautiful human beings. Some of them gallant. A few even noble. But why do we even have need of such concepts? Why are so many of those others now still so dear to me? And why, in retrospect, do so many seem to have been so tedious and dreary at their best? And some, quite a lot, the worst of them, so hideous? How could that be? Why do I remember them at all? Why do I have this impression that I *am*. That anything *is*? Why is that?

But, oh, yes, everything I read these days constantly assures me that such is the reality of what I am, and I have no reason to doubt it. But there's something I might as well fess up to. As important as knowing my true identity is to me, for some strange reason, I take only cold comfort in those assurances. I mean, those assurances that I am merely concatenations of tiny synaptic plozions and combustions, devoid of all pretense to either sound or fury and surely signifying nothing. Worse yet, this scientific truth would not so much diminish, as utterly annihilate me. And so it is that, science having placed me and my fellow man among the vanquished, I find myself climbing up on the mountain, looking around from the high ground for any sign that there's hope anywhere for the lot of us. And nothing do I see from up there but red lanterns on the levee.

That's what Dr. Harwood said I'd find myself doing someday, looking around in desperate hope. I learned also from him that if I am to come to safe harbor somewhere, I must first abandon all hope of it, and look the other way—out into the unknown. And the greatest of the unknowns is the answer to the simple-seeming question that science, ever true to its calling, never asks, but children always do. The simple, little question—*why*? A question which, of course, no one can answer, but which, all alone, may be justification enough. Reason enough for us to look around in hope.

Now, on a somewhat lighter note, you will certainly have long ago divined that I am a strong proponent of the liberal arts. Not because they make one smarter. Oh, hell no! To be smart is only to be slick. It's only an appearance. A veneer. A patina. It's because liberal learning—that's to say, the long, slow process of self-education, a journey, as they say, and not a destination and, by definition, unending, ever-continuing—holds out at least the remote *possibility* that we might, just *might*, somehow, eventually, hopefully even before we destroy ourselves, muddle our way through to something resembling a kind of wisdom. To a society that justifies its own aspirations.

But people do think that to be smart is something of great importance. And they tend to see that as the end and purpose of education. Which they see as formal training in an institution. Preferably, a trade school. I'm continuously told that it's a lack of education that makes so many of us poor. So many of us criminals. That produces so much violence. That accounts for the very widespread, because imminently human, choice we make in favor of indolence, deceit, and cupidity, conjoined in most cases with the proclivity to active, destructive malice.

Do I think education is the solution to those and our other similar social problems? I do not! But I hear it all the time.

Especially from politicians. It's a standard platform platitude. Learning just *might* conceivably help a little, but what the politicians call *education* never will. The majority of the electorate is already over-burdened with it. The enormous percentage of our population which either is, or should be, incarcerated to protect the general public, already either knows, or is in the process of learning, everything it wants and needs to know to ply its trade. Our jails have become our trade schools and our penitentiaries our institutions of higher learning. And both are provided to our criminal masses by the state without tuition and with free room and board.

I read recently that some eighty percent of those now in jail have yet to earn their first dollar, their first wage of any kind. Do you find that fact remarkable? I did. But being of a liberal mind, I shouldn't have, because they're only exercising their basic, inalienable right as human beings to be the best they can be. To be what they want to be. What nature intended them to be. And not one damned thing will change them. Nor, in theory, if we truly believe, as some do, that each of us should at all costs be permitted to be himself, should it. Which is to say, in the freedom of the individual.

Never mind that, as a general rule and in contravention of the criminal's god-given, inalienable right to be what nature and nature's god has made him, organized society will nevertheless inflict upon him the consequences of society's own, particular, collective *lex talionis*—consequences which differ not a great deal from those once imposed in atavistic societies by those who, feeling themselves personally and individually offended, resorted to self help, just as many still do in this still largely atavistic world of ours.

But getting back to smartness. Think of *smart* as being a great metropolis, just teeming with hordes and hordes of bright and busy people, all of them pushing and shoving and ever on the make. Wise, on the other hand, is just a contented little country town, somewhere way off by itself, where a few quite normal people can be seen strolling together its pleasant streets. Of course, you won't find either of these two, altogether dissimilar places on any map. Cartographers don't make such maps. They don't because there's no demand for them. But if they did, such a map might, I think, show these two places to be separated by a great mass of jagged mountain ranges, and from the legend at the bottom, you might learn that the journey from Smart to Wise is the long, hard journey of a lifetime—if, indeed, one is lucky enough to find one's way there at all. Come to think of it, I believe I heard someone say that you can't actually get from Smart to Wise. You have to go somewhere else and start from there. But then, how would I know? I've never been anywhere near either place.

If you think I don't know how to pontificate, you haven't been paying attention in church. Ha! The pope now, he wouldn't like for this to get around, but just between us, he's become rather dependent on me. And not just for the well-wishes I send him, but for the heavy-duty kind of stuff I'm accustomed to fire off. He picks up on it to use in his sermons. He's told me so himself. Charlton, he said, if it weren't for you, come Sundays, I just don't know what I'd do. I'd have to call in sick, I guess, because I couldn't very well get up there and deliver my morning homily without including at least one observation of over-arching, transcendent importance, could I?

Here's something else the Pope confided to me. The pope admitted to me just the other day that, even when he is about to speak from the cathedra, the first thing he does before ever he opens his mouth is ask himself, I wonder what Charlton would say. He went on to confess that it was not until then that the sure sense of his own personal infallibility would come over him and he could cut loose and speak his mind.

You've just heard me say that almost nothing can be taught, so you may be a bit surprised to hear that I spent much of this morning thinking back on all the highly successful teachers I've had. I guess that's what I've been gradually getting around to since we sat down. All the great teachers I've had in all those wonderful twenty years I spent in the seven schools I attended between 1928 and 1948. That's right, if I've not lost count, and left one out, I've had seven different schoolings in seven different academic settings. And I not only graduated from all of them, but from all of them I learned something of value.

Grammar school at South Highlands here in hometown. The Lawrenceville School. Yale University. The Field Artillery School, at Ft. Sill. The Engineer School, which was then at Ft. Belvoir. The

Infantry School, at Ft. Benning, Georgia. And finally, there was the Tulane Law School, in New Orleans. Yes, you heard me, three military schools. I'm a World War II graduate of the Artillery School, the Infantry School and the Engineer School. I may be the only man alive who can claim the distinction of being a diplomat of all three of the training schools for officers in those three basic disciplines. Disciplines? Yes, *disciplines*! Academia throws the word around a lot, but it's the military that practices it. That knows what it means.

At the time I went through the Infantry School, the war had not long been over, and I was there on detached duty awaiting demobilization, so, most regrettably, I never actually wore the crossed rifles. But I was privileged to wear an Engineer's castles, and a Tank Destroyer's badge, whatever that was, and, of course, the crossed cannons of the Field Artillery, my real service. And remember now, I was also a corporal in the Military Police, and so I wore that badge, too. What *was* that badge the MPs wore? Can't remember.

Anyway, as I thought of those teachers who long ago tried to teach me something, Chaucer's Clerk of Oxenford came to mind. Just think of the beautiful picture the poet of Canterbury left with us of that little Clerk. Although Chaucer had other lovely things to say about that modest, unassuming little man, the Prologue goes straight to who he was. In just seven, sweet words Chaucer captures the very essence of a man who was born to teach. Those words he wrote of the Clerk of Oxenford have come down to us from the very beginnings of modern English "... *gladly wolde he lerne, and gladly teach*." Now, *that's* a teacher! And that's Canterbury, too, our first vernacular. Chaucer's splendid, antique quiver stuffed full with golden arrows, every one of which, when loosed, flies straight to the mark. Like those names that Dickens used to pen his people down.

Thinking back on all those devoted teachers who did their patient best with me, I remember only one for whom I had no respect. One whom I quickly came to despise. No, that's too strong. The one teacher for whom, shall I say, I felt a certain *distaste*. Yes, that's more what I felt—distaste. He taught at Yale. Well, no, he didn't *teach* at Yale. He was a member of the English Department, when I was a student there, and he *did* meet with classes. But only a few, I suspect. And with them, only occasionally. But as he was even then becoming a rather distinguished scholar, his career-goals lay elsewhere, and he simply couldn't be bothered with teaching. Probably not at any level, but certainly not at the undergraduate level. Classroom teaching was something for which, may I say, that awful man obviously felt a certain distaste? Yes, I can say that of him because it's quite true. He was most certainly *not* Chaucer's Clerk of Oxenford. The same Oxenford, by the way, which sent Mr. Spencer to Lawrenceville.

Oh, yes, I haven't mentioned it but I remember his name. I know it quite well, but you'll never hear it from me. Never! My lips are sealed. Besides, let's not forget Laertius! You know, those immortal words that commence with *De mortuis*?

But now, about quivers and golden arrows. You wouldn't think it, but Charles Dickens had a quiver of his own and it, too, was stuffed full of golden arrows. Of course, as you know, his arrows were the names he gave his characters. The names by which he introduced them and brought them to instant life. Names that, as I say, flew straight to the mark. And he drew them all, or certainly most of them, from that quiver of his that he spent much of his life stuffing full of names that caught his ear. Dickens kept a memorandum book, you see, a book in which, year after year, as he found them, he wrote down every name that came to him for which he thought he'd maybe someday have a use. Names that, just in themselves, bespoke a human characteristic, but sometimes even the whole of a character.

He kept adding to that list, so that, as I remember, at the end he had more than a thousand names in there! Imagine that! Names that would more than suggest—names that were imbued with, and so would be certain to instantly evoke in his reader, a strong sense of the persons who would bear them. Lovely names for lovely people. Pickwick. Mr. Pickwick! Disagreeable names for disagreeable people. People like—like Pecksniff. Seth Pecksniff. And Pottle. Yes, by all means, Pottle! Don't leave him out. Fred Pottle!

I wonder now, if I actually remember reading that about Dickens, or if I only *think* I remember reading it. It seems far too specific to be something entirely of my own confection. But that sort of uncertainty is a problem I'm often faced with now—now that I'm devoting this last remainder of my life to reminiscing. But no, Dickens' list *must* be something I actually remember. Something that actually *was*. It's not the kind of thing that would ever conceive itself in my mind. Well—mind or brain, again the choice is yours. But we can all sleep at night because science is now hard at work on the question, and, someday soon we'll surely have the answer. An answer, however, surely also to be in effect another question. In any case, I doubt very much that the answer will have any great effect on life as we know it.

You just now heard me use the word *problem*. You almost never hear that word anymore, an absence which would lead one to believe that the matter to which it once related, its objective correlative you might say, has quite gone away. The troubles of mankind that require correction have quite disappeared—and never, *ever* to return, thank God! *Problems* must have come to be seen as altogether too intractable for the modern mind. To pose too many—well, *problems*. So now, in the place of *problems*, what do we have? Why, nature abhorring a vacuum as she does, *problems* have been replaced by—what is it they now say? Ah, yes, by —*issues*! We hear it even from the better minds. Even on Public Radio. *The issues America cares about most*? And *issues*, of course, unlike problems, need not be squarely faced and dealt with. Need not be solved, as problems must. They need only be *considered*. Debated. Tabled. Pigeonholed. Returned to committee. Left to the next Congress. The next President. The next generation. Like the national debt. Like the twelve million or more illegal aliens we've got on board. How nice!

In September of 1928, I began my formal schooling at the South Highlands School. It was our school and only two blocks from my home. It housed the first seven grades, and at first I'd walk there. But then, as I grew older, I would more likely skate to school or ride my bike. At first I'd take my lunch in a paper bag but then we had a cafeteria. Our teachers were all women, and all very able, and all tenaciously dedicated to the profession of teaching. In consequence of which, they were held by our little community to be, themselves, persons of consequence. Worthy people. People glad to teach.

It would not be until my last year in college that I would run afoul of that fellow I told you about. The one person I was to encounter in the whole of my academic life who was wholly unworthy of the honorific *teacher*. A pedant who, doing nothing gladly, could not gladly teach, and who, in consequence, could not teach at all. Who, at the first meeting of our intimate little class of four seniors—*The History of the English Language*, that was the title and material of the course—made it plain that he would have small time for the small change he considered us to be. But let's be done with minor devils and talk of demigods.

As I think you already know, for five years, from 1935 until June of 1940, I was a student at what was then an all-boys boarding school in the East. In those days it was called a prep school. I don't know what people would call it now. I'll have to ask. And I remember almost every one of the grand teachers I had there. Most of them by name. I was then a brand new and almost empty bucket and there at Lawrenceville, that's where I went to the well.

I hope you don't mind, but that is *not* a grandiloquence. It is a simple statement of fact. Lawrenceville was then the most nearly perfect environment for a boy that could possibly have been imagined, and the five years I spent there were the best of all possible times. The most nearly perfect time of my life. And there were five full years of it. It all began with our new Headmaster, Allan Heely, who, though not a classroom teacher himself, saw to it that on that campus were to be found not only the best of formal, classroom teaching, but an enormous variety of extraneous, literate voices brought there by him from time to time and from every point on the cultural compass.

Let me tell you a bit about just a couple of my teachers there, Dr. Harwood and Mr. Spencer. Save only in my memory of them, neither could ever be regarded as great, historic monuments to the profession. Teachers at that mid-level almost never are. But neither were they teachers of just the common, or garden, variety either. One of them, Mr. Charles Spencer, was never my classroom teacher at all. But he nevertheless made a most memorable impression on me. And not only on me, but on Moment and Higgins and Flemer and Green, the four boys who became my closest friends.

By the way, Charlie Higgins showed up again the other evening. It was while you were jabbering away about something or other. But then, you never knew Higgins, so you couldn't have seen him anyway. Generally, when he comes, it's Charlie himself I see, but this time was different. It wasn't actually Charlie I saw but a vision of him, the kind of fleeting vision I sometimes have. This time, it was just his reflection out there on the pool, shimmering for a few moments on the still surface of the water. But then a little breeze came up—just a little whisper of wind that wrinkled up the water, and he was gone. One moment he was there and the next he wasn't, the way it's always been.

But now, about Dr. Harwood, Dr. Floyd C. Harwood. I want to say that Dr. Harwood taught Latin but that would be so inadequate as to be quite incorrect. It would put you on altogether the wrong scent. And I'm someone who knows, because in every one of the five years I was there at that school, I took a course in what was probably described in the syllabus as a Latin course of some sort. Incidentally, at that time, in that place, five years of high school Latin was nothing unusual. Lots of boys did that. And on many a college campus of that era there was no major more popular than English, can you believe that? That was my college major—English literature.

But anyway—two of those five years were spent in Dr. Harwood's classroom, and I assure you that it was *not* Latin that we studied. No, indeed, we studied literature. Mostly poetry, but other literature as well. A literature which happened, and not altogether coincidentally, to be written in the Latin language, the language of Rome. And it was that literature to which Dr. Harwood directed our attention. And it was the understanding of those texts and their translation into something resembling a literate, and if possible, even a poetic English, that Dr. Harwood would have us attempt.

What I'm trying to say is that the emphasis in his class was certainly not on the *subject* called Latin. Not on its grammar or vocabulary. It was on that ancient literature, written in a noble language, which it is our misfortune to no longer speak. Reading those ancients who wrote in Latin gave me to believe that, although the landscape of my own life has been in large part peopled by pygmies and midget runts—among whom, needless to say, I feel myself comfortably at home— yet, there was once a very real time when there had indeed been giants in the earth. I was to experience again that same numinous sense of the chthonian past when I visited Stonehenge some years ago. I understand it's roped off now, but when I was there, one could walk about anywhere among those enormous stones and put his hand on what those giants had done before they went to earth. That's precisely what Dr. Harwood had us to do in his classes—bring back something, if only the ghost, of those giants who once-upon-a-time had inhabited the earth.

Dr. Harwood also acted as House Master of a Circle House, the Woodhull, but I never came to know him other than in his classroom. But I remember him so well, and, even at a distance of almost seventy years, with such a deep respect, and yes, fondness, too, that, not long ago, I tried to learn something of the man beyond the dedicated teacher I'd known only in the classroom. I thought—mistakenly as it turned out—that because he was for me so unusual, there must certainly have been something of great interest about him that I hadn't known while I was in School. Something in his background—whence and why he'd come to the School in the first place, that sort of thing.

So I bestirred myself and made inquiry of a new friend at Lawrenceville, Jacqi Haun. Jacqi sleuthed about among her archives and found that Dr. Harwood's life had actually been rather uneventful. He'd been born in 1893, the year before my father's birth, and he died in Connecticut in 1972, the year before my father's death. He'd been a professor of the classics at Yale and he came to Lawrenceville in 1934. That was just the year before I arrived there myself, so we were both newcomers. It seems that the only unusual thing about Dr. Harwood, the thing that makes him still glow in my eyes, was the simple joy with which he taught the classics. The shear magnitude of the happiness he'd found every day in simply being a teacher.

Thinking of my father, he died on August 8th of 1973, and August 8th happened to be the same day and the same month that my dear friend Burt Trichel also died. Burt died in 2005, at age 91. If I haven't mentioned him before, I should have, because if B. F.

was my life-long friend, then Burt was the other great friend of the last half of my life. For more than the last forty years he lived, Burt and I hunted and fished and cooked and camped and traveled together, and all that time we never had a cross word. Not one! That was because of him. Because of who he was, not on account of me! I still miss him every day. It's painful, of course, but it's the kind of pain that good memories bring and you hope never goes away.

Burt was born in a house at the far edge of Harrisonburg, a little country town in east-central Louisiana. Beyond Burt's house lay nothing but the big woods where Burt's father shot squirrels all year round. Those families who first crossed the Appalachians to settle all that trackless forest that then lay east of the Mississippi, they lived off squirrel. Squirrel was the mainstay of their foraged table, and even as late as Burt's country boyhood, squirrel was still a staple. Burt's father likely shot rabbits for the table, too, but I'm not as sure about that.

Speaking of rabbits, that brings to mind an old codger Burt was always talking about from down there. He lived in the country, three or four miles outside of Harrisonburg. Can't think of his name, but he was a very famous character in those parts a hundred years ago. Burt had a lot of stories about him and one of them was about him and rabbits. Don't know why I can't think of his name. Burt could call it if he were here, but unfortunately, he's not. Anyhow, it was another of those names straight out of Dickens. If I could only say his name, you'd know in a flash just who he was.

Anyhow, this old man lived out in the woods, five or six miles from town, and he'd walk into town every Saturday morning and park himself on a bench there at the courthouse, watching the people come and go. Now a lot of people talk too much, have you ever noticed that? Well, they do! Take my word for it. But not this old fellow, he didn't talk much at all, but when he did, people listened. That's because he could foretell the future. Oh, he'd didn't read chicken entrails or anything archaic like that. Oh, no, he was scientific about it. His forecasts were based on observation. For instance, because of him, the people in Harrisonburg knew the Great Depression was over a good year before news of it appeared on the pages of *The New York Times*.

It was on a Saturday morning in 1938, I think it was, that he announced to the crowd gathered around his bench in the park his finding that the depression was over. And not only did he assure them that the Great Depression was history, he told them how he'd learned it was. It seems that, as he was walking the rails to town that morning, on three separate occasions a rabbit had run across the tracks out ahead of him and not one single soul, not even one man, was chasing after any one of the three.

And not only did he predict the *end* of the Great Depression, he had also accurately predicted its *beginning*. This was in 1928 when he made that prediction. When the post-war boom was at its height and money and motorcars were everywhere, even there in Harrisonburg. He was right about it, too, of course, but that was early in his fame, so half the people in town didn't believe him when he told them how he knew there was a bad depression just ahead. Can't much blame them either, because it didn't make much sense.

Here's how this rustic old natural philosopher explained how he knew that hard times lay ahead. That despite the appearances, the country was about to go slap to hell. It was a ratiocination worthy of Holmes. Burt could quote him because he was there in the park when that old man said it. *There's too blamed many people out there riding on rubber and farting through silk. Things just can't go on like this much longer.*

When I'm hunting or fishing, that's when I miss Burt the most, so that's when I make it a point to say a few words to him. When just the two of us are out there somewhere together. When I drive out to the lake by myself to fish a while, or clean up the camp, or fire up the tractor and hog-off the place—those are the times I talk with Burt. Talk with him out loud, too. Call him by name, like I used to do all those years the two of us would go out there together. Just a few words out loud, and for a moment everything is back the way it was. For a while, anyway.

You don't do that? Not even when you need to make sure that someone's still around? Still there, somewhere? You don't sometimes speak out loud to the people with whom you shared the best times of your life? Well, let me assure you that for anyone like me, anyone for whom the past is not dead and gone but a living presence, speaking to the dead is an entirely normal thing to do. It's something I do all the time and I'm normal. If you don't believe it, just ask around. Ask anybody, they'll tell you I'm normal. Well, let's *hope* they would.

Even when Burt became so blind he couldn't see to string up his own rod, I'd still take him with me out to Lake Bistineau. He was house-bound, so I'd dream up some unlikely reason why the two of us had to drive out to the camp. We really didn't need any reason. He was always ready to go. Burt was a doctor, and he knew he was dying. On one of the last trips we made out there—it's not far, only a thirty minute drive—he told me straight out just how he felt. He said it in plain words, in the same perfectly matter of fact way he might have asked me to pass the sugar. I couldn't have done that. I'm too emotional. Burt said, *Pa, I don't know what my life would have been without you. I don't know what I'd have done all these years if you hadn't been around.* Like most everybody, Burt called me, Pa.

But I can quote him *verbo ad verbum,* you see. That's how much what he said meant to me. My father was much the same kind of man as Burt. He said it out plain, too, so that I'd be sure to know. But Papa didn't say it at the end like Burt did. At the end, all Papa said to me was, *Pa, I don't think I'm going to make it.* I'd declined life support. Then he went into a coma and lived for ten more days before he died. No, what Papa had wanted me to know, he'd already told me. It was of such importance to him that he said it over and over again, for ten years or more before he died. And what he said to me was always the same thing, *Pa, you're the best friend I ever had.*

I wouldn't care to live forever, God knows. In this old carcass? Who in his right mind would? But if I wanted to, I could. On just those few words said to me by my father. On just those words alone, I could live on forever.

But now, back to Dr. Harwood. My eyes can clearly see him now as he was in those peaceful, happy days when he would walk from his classroom back across The Circle to the Woodhull, the Circle House of which he was Master. He's just finished teaching a class. I know that, because he's still full of the joy of it. He looks so jaunty out there on the grass, bouncing right along, whistling away at some tune or other, as happy as a school boy with a new hoop. Because Dr. Harwood is in love, you see. Still in love with all those musty old Latin poets. Never mind that they know nothing for him.

So it's no trouble for me to remember the impression that made on me—the sight of him going so happily home after classes—that clear evidence of that love of his for those ancient writers of that timeless literature—because it was an impression indelibly inscribed on my young boy's consciousness, and so, of as I said, it's still here with me. Even after all these years. Dr. Harwood, whistling and singing his way across the campus, hopelessly in love.

I took no more Latin in college. Five years of it seemed like enough. And, besides that, my friend Jack Moment had been trying hard to entice me into learning Greek. But anyway, by the time I'd finished Lawrenceville, I'd read all of *The Aeneid,* of course, and that last year with Dr. Harwood, I believe we'd had a look at Cicero and Horace and Ovid. Those are the only writers I seem to recall.

But for a long time thereafter, whenever the occasion arose, I would quote—quote instinctively and accurately, too—a dozen or more of those phrases from *The Aeneid.* Aphorisms which set out so succinctly something of value that can't be taught but only learned. And even then, best learnt from that best of all teachers, one's own personal experience. Phrases like, *Una spes victis, nullam sperare salutem.* Which, if you don't know it, assures us that there's but one hope left for the vanquished, and that's to forgo all hope. To make do without it. That's the kind of wisdom Dr. Harwood said we'd be in need of someday. Someday when we were truly down and out. He was quite right, of course. I've been there myself. More than once.

But I seem to have remembered Virgil's short, biting dicta best. That mordant pungency with which he could fix a matter forever in your head. *Dis aliter visum!* Or, *Dux femina facti!* The both of which would have us to believe that fate, like fault, lies, not in the stars, nor yet in ourselves, dear Brutus, but, rather, either in the eyes of the gods, or, of equal probability, in the malefaction of some woman. Everywhere you look in that Latin literature of the classical period, there are fingerprints left on it by writers with eyes as shrewd and sensibilities as refined as any that have come along since. Saving Shakespeare, of course. Shakespeare trumps them all.

And then, for a couple of years, there was a remarkable Englishman there on the faculty at Lawrenceville. His name was Charles Spencer and he taught English literature. I never took a course with him but I wish I had. In his classroom, he must have been as riveting as he most certainly was in all the teaching he did outside it. He was a true force of nature, simply driven to learn and to pass on to others all the good stuff he'd come across.

So let me tell you just a bit about this Englishman, this Mr. Spencer who came to Lawrenceville in September of 1937. Charlie Higgins came to Lawrenceville at the same time, so it was during that fall that I first met them both. I believe I've mentioned Higgins a time or two already. I should have, because he was about the dearest of the four dear friends I had up there. We were roommates my last year at school, and the two of us, along with Jack Moment and Johnny Green and Bill Flemer, went on together to Yale. After my own father, Charlie was perhaps the most highly *principled* person I ever knew. Well, that I ever came to know well enough to be certain of how deep it ran.

It's only thanks to Jacqi Haun of Lawrenceville that I now know a great deal more about Mr. Spencer than I ever knew about him during the two years he was at Lawrenceville. In fact, I now have a rather full account of his life, an account that contains far more than I could remember to tell or you have time to hear. It makes a fascinating story in itself, and if I should ever get around to writing that book, I could very well include that brief biography of him that Jacqi sent me. Maybe put it in that appendix if I get around to it. I think that anyone who went to the back of the book to read it would be glad they did, if only for the *vitae*.

But in addition to an extensive CV detailing the career of an extraordinarily interesting and widely traveled English school master during the first forty years of the last century, there's quite a lot of rather personal stuff in there, too. Stuff from him and stuff about him. He was an athlete and an intellectual and he had eyes and ears that reached out in every direction. Fact is, that appendix would make for better reading than anything that I could ever write about him. You get a good sense from it of how restless he was. And of how dissatisfied he was with himself.

But I'll tell you the story very briefly. Mr. Spencer came to us by way of Magdalen College, Oxford. The same Oxenford, mind you, that gave us Chaucer's Clerk. He taught at Stowe quite a while, and it was after that, as I remember, that he worked at the Talks Department at the BBC. Then, following some other assignments of a similar nature, he came on various missions several times to the States.

There's something, too, I recall about Mr. Spencer having spent some time in this country as a Commonwealth Fund Fellow in Education, whatever *that* is. That must have been in the early thirties, and I believe he lived for the most part in Chicago, but also for a while at Yale. But in any case, his work took him all around the country. I'm also pretty sure those *vitae* say that it was in New York that he crossed paths with the man who was then our grand Head Master. That was Allan Heely, and it was Heely's genius to have quickly recognized Mr. Spencer for the highly exceptional man he was, because, soon enough, the arrangements were made that brought him home to Lawrenceville.

And no sooner had Mr. Spencer settled himself down on our campus, than he began to answer to the call of his own very singular nature, because he began to sort out and to collect around himself a little group of us boys. Boys he recognized as the very kind of sponges he was in want of. Boys who were naturally curious, who sopped up everything they could find around them. Who could never get enough. And being, as I say, a born sponge himself, he knew one when he saw one. I mean that he knew the earmarks of the breed. Although he kept classes, I'm not sure that any of the five of us who were so close were ever actually enrolled in any of them. I certainly wasn't. So how he found us out, I have no idea. As for how many of us there were in our little group, I'm not sure about that either. Bill Flemer remembers us as calling ourselves *The Twenty Club*. I seem to recall that name myself, but *twen*ty? Memory doesn't see so many. I do have a marvelous memory but it's not perfect. Not quite.

In any event, we were a wholly unofficial, completely ad hoc, consortium of off-beats. And we'd just circle up, wherever and whenever, I have no idea how. And that's when Mr. Spencer would start talking to us. Start showing us things. Not about English literature or anything you'd ever be apt to learn about in the classroom. No, it was nothing at all like that. It was always about other kinds of things he'd want to let fly. All sorts of things that he'd come across and found interesting in his own life. That's what he'd share with us. Things he'd learned himself. Experienced personally. Put himself in the way of. Right now, I can remember only two or three of them, but if I thought awhile, I'm sure I could remember others.

For instance, he introduced us to the Bauhaus. In fact we received a full tutorial on the Bauhaus. Several full sessions on the Bauhaus, as I recall. The Bauhaus was the then still-new, seminal school of architecture and design which, along with the ill-fated new German republic, had begun its life at Weimar only twelve or fifteen years earlier. And although the Bauhaus was a modernism of enormous importance, and, I'm sure, much bruited in the press, it was not a movement of which, country boy that I was, I'd ever even heard. Now, by *tutorial* I mean that Mr. Spencer told us all about its provenance, about Gropius and the other people who'd inspired it. About the aesthetic principles and hard, practical thinking that underlay its program. And along the way, we learned about Le Corbusier, of course, and the international style and all such as that. In short, we got a good taste of that whole new development in our culture. The new form and style which had seized the imagination of the West. The theory and practice of functionalism.

Mr. Spencer had been there to the Bauhaus himself, you see. Where he got them, I don't know, but he was able to produce photographs of the place, and walk us around it. We could see examples of the kind of art it produced. As I remember, he even had a few pieces of it, so we learned not only with our ears, but with our eyes and with our hands as well. He did much the same thing with Seurat, and with the whole of the theory and practice of Pointillism. We were given a carefully conducted walking tour of *La Grand Jatte*. He escorted us all over and around that great painting in painstaking detail, inch by ever-more-fascinating inch. Pretty heady stuff for a kid from the hinterlands, believe you me!

And all this and more, you understand, from a driven man who was simply not content with teaching only English literature but felt himself compelled to share with others absolutely everything of cultural value that he'd ever learned. That's why it was that we boys quickly became, quite simply, an array of black iron filings, every one of us glued tight to the draw of this magnetic, infinitely humane teacher, who had so much to give to anyone who'd listen.

Even though my memory is less clear about the details of it, there's something else that Mr. Spencer did that might interest you. Something very typical of him as a teacher. Jack Moment himself assured me recently that it happened the way I remember, so I'll go ahead with it.

This story concerns another Englishman, Alistair Cooke. That's right, the Alistair Cooke who many years later became the host of BBC's *Masterpiece Theatre*. But back then, he was an unknown Brit not long arrived in this country. It turned out that he loved our country so well that he stayed on and became a citizen. That's the very same avuncular gentleman you found so appealing, sitting there in that armchair in his cashmere jacket, that you wanted to reach out and touch him.

I've looked to see and I've found that Alistair Cooke first came to America with the British Broadcasting Company and that he arrived here at about the same time as Mr. Spencer came to Lawrenceville. I'm only guessing now, but I think it likely that the two of them would have known each other through the common connection they had with the BBC. I know without doubt that Mr. Cooke was on the campus at Lawrenceville during the period 1937 to 1939 and almost certainly more than just once or twice. That's how well I remember his face and voice and manner. In fact, when I first saw him appear on TV to introduce some *Masterpiece Theatre* production, I stood up and hollered right out loud, *My God! Why, I know him! That's Mr. Spencer's friend! That's Mr.—Mr.—what-was-his-name?* So that's why I'd be pretty sure that it was at Mr. Spencer's invitation that Alistair Cooke showed up there at Lawrenceville.

But I also have Alistair Cooke connected with another faculty member, Mr. Erdman Harris. Mr. Harris, in addition to his duties as both the head and the whole of the Religion Department, was an accomplished amateur pianist and composer, and one of his works was a one act light *opéretta bouffe*, maybe thirty minutes long, which he'd set in the not-altogether-mythical land he named *Lawrencia*.

I know there was some role I sang in it because I can see myself now, up on the stage at a rehearsal in Mem Hall. Well, it was hardly a stage, it was just a somewhat elevated rostrum, and I'm doing my best with the dark lyrics of a song I sang in the show. The song begins, *Every silver lining lines a black, black cloud*, and it's sung in ominous, descending notes in a minor key. It was a great idea for a song, and by the way, I can still sing it, if you'd like to hear? No? You'd rather hear about Alistair Cooke? Well, yes, I do—I quite understand. Oh, no! My feelings aren't hurt one bit—not at all!

So there I am, looking out over the near-empty house, and who does my memory see sitting out there but Mr. Cooke! And when I see him, I don't have to wonder who he is, because I already know. It's strange how in just the simple course of talking about Mr. Cooke that little scene suddenly appeared to me of its own volition and played itself out in my mind. Some memories are of the sort that instinct tells us we can trust, and that memory of Mr. Cooke—sitting alone there in Mem Hall—that's one I know in my bones I can trust.

Now, here also, I can be quite specific. It was at one of our gatherings around Mr. Spencer that I learned for the first time the hard truth about the American cowboy. The cowboy who'd been the icon of my boyhood's sole religious instinct. And, of all the unlikely people in the world to learn it from, I had to learn the truth from Mr. Alistair Cooke, that mild natured and elegantly mannered gentleman who'd come to us fresh from England. Yes, it was Mr. Cooke who informed us that the cowboy of America's mythic West, the silent protagonist of all the silent movies I'd ever seen, the hero back then of every little boy's dreams, the very same cowboy, in fact, that, as a little boy myself, I had so much hoped that one day I'd become—that cowboy had never existed at all. He was a myth.

It must have become obvious to me that Mr. Cooke had a deep personal interest in his subject, and that he'd made a long study of it. That, from everything he said, he knew the cowboy like the cowboy knew the back of his horse. I wouldn't have known then, but

I suspect it now, that his interest arose out of the fact that his was the last generation of European men and boys to have themselves become enamored of our Wild West. By European, I mean to include the Russians, of course. I'm also satisfied that my own generation of American boys was the last to have done the same.

But to put quite bluntly what Mr. Cooke, given the youth of his audience and his own innate kindliness, would certainly have put with greater delicacy, the historical American cowboy was, in fact, little more than a working stiff. A bloke with no pretensions to grandeur of any kind. A common laborer, in fact. And one almost as likely to have been little more than a kid and one all bunged up to boot.

It was hard for me to do, but I did it. I believed him. I knew as he spoke—knew it where knowledge lies, in my heart of hearts—that Mr. Cooke was right. Nothing is quite so hard, I'm told, as to become an apostate. To forswear one's religion. But that exactly what I did. And I did it for the best of reasons. I did it because, after hearing the un-sworn testimony of Mr. Cooke, I simply didn't believe it any more.

Now, all that was *then*, of course, and *then* was *then*, but *now* is *now*. And when I think about the American cowboy now, I'm not thinking of a little boy's idol at all. And I'm not thinking of Mr. Cooke's farm hand, either. I'm thinking about our forefathers who labored their lives away on the land. About what unlikely raw material they actually were for the myths that imagination made of them. How like man it was to make myth of the hard, physical labor he could not then avoid. To make the quotidian, timeless. To take a commoner—a lowly commoner, with neither sword nor pistol by his side—and make of him a prince. Just imagine it! All that bright flourish of trumpets, that fanfare for just a common, ordinary man! And so I guess I'm really thinking of man's strongly felt need to be something better than what he sees himself to be. The aspiration of all art, to take a piece of common clay and make of it a nobleman. His art may well be the sole justification for man's presence on this planet. I think that's very likely.

Those are the kinds of thoughts that leave me lost between the great joy I sometimes feel for us all and the infinite sadness I feel for people like Mr. Spencer. There's something very sad about Mr. Spencer. Something I suppose I should have told you right at the beginning, so I'd better tell it now and get it over with. Accurately sensing the onset of the war, in the spring of 1939 he went home to England, became an officer in the Royal Marines, and after two promotions, the last one to Captain, and following some kind of service in North Africa, he returned to England, where, sometime in October or November of 1941, for God knows what reason, he killed himself. Shot himself with his own service pistol. That's what I understand.

Why did he elect to end his life? I couldn't possibly tell you that, but he was not the only driven teacher I had who would do so, he was just the first. But who among those of us who knew him could reasonably have anticipated that our Mr. Spencer would ever do such a thing as that? But, then, who, a hundred years ago, could have guessed that the finest Italian tenor of the coming century would be a Swede? I know this much about Mr. Spencer. He had a grand and glorious sense of humor and he could laugh right out loud. At you, at himself or at anyone or anything. That made it possible for us to laugh, too, at anything he did, and that's the part of him that I remember best.

I suppose some smart people would say that his suicide was inevitable. The psychological biographer might likely aver, along with the usual hypotheses and following many a rankly conjectural, *it's likely that*, and, *we can well imagine that*, and similar imprecations, and not unreasonably either, that his death was the dark, and balancing, side of his intense zest for life. That it was an essential part, you might even say, the inevitable result of his insatiability, his infectious restlessness and, yes, his profound dissatisfaction with so much that he saw around him.

His family may know more but the facts known to me are few and simple. In spite of his enormous love of life, he chose to end it. His death by his own hand was, when I knew him, to occur in what was then the future, and the future is an altogether unknown god, and unknown gods are notorious impostors and never cast in the play of reason, and the future tense itself is a logical abomination. So all I can say with any certainty is that one day this extraordinary man, for reasons entirely his own, left us and walked off through the twilight and into the dark of the night.

That brings me to Gene O'Neill, who also was buried at the crossroads. Like Mr. Spencer, Gene also killed himself—opened his veins and bled to death. This is Eugene O'Neill, Jr. I'm talking about. The son of the playwright. From September of 1941 until I graduated, I was studying Greek literature with him the whole time. I'm including the summertime, of course, because, following Pearl Harbor, there were no vacations taken at Yale. School was in constant session, year-round.

The first year we spent reading the *Iliad*. There were only four or five of us in the class, and we met for an hour three times a week. As I recall it, our assignment for each class was to prepare some eighty lines or so from the poem. He'd ask each of us in turn to read ten or fifteen lines aloud in the Greek, and then to render those same lines in our own rough translation into English. Following that, we'd use whatever time was left in a general discussion of the material, including elucidation and commentary by Mr. O'Neill.

I don't recall any homework other than the preparation of the assigned text, but if you've ever done that sort of thing, that was work enough. I'd be pretty sure we were given an occasional written test in class. And I'm imagining that sometimes we'd have been asked to translate some text we'd not previously seen. We must have been. But be careful, though. There's more conjecture than memory in what I've just said there.

Within three weeks after he'd first laid eyes on me, Mr. O'Neill knew that I would never be content with a literal, word for word, translation of anything I read in the Greek. I would be trying my dead-level best to do better than that. I'd be trying to make something actually resembling poetry—English poetry—out of Homer's Greek. Not that I never made any raw errors in my translations! Oh, no, I'm sure I must have, but then, as every sinner reminds himself, even Homer nods.

But O'Neill knew that, too, and he also knew that, excusing the occasional mental lapse, I could read and parse and understand the stuff quite well enough for his purposes. And *I* knew that *he* knew that I could do it, so that gave me the license to take the little liberties that I *knew* from my own experience with Latin I *had* to take if I were to have any hope of doing what it was I wanted to do. That is, to produce in the sensibilities of the reader of my English an effect at least somewhat akin to the effect I *presumed* might, conceivably, have been the effect of Homer on the Greeks. I mean, the effect of hearing Homer's story of Achilles, as, they would have heard it in their own day, sung out loud.

Now, that's aiming awfully high for a boy of nineteen, but that wasn't my first prance around the pasture. I'd already learned to aim high. Learned it from Dr. Hardwood, so I was not unfamiliar with the drill. Now, you might be thinking to yourself something like this. *Where does old Lyons there get off thinking he could possibly know what some old Greek fellow would have thought about this Achilles guy twenty-five hundred years ago?*

Well, I'll tell you. That old Greek fellow was the very same animal as me. We were born no different. Science assures us of that, and there's every reason to believe, and none to doubt, that science is absolutely right. And we know without doubt that Homer's poetry had meaning not only for that old Greek fellow but for all the Greeks ever since. And by no means just the Greeks. We can take judicial notice of that.

Homer's poetry also has meaning for me. And because we are one and the same animal, that old Greek fellow and me, I conclude that those two meanings, that ancient Greek fellow's and mine, must reasonably be, in fact, *are,* of necessity, very much the same.

Let me tell you something. When you read those Greeks and those Romans for a while, when you get somewhat familiar with them, they cease to be strangers. They really do. They become people you know. If you doubt it, just take off a few years and listen to the way they talk. Listen close to what they say. If you do that, you finally even begin to hear their language as your own. To see their everyday life and their everyday concerns as much like yours.

Oh, sure, owing to several factors everybody knows about, not everything survives translation. Of course not, but much does. The story of Achilles does. The story from which we learn what we seem never to learn—that none of us ever seems to learn anything.

Save through his own suffering, suffering being perhaps better understood here in the sense of enduring the experience of human anguish. Now, *that* story, the story of learning through suffering, that *does* survive translation. And that's why I didn't see it then as presumptuous of me to have aimed so high. And I still don't.

Anyhow, much later on, Mr. O'Neill discussed with me a theory he had regarding some special significance to be found, so he thought, in the placement within the line of the caesura in Homeric poetry. I can't recall any more than that, but he went on to offer me a job. He had some student-help funds he said he could use to pay me for it, if I would undertake to make a line-by-line analysis of the caesuras in the *Illiad*. He was looking for statistical data to support that theory of his. Oh, sure, I was flattered, and it would have been a great opportunity for me, but I had to turn it down. I was already up to my eyeballs with singing, and anyway, my mind was on getting in the army. So I turned him down and took ROTC instead.

There was a time when O'Neill and I were both singing in the college choir, the Battell. All male, of course, and well paid, since it was very handsomely endowed. Gene was a big man with a big bass voice. It was as black as tar and absolutely *thunderous*—as large and unruly as was the man himself. Unfortunately, he sang with a thrumming wobble that would occasionally straddle an octave. I was singing first tenor and sitting directly across from him, so I was favored with the full brunt of it.

But he didn't stay long at Yale. It wasn't in his nature to act your usual company man. But you've probably suspected that already. There's something else I guess I should tell you. Gene was a drinker. The very worst kind, too—an Irish drinker—and no doubt that had something to do with his fall. But he did continue teaching after he left Yale. For a while. Where, I don't know, but not very successfully. At least, that's what I read somewhere. A few years after the war, he wound up in New York and was beginning to make something of a name for himself, maybe even entering a new career. He began to appear as a personality on radio, and later on television, then in its infancy. But soon after that the roof fell in on him

But I have no trouble at all seeing him as he would have appeared on television. A fixed star in that firmament, that's what he would have become. That is, if he could have done a better job of holding himself together. Not only was he something of a polymath, he was a naturally prepossessing, ready-made, full-blown, highly colorful character. Add to that, the prominence given him by his father's name, and you've got someone audiences would not only take to at once but never forget. And more impressive than anything else perhaps, was that big, base drum he had for a voice. I can hear him now on TV, sounding more like the voice of God even than Sarastro does himself, in The Flute. He could have become an enormous success, but given his nature, he was never meant to become a fixed star—only a meteorite. But when I knew him, I wouldn't have seen that.

Jack Moment read Aristophanes under Gene, so Jack knew him, too. Two years ago, when Jack and I got back in touch, we did a lot of visiting back and forth, most of it by E-mail. And most of it about the boyhood we'd spent together. Nostalgia, for the most part, but now and again something specific about a few of the more interesting people that lay in our common past. O'Neill's name came up more than once. There were three or four of those messages from Jack in which he remembered something of Gene. I've got one right here with me. Listen to this. This is March 9, 2005.

After the war I bumped into O'Neill a few times, too. I lived right across the street from the Minetta Tavern (locale for "The Iceman Cometh") where he was occasionally seen in the days when he was doing a radio show on public radio or some such.

And here's what I fired right back.

Jack, I think our teacher—our most excellent teacher—first lost his artificial horizon, then his needle, ball and airspeed, spun in, crashed himself against the rocks and died. I would imagine that, soon after we knew him, he had made himself a "difficulty" at Yale, gone on to New York and by about 1947 or 48 (when indeed there was TV in New York) developed of himself, for a short while, a television and radio persona for which there was an audience and hence a market, blown it all by being who he was, whereupon he became the half-mad, alcoholic, penniless bum who, much as he had aspired to be otherwise, left no shadow of himself, even on a sunny day."

  I've been holding forth entirely too long now on those old poets who only wrote in Greek and Latin, so what say we talk about something else? Take up some brand new subject? Something completely new and refreshing, right? Right! Let's see now—for a change, why don't we talk for a while about *English* literature?
  I read somewhere recently that not one college student in twenty now majors in English. Would it surprise you to learn that only seventy years ago on campuses scattered all over this country there was no major course of study more popular than English? That was sure true at Yale. Even boys from other disciplines would frequently register for some English course. I understand that Yale's English Department now offers three prizes in English composition, but when I was at Yale there were only two. One was a competition open only to Freshmen called the Freshman Essay Contest. The prize was $250.00 cash. The other was the Ralph G. Paine Memorial Prize for prose style. It seems to me only Seniors were eligible for that one. The winner of it received a check for $500.00. That would be about the equivalent of $2,000.00 today. It wasn't necessary that you be an English major either to enter either one. Anyone could enter. Besides the money, there was not a little prestige riding on it, so the competition for those prizes was right smart.
  I may have mentioned to you once or twice a man named Maynard Mack and about his connection with New Criticism. Although I was not in the bedroom when this literary movement was being conceived and although I had not arrived at Yale in time for the lying-in, at least I was right there soon after that precocious little tyke was born. As I may have told you, it was Maynard Mack who took me into the delivery room and introduced us. New Criticism was to become, in our country anyway, and for the remainder of the last century, far and away the dominant, formal discipline used in the teaching of literature in the academy, and Maynard was the teacher who first instructed me in its basic principles and taught me a little of how to practice it.

Like everything else, the way in which it's been practiced must certainly have evolved over the last sixty-five years, so I don't know how they're teaching it to freshmen now. But as I learned it from Maynard, it was one of the richest intellectual experiences of my life. If you don't know much about it, New Criticism limits itself to a strict examination of the text itself. It eschews any foreign matter, all extraneous considerations, so it's pretty dense stuff. A black hole is likely the way in which its critics think of it. But my own first experience of New Criticism, of the hands-on, practical use of that critical methodology, was under the tutelage of Maynard Mack. So when I think of it now, it was the specific *methods* Maynard himself used that now come first to mind. He made us feel that, together, we had set sail on a voyage of discovery. The discovery of the materials and designs of the rhetoric that makes literature always so distinctly, and often, so subtly, different from other writing.

Now, Maynard's method required that he be in no hurry, so neither were we. That was because his was the so-called Socratic method—that painstaking and highly personal pedagogy that works best with a small, tightly focused class, and preferably in a tight little classroom, too. Only once—and this was much later, and not at Yale but at Tulane Law School—have I seen it used successfully with a large group of students. And not only were his classes large, but that distinguished professor of law I knew at Tulane met with them, not, like Maynard, in a some modest space, but in a rather large lecture hall. I've never seen that even attempted anywhere else. But there at Tulane, we were in the hands of an absolute master at it.

Anyhow, my Freshman year at Yale, I had one five-hour class a week with Maynard. One to six every Friday afternoon. That was when I trained myself to see all writing with other eyes. It's very time consuming, as you know, but, for better or worse, you come out of it with reading habits you never lose.

Maynard was a coroner, you see, and we were a coroner's jury. At one o'clock, we'd gather in the intimacy of that small study in Davenport that served as our classroom. There were two or three big bay windows that looked down from the second floor onto the courtyard of the college. I can shut my eyes right now and go through the entrance to Davenport and turn to the right and walk up the stairs to that little room and place my papers on that oval table and sit down. Maynard is sure to be sitting there already, waiting to begin the inquest.

Figuratively speaking, that table would then become the surgery where some work of literature would be laid out. Typically, it would be poetry. That was because of poetry's high specific gravity. Its greater density, relative to the flab of prose. As you well know, in a poem, any little word might well weigh a ton. The same with song. For every little movement has a meaning all its own, certainly you know that.

Here's something about poems that might interest you. Whatever it was we might call the work we were studying—poetry, short story, novella—it was, in point of hard, lexical fact, a *poem*. That comes about because, at its root, the word *poem* can have as its referent, prose as well as prosody. Nowadays, of course, most people understand *poem* to mean, specifically, a piece of *prosody*. Something metered, probably rhymed, too, but *poem* need not mean just that. The root of the word, that is, the Greek word, ποιέιν, means, quite simply, to *make* or do, and so you can see that a poem becomes simply a thing that has been made. Something not in being until made by man. Unless, of course, it be a tree—in which case, there's an old song in which the singer, either overcome by the bathos of the moment, or persuaded by the pathetic fallacy, assures us that it would have been made by God.

But the root of our word poem, is *to mak*e, and even now, I suppose, it hasn't altogether lost that generalized meaning. I'm not sure of my dates here, but I believe that even as recently as the late eighteen hundreds, European writers of prose were often called *poets*. That must certainly have been true during German Romanticism, because German intellectuals saw themselves as being the true and direct heirs of Hellenism. The great Russian writers of the time, they did too. And not only writers. Composers, painters, sculptors. Anyone who made anything that might have been seen as a work of art would often have been referred to, indifferently, as a *poet*. You've heard that usage yourself, and if you've sometimes wondered why, well, that's the reason for it.

But the identity of the poet who'd made the poem was a matter of no interest at all to New Criticism. Nothing in its provenance was. Only what lay within the four corners of the page. So, every time we met, the poem we were studying would be laid out there on the table before us—cold as a corpse on a slab. A bit macabre, I'm afraid, but that's the way it was. But why not? Let's *do*! Let's think of that poem as a corpse. The corpse of a song. The remains of a song that once sung itself out loud, but now lies mute. Mute as the swan and a body unclaimed. Like the body of that girl in St. James Infirmary, stretched out on a long, white table, so sweet, so cold, so bare. I don't hear that song anymore and that's too bad.

Well, each poem *did* have a title, of course. Each corpse did have a name. Some rough means of identifying it, like the names on the tags tied to the great toes of the dead in the morgue. But although their titles revealed little or nothing of whence they came, and were even sometimes flat-out misleading, those poems were not strangers to us. We'd been studying them pretty hard all the week long. Each of us had, back in his digs. And we'd come to class prepared with a lengthy essay in which we criticized that poem. An essay we'd spent the week writing and in which we'd placed all our hopes and dreams for the week.

Maynard would not merely grade those ten essays, he would carefully study over them, before returning them to us the following Friday. Every page would be covered with brief approvals, disapprovals, suggestions, observations, analogies, even incidental intelligences, some seemingly quite remote. Then, too, there'd be the odd question mark, without explanation but suggesting we'd do well to look and see for ourselves the questionable thing we'd done. Or the horrible mess we'd made, just here. And all of this would be writ with a red pencil and in a fair hand. Each of us was turning in some four thousand words or more for Maynard to read, and most of it in long hand, too. Well, one of us, Lorenzo Semple, never wrote less than ten thousand words, but he used a typewriter. Used it like a machine gun to mow us all down.

Just imagine having to go through all that stuff! That's what Maynard did and he did it every week. That'll tell you the kind of man and teacher we had in Maynard Mack. Then would begin the coroner's inquest, revealing the uses of irony or of ambiguity. Whatever. But it was always some lesson in the anatomy of literature.

But I can see you don't want to hear any more about New Criticism, so I'll move along to two other professors I knew at Yale. Being both of them stars of the first magnitude and all ablaze with glitz and glitter, they lit up our sky. I'll tell you about Tinker first. The great and illustrous Professor Tinker!

Oh, before I get into those two men at Yale, I want to return briefly to someone I only just mentioned. That professor at Tulane, who never strayed an inch away from the Socratic method he used as though it were something he'd devised himself. He must have been born possessed of some special feeling for it, some peculiar genius. It was just the language he spoke.

That professor was my tennis partner while I was in law school. Ferd Stone. Ferdinand Stone, and Ferd taught torts. He likely taught other subjects as well, but torts was the only course I had under him. And that was too bad, too, because every meeting of our torts class saw a teaching tour de force come from Ferd. Of course now, the material of torts must make it a particularly attractive subject for the fine legal mind to teach, anyway, no doubt of that. And there's no doubt, either, that Ferd's was a very fine legal mind. Not only that, the law of tort must be the *first* law we had gumption enough to work out for ourselves. And not only the first, but to my mind, it's the most *basic* of all our law. After all, that's where it begins, doesn't it, with us in a state of nature? How's this for an early headline? *Two men in jungle attempt to take rational account of the consequences of acting like the animals they are!*

The law of tort *does* come ready-made for Socrates, I'll grant you that, but not just anyone can teach it that way. Few, in fact, could have taught it the way Ferd did. In his class of some forty, things would begin with one of us up on his feet. He'd be acting as deputy for the rest of us. That was one of the ways in which Ferd brought about the sense of intimacy his teaching required.

Then, between that fellow on his feet and Ferd would begin the talking over of a fictitious injury caused by one of them to the other. You could hear it going on, the balancing of the a priori with the a posteriori. And then Ferd would turn to another corner of the room and invite another member of the class to stand and express *his* opinion, the opinion of a witness, and that's when the weighing and the melding would begin in earnest. Though not determinative, of course—this being, ostensibly at least, the civil, and not the common law we were learning—there'd be a glancing look, now and then, back in the direction of the early cases. All of this at first as if by the onset of a magic, but then, by and by, through a seeming inevitability, a certain reasonableness would begin to appear, to make itself known. Never, you must remember, in consequence of any dogma Ferd laid down. Always the consequence of that leisurely discussion being had between him and one or two or three of the rest of us. Until, what had begun as a casual little colloquy would slowly develop into a full blown dialogue of the kind you might find in Plato. And that scene would play itself out, until the moment came, that moment so devoutly to be wished for, when that certain reasonableness I just mentioned would have metamorphosed into, and clearly emerge as, the very law of tort itself. Read again a chapter of *The Critique of Pure Reason*, and you've not only just spent an hour with Ferd, you've also climbed to the top of the highest ground around. Ferd has brought you with him, step by slowly advancing step, to the highest principles of a reasoned and humane justice for us all.

How would I compare all these wonderful teachers who've tried their best to teach me something? Well, I wouldn't! I'd never even *think* to compare any one of them with any other. No more than I'd ever compare one wonderful composer with another. Oh, yes, I know, everyone does. Writers make a little industry of it. Even good writers. But I don't. A good teacher, like a good composer, is an absolute. Each one a decent, dedicated man who, in the event, could teach me nothing, but from whom I would learn so much. So, if I see each as being an absolute, shouldn't I just demur, and simply say that each is *incomparable*?

But now, on to the great Tinker! The long ago much renowned, but now altogether forgotten, Sterling Professor of English at Yale, *Chauncey Brewster Tinker*! Just listen to that name! Tinker's was another of those extravagant names of the sort that

Dickens used to such good advantage. And how about his name? *Three consecutive trochees!* You won't find a name like that on many pages of the phone book! After one month in his class, I find that I wrote this in my diary.

> *October 7, 1942*
> *Battell is back to 60 voices and sounds great. Jim Howard finished his thesis on his honeymoon! Tinker's course on "Age of Johnson" will be quite an experience.*

Tinker's lecture course, *The Age of Johnson,* was, and was by far, the most famous course being given at Yale in the years when I was there. He was a rather considerable scholar, too, but it was as a lecturer that he shone brightest. He was at the opposite pole of the universe from Maynard Mack. Maynard was a quiet, modest man, modest even of stature, and in no need of attention. He'd just sit there quietly, joining with us in our investigation of this use of irony or that appearance of some subtle allusion. Or so he made it seem.

But not Tinker! He was all sharp angles and cutting edges and brittle in his points. No part of Tinker was blunted, nothing of him was smooth or round or soft. And on his feet—and it was always on his feet that he taught—his every appearance promised a bravura display of the studied dash and elaboration of the techniques he'd worked out and used to teach.

My father was the exact opposite of Tinker. Papa was the *least* prickly of men. He had *no* cutting edges. He antagonized no one. But simply because he wore a velvet overcoat and suede gloves, don't think he himself was soft. He wasn't. Under all that benign exterior—which, by the way, and oddly, too, was not a prevarication but who he actually was—was an iron will. As you might have guessed, Tinker could be a mite abrupt, even confrontational, but that was never Papa's way of getting to the place he wanted to go. In reaching the best approximation possible of the hard fact and basic truth of the matter, Papa was much more like Ferd. I see I keep turning aside to Papa. Comparing him with other men. And don't tell me that there's something wrong with that. Nothing is more natural.

In Tinker, one saw teaching as performance art. At the appointed hour his assistants would close the doors to the hall and talk would fall away to a murmur before a hush settled down on the house, and then, hard on that hush, and on precisely the correct count, the curtain, as it were, would rise, and as it did, there would be revealed the Great Man Himself, striding purposefully in from the wings, pushing his light bulb of a nose ahead of him, his one and only hand prop an extremely large, black book containing, one always presumed, his notes for the lecture upon which he was about to embark, that big, black book, as I say, under his arm, and proceeding, as he then did, directly across the stage to the lectern, at which he'd stand for a long, carefully calculated interval, erect and severe, straight and stiff as a flagpole bearing the Stars and Stripes, gathering in with his eyes his audience to his breast, before slowly opening wide his lecture book and placing it on the lectern before him, at which point, the audience having become now more still than even death itself, he'd commence to speak, and to speak in a subdued, but yet, somehow authoritative, voice, to speak, as I say, calmly and, surprisingly enough given the attention he'd previously called to it, without reference to, or even notice taken of, his lecture book, a book now, as it was quite large, seen peering out over the top and sides of the lectern. Just so did the Great Man—as so many, but by no means all, conductors of orchestra do—make it known to the world that although the score was plainly there for him to consult had he but wished, he had in fact no need to do so, but would conduct the entire program as though he'd written the music himself, which of course in our case he had, being careful in his scoring to hoard and hold back his trumpets and trombones so as to release them upon us in just the crucial, resolving chords. All this and more he did, before abandoning the lectern itself to visit, as he spoke, each and every quadrant and corner of the stage he held, all according to a carefully devised blocking he'd laid out and choreographed for himself, the purpose of which was, quite apparently, to place himself at locations here and there about the stage he thought best suited to his text of the moment. And so it was that with just such wiles he sought to enlighten us as to that certain atmosphere of skeptical expectancy that came to be called The Enlightenment.

You might be hearing all that from me as just wild, extravagant talk, and to the undiscerning eye, that may have been what his lectures seemed—just wild, extravagant talk! But it wasn't. Every word of what he said was to the point. What's more, his purpose was to make it memorable. So if there *was* madness in it, it was the madness that was made to mesmerize, for that's what he used it for. That's how he kept the hall packed for his lectures, even to the last one he gave. Those lectures comprised the whole of the then-famous course called *The Age of Johnson*. I'm not entirely sure of this, but those very lectures I heard myself and have tried, but failed, adequately to describe, were very probably the performances of them that Tinker gave the last time he ever taught that course. The last time the *The Great Tinker* would ever appear onstage to deliver them. The last time they were ever heard by living man. I wonder if that's so. I suspect it is.

But there's something you should know. It's possible that not every word of what I've just told you was the literal truth. But most of is. His prominent nose, with that large, gnarly knot of flesh drooping from the end of it, that certainly was. His posture, his mien, his austerity, the whole general affect I've tried to indicate, I think I was right-on about all of that. And that hand prop on which I've anchored his performance—that large, black lecture book—that too is a hard fact I'd bet my life on. But other than that, what I've told you is only an impressionistic rendering of the Tinker I remember seeing on the podium, of the strong impression he made on me at the time, an impression still sharply defined and embedded here in memory.

Professor Tinker was a Fellow of Davenport College and he had quarters in the first entranceway to your left as you came in through the York Street entrance. My own room was hard by his. Mine was up the stairs in the first entranceway to your right as you entered, so I saw him often, as he came and went. Saw him in the dining hall, too, almost every day, and I was even in his quarters a time or two. He kept office hours and I went in to talk with him about something or other. So, though only remembered impressions, the things I've told you are certainly not fabrications. Not things I made up out of whole cloth, oh, no indeed!

I couldn't possibly tell you what grade I actually received in Tinker's course, but, thanks to my trusty diary here, I can tell you what, at the end of the course, I *thought* my grade would be. Here's what I have for the 23rd of January.

> *January 23, 1943*
> *Tinker threw a "toughy" at us in "Age of Johnson"*
> *By way of a final exam. Anticipate a "B" in his*
> *course. Norm and I stepped out with a couple of New*
> *Haven Hospital nurses*

Ah! I see I let slip a little incidental social intelligence in this one and I can't let that pass without a passing comment or two. A brief aberration from those teachers I knew at Yale, but surely that's something you're used to by now.

All these evenings we've passed together and I think I've never even so much as mentioned romance. But, oh, my! *Stepping out* with *girls!* Do tell! But I'm not ashamed of it. Not that I was the kind of young man who was then commonly called a *wolf.* If you're not familiar with that usage, sixty-five years ago, a wolf was the word we used for an openly predatory male and a wolf was most certainly not what I was. But, yes, when it comes to women, I've always been their celebrant and nothing at all like the celibate my silence may have led you to believe.

Briefly stated, like every other intelligent life-form of the male sex, the female has been for me both the bane and the blessing of life. So when my diary mentions *hospital nurses,* that gives you only a peek at the flourishing social life I led at Yale. Now, I'm not going to let you see this for yourself, but, short as it is, my diary is literally *peppered* with an enormous variety of such romantic trystings. Oh, yes indeed, I could tell you some stories about women that would make you blush-up like a red cabbage and turn your head away. But not shut your ears. No, you'd never do a thing so unnatural as that, not if I know you.

I'll reveal this much. There were two women I ran afoul of in my younger days you'd find especially fascinating. Both were in the long-term care of psychiatrists, so they were permitted to roam about and feed freely in the larger society, that being the grazing ground of choice for sociopaths and ethical idiots of precisely whatever persuasion. Since I never saw much improvement in either one of those ladies, it seemed to me that those psychiatrists would have done better to have institutionalized the both of them somewhere other than with the public.

But that's not what psychiatrists hire out to do. That must be why they apparently feel so little responsibility to the public. Well, there *is* one exception. Psychiatrists are like priests at confession, you see, so when they do become aware that a murder is about to come down, well, then in that case they will, albeit with much reluctance and delay, make a report to the authorities. At least, that's what I understand they do. But just hearing from me about those two women would make your ears curl up, your hair turn green and your teeth go blood red in your mouth and fall out. But I'm not a psychiatrist, God knows, so that's not the reason you won't hear those stories from me.

No, my silence is owing entirely to the customs of the age in which I grew up. When it comes to our personal relationships with women, mum's the word for the men of my generation. We might have kissed, but we never told. Well, almost never. But we would certainly *never* have described it in the explicitly gynecological terms which nowadays are *de rigueur*. That is, if you don't want your audience to be hissing at you as they walk out. No, my generation of men grew up in the dark of the long shadow cast ahead by the days of our fathers, when swains came courting on horseback and never, *ever*, spoke ill of a lady. Which is what *all* women were conclusively presumed by our fathers to be, whatever the evidence to the contrary

In those days, women were a thing apart. But not *too* far apart, mind you, because, even back then, it was common knowledge that men and women *do* successfully interbreed. But were you aware that they are the *only* two separate and distinct animal species ever known to do so? Well, they are!

But getting back to the subject, I'll just introduce you to Billy Phelps, and then I'll quit and let you talk a while. I'd heard him speak several times at Sunday chapel at Lawrenceville. It seems to me now that he came there almost every year. I sang in the school choir and so I was right there behind him when he spoke. I also met and talked with him after the service one Sunday in the Head Master's study in Foundation House. So I had a strong impression of Billy even before I got to Yale.

Billy was William Lyon Phelps, and he was the most famous of all the famous emeritus professors still around the campus when I was there. The ultimate rara avis. More than a hundred years ago, he changed forever the way English would be taught. Changed *what* was taught as well. Even what was considered to be English literature. Look him up yourself, you'll see. But let me read you this entry I've found in my diary.

> *October 9, 1942*
> *Jud Pearson asked me for lunch with Billy Phelps –*
> *an amazing old gentleman of course. One forgives*
> *him his high opinion of himself because it is equally*
> *high of everybody else. A perfect optimist.*

Although not, I believe, an ordained minister, Billy was a natural preacher. One of the inspirational, or motivational sort. He preached self-reliance in the pursuit of your highest aspiration. Upwards and onwards to the stars! *Excelsior*! All of it good stuff for boys to hear. And again at Yale, as at Lawrenceville, I was in the choir and heard him at least once every year. Let me read you this.

> *May 2, 1943*
> *Billy Phelps talked in Battell this morning – almost*
> *certainly the last time I will see & hear him; he is*
> *much fallen off in power, but still too big for personal*
> *modesty of our vacuous modern kind.*

Less than four months later, on August 21, 1943. Billy died. He was born in 1865, the same year as my Grandfather Lyons. That was the year that our President Lincoln was killed, you know. When Billy died, I was at the artillery's Officer Candidate School at Ft. Sill, and I'd be curious as to how I might have learned, way out there, of Billy's death, but I did. But every Sunday paper in the land would have carried some mention of it, and perhaps I was able to see a paper that morning. I was still keeping my diary and here's what it has for that Sunday, the day immediately following the day he died.

> *August 22, 1943*
> *Billy Phelps died yesterday. "De mortuis . . ." but what evil thing can be said of his generosity & all-pervading optimism? He was a strange old man. As a young man, I suppose he was magnificent.*

Billy? I can call him that now, but I doubt that I did so back then. But anyway, Billy was both ebullient and voluble. In fact, he was both in the extreme, but in him, neither was any great fault. Not in my view, anyway. He was so well intentioned, you see. But it *is* true that Billy talked too much. And if the whole truth be told, far too much for most who heard him. He was something of a machine, you might say. A regular talking machine, droning on and on, and I could understand how that would turn some people off. Back in those days, though, you saw quite a lot of gabby old guys like him. Old men with hairy ears, who'd talk your arm off. Some of them would even go so far as to grab hold of you, lest you attempt to escape. They'd grab your coat lapels with both hands. Honest to God! But you and me, now—that's not something we need worry our heads about, is it? No, nowadays, there just don't seem to be any garrulous old geezers like him still left around. I suppose it's been twenty years or more since I saw the last one.

And that makes me wonder about something. Where in the world do you think all those old fossils went to when they disappeared? It might not hurt to have a quick go at the fossil record. It's on the Internet now, you know. Dial up *fossil record dot org*, and then click on *old fossils*. Now, don't you let me forget!

Opus 7

Humoresque

    There was something I had in mind to tell you when you came and sat down, but I'm danged if I can remember what it was. But anyway, here's that picture I promised you of my black dog, Scout.

She's not been gone so long that I find it easy to talk about her even yet, but I can show you what she looked like. You wouldn't believe the wild joy that would seize her every morning when she'd see me coming. I'm not over her yet, and I don't expect I ever will be.

That's Scout on the right, me on the left. This was taken on Scout's very first duck hunt, December 1, 2002. Peggy took it from the duck blind we call *The Doctor's Lounge*. That's the unusual name we gave to the blind that me and two ER doctors built on one of the duck ponds we've got out there on a place in the Texas Panhandle we call *The Promised Land*. It's too bad that that's all you can see of that beautiful pond. Just it's west end. It's my second most favorite of the four or five places there where we can shoot ducks. Now, Burt's Blind! That may be my favorite place to hunt!

And while I'm at it with pictures of dogs, here's one of Peggy's dog Meg. That's Peggy and me with her. This was shot about thirty years ago, right over there, just the other side of those azaleas,

Oh, you noticed my hair, did you? Yeah, I know, it's too long. I've never let my hair get long like that. Except for those few years around the time that picture was taken. Here's what happened.

My oldest daughter, Susybelle—she's named after her mother—but anyhow, Susybelle called me one day to invite me to have lunch with her and all four of her sisters. She wanted me to meet them at noon the next day at the Bamboo Grill. The Bamboo used to be a Chinese restaurant on Centenary. It's not there any more. Few things are. Invite me out to lunch? All five of them? Kind of scary when you think of it.

But being the dutiful father I am, I showed up on time, and when we'd finished ordering, that's when Sue announced that Laurie had something important to say. A favor they all wanted to ask of me. Now put yourself in my place. Can you think of anything more ominous than that? Anything better calculated to make a man's hair stand up on end, his teeth rattle and his heart fall down and go bump at his feet like a stone? No, it was one of those dire moments that every father of daughters hopes never to see but invariable does.

Laurie is not only a very able attorney, she practices before the bench and she comes to court prepared. All this happened a long time ago and I won't attempt to reproduce in any detail the argument she made, only its general tenor and effect. My daughters all loved and admired me very much, that's the first thing Laurie said. That was said solely to get my attention, but I couldn't help myself. I was instantly transfixed. They also wanted to assure me that I hadn't lost all my looks. Not yet. Even if I had gotten a bit older and my clothes didn't look very nice. But I could look a lot handsomer, she assured me, if only I'd just let my hair grow out long the way all the real men had begun wearing theirs. It wasn't much to ask, and anyway, couldn't I please do that one little thing just for them? It would give them all so much pleasure and mean so much if only I would?

What choice does a man have in the face of rhetoric like that? Why, of course I'd do it! I'd let it grow out till it drug along the ground! Piece of cake! With that, they all five went out of their minds. In fact, Susybelle became so ecstatic that when we'd eaten and the waiter had slipped me the check, she reached over herself and grabbed that check right out of my hand. She paid it, too! Cash money! Nothing like that had ever happened to me before. Can't say it's happened since then either. It was staggering. The kind of thing that'll make a daddy gulp and cry out for absolution every time.

Our physical appearance seems to be much of who we are. For not a few of us, it's *all* we are. My head may be completely empty, but by God! just look at my gorgeous mane of flowing hair!

The Promised Land? Oh, it's nothing much—just a wild, scruffy, worthless piece of sand, out there in the Texas Panhandle. A couple of sections that I hunted for more than thirty years. I fell in love with it, and finally I was lucky enough to own it. Two hundred years ago, when my Havard and Stafford forebearers were first settling on their land down in Rapides Parish, The Promised Land still belonged to the Indians. The Texas Panhandle of those days is not something I remember, of course, but it doesn't take much imagination to visualize it the way it was before the white man appeared on the scene.

From the Panhandle north once stretched a vast and virginal sea of grass, wave after wave of it, all the way up almost to Canada. And from east to west, all the way from the Mississippi to the foothills of the Rockies. Those were the grasslands that once covered the whole of that flat and almost treeless prairie that came to be called The Great Plains. The Promised Land lies right at the extreme south end of what was once almost nothing but grass, the very beach where that whole great ocean of grass began.

The TPL is what it's called by the boys who now own it, and it lies not far at all from the elevation that separated the once Great Plains into its two distinct parts. And not far west, either, of the hundredth meridian, the longitude which roughly tracks that same critical elevation and is said to have separated the short-grass prairie to the west from the long-grass prairie that ran downhill to the Mississippi basin. But if you drove by The Promised Land right now, you wouldn't look at it twice. No one would. Although there was a time when I held legal title to her, I never once claimed that I owned her. She owned me. She claimed me the day I first set eyes on her. She was just sitting there, like Scout used to do, waiting for me to show up. We just *think* we own the land. We don't. We always go off somewhere into the unknown but the land, she stays.

I've been hunting quail and ducks out there for almost forty years now. Doves? Oh, yes. Turkeys, too. We've been covered up with them the last few years. Sometimes a flock of Canada geese will roost in our main marsh for a while. Only once have I ever seen Snows. As often as not, during the fall and winter you can hear the barbaric yawps of the Sandhill Cranes, and when you look up, there they are right over you, right up there plastered against the roof of that beautiful world. Now me, I only hunt things that fly. But the place is covered with deer, and I love looking at them. Both white tails and mulies, but they get left alone. At least, by me they do.

I've never been to sub-Saharan Africa, but it looks to me like the African bush. There's a great toss and tumult of high sand hills sprawled all across the south end of the place. Same as those you see in Nebraska. Whether they were deposited there by wind, like loess, or just alluvium, I'm not geologist enough to be sure, but it's most likely that when the river scoured out the Palo Dura Canyon, it brought all that sand down with it and dumped it off there.

The north boundary of the place—well, that just happens to be the main branch of the Red River, the same Red River that you can see flowing past you right here in hometown. Just before it reaches The Promised Land, it comes flowing out of the famous Palo Duro Canyon, only thirty miles or so to the west. But where it passes us, that river bears a different name, the kind of name a river needs to have if it's going to flow through the Panhandle. Out in the Panhandle, it's called the Prairie Dog Town Fork of the Red. That's because even as recently as a hundred years ago, that whole country was one enormous prairie dog town, stretching from The Promised Land north all the way up into Nebraska. But isn't that a terrific name for a river? Lots of people now have heard that name, Prairie Dog Town Fork of the Red. That's mostly owing to Larry McMurtry. *Lonesome Dove*, if you remember. Although they're otherwise nothing at all alike, because of their place in our country's literature, you might think of the Prairie Dog Town Fork as being The Big Two-Hearted River of the southwest.

There are three short bits of shelterbelt still left there, planted after the Dust Bowl. I knew something of the Dust Bowl myself. All through the mid-thirties it was constantly in the papers, and every summer driving to and from Wisconsin it was a visible presence off to the west. Not only that, we could literally *feel* the dust. It was always in the air around us, often as far east as the Atlantic seaboard.

The Dust Bowl so much affected me that it became the inspiration for the first piece of writing I ever had published in a literary magazine. A very short story called *Sand*. It was a description of the moving, blowing sand and dust that for years covered that vast area of our Midwest. It did have a plot, as I remember, but the plot was not set out as explicit narrative. It lay half-hidden, submerged in a description of the physical desolation taking place.

There's even an old dugout on The Promised Land. It's dug into the side of a hill above Scuddayskill. Right out in front of it, there's an old abandoned home site, and I'd imagine that those early settlers used that dugout to shelter their livestock. They could even have lived in there themselves, until they could build something better. Oh, that dugout, it's the real thing, all right, and it's still there, even after all these years. I think Quanah Parker might have set his eyes on that dugout, riding by on day on his pony. Maybe Blue Duck did, too. But Quanah Parker rode over that whole country out there, so I'd be pretty sure that Quanah would at least passed somewhere close around The Promised Land.

The Doctors' Lounge? Yeah, that *is* an unusual name for a duck blind. As I said, two ER doctors named it that. They're my in-law nephews-in-law. What? You never heard of such a thing? Look here now, anybody who's related to my wife is my in-law, right? And my wife's got nieces—three of them, right? And they've all got husbands, right? Well, their husbands are not my wife's nephews, are they? No, they're my wife's nephews-in-law. So there now!

Oh, I know. Relationships like that exist only down here in the South. The Deep South! You can look around up North all you want to and you won't find a single in-law nephew-in-law, not one! You'd be lucky if you happened up on anybody up there who knows what one is. Who ever even *heard* of an in-law nephew-in-law. They don't really seem to care that much about claiming kin up there. Nothing wrong with it, I suppose, it's just how they are.

The Promised Land is located just west of what's now a tiny, little settlement called Estelline. Estelline's in Hall County, and Hall County is only one of the more than twenty counties out there in the Panhandle that have been losing population for the last fifty years or more. The population of Estelline stands now at only 168, but I'm told that as recently as only eighty years ago, when so much more of that land was in crops, Estelline boasted a population of over a thousand. It had a moving picture theatre, a big general store, two or three eating places, a post office, a gin, and some other business enterprises. Nowadays, the population of Estelline makes do with two liquor stores, a gin, a gas pump, and a post office. Oh, and there's a police station, too. But Estelline now, it's altogether different from Hall County or any of the rest of that world out there. It's been flat holding its own, population wise. And thereby hangs a long, tall tale I'll spin for you if you'll sit still a while and listen.

That whole Panhandle country out there is dry as a bone. For a hundred miles in every direction not only does it never rain, there's no place out there a man can buy a drink. Not even a beer. Can you imagine that? Except in Estelline. Estelline is different. If you're heading out west, towards Denver, and you don't stop and wet your whistle in Estelline, then you can look forward to a hundred more parched miles of Texas highway before you get another chance. That's how far it is to Amarillo. That's one of the things that makes Estelline so well known out there. Those liquor stores, they do draw a crowd! I've been noticing that you drink some. Well, if you don't mind my saying so, you drink a *whole lot*, so you're somebody who can understand why so many people are drawn to Estelline.

But legal liquor is not the only thing that makes Estelline unique of its kind out there in the Panhandle. It's the population. For more than thirty years now, the population of Estelline has held steady at precisely 168. I mean it has not fluctuated one iota. Not by so little as even one person! It's been in all the papers out there. I know that for a fact. Even the Denver *Post*. It ran a whole series on that highly anomalous statistic.

I'm sure that was how Estelline first came to the attention of the scientific community. The statisticians were the first to arrive, but not far behind came the geneticists. Especially those engaged in some brand new sub-discipline called *population genetics*. Several studies and two doctoral dissertations have already been published as a direct result of those investigations. DNA samplings of 100% of the population of Estelline were taken. That was the first thing they did, of course. They did it all over again, too, after every birth. Naturally, they gave very special attention both to variations resident on the Y chromosome and to those variations that reside in the mitochondria.

In short, nothing was left unexamined that might offer a scientific explanation for the hard fact of that troublesome zero population variance, a variance that took place over a very, very long and ever increasing span of years. Those scientists left nothing to chance. Nothing!

They ran four separate, carefully designed and highly sophisticated computer programs. Ran them concurrently, I was told. And yet, even after analysis and assessment of all those hard data, teams of experts were none of them able to locate *any* genetic character which would account for this unprecedented, anti-historical condition of zero population variation.

Now, there *was* one possible explanation that was suggested. But it didn't come from the scientists, it was suggested by someone who was a resident of the locality. Someone who, I was first told, wished to remain anonymous. But that suggestion came to nothing, too. I heard that it was at first discountenanced by the scientific experts as being merely anecdotal in character and lacking the supported of data. Then, finally, it was cast aside altogether, as being amenable neither to verification through repetition nor to double-blind testing.

But not wishing to omit anything from this highly exotic tale of mystery and intrigue, I'll go ahead and tell you something else I heard. And hold your hat, because this may well be the most startling part of the whole story. But here's how I heard it from someone I trust, and it sounded reasonable enough to me. But then, who am I to know? It was two years ago that for the first time I learned exactly what it was that had been suggested to those learned scientists by that anonymous person they'd seen lurking about in the shadows and who only once came out to speak.

Well, it turned out that she wasn't so anonymous after all. In the meantime, someone had outed her. She lives in a squalid little hut at the far edge of town. I've seen it myself, so I know. There's a crudely hand-lettered sign staked in the bare dirt out front which says that Sybil's inside and she reads palms and tells fortunes and can cast a spell. Sybil Verdad! A squat five foot, her skin the exact reddish brown of mahogany and her face adorned with a moustache of which a sergeant of horse guard would be proud, she's obviously Tex-Mex and about eighty I'd say. But she still gets around pretty good. You should see her, digging down in those trash barrels on the town square. Throwing garbage over her shoulder, left and right like a possum at play under the full of the moon.

Anyway, she'd told them that she'd thought nothing of it at first. Probably just a coincidence, that's what she'd told herself. But finally, about the fifteenth time it happened, she couldn't help but notice. She told those experts that what she'd noticed, and what she'd thought a little peculiar, was that every time a baby was born, a man left town.

Do you believe that story? Yes, I thought you would. I did, too. At least for a while. In fact, it made perfect sense—that is, until it was explained to me that it was just too simple. And it wasn't just anybody who explained it to me either, it was a high-ranking, modern theorist of my acquaintance. Someone who's steeped in Critical Theory, and if you know anything at all about Critical Theory, you'll understand that he had to have got it right.

Anyway, after I offered him that explanation, he condemned it as being too simplistic. That was the very word he used, *simplistic*. I would have said that that explanation was too simple myself, but the word *simple* has just flat disappeared from the language. You never hear it anymore. Never! Apparently from what I read and hear nothing is simple anymore. That's because what was once thought *simple* is now automatically judged to be *simplistic*. So that perfectly good, old-fashioned word *simple* has no further use for us. I think it safe to say that *simplistic* is simply—no, no, what *could* I be thinking! I think it safe to say that *simplistic* is neither more nor less that the hypertrophication of the not so simple word, *simple*. In other words, if I understand our modern folklorists, the idea, the very notion that anything could possibly be simple, has just got too damn big for its britches. And so off with its head!

So to conclude, I've learned this much. For most people, nothing is ever simple. They don't seem to want it that way. So I've learned to avoid the expression altogether. To never even use the word *simple*. Never, of course, unless I'm among friends. Among the kind of people I can trust to keep a confidence. You know—closet heathens like me? You *are* a closet heathen, aren't you?

Octet for male voices:
The Society of Orpheus and Bacchus

    After you left last evening, I thought of something else that happened as we were going down to Rio on the *Brazil*. We'd been gone from New York only a few days when, out of the blue, I was invited to sit in and rehearse with a small group I'd never even heard of. They'd been formed only the year before, I think, and they called themselves the O&Bs. Irv Walradt was their leader and it was Irv who asked me. They were in need of a second top tenor, that's why they asked me. The other seven were all members of the Glee Club, so they were right there on board. At the end of that rehearsal, they asked me if I'd like to join up, and I said I would. That's how I became a member of the Society of Orpheus and Bacchus. What a difference a day made, twenty four little hours.

    When I joined the O&Bs, that made the third group I was singing with at Yale. When I first went there, right away Sam Ross and I were singing with the Freshman Glee Club. Sam was my close South Carolina friend from Lawrenceville. That's also when Shearen Elebash and I first became friends, singing with the Freshman Club. Shearen was from Montgomery, and he and Sam and I were especially close all through college. We all three like to sing and we spoke the same language—Southern. Then, in about February of 1941, when it was definite that the Glee Club would tour South America that coming summer, Barty promoted all three of us from the Freshman Club to the varsity. There was another Freshman he also elevated, Steve Stack. That was a considerable distinction for the four of us, to be piped aboard the varsity when merely Freshmen.

    So when I joined the O&Bs, I was already singing both with the Glee Club and with the choir at Battell Chapel. The Battell was the official choir of Yale University. Naturally, this being 1940, it was an all male choir. When I joined, it was composed mostly of people from the music school and older members of the faculty. Battell Chapel itself was quite handsomely endowed, so the choir was very, very well paid. Not much later, I began singing also as the first tenor in the quartet that was paid to sing at noon every week day in Dwight Chapel. Dwight was the other chapel on the Old Campus. My diary's got some interesting things in it about singing in Dwight and Battell. Remind me to tell you about that. But anyhow, I was singing somewhere almost all the time. I loved it, but I wonder now how I ever managed to make it through school.

Here's a picture of the Society of Orpheus and Bacchus, This was us as we were early in 1942. Have a look.

I look so sober here you probably don't recognize me, but I'm that blonde fellow standing back-right. There at my right shoulder, that's Frank Lebar. Frank sang bass. Our other bass is that excellent young man who's sitting on the arm of that chair second from the right. He's Ed Friedman. Ed's the one I felt closest to and remember the best. Ed and I have been talking back and forth quite a lot lately.

My diary's got maybe as much to say about the O&Bs as it does about the Yale Glee Club itself. I'll read just a little of it to give you an idea of how we passed the time away back in those days.

> *Wednesday, February 4, 1942.*
> *O&B's had cocktails and dinner and a long evening of song with Prof. Havermeyer, Associate Dean of Sheff.*

> *Saturday, February 14, 1942.*
> *Sang as special attraction with the Freshman Glee Club at Grey Court College—brand new school near Danbury. They have no idea how to run the place. In at 4:30 this morning.*

> *Sunday, February 15, 1942.*
> *Made rehearsal & service this morning. Concert with Jane Pickens tonight at Town Hall. Buffet supper at Ed Friedman's afterwards. Mr. Friedman a wonderful man. Back at 4:00 this morning.*

All I can remember about that Town Hall concert is Jane Pickens herself. I have the impression that when it came time to perform, she was one very serious lady. But what I *do* remember very well is that afterwards, two or three of us drove uptown somewhere with Ed to his family's town house and that I met and spent a happy hour or two with Ed's father. I say here only that he was a *wonderful* man. Well, believe me, he was that and more.

I'm obviously rather proud of myself for having not missed that choir rehearsal and Sunday morning service at Battell. I had a right to be. I hadn't gotten home from Danbury until 4:30 that morning, and the very next night I was at it until four in the morning again! Those were the days, my friend, we thought they'd never end!

Luther Noss was our organist and choir director. Just in the nick of time, Paul Hindemith had flown Hitler's Germany and landed at Yale. One day when I was on my way back to Davenport and had just crossed the street from Calhoun and was passing

Battell, Mr. Noss stopped me and introduced me to the gentleman who was with him. It was Hindemith. I was even more ignorant of such things then than I am now, so Mr. Hindemith couldn't have meant much more to me than just a name I'd heard. I'm even a bit surprised that I've remembered it, but I do. Very clearly, in fact.

Here in hometown, when I was little and went downtown to the movies, those silent films were always accompanied by an organ. In the big cities, they sometimes even had small orchestras that did that. Fifty years before that, lots and lots of legitimate theatre was accompanied by incidental music played from the pit. Most of it was written just for that one particular show.

As you know, those little orchestras that set the mood for those silent films were what morphed into the modern movie sound track. Some could even boast a few strings, but all I ever heard here in hometown was an organ. That's what the Strand had, a big organ. The Majestic had an organ, too, but not nearly so grand. And I do seem to remember hearing a piano somewhere, probably up in our little movie house in Chetek. You may know this yourself, but at one time Hindemith played some instrument or other for silent movies like that. So did Shostakovich. But just to visualize Hindemith and Shostakovich down there in the pit, playing for a silent movie,

I find that rather reassuring myself. By that I mean, if genius of that order can sit in the pit unrecognized, then there might be some hope for the rest of us. I've even heard somewhere that Brahms himself once played piano in a bar. And not a very fancy bar either, so there!

He later became dean of the Yale Music School. Not Brahms—Mr. Noss. I can see him now, sitting there at the organ every Sunday, conducting us with his free hand. That is, on those brief interludes when the music would let him. Otherwise, just with his head and his body and eyes. He could always somehow manage to let us know what he was thinking. We didn't just sing on Sundays in Battell. Once a week we'd rehearse for a couple of hours, too.

I think that concert we gave in Town Hall with Jane Pickens was one given by the Glee Club, but I'm not sure about that. It could have been the O&Bs who sang with her. Jane Pickens? She was the principal singer with the Pickens Sisters. If you never heard of them, they were then the ne plus ultra of female vocal trios. Bigger than the Andrews Sisters! The Dixie Chicks? Never heard of them.

But Jane Pickens, now! We can flip back a couple of pages and look what we find!

> *Wednesday, February 11, 1942.*
> *Two rehearsals with Miss Jane Pickens—of Pickens Sisters fame—who is to appear on Town Hall Program with us. Very attractive, Georgia, deep red hair.*

I can't tell from this whether I was singing with the Glee Club or the O&Bs, but I'm satisfied those Wednesday rehearsals would have taken place in New York. Probably right there in Town Hall. Miss Jane Pickens was too great a luminary ever to have taken the train up to New Haven. Not that she would have felt it something beneath her. Far from it. She was a real person. She was from Georgia, you notice, and don't forget, she was red-headed like my mother. And like my mother, she was every bit the artist.

> *Sunday, April 26, 1942.*
> *O&B's sang over WTIC this afternoon.*

> *Monday, May 4, 1942.*
> *O&B's sang over WOCD; our reputation and following increases!*

> *Friday, May 8, 1942.*
> *O&B's sang with Tommy Dorsey in Hartford from the stage of the Strand Theatre. The half hour program was broadcast, being designed to launch a bond drive.*

What! You say you've never heard of T. Dorsey? *Incroyable!* Then you've probably never heard of Glenn Miller either. Well, let me tell you, beginning about seventy years ago, in the early days of radio, that's when the dance bands became the rage of this whole country. The dance band and jazz music. And Glenn Miller and Tommy Dorsey were probably the two biggest of the big. It must have been sometime in 1942 that Glenn Miller's Air Corps band came to be permanently stationed at Yale. I can see and hear them now, marching up and down on the New Haven Green and playing for us every day in the Commons.

Like every other college campus, the whole place was turning to uniforms, and Miller and his orchestra—well, it was something between a military band and a dance band—but at meal time, they'd play there in the Freshman Commons. I was supposed to eat my meals at Davenport, but I'd sometimes give up lunch just to listen. They played from up in a little balcony at one end of that great, long dining hall, and Glenn Miller himself would be up there, stick in hand. Two years later he was dead. The plane he was on just disappeared somewhere over France.

There were two other groups of musicians that passed through Yale about that time. There was a quartet of Aussies, all turned out in their Aussie uniforms. I followed them around everywhere, until I could sing *Waltzing Matilda* just as good as they could. Then for maybe a week, there were some Russians from The Red Army Chorus. They were in their army uniforms, about a dozen of them. They'd sing in some of the colleges, but mostly they'd stand out on the green that then stretched out in front of the Sterling Library. They featured a genuine counter bass, the first such *profondo* voice I'd ever heard. He wasn't tall the way basses tend to be, with long cords. No. he was a little red fire plug, a stump. I couldn't stay away from him. I just had to stand there beside him, listening to him as he bumbled and rumbled his way along, down there an octave below everybody else.

There's a lot of other good stuff like that in my diary about the O&Bs. Here's one more that might interest you.

> *Thursday, May 14, 1942.*
> *Ralph Levy, who has been doing most of the work in the O&B's in direction & interpretation, will someday amount to something in the theatrical world, I think.*

Ralph Levy is the very serious young man you see sitting front and center in this picture. I must have been clairvoyant when I wrote that. I sent Ed Friedman a whole clutch of notes I'd made in my diary about the O&Bs and when he saw that prognosis I'd made for Ralph, he wrote me right back. Here, let me read you what Ed said.

> *Dear Charlton,*
>
> *Thank you for your "notes." I was especially interested in Ralph because we had been close friends in College right from freshman year when Ralph was the freshman glee club soloist. We visited each other in summer and I would spend a couple of weeks at his camp where he was the drama councilor and singing coach. While at "Camp Kewanee" we would put on a show. One summer it was a review, a musical extravaganza with original words and music by the campers. I even remember some of the songs. Another summer we put on "Pirates of Penzance" where I was "the very model of a modern major general."*
>
> *Ralph was a genius and I knew it then. He was very fond of my dad who was a vp of Warner Bros. Pictures. After college I went to Med School and put away childish things except for singing. Ralph never answered letters; I never saw him again. Via the grapevine I heard he was married and directing Jack Benny and that he had become the Ballet Russe's manager. Period.*
>
> *Medical school, marriage, parenting, teaching, practice took their toll. I didn't even know that Ralph had died. We had a mutual friend, Leonard Silverstein in your class '43. Len was friendly with my brother in law and I would hear about him from time to time but nil about Ralph.*
>
> *******
>
> *Thanks for your friendship—keep in touch.*
> *Ed*

When I read Ed's letter, I went straight to the Net and there Ralph was in all his glory. A pioneer in television. Twice winner of an Emmy for direction. Director of the pilot that gave birth to *I Love Lucy*. Lots of other stuff like that. Ralph lived until 2001. He worked until he died. Look him up!

Well, before I sign off, I guess there *is* one more entry you ought to hear. This was one I made in March of 1943. It was written just before I took my Senior comprehensive exams in order to graduate and go into the Army. That makes this the very last thing I ever whispered privately to my diary about the O&Bs. Appropriately enough I suppose, the very last sentence of this final entry on that subject pretty accurately sums us up.

> *March 1, 1943.*
> *The O&B's are all new (except Colby, Bill & I): Bill Collins & Pete Wood, Ken McDonald & Colby Stearns, "Rocky" Rockwell & Willie Munro, Hank Beuhner and I. We sound well enough when not drunk.*

The Colonel McCabe March

Like most little boys of my generation, I was completely fascinated by the idea of putting on a parachute and jumping out of an airplane. In my imagination—and mine was very active, believe me—I could just see myself as I casually jumped out the door of the plane and parachuted back to earth. Interestingly enough, there did come a time when, at least for a few days, I thought that I was about to do just that. It was in early June of 1944, about the time of the Normandy invasion and I was with the 419th at Camp Gordon. That turned out to be a summer when all sorts of really wild and wooly, wholly unexpected things came to pass. Including getting married. And going AWOL for three days. The two being not unconnected. And oh, yes! I became an Engineer Office that summer, too.

It must have been late in May when I got orders to go to the jump school at Fort Benning. Apparently, somebody high up in the chain of command got the bright idea that forward observers in armored artillery should be jump-qualified. There was a school for that at Benning, and Benning was just over on the other side of Georgia, just outside of Columbus, so that's where I was given orders to go. It happened that I had some leave time coming and that's how I got a delay en route and came to spend two or three days at home. And how I came to meet Susybelle, my first wife.

One night while I was home, I went down to the old Zephyr Room in the Captain Shreve Hotel and ran into a home-town girl I scarcely knew. She was Susybelle Wilkinson and she was a student at the University of Texas. In those days Texas didn't have but one campus and that was at Austin. It just happened that Susybelle was home on a short vacation herself, and after dancing with her, I asked her for a date the next night. Susybelle and I had supper at home with my parents, after which I promptly went sound to sleep. I did! I went slap to sleep, sitting there in a chair, before taking her home. That was the first, last and only date we ever had.

The next morning I had a wire from battalion canceling my orders to go to Benning and ordering me to return to the 419th. Nothing strange there. The Army got some new idea every day.

Back at Gordon, I learned that the Tenth Armored had been alerted to go overseas. Nothing definite as to when we'd go, just get ready. But we were already ready. We'd *been* ready for months and months. Fact is, we were *over* trained. That's hard on morale, repeating the same old maneuvers, running the same firing exercises over and over again. Digging the same dirt out of the same foxholes. Working the same map and compass problems every night. Boredom is a life sentence and there's nothing harder on the men.

Those were the circumstances in which I embarked upon two courses of action that would have profound effects on my future. One was for the long term, the other for the short. Susybelle had gone back to Austin for summer school, and I'd started writing to her. One day I finally plucked up courage enough to go in to see Colonel McCabe and ask him outright if I'd be leaving with the division. In those days that sort of thing simply wasn't done. You spoke to colonels only when colonels spoke to you. But I did it anyway. Boldness like that's now a thing of the past. Been knocked out of me. But back then I could get a little reckless. Fact is, I was a great taker of high risks all the time I was young. To get right down to it, I was what you'd call a wild ass. Even for a civilian I was wild. And a civilian is all I ever amounted to in the Army anyway.

I think I told you that from the day I reported I'd been an officer they didn't need in the battery. A supernumerary outranked by everybody. So I had no reason to hope he'd pick me of all people. Not over those other two forward observers. Besides, I'd been the only one in the battery sent to that parachute school and that in itself meant I was the one most expendable. But as I say, I was writing to Susybelle, and I wanted some idea how long I could expect to be here in the States. I wasn't in his office two minutes. No, I'd not be going. When the division left, I'd be transferred out somewhere else. Where, Colonel McCabe didn't know. That would be up to Division Artillery.

Not long after that I saw a notice from the Corps of Engineers that was posted in battalion headquarters. It said that Combat Engineer Officers were badly needed over there in the ETO and they were looking for commissioned officers from any other combat branch who'd be willing to transfer to the engineers. You'd be given a month's intensive course at the Engineer School at Fort Belvoir. Land mines, shaped charges, barbed wire and Bailey bridges, all that engineer stuff. After which, you could expect to be sent overseas almost immediately. I knew nothing at all about the engineers, but now, about this going overseas—that was something I thought I knew something about, so I signed up.

As I say, about that time I was writing Susybelle pretty regular. Then that day came when I called her and asked her to marry me. Just like that. Two nights later, she called me back and asked if I still meant what I'd said. I said that I did. She said, Well then, I will. The next thing I knew, she'd left school down at Austin and was out on Long Island with her parents. Her father was Scott Wilkinson. Scott was a lawyer here who'd been in the Army in the First World War and he'd stayed active in the reserve. He was one of those who'd gone back on active duty a year before Pearl Harbor. At that time in 1944, Scott was a full colonel in command of an AA outfit out on Long Island.

Susybelle hadn't been out there on Long Island but a week or two when I had a call from her. Her mother had arranged everything. We were all set to be married on Saturday, August 12th. The wedding would be in St. Bartholomew's Episcopal Church in New York. Everybody would be staying at the Waldorf, just a couple of blocks down Park from the church. Everything had been taken care of. I told her I'd see her at the altar.

This was toward the end of July, mind you, only a couple of weeks before the wedding. The first thing I had to do was get a railroad ticket to New York. But I found I couldn't take a train from Augusta to New York because there wasn't one. I'm not sure of this, but it seems to me I had to drive up to Aiken, South Carolina and catch a fast train that came through there on its way to New York from Florida.

Next thing, I had to get a three-day pass, and right there was where I ran into a difficulty I hadn't at all expected. It just happened that at that time I wasn't assigned to my battery. I was working shifts with two other Second Lieutenants, one from each of the other battalions, and the three of us were on battalion duty twenty-four hours a day packing up stuff like gun sights and binoculars. Things that needed special packing for shipment overseas. So I couldn't go to my Battery Commander for a pass. But then, when I went to battalion for one, I was turned down. This was wholly unexpected. So what did I do? What any self-respecting groom would do, I hauled off and went AWOL. Those other two lieutenants took my shift. Covered for me while I was gone. I'm pretty sure one of them was Carl Barton. I don't remember who the other one was.

Incidentally, Colonel McCabe was a native of South Carolina. He was also a West Pointer and as fine an officer as you'd ever hope to serve under. He wasn't much to look at. Not physically. He was only about five foot seven as I recall and he couldn't have weighed more than a hundred and thirty or forty. He was so quiet you'd hardly notice him. But there was a lot more there than met the eye. Because he was some tough. It's hard to say what a real man is, but of all the real men I've ever known myself, not one of them went in much for mouth. For show neither. But as I say, there really wasn't that much to Colonel McCabe. He looked kind of like that ninety-seven pound weakling they used to advertise in all the magazines. But when I first reported in to the 419th, I found out right quick that everybody in the battalion thought the world of him.

But not one of us gave him a chance of ever actually going overseas. We thought he could never pass the physical proficiency tests we were being given. The last one we all had to pass to be certified for duty overseas was a march. This was in July, and believe me, in a Georgia July it gets hotter than the hinges of hell. But we had this forced march coming up. All of us, the whole battalion, formed up out there on the parade ground. Steel helmets. Full field packs. All of us carrying a rifle of course. And little old Colonel McCabe standing out there in front, ready to lead the way.

I can't certify as to the exact details, but it seems to me we were required to make something like eight or ten miles around that parade ground. And we had to do it in so many minutes. I don't remember how many, but we had to be at a slow trot for the most part in order to make it. As I say, when we started out we thought it was only a matter of time before he'd have to drop out. And we all knew that failure would have about killed him. I don't think anyone who was there and is now still alive will have forgotten that march.

But I made it up to New York OK, AWOL and all. My mother and father were there. How they got railway tickets I'll never know. And my brother, he made it, too, from Great Lakes. I had only one friend from school who was there at my wedding. He was Frank Sommer. Frank was a full bore 4-F in the draft and none of the services would even talk to him. That's why Frank could be there.

So we got married and got safely back to that little room and a bath I'd rented in Augusta. Our first home. It was near The Partridge Inn, and when we got there, it was around four o'clock AM on that Monday morning. I'd been AWOL quite a while by then. Gone AWOL for three whole nerve-wracking days, and I was getting awful nervous, so I didn't hang around there for long.

I kissed Susybelle goodbye and headed straight out to Camp Gordon, and it's a damn good thing I did. Because when I walked into battalion headquarters—this was well after five o'clock in the morning—the first thing I saw posted on the board was that I'd been made battalion Officer of the Day for that very Monday. Now the first thing the OD does is take reveille, and reveille was just about to happen. Right out in front of battalion headquarters. If I'd delayed at all after settling Susybelle down in our little apartment, reveille would have taken place without me, and that would have been a somewhat untoward event leading inevitably to my own immediate court martial.

When I left for New York, I hadn't drawn OD for that Monday. Maybe there'd been a bed check while I was gone, I don't know. But someone had made a change. While I was gone AWOL, I'd been made OD, and I think it was most likely Colonel McCabe himself who'd done it. He knew I'd slipped off and he was fully expecting to catch me. But he didn't! Because there I was! In the proper uniform and cool as a cucumber. Out in front of battalion headquarters, striding back and forth, impatiently looking at my watch, ready for battalion reveille that was scheduled for six o'clock. I could hardly wait to take the First Sergeant's salute, which I did with my usual grace, strength and agility—thereby saving my ass.

The funny thing is, on that very same day, orders came through sending me to the Engineer School at Fort Belvoir. So that Monday night turned out to be the only night Susybelle and I spent in our first home, in our cozy little apartment there in Augusta at the beginning of our marriage. The next morning, we packed up and drove up to Fort Belvoir, where I was to become, for a few months anyway, nominally an Engineer.

A hasty war marriage? Oh, yes! *Very* hasty. Regrets? About other events in my life I've got plenty, but going AWOL to marry Susybelle, that's not one of them. Looking back on it, I can only regard those twenty-five years that it lasted, those fine, long, happy years, and those six wonderful children that came along—every bit of it a direct result of my taking a calculated risk by going AWOL— I can only see all that as having been a perfectly beautiful time of my life and among the best hands the Fates ever dealt me. Yes, it did come to an end, but we struck a perfectly good chord in the beginning. It was just a chord that we both managed somehow to lose. But those are private matters and best left unsaid.

I have a good friend here named Jack Kennedy. Jack and I've been lunch-time bridge companions for more than forty years. In the war, Jack also served with an Armored Division, the Sixth Armored. Jack's a graduate of West Point himself and wears a Silver Star. A few years ago, he was telling me about some of his experiences as a cadet there at the Point. It turned out that I knew some of his classmates. We'd gone over there to West Point a number of times to shoot against them when I was on the Yale skeet team. We liked going there because we could shoot as much as wanted to and do it for free. I mentioned to Jack that I'd served for a while in the States under an officer named McCabe who'd graduated only a few years ahead of him and I was wondering what had happened to him— whether he might still be living. Jack said he'd get in touch with his alumni association and find out what he could.

Sure enough, a few days later, Jack sat down at the bridge table and told me that after the war, McCabe, Lieutenant Colonel Robert McCabe, had worked as an engineer for the South Carolina Highway Department, but he'd died as a rather young man. In the seventies I think Jack said. If I neglected to mention it, McCabe did succeed in making that march and he did go overseas in command of the 419th. Jack also said he'd been awarded the Distinguished Service Cross and all kinds of other medals. A Silver Star or two, I don't know. Don't quote me on that, but I know that the gist of it has got to be right. Because that's just what Colonel McCabe always was. You would have seen it yourself. Colonel McCabe was meant by nature to be a soldier. But the fact that he quietly also became a war hero, now that's a part of it he took care of all by himself,

The moon shines tonight on pretty Redwing ...

If you were wondering whose voice that was you heard when you walked up, that was Nan Merriman. If you don't know her, Nan was a great mezzo soprano of fifty years ago and she was as beautiful herself as her perfectly beautiful voice. Although Nan and I were of the same age and good friends, she was really the friend of my parents. That was a Spanish song she was singing. One of some ten she recorded more than fifty years ago for Angel. She also made an Angel recording of French songs about the same time. I still have those two old vinyl records, but now I've got every one of those same songs on a disk. Here's a picture of Nan, the only one I have.

This was taken on January 29, 1953, close to the time she made those two records. I told you what a lovely person she was. The last thing I heard was that she'd hidden herself away somewhere out there in California. She just might still be alive for all I know.

Here she is singing at a banquet in the Crystal Ball Room of the old Washington Hotel downtown. They're both gone now. That room was plumb full of oil men who'd come here from all over the country to honor my father for what he'd meant to the industry.

One day my mother happened to mention to Nan something about this big testimonial dinner, and Nan asked my mother if she could come and sing. So she and my mother schemed it up between them as a surprise. And it was, too. Papa had no idea Nan was even in town. Not until they were announced and she and Ralph walked out. That's Ralph there at the piano, Ralph Linsley. First, she sang some Bizet's songs and then *The Kerry Dance*. But then she concluded with a song I doubt has ever been heard anywhere since. *The Moon Shines Tonight on Pretty Redwing*. That was Papa's favorite song when he was a boy. Mama had asked Nan to sing it.

Nan herself—I mean in her own person—was as warm as the music she loved. She had that special warmth that comes with a large and beautiful humanity. She wouldn't sing a note without first spending a long, long time warming up. I always thought that a bit odd. Even when she'd come over to our house and we'd all gather around the piano to sing, the way we always did, Nan would just stand there and listen. How she could bring herself to just stand there and not sing, I have no idea. Me, now, I've never warmed up to do anything, let alone to sing. And I've spent my whole life singing. But when you're like me and most of your singing has been done in bathtubs and barrooms, then such an extravagance as *warming up the old instrument* would hardly seem necessary, right?

The Moon Shines Tonight! Papa's favorite and it could even be the song Nan's singing in this picture. Hers was not an enormous voice. One that would fill a coliseum. No, but it was a perfectly gorgeous garment that she wore whenever she came out onstage. It was of the texture of goose down, and at her command might be of any and every hue of the rainbow. A garment she wore with the quiet pride of the fine artist she was.

Over the top, am I? Not at all! Toscanni thought the same. Nan was Toscanni's favorite mezzo. Why did she come here year after year to spend two or three weeks with my parents? They were almost old by then, a whole generation older than she. I'll tell you why. Being around my mother and father would give anyone the ridiculous notion that to be a human being and in the company of other human beings was plumb OK. A very fine thing indeed.

Listening to Nan sing just now, it seemed to me I could see and hear her both at the same time. I could clearly see her, sitting right here around the pool the way she used to do. And I could see again her own lovely self and hear again the beautiful musical instrument she also was. That's when I'm reminded that no musical instrument ever made by man even *approaches* the glorious sound made by the instrument we're all born with—our own, human voice. Nan had a gorgeous vibrato that was as soft and delicious as a red velvet cake. I wish you could have heard her sing in person.

I ought to tell you that that last song she sang, *The Moon Shines Tonight*, was not only Papa's *favorite* song, it was the *only* music of any kind in which my father ever took the slightest interest. It's not too much to say that for my father music simply did not exist. I suppose that when he was a boy, it would have been unusual for him to have heard music of any kind. Maybe a steam calliope on a passing stern wheeler or a wheezy old pump organ in that tiny Episcopal church—it's really only a chapel—he attended as a boy. That little church is still standing there in Melville. It's only a block or two from the Atchafalaya.

But somewhere along the way he'd heard that song. Maybe it was later, when he was serving in the Army in the First World War. But wherever it was, he never forgot it. If you don't know it, it's a song about a young Indian maiden, Little Redwing, and a hundred years ago it had a sudden, and perfectly enormous popularity in rural precincts all over the world. But other than that one song, music was a blank place in my father's awareness. We all have them, you know. Places in us that for some reason seem to remain forever blank. Papa would have applauded Mark Twain had he heard Twain say—as he did—that Wagner's music was better than it sounds. Only Papa would have extended that sentiment to include almost any music. Any music, that is, except that one song, *The Moon Shines Tonight on Pretty Redwing*.

Here's Papa in 1916, the year he graduated from the Tulane Law School. You can see his whole class here, seven of them.

Papa's the very pleasant looking fellow you see there, the second from the right. In 1948 I graduated from that same law school myself, and our class picture was taken with all of us standing on those same stone steps you see there in the picture.

When Papa graduated, he didn't have money enough to open a law office on his own. In fact, he didn't have any money at all. Later on, when he went up to Wisconsin to marry my mother, he had all of two hundred bucks in his pocket. He wouldn't have had that if his Aunt Sally hadn't lent it to him. And get this! My mother had half of that spent before she even said *I do*. Papa said she spent it on ice cream at the drug store over in Chetek.

A week after they were married, they were both hard at work teaching school in Pollock, Louisiana. Pollock's a little country town in the piney woods down in the central part of the state. It was a sawmill town then and I imagine it still is. Saving the time Papa spent in the army, that's where they both lived for a while, pinching pennies until they'd squirreled away enough money to make the great leap of faith. I'm not exactly sure when that was but probably in 1919. But they just hauled off and gambled everything. Left their jobs and moved to Winnfield, Louisiana. Winnfield was a much bigger town located not too far away. That's where Papa began his practice of the law.

Papa said that when they first went to Pollock, there was only one room in the whole place they could rent to live in. It was a little backroom in an old ramshackle of a house overhanging a creek bottom out at the edge of town. It was in a house built up on stilts, on thin wooden pilings that raised it high up off the ground. That was to keep it up out of the water when the creek rose. That was a very common practice in low-lying areas all through the state back then. I suppose it still is in lots of places.

At that time in central Louisiana, and even much later on, for most of the year the hogs were turned loose to run wild in the woods. Hogs'll go feral as quick as cats you know, and those feral hogs would sometimes come right up around the house at night, looking for the garbage thrown off the back porch. They'd even come right up under the house and rub their backs against those pilings. Papa said that those hogs would sometimes rub up against those pilings so hard the whole house would shake. It would teeter back and forth and sway around in the air something awful, like it might fall down any minute. My parents used to laugh about that a lot. They said the hogs got so bad one night that Mother was literally shaken right out of bed. Those were times they never forgot. They called those times *the good old days,* and they'd laugh and laugh. Laugh right out loud together every time they'd talk about it. That's where they began their life together. That was their first home, in that shack perched up on stilts in absolutely the poorest part of town.

Here's a picture of my mother the way she looked when she was teaching school in Pollock.

This was taken in 1918 when my father was off in the army and she was there alone, teaching school without him. But why don't you just forget my mother for a minute. Don't look at her at all, but just cast your eyes on that little corner of Pollock you can see there behind her. Focus on that and then let yourself drift back a ways in time. Let your imagination put yourself in that scene. Don't you get something of a feel for what it must have been like, living there in Pollock ninety years ago?

When they'd finally scraped together enough to live on for a few weeks, that's when they made the move to Winnfield. They went there bone poor, but they went there young. Nothing wrong with being young and poor. Not then. Not now. The main thing is not to quit, and there wasn't any of that in either one of them. And they had something else in common. Two natural dispositions that would serve them well all their lives, those being high hopes and noble aspirations—without which no two young people should ever want to start out life together anyhow. But most important of all was the plain and simple fact that they knew they had each other.

Here's Papa in 1922, a couple of years after he began practicing law in Shreveport. All the time I was a boy growing up, it wasn't uncommon for some older lady to draw me aside and confide in me that my father was the handsomest man she ever saw.

After Papa hung out his shingle in Winnfield, it wasn't long before he caught the eye of an astute older lawyer in Shreveport named Judge George Wallace. After Papa had bested him in court the second time, Judge Wallace invited him to come to Shreveport and be his law partner. That's the kind of man my father was. Everybody wanted to be his partner. You would, too, if you'd ever known him.

My mother was always quick to judge and often wrong, but Papa, now—he was just the opposite. He was slow to act but he rarely made a mistake. Oh, he could be wrong! He wasn't some god, I'm not suggesting that. In fact, he was almost *too* human. So he made mistakes of course. But not big ones, not generally anyway. And not very often either. Let me put it to you this way. If you spend enough time out in the woods, sooner or later the day will come along when you look up and there's a squirrel falling out of a tree.

I've got two or three other pictures here of Papa I want to show you. This first one is a 1952 picture of him with Ike.

This was when Eisenhower was running for president the first time. He'd stopped off here at my father's invitation. At that time Papa was head of an organization that called itself *Democrats for Eisenhower*. Why Democrats and not Republicans? It's not far off the mark to say that at that time there *weren't* any Republicans in our state. Well, there were a few *professional* Republicans if you want to count them. But certainly there weren't any capable of making their presence felt. Our new airport had just been opened for traffic and that's where Ike made his speech, out there at the new airport.

In 1973, soon after Papa died, I had a call from the archivist at the LSU Library in Baton Rouge. I don't recall his name, but he came up here, and together we went over some of the stuff Papa had. Afterwards, he sent me a list of the things he'd like very much to have for their archives. Files and scrapbooks. Photos. Things like that. A few months later, I took it all down to Baton Rouge and gave it to LSU. I don't think you'd really have much interest in seeing it. It was mostly just political stuff. But there were a lot of pictures of Papa I wish I'd kept to leave with the children. Just recently, I did arrange to have some of them scanned, and I've got a couple of photos here of Papa with Mr. Reagan. But before I show them to you there are some things you might like to know about them first.

The first one I'll show you was taken at the convention that nominated Goldwater in 1964. The two of them are down on the floor of the convention, and it looks to me like Papa must be taking Mr. Reagan around to meet the southern delegations.

By the way, that 1964 convention was the one at which Reagan delivered his famous *Rendezvous With Destiny* speech. If you remember it, that was the speech that catapulted Reagan into our country's political empyrean. In fact, I believe that picture of them at the convention was taken the same night that Reagan gave that speech. Probably just before or just after he gave it.

Mr. Reagan and Papa already knew each other somehow. How or where they met I've no idea, but that same year, 1964, that was the year Papa was running for governor, and Mr. and Mrs. Reagan came and spent three days in South Louisiana campaigning for him. This other picture is one taken of them in New Orleans.

AUG • 64

Mrs. Reagan was standing there also but she's just barely off camera. That's Tom Stagg you see in the middle. I don't know who that other fellow is, but he doesn't look much like a barrel of laughs, does he? There are a lot of other pictures of Papa down there where these came from. Other things, too, in those archives. Just go to the LSU Libraries in Baton Rouge and ask to see the Charlton Havard Lyons, Sr. Papers. They're cataloged as Mss. 3075 in their Louisiana and Lower Mississippi Valley Collections.

As I say, Mr. and Mrs. Reagan came here to Louisiana and campaigned for Papa, but the truly interesting thing about that was not the speeches he made in New Orleans and in Lafayette, but how the Reagans got here from California. It would be two or three years yet before Reagan became governor of California and at that time the Reagans didn't fly. Mr. Reagan simply *refused* to fly—anywhere. No, they came all that way from California by train. By *passenger* train, if you didn't hear me! And they went back home the same way. Imagine that! Much later and they couldn't have done that. In 1964, the passenger train, the train that we'd ridden everywhere all our lives, had become a highly endangered species. The first thing to go was real buttermilk, and then came the passenger train. Both now dead! God knows who'll be next! Ah, yes, it's my morning paper! A society that watches, inattentive and uncaring, over the demise not only of buttermilk and the passenger train but of the morning newspaper as well—why, you can rest assured that that society is well on its way back to another dark age. Unless we are successful first in our ongoing, Herculean efforts to destroy the human race with illegal drugs and violent crime. Not to mention, O Horatio, the blowing up the whole of the planet by some cunning means as yet undreamed of by our superhuman computers.

I've had small experience of the politics of foreign parts, but I've had a rather large and hands-on experience of the politics practiced here in my home state, and believe me, no subhuman enterprise is so fired up with raw emotion, devoid of principle or fraught with horrific waste as what goes on here every day. I think I'll leave it at that. High blood pressure, you know.

If you think of a typical candidate for public office, you'd never think of my father. Not ever. He was that highly unusual combination of a principled and a practical man. He always aimed high, but he never tilted at windmills. But the thing that endeared him the most to everyone who knew him was his total acceptance of all the rest of humanity. He could find some excuse for almost all of us but he never had to make any for himself. I'm the opposite.

My mother had her own little tool kit and she knew how to use it, too. She could make all sorts of small repairs around the house herself. She said her grandmother, Mary Scally, had taught her that when she was a girl growing up out on her grandmother's farm. But Papa would scratch his head over a light bulb. Well, that's stretching it a bit—but not much. Worse still, he cared very little for the arts, the very thing that was so dear to my mother. Oh, he'd look where she'd told him to look, and he'd look hard, too. He'd try his best, but bless his heart, he just couldn't see it. My parents spent a lot of time in New York and when they were there, he'd go with her wherever she went. To plays and concerts, almost anywhere, but for some reason he drew the line at opera. Opera was just too much, Too outright silly for him. He wasn't at all silly. But he could laugh! My God, how Papa could laugh!

He was forever reconnoitering the terrain of the possible. Always asking questions. But you never felt that it was a question to which he already had the answer. He'd actually *listen*. Listen hard to what people had to say. And all this time he'd be thinking and thinking and by and by he'd have a position worked out. The answer that he was satisfied was the most tenable under all the facts and circumstances. And in doing that, he'd always be looking for the highest principle that could be grasped by the commonality of us. The highest ground that could not only be taken but held. Oh, he could make mistakes! I saw him make several myself and I told him so. That's one of the reasons he could trust me. I wasn't like those sycophants—those hangers-on and yes-men who were always around him. He knew that if he came to me, he'd get it straight.

No, there was nothing quixotic about my father. He was forever looking for ways to improve matters. But he never attempted the impossible. He may have been always looking up for some higher ground to stand on, but he was perfectly well aware of all the dangers that lurked below. Of all the snakes that slithered around his

his feet. How he could do that, I don't know, but he could. He could somehow look every way at once. Look up and down and all around, while at the same time never losing track of the stars.

My father was as indomitable as he was quiet and modest. He simply could *not* visualize defeat. He *never* gave up. His last words to me—this was only hours before he lapsed into that last long coma—were, *Pa, I don't think I'm going to make it.* Then, for seven days and nights, he fought off death the way a child fights off sleep,

My mother died in 1971 and until his own death from metastatic cancer of the prostate two years later, not a day went by but what my father wept for her. I mean he'd sob and sob his heart away, till I thought he was never going to stop. It's heartrending to watch your father suffer like that, but to my credit, I never turned away from him, not once. It wasn't just because I knew I was the best friend he'd ever had and he needed me there—it wasn't just that. It was more because I knew it was an experience I'd never forget. Never *want* to forget. Seeing my father like that, a man after all those years still so full of love for my wonderful mother. It made my own low regard for humanity seem somehow childish and trifling. And so altogether *wrong*! I'd always been able to look to my father for that, and I didn't want to forget it when he was gone. The feeling that there might be something to be said for us after all.

Forgive me if I've told you this before, but it's just about the most important thing a man could ever possibly say about his father. Or ever ask himself about anyone for that matter. Taken all in all, is this someone who lifts you up—or pulls you down?

As you now know better than anyone, here lately I've been thinking a lot about my life. Asking myself whether, worthless as I am, it was one worth living. That's what you do when you find yourself in my position, looking out ahead into the gloaming. And you know what I do when I ask myself that question? I do what I've always done my whole life. Whenever I find myself suddenly in doubt. I go straight to the top, to the head man, to the ultimate authority on anything and everything. Which is to say, I consult my own opinion. And in my opinion, my life certainly *has* been worth living. And that's been owing for the most part to my parents.

Nowadays, there are lots and lots of men out there who never had a father they could trust. That's very hurtful to a little boy. He knows very well he's missing something, missing a father he could trust. That's why so many men, when they grow up, spend the rest of their lives searching for someone—anyone at all—they can trust.

If you'd ever met him, you'd be like everybody else who ever did. You'd know right away that in my father's eyes you were seen as someone rather beautiful and nice. He doesn't sound human? Oh, he was human all right. The man never lived whose broad and simple, all-embracing humanity was more clearly evident, more immediately understood by everyone he touched, than was my father's. No, no one could have been more human than he. And in that, my mother, in her own distinctive and quite different way, was, strange to say, very much like him.

A few weeks ago, my youngest daughter, Marian, sang *Summertime* for her mother at her mother's funeral. When I was growing up, I was like that baby in Gershwin's song. It was then always summer for me, too. Because I always knew that there was nothing that was ever going to harm me. Harm *me*? No, *sir*! Not with *my* parents, not with two people like them standing by.

Come to the church in the wildwood ...

There are not one but two chapels on the Old Campus at Yale, Dwight Chapel and Battell, and I spent quite a lot of time in both of them. Just as I'd done at Lawrenceville, I sang in the choir all the way through Yale. A lot of that time wasn't spent listening or praying, it was spent singing. But not all of it. There was a lot of preaching that went on in those places, too. When I was at Yale, a short service was held in Dwight Chapel every weekday at noon. It lasted only about thirty minutes, and that's where you could generally find me at that time of day, there in Dwight, singing first tenor in a male quartet. And for very good pay, I might add.

Dwight Chapel lies, as I recall, almost directly under the great bells in the carillon of Harkness Tower. Harkness Tower is the Gothic campanile we would hear off and on all day long, tolling out the time. You may remember that some time back I showed you a line drawing of Harkness. That drawing I showed you was Jack Moment's impression of it—the way his psyche saw it forty years or more after he and I were there.

I can clearly remember a famous recording of the *1812 Overture* that was made fifty years or more ago and in which those Harkness bells were the bells that had been dubbed-in, peeling away as part of that great clamor we hear towards the end of the piece. The cannon fire had been provided by guns at West Point, French seventy-fives, as I recall.

Those bells were loud, too. So loud we could sometimes hardly hear ourselves singing in the chapel down below. I've been looking here in my journal and I'm a bit surprised to see that I actually stopped long enough a few times to scribble down something in the way of my own impression of a few of those daily services held at Dwight. Here are some of the things I wrote down.

Monday, February 2, 1942.
Reinhold Niebuhr spoke in daily chapel today, speaks again tomorrow, he has an excellent idea: Christian contrition with resolute action. Main Chance?

> *Thursday, February 12, 1942.*
>
> *The Rev. Richard Roberts has been speaking in chapel this week. Very, very good. The old school type with a defunct or moribund (during my time) religion.*

> *Wednesday, April 15, 1942.*
>
> *An itinerant churchman today addressed a congregation of seven, and a subsidized choir of twelve, on "the church: a vital institution".*

Yes, I know. I said just now that when I sang in daily chapel, the choir consisted of a mere quartet, and that *is* the way I remember it. There *were* only four of us. But looking at what I've written here, I suppose the explanation must be that in the spring of 1942 there were twelve of us making up the choir, but that later on, we were reduced to a quartet. That must have been due to the war.

> *Thursday, April 16, 1942.*
>
> *Perhaps we moderns lack most the conviction of the existence of a panacea. The churchman spoke today on the things that are seen and those that are unseen. The congregation was, once again, seen only with difficulty.*

Most of the entries I made that relate to the Sunday services held in Battell Chapel have to do only with the choir and what we sang and not with the rest of the service, but I've found two or three exceptions.

> *Sunday, March 8, 1942.*
>
> *Norman Thomas spoke in Battell this morning—a man with pure conviction.*

Norman Thomas? That's just a name to you? Well, he was once someone very, very well known. All through the thirties and forties he was the Socialist Party's candidate for President. He was perhaps the most genuinely altruistic public speaker I ever heard. I heard him speak a lot, and I never missed a word because I was always sitting right there in the choir. He also spoke more than once at Lawrenceville while I was there. I even met him, shook hands with him over at Foundation House. We heard from everybody, all sorts of people, while I was there at school. Anybody worth listening to. Allan Heely was responsible for that. That was the kind of Headmaster he was. And the kind of school he made for us.

So when I listened to Mr. Thomas there in Battell, that didn't represent my first exposure to that good man's vision of the utopia that could be ours. What do I think? I think there just might be a gene for goodness. How else would you explain it? I certainly hope so and I hope they find it in time. Because it's getting late. I think that I'd be more inclined to agree with Mr. Thomas if man were even a slightly different animal from the one he seems to me to be. I think that right there where I was, there at Lawrenceville in the nineteen-thirties, that was as close to utopia as I'll ever get.

> *Sunday, August 23, 1942.*
> *A young rabbi spoke at Battell this morning: better than most of the protestant preachers.*

> *Sunday, November 1, 1942.*
> *'Uncle Sid' Lovett gave an excellent sermon at the service in commemoration of Yale's war dead. Two members of my class so far have taken a dive—or in the quaint phrase, gone West.*

I don't know who those two boys could have been that early in the war. Also, I can hardly believe I wrote that. I wasn't that callous. I'm certain it must have been sheer bravado. Whistling in the dark, to ward off what we all knew was coming.

> *Sunday, February 28, 1943.*
> *Reinhold Niebuhr gave one of his evolved, masterly sermons this morning; he is lucidly deep & extemporaneous.*

Here's a little rhyme I wrote about a typical Sunday service in Battell. About the strange goings-on I witnessed there. It begins, as it should, with the processional and moves smartly on from there. When I found this, it was tucked away in an old notebook and there wasn't the sign of a date on it. However, I can see from internal evidence that it must have been written in my sophomore year. I didn't recollect that the robes worn by the choir at Battell were a deep sky blue, but apparently they were. I can also see that I intended this as a poem in that rather tiresome mode in which so many poems have for a long time now been written. By that, I mean I used a brevity of address and spoke myself in an obscure idiom designed to produce a poem which would be all but incomprehensible to even the most intrepid of my fellow poetasters.

Battell Chapel

Cyanic band accomplishes ascent
Nearer heaven, hymning the gold and blue:
There lo! mounting the rostrum, subsequent
Coryphaei of Christ's Life and Works review.
Marvelous by the lone sea washes stand
Simon and Peter casting nets, mark ye!
Descending miracle there by the strand,
Thrice calling: Corn, abideth not with thee.
The pulpit's voice singeth before wine-dark—
Revelation! The fane moves, shudders long.
Profane iron that shatters melody
With harsh wheels or bears burden to the song.

Opus 8

Harold in Jersey

    Haven't you heard me speak of the five of us who were the very closest of friends all through school and college? Higgins and Moment, Johnny Green and Bill Flemer and me? I told you some time ago, I think, that Jack Moment died last Thanksgiving day. But at least that left two of us, two leaves upon the tree. Flemer and me. Well, I just learned yesterday that Bill Flemer's also gone. Died some time around the first of May. So now there's just me.
    Bill's death got me thinking again about Lawrenceville. Did I tell you that for the first two years I was there, I lived in Davidson House? Davidson was one of the three dormitories in Lower that were then in use. They called them *houses,* but they were actually just dormitories. They were where we First and Second Formers slept. They were all under one roof in a building called Lower School. Lower's proper name was *The Alumni War Memorial Building*. The alumni must have named it that in the hope that the Lawrenceville boys who'd died in *The Great War* wouldn't be forgotten. That's what we called the first of those two World Wars that were fought in the first half of the last century, *The Great War*.
    I don't remember seeing one, but almost certainly there was a plaque hanging somewhere around Lower with their names on it, the names of the Lawrenceville boys who'd died in that war. They've all been forgotten now of course, but they'd all been forgotten even then. That's how quickly we forget. I wonder who they were. What their names would have sounded like if I'd taken the trouble to stand there before that plaque and read them out aloud.
    Our class graduated in June of 1940, and it wasn't long at all before a friend of mine who'd graduated with me was killed in our war. Derrick was the first. Derrick Vail. Derrick never went to college at all. From Lawrenceville, he went straight up to Canada to sign on with the RCAF. That's the Royal Canadian Air Force. Here's all I know for sure. By February of 1941 Derrick was something called an *Air Cadet* in the RCAF, and by sometime that

October he was an RCAF *Sergeant Pilot*. He went overseas in November of 1941 and was killed in action on February 22, 1942.

> *March 30, 1942.*
> *The glee club sang a bang-up concert in Washington in spite of my absence. I think I have not recorded the death of Derrick Vail—shot down, presumably. I liked him extremely well.*

We'd only just entered the war, but eleven months after making that entry in my diary, I made two more to the same effect.

> *February 23, 1943.*
> *Ed Lowery (my class at L'ville) was recently killed in a bomber crash in the West; he was an Army Lieutenant pilot. There is considerable talk that our whole class will graduate in May; I'm damned sick of hanging on.*

If you don't understand just what I meant by the words, *damned sick of hanging on*, I can tell you right quick. I was damned sick of that whole year I'd spent trying to stay in school when we were at war. After Pearl Harbor, nothing was the same, you see. Nothing! The very first entry I made in my diary is the one I made on January 3, 1942, when I was on my way back to Yale. Here's what I wrote. *Pondered coming home if R.O.T.C. doesn't pan out something definite.* From that moment on, school was not where I really wanted to be. I could hardly keep my mind on my studies. All I really wanted to do was drop everything and enlist. That may be hard for you to understand now, but that's how it was back then.

> *February 24, 1943.*
> *Jeff Wiedeman told me that Parker Toms (L'40) was shot down as member of R.A.F., leaving a wife & baby in Canada. Heard Vronsky & Babin at the pianos in Woolsey. Parker was the third of our class to die in a plane.*

I gave that entry to Jacqi Haun and asked her if she'd trouble to look in her files and see what she could come up with in the way of more details about Parker's death,. Here's what she told me.

George Parker Toms' file had in it a wedding announcement, a black-trimmed thank you note from his widow following his death, and a handwritten note in pencil that said his son (which turned out to be a daughter on further research) was born December 25, 1942, and that Parker had been killed January 20, 1943, in a plane crash. This date is contradicted by a notice in the Lawrentian, *which says 'George Parker Toms, Jr., L'40. Joined the Royal Air Force Eagle Squadron in Canada in February 1941, winning his wings in December of that year. He arrived in England in March of last year, completing his training and then being transferred to the Sixth Pursuit Wing of the US. Army Air Force as a Second Lieutenant. He was killed January 15, 1943, in a flying accident somewhere in the British Isles.'*

Further research into our official alumni war records confirmed that the Jan. 15 date is correct and that the son was actually a daughter named Wendy.

Haven't I told you about Jacqi? She's that indefatigable Archivist at The Bunn Library at Lawrenceville. Here's what she had to report about Ed Lowery. Parker and Ed both became flyers early in the war and both were killed in training—in what during the war was called *operational* flying. Parker died overseas, Ed here in the States. Neither one was killed in actual combat. What difference did that make? None. Operations or combat—in the war, it was all pretty much one and the same. Just *learning* to fly was dangerous enough. Just taxiing out put your life in the hands of the Fates.

While I was doing this research, I also came across the notice for Ed Lowery's death, which happened at 2:15 a.m. on November 30, 1942, in a plane flown by Henry Bunn, after whom our own Bunn Library is named. The Winter 1943 Lawrentian *has entries for both Lt. Bunn and Lt. Lowery on the same page, telling the story of how their plane crashed in a snowstorm. If I understand the sequence correctly, this makes Derrick Vail the first lost from the class of 1940, Lowery the second and then Toms the third.*

If Ed was already a lieutenant in November of 1942, he must have done the same as Parker and so many others did and quit school even before Pearl Harbor. Unless he went into uniform straight out of school and never went to college at all. That's what Derrick did. Did you notice what she said about The Bunn Library? It's named after the same Henry Bunn who went in with Ed.

I loved that school, loved it with all my heart. I still do. But I had a tough time of it at first. In fact, I didn't think I'd make it. I thought that every day would be my last. Oh, it wasn't the classes and the sports and the other activities—that was my briar patch. Maybe that was all that kept me going. That, and pride.

As I remember it, during the day I was—well, I was OK. I could get through the day all right. It was when night set in—when the lights went out and I was left to lie there in the dark of that long, silent room with some twenty-five other boys—that's when the agony would begin. There I was, every night, lying there on my narrow little cot, in my little cubicle, its thin, plywood walls reaching up only head-high, hearing every cough, every sneeze, every sound that any of the other boys made. So I knew that every boy in the House could hear me, too. That's when I'd suffer this terrible fear, this mortal shame, that the other boys would hear me when I began to cry. But I cried anyway. I couldn't help it, I had to.

Beginning in November, when it began to get really, really cold, almost every night after lights out, I'd lie there weeping until I went to sleep. When I found myself there in the silence and the dark, that's when that terrible, terrible homesickness would rack me and turn all my pride to pulp. All I could do to get through the night was to lie there on my stomach—face down with my pillow pulled up over my head, holding it down with my two arms, trying to stifle the sound of it as best I could. That's when I'd literally drown in homesickness, trying to strangle my sobs so no one would hear.

When I went up there, I was not a tough little kid, you see. Not at all! But I did manage somehow to tough it out till Christmas.

But when I went home for that first Christmas vacation, I went feeling sure I could never make myself go back up there again. But I did. I don't recall that my homesickness was ever discussed while I was there at home. In fact, I'd be pretty sure it wasn't. I wouldn't have said anything about it of course. I couldn't. It wasn't manly. But don't think for a minute my parents weren't aware of it! *They* knew! But to take recognition of weakness was just not their way. And besides, they trusted me. Trusted me to be the person they always saw me as. So what else could I do but go back?

So that's what I did, I went back. My two legs like lead, I climbed those steps back up onto that train. And that January, when the weather turned ever colder and colder, I became ever more forlorn, ever more wretched, week after lonely week. That's how I passed the whole of that first winter up there. Dying off a little more each day. Then came spring vacation and I was home again. It lasted for ten days, and when it came time again for me to get back on that train and go back to Lawrenceville, I suddenly realized that the whole world had changed. By some miracle, the sickness had gone off and left me and I *wanted* to go back! The horror was past!

But it was a close thing. A very close thing! I could just as easily have failed my parents and squandered my patrimony. I ask myself now how did I ever manage to make it through? I think that more than anything else it was because of my fear of failing my parents. That was something that, as a child, I felt that I absolutely must never do! Maybe I've told you, but I had this keen sense of all that enormous hope and confidence and aspiration that they'd always placed in me. But especially when they sent me away from our home at such a young age to that strange, new world up there in Jersey. You might say that I survived solely because of this sense of myself that I'd been given. My only identity. Without which I was *nothing*. I got that *self* of mine from my parents. I got it because of who *they* were. Certainly not because of who *I* was. Because I wasn't much. Like the song says, I was just a poor wayfaring stranger in a world of woe.

Although they may have tried, I'm not sure my parents actually ever *taught* me anything. They simply weren't didactic in that way. But I learned from them. Learned just from living in the home they made for me. And to this day, those beautiful things I learned from my parents are all that I consider really worth knowing, all that gives me hope when I get up on the levee and look around.

When I arrived back at school that spring, Davidson House hadn't changed. The same long corridor between two rows of tiny cubicles—tight, little Spartan spaces where, behind a cloth drape, each boy lived a life he could only with difficulty call his own. But if Davidson hadn't changed, I *had*, and, beginning with that spring of 1936, the next four years in that school were heaven itself to me.

In Lower there was a little room that contained a few shelves of books. Maybe three hundred titles. All of them, of course, books written for boys. By the end of my second year, I'd not only opened every one of those books, I'd probably read a fourth of them to the end. That was my first exposure to the stories of Owen Johnson. To Dink Stover and the Tennessee Shad. Scott Fitzgerald said that for him and all the boys of his generation Johnson's *Stover At Yale* was their *how-to* book, their bible. They even quoted from it. And I'll bet you've never even heard of Dink Stover. No, I thought not.

As you know, I wound up at Yale, but during almost the whole of the five years I spent at Lawrenceville, I'd planned to go to Princeton. Almost everybody from school went there. But Higgins had been after me to go to Yale with him. And Flemer and Green and Moment, they were all leaning towards Yale, too, and the four of them were by far the closest friends I had. So in early 1940, when Nelson Boice, a friend of mine already at Yale, invited me to come up there for a weekend, I went. When I returned, it was decided that the five of us would be staying on together, but this time up at Yale.

Among the books I found in that little library were a few about the American West. That was a time and place that had always enthralled me. Maybe I've told you. Among the books there that got my close attention was one written by Owen Wister. *The Virginian*. By coincidence, only seven years later when I was at Camp Gordon with a firing battery of the 419th, our battery's ammunition sergeant was named Wister, and it turned out that Sergeant Wister was one of Owen Wister's two sons. When we were out in bivouac and not sleeping in the barracks—which was half the time—that's when I was able to talk with him about his father and about that book.

The Virginian was the source, you know, of that immortal line, *When you call me that, mister—smile.* I may have that a little wrong but you can look it up. Sergeant Wister was Carl to his family but he was always *Sergeant Wister* to me, of course. I found out last year that he died some years ago, but I have been in touch with his son.

One of the House Masters in Lower—I want to say it was Mr. Herrick—had a personal interest in theatre, and we did one-act plays on a little stage we made ourselves, down in the basement. I can remember playing a part in one of those plays. It was called *In the Zone*. All the action takes place in the crew's quarters of a tramp steamer during The Great War. The Zone of the title was the zone in which merchant ships were subject to attack by German U-boats. I played a seaman named Smitty. Isn't memory a wonderful thing? Why in the world would I remember a little thing like that? *In the Zone* was written by Eugene O'Neil, and a son of his, Eugene, Jr., was to be my professor of Greek all the way through college. Didn't I tell you something about him a while back? It seems to me I did.

Another play we did was one written by a man who only six or eight years before had been teaching there at Lawrenceville. He was a French teacher. I think that play might even have been written while he was there, because it was called *The Happy Journey to Trenton and Camden*. It was a play that required nothing at all in the way of a set, and the only props we used were four very spare, upright chairs, the kind you used to see in ice cream parlors. The kind that had those stiff wire backs. The playwright gave the stage entirely to the actors, just as he did later when he wrote *Our Town*.

Thinking of that second year I spent in Lower brings Bob Wilson to mind. Bob came to Lawrenceville as a First Former in 1936. He wasn't in Davidson, he was in Ross, Perry Ross, so I probably didn't get to know Bob right off. Now I have no recollection of this at all, but looking through the 1937 Olla Pod the other day, I saw that the year we were both in Lower, Bob and I played together on the Lower School's football and basketball teams. I see that those teams were composed of boys from all three of the houses in Lower and the Olla Pod calls us the *Junior Varsity*, so all of our games must have been played against other schools. That's likely how I first got to know Bob, playing football that fall.

He was an absolutely straight-on guy. Your first thought on seeing him was, *Wow! Now there's an athlete!* And you'd be right. But pretty soon it was the strength of his character that held your attention. That stalwart, fearless disposition we should want in our leaders but all too seldom elect. It's become very apparent that what we prefer in our politicians is pap, and there was none of that in Bob. He was a man. Even then, when he was a boy, Bob was a man.

I can remember his voice. It was preternaturally deep and dark. Even in Lower School, it sounded mature. More like the voice of the viola than the violin. Unfortunately, the voice of the viola is too much like the voice of reason—it's generally too submerged, too deeply embedded in the musical discourse to be heard above the din. It's a shame, too, that we don't hear it featured more often. It's so nice, for a change, to listen to someone who's not screaming at you. Someone to whom you naturally want to lean in closer so you can hear. That's why I've got such a special affection for the viola. It doesn't call attention to itself. No, it just serves to hold everything together and that's the kind of boy I remember Bob as being.

In any event, Bob and I got to be fairly close. Close enough, so that, in the spring of 1937 when the baseball season began, I was one of three or four boys in Lower that Bob invited to go down with him to Philadelphia one weekend to watch the Phillies play. It was a spring-training game, I guess it was, and they played in the afternoon. Baseball wasn't played at night back then. It wasn't played indoors either. And in those days it was played by actual teams. Year after year, the same men playing the same positions. There's no such thing as a *team* anymore. All you've got now is a *program*! A front office, and a bench full of billionaires, most of them waiting to hire on somewhere else. So who cares anymore!

When we went down to Philadelphia with Bob, we sat in a box right behind the dugout on the third base line. Bob's father was Jimmy Wilson. He'd been a major league catcher himself, but at that time—this was in 1937—he was managing the Phillies. I believe he may have been what used to be called a player-manager. You don't see those anymore either. I know he was still doing a little catching because when Bob showed up with some of his friends from school, Mr. Wilson went behind the plate himself and caught the first three or four innings. I remember that very well. I'm not quite sure, but I think Bob was an only child. Anyhow, Mr. Wilson was very proud of him. Boys are very quick to notice that sort of thing.

Bob was stout as a stump and quick as a cat. In short, he was one hell of an athlete. He was a natural at everything, but at baseball he was phenomenal. When only a Third Former, he could not only *catch* major league pitching, he could *hit* it, too. Hard! Behind the plate, he was in total command of the field. And that wasn't just my opinion. Lefty Page thought so, too. He told me so himself.

I was in Dawes House that year. In a double with Bob McConnell, and Lefty's apartment was right next door. Lefty was our assistant house master and he coached the varsity pitching staff. He wasn't long out of Harvard where he'd been a standout pitcher, and he could still take the mound himself. Lefty said that Bob could play in the big leagues right then. Lefty was Warren K. Page, and not long after the war, he became the Guns and Ammunition Editor of *Field and Stream* magazine. I read his stuff for years. I just thought I'd throw that in—in case you were interested.

My son went to Lawrenceville all five years—same as me—and he says the boys he came to know there in school mean more to him now than most of the ones he met later on in college. Of course now, he went to Harvard, and maybe that'll tell you something. But seriously, my own experience was the same as Bud's. You're far more impressionable during your high school years than you ever are later on. Between high school and college, our center of gravity seems to migrate from the heart up to the head. We begin to *feel* less and less and to *think* more and more. *Tant pis!*

I'd known Jack Moment and Johnny Green from Lower School and we were already close, but it wasn't until the Third Form that Charlie Higgins and Bill Flemer showed up at Lawrenceville. And right away, they, too, became my friends. So that's how it all began. And now that Flemer's gone, there's only me that's left alive. I can't get it out of my head. Bill was still living there in Princeton when he died. Had to carry oxygen with him. He told me that a year ago. I got to tell you—I'm thinking more and more about that book.

I'd give anything if I could describe Charlie Higgins to you but I can't. I don't even have a picture of him handy to show you.

The only picture I have of him is the one in the 1940 Olla Pod. That's the Lawrenceville yearbook, and back then about a third of it was given over to Fifth Formers. Those were the seniors who were graduating that year. Each Fifth Former was allotted a full page. Some vitae, a block of text and a picture. I was going through our year book again this morning, looking at that picture of Charlie in there. But, no, I wouldn't attempt to *describe* him. But I will tell you a little bit about the space he inhabited, if that makes any sense.

Higgins wasn't perfect, Lord knows, but he was that next rarest thing—a perfectionist. Which is to say, he was an idealist. I don't mean that he was an idealist in the philosophical sense. The notion that the *idea,* the *concept,* of an object is its only true reality. No, I mean idealist in its common, everyday sense as being the sort of person who's given over to man's highest aspirations for the tribe. Most of us see perfection in anything as being merely some human ideal. Why did I just say *merely,* when the *ideal* is so infinitely beautiful as to be *almost* beyond human imagining? But for Higgins, it wasn't. No, not at all. Because Higgins, unlike most of us, was somehow always able to imagine it. Not only to imagine it, but to see it as being something actually attainable. Something well within our grasp. Thinking back on it, his idealism was likely the very quality in him that attracted me the most. Not only me, but all four of us who became his closest, dearest friends.

Tell me something. Why do we humans always shy away from admitting even the *possibility* of perfection? I don't know why, but we do. But Higgins didn't! He didn't shy away. Oh, no, that's what he was all about. What he was bent on. That may have been what interested him so much in the arts, because they do seem to offer some possibility of at least a limited kind of perfection. His own art was photography, and in that, as in all else, he was an idealist. I'd sometimes go over with him to the darkroom and keep him company, and that was when you could see it best. You could see it there in his eyes, as his prints would magically appear out of the nothingness. He'd be standing there transfixed, always hopeful, always expecting the magic of absolute perfection.

That last year at school Charlie and Andy Underhill and I roomed together in a triple in Upper. I was just looking at it this morning, and on Charlie's page in the Olla Pod there was something that popped right out at me and brought it all back like it only happened yesterday. Here's what it said. *With his two roommates, Charlie Lyons and Andy Underhill, Charlie Higgins makes the third party to one of the most remarkable trios in the School.*

That picture of Charlie is on that same page, and I can't get it out of my mind. There's a profound sadness I see in the way he looks in that picture. Maybe if you saw it, you'd think he just looks—well, *pensive*. But whatever you call it, it's like all my memories of him. He seems to be looking at something *out there*. Something he can see but no on else can. And to me it's always something that seems to sadden him. One of these days I'm going to show you that one picture I have of Higgins if it's the last thing I do.

Whenever he'd get that sad look, that's when I'd take it on myself to jolly him up, and in all modesty, I've got to admit that I was pretty good at it. I could almost always coax something resembling a smile out of him. It might be a little wan, but it was better than nothing. The way I'd generally make him smile was by doing some of my patented cavorting around, making monkeyshines or talking some sort of silly nonsense. Of course now, he knew perfectly well that, despite appearances to the contrary, I was as concerned as he was himself, so he could never quite understand how I could let myself get so damned giddy in the head—be so lighthearted and quick to act the fool—when there was all that serious business at hand. That's when he'd say I was his *blithe spirit*—when, completely against his every instinct, I'd make him laugh in spite of himself. He didn't get that moniker he used for me from that play, it hadn't been written yet. He got it from Shelley.

Charlie came from Wilmington. Wilmington, Delaware, where the DuPonts live. His people were pretty prominent down there. We were aware of that of course, but none of us paid it any mind—Charlie least of all. There were lots of boys like him in school back then. Boys from big, important families. But the school's no longer just for boys. They've got girls up there now. Most of them, I'd think, are from the North, so I worry about them a lot. Mainly, I wonder if those girls they've got up there now still do girl things, like use mascara or say *Yes, ma'am*.

Sunday was the one day we had all to ourselves, but Higgins just hated Sundays. You see, that was the day his mother was most apt to show up. Our windows looked right out over the Esplanade and Charlie would be on pins and needles, watching out for her. When she'd arrive down there in front of Upper, she'd be bringing something for Charlie. A new armchair, a cashmere jacket. It was always something. Charlie was an only child. His mother's whole existence, and she just couldn't keep her hands off him. It was comical all right, but it was also something rather touching to see.

So me, I just loved her all the more for that, but those visits embarrassed the living hell out of Charlie. He was more than embarrassed, he was *humiliated*. Whenever the Higgins' limo would make its appearance, it seems like half our class would have picked that very time to be out there on the Esplanade, loafing around. The Higgins limo was a great, long, gun-metal Cadillac of extraordinary elegance and grandeur, and the Higgins' chauffeur—there was no postillion, just the driver—but he'd be in full livery, perched up there on the driver's seat stiff as a poker, and she'd be sitting in the back like a queen. Everybody would stop whatever they were doing and watch. Charlie loved his mother of course, but sometimes it was all he could do not to run off somewhere and hide when she came.

During the twenties and thirties, when the insanity of *The Great War* was still much on everyone's mind, there was an equally insane notion being bandied about that the big makers of munitions had been the cause of that war. Krupp and DuPont were the ones always mentioned by name. They'd somehow managed to start the whole damned thing just to make a market for their munitions. You get the idea. You don't believe that? Well, it's true. I mean that there was such a notion abroad, not that the notion itself was true. It's what you used to hear referred to as *vulgar error*. The modern equivalent, a bit sanitized as modern equivalents tend to be, would, I suppose, be an *urban legend*. But by whatever name, no patent error of fact is ever so incredible but what hapless millions will believe it. Hercules Powder Company is the name in which DuPont has always manufactured its munitions, and it was Charlie's father, Mr. Charles A. Higgins, Sr., who, through all that rumor-mongering, suffered the public discomfort of serving as president of Hercules.

The boys in school at that time tended to be rather apolitical and I certainly was. I lived in an ivory tower, as far above it all as I could get. Or I tried to. But that wasn't Charlie. Charlie always had the latest edition of *The New Republic* tucked under his arm, and he'd pull it out and quote you stuff from it. At great length, if you'd listen. He was the human social conscience personified, and as you may have already guessed, the conscience with which Charlie was afflicted was of a particularly virulent strain, intense and purposeful. I think everyone of us who knew him would agree that he was an ideologue, but unlike so many of that importunate breed, he was neither a dilettante nor an insufferable boor. Least of all was he among the militant of the type. He was pure, but he was neither unreasoning nor unreasonable. He was just a very good person, someone interested, not in his own but in the common good. And. as is so typical of the people of that bent, he was always not a little mystified that others were not nearly so obsessed as he was with such arcane, abstruse and, well, such wholly irrelevant matters as human rights and social justice.

But that doesn't adequately describe him either. It's not even close. Nowadays, men are apt to say of someone they like and admire that he's a regular fellow. Or a good guy—something like that. But that wouldn't do for Higgins. Not at all! You didn't know him, and I myself, I've forgotten most of what I should be telling you now about him, but you can just take this much from me—Charlie Higgins was a gentleman first and last. What my father's generation might have called a gentleman of the *old* school, but my generation always spoke of as a real prince of a fellow. And that's just what my old school mate was, a prince. Higgins was a prince.

But now to wind up about Bob Wilson. When I graduated in 1940, I'm sure that Bob had already been elected President of his class and at Lawrenceville that meant he'd be the President of the whole school for the coming year. A year later he went on to Princeton. I seem to remember seeing him there once myself. Half my own class from Lawrenceville had gone to Princeton. Underhill had, so I'd drop in there every chance I got. And then somewhere along, I learned that Bob had been killed. But that's all I knew about it until I went to Jacqi Haun, and here's what I found out from her.

Bob's name was Robert James Wilson and he stayed at Princeton just long enough to finish his freshman year. Then he left Princeton to enlist in the Army Air Corps. For a year he trained as a bombardier at a base somewhere out around Midland, Texas, and then he was sent to Clovis, New Mexico. At Clovis, he received some more training, this time as both navigator and bombardier on the B-29.

But to get to the point. Having left our noble school as its President in June of 1941, only a little more than three years later, it was in either November or December of 1944, Bob Wilson died out there in the Pacific. It happened somewhere high up over the Bay of Bengal. Let me show you this little excerpt about Bob taken from a memoir written by someone whose name Jacqi gave me—what was his name? Barton Biggs, that's it. That name sounds vaguely familiar but I don't know him. This is all that Jacqi sent me. Here, read this.

On an extra credit flight over the Bay of Bengal [India], just off Gillies' Head, his plane, a Superfortress, exploded and crashed into the bay. The water is very deep there, and they never found a trace of the plane or the men. Apparently, until his own death about a year later, Bob's father, Jimmy Wilson [coach of the Cincinnati Reds] continued to believe his son had survived the crash and had reached one of the jungle islands nearby.

Even now, thinking about Bob Wilson, it's hard to realize—let alone accept—that a life that promised so much could be so suddenly extinguished, and extinguished in just one brief flash of light, high up in the sky over the Indian Ocean, clear around on the far other side of this lonesome world.

Escales: Ports of Call

If you remember, one evening some time back I was telling you about that concert tour the Yale Glee Club made of South America in 1941. I told you only how it began. Well, now I want to tell you the rest of the story. It won't take long, I promise.

Immediately after the second of those two formal evening concerts in Rio, we boarded a train at midnight that took us to São Paulo. São Paulo is now the largest city in the southern hemisphere, did you know that? We sang there at nine that night and once again we left right after the concert, this time by special train. We were the only passengers on board when we headed back to the coast, to Santos. At that time there was more coffee shipped out of Santos than out of all the other coffee ports in the world combined. Right there above Santos the coastline is so severe, so steep, so precipitous, that, quite literally, our train had to be slowly lowered down to the level of the station by cogs laid between the tracks.

It was on July 5th that we arrived in Santos, and what did we do when we got there but climb right back on board the *Brazil*! We'd left her back in Rio, you remember, but Santos was her next port of call on her way down the coast of Brazil to Uruguay. That's where we were to sing next, in Montevideo.

A day and a half of steady steaming gets you from Santos to Montevideo, where we were scheduled to sing on the night of the 7th. We badly needed the rest and we could have slept in, but we didn't. No, we were all up especially early that morning. I can see us now, strung out along the starboard rail as the *Brazil* coasted close inshore on her approach to the harbor. The war had begun in September of 1939, and we were waiting to catch our first sight of it.

Hostilities had hardly begun when the *Admiral Graf Spee* was sinking enemy shipping in the South Atlantic. If you've never heard of her, the *Graf Spee* was a much feared German pocket battleship. She, along with the *Bismarck*, was the most famous of all the ships in the whole German navy. Both those battle ships died early. The *Bismarck* had been sunk only the month before, as all of us stood there on deck, looking at the ghost of the *Graf Spee*.

The first real naval battle of the war was between the *Graf Spee* and three smaller British men of war, and it had taken place very close to where we were, in the estuary of the River Plate. I'll spare you the details, but her captain, Hans Langsdorff, had scuttled her not far out of Montevideo. I can still see the head and shoulders of the *Graf Spee's* bony carcass. She was right there between us and the shore, only a couple of hundred yards to starboard. Right there! All of her superstructure and even a bit of her deck still showing, her captain having sunk and abandoned her, half-buried in the sea. It gave us all a sense that something dreadful had happened there. And that something equally dark and dreadful was impending over our own lives. The silence was eerie. No one said a word, as we sailed past the grave of the *Graf Spee* to sing concerts that night, and the next, in Montevideo. We sang in a handsome hall called the Auditorio del Sedro, just as though nothing at all had happened.

Although he had doubtless saved the lives of all his crew, Langsdorff, by electing to send his wounded ship to her shallow grave, had also effectively sent himself to his. He and the skeleton crew he had with him, after opening the veins of that great gray vessel up to the ocean, had made their way in a small boat across the broad mouth of the Plate to Buenos Aires. Langsdorff went straight to a hotel and, as I understand it, wrote some letters to his family, before picking up his pistol, lying down on his ship's battle ensign and blowing his brains out.

I've always wondered what he might have said in those letters he wrote home. Maybe there are scholars somewhere in Germany who know. I'd like myself to think that he killed himself to protect his family. That's what Rommel did. Maybe Langsdorff had come to realize who Hitler actually was, maybe not. But think about it now. That Adolph Hitler we all see as so malign, was he not one of us? Of course he was! And more than that, someone beloved, even idolized by millions. No doubt tens of thousands still do. Oh, yes, Hitler was one of our own all right. One of our very own!

You don't understand that at all, do you? But I've got to say it, got to constantly remind myself of it, because I believe it's true. Even looking down from my ivory tower, I see myself as part of the main whether I like it or not. But being part of the main doesn't, in itself, make us responsible for the acts of all those others, does it? Bearing the burden of our own is quite enough, don't you think?

Oh, yes, I am quite sensible of the enormous efforts made since the war by the Germans—especially the people of West Germany—to acknowledge the horror their country became under Hitler. The enormous damage their country did to a very large part of the world. I have the distinct impression that they've made every admission, performed every act of contrition and remorse that I could have reasonably expected, ever imagined. And most of it coming from people not themselves responsible. But then, these Germans of today *are* the descendants of that highly cultured, hard working people I so much admired when I was a boy, so there's got to be *something* left of that.

For a long time I hated the living hell out of that country and every damned person in it, but now I think I'm OK with it. I can certainly exonerate all of those who played no part in committing those ghastly crimes. For instance, those hundreds and hundreds of little children we found warehoused there in Bad Heilbrunn when we first moved in. Most of them had been brought—God knows how!—from the firestorm that had been Hamburg. Only a few of them had mothers left. And those little children, they, too, were among those who were left to apologize! My God Almighty!

Here's a couple of scraps from *El Dia*, Montevideo's leading newspaper. This is from the July 8th edition.

> *It should be pointed out that the presence of this chorus in Montevideo is one of the most pleasing and the most positive aspects of the cultural exchange which is taking place between Uruguay and the United States. The Yale students are typical exponents of the North American colleges. Tall, gay, with an air of tranquil ease, they showed by their manners the characteristic freedom and poise of the North American. Even while still on board ship, waiting to land, they sang several beautiful songs of their country.*

The writer then went on and on, expatiating on the virtuosity of our singing. If I haven't mentioned it, not only did we sing regular formal concerts at night—two such in Montevideo—but during the day we'd go about to schools and colleges and that's where we'd sing and mix with people our own age. Just listen to this little sound-bite from a very lengthy piece that appeared in *El Dia* on July 9th, the next day. This was by no means all of it. The writer went on and on in the same vein.

> *North American and Uruguayian students were gathered together yesterday in the University in a beautiful act of brotherhood. The Yale Glee Club in a public function organized by the Uruguay Student Federatio, was welcomed and honored in the university assembly hall. Our students wished to express the pleasure which they feel in the visit of these boys who have come to Montevideo to ring an example of the spirit of American youth, a pleasant mission of cultural exchange.*
>
> *It ought to be said that we have never seen such a large crowd as gathered yesterday in the assembly hall of the university. Students from all schools and departments, from private schools such as the Crandon Institute and Licee Francais, came in great numbers to welcome these friendl guests. The orchestra and the gallery were filled to the top and even the entrance stairways were crowded. When the Yale students appeared on the platform the unanimous ovation lasting for several minutes expressed the respect o these Uruguayian colleagues.*

That was the sort of reception we received from young people all over South America. Here are snippets from each of the two papers in São Paulo, but I have eight single-spaced pages of encomia like these from papers everywhere we went. This is from the *Diario de São Paulo*.

> *The discipline, perfect pitch, perfect taste with which the program was chosen deserves the highest praise. A beautiful concert and even more a beautiful lesson to us.*

And from the *Correio Paulistano*.

> *Much was expected of this chorus for its fame had preceded it from the United States and there were excellent reports of its concerts in Rio. Yet this performance far surpassed all expectations and each number called forth a thunder of applause. The theatre yesterday was too small to hold the multitudes that wished to attend this concert. The enthusiasm and applause lasted through the entire performance.*

From Montevideo, we went to Buenos Aires for six days, with over-night side trips to sing in La Plata and Rosario. Then, off by train across the Argentine pampas to sing in Mendoza, a wine city at the foothills of the Andes. From there we crossed the Andes. Not all the way by train as scheduled but partly by bus. A stretch of track had been taken out by an avalanche a few days before we got there. We sang two formal concerts in Santiago, then five days of sight-seeing, a lot of singing to our peers and not a little socializing.

One of those social events was a large dinner party held for us one evening by our ambassador to Chile. All our ambassadors everywhere had honored us in some way, generally with a reception for the more important locals held in the embassy. Our ambassador to Chile was different, and so was the party he gave us for us in his home. His name was Claude Bowers, and not only was he an orator and diplomat but he was a writer of some importance. He'd previously been Roosevelt's ambassador to Spain, but that was during the Spanish Civil War. It seems to me he had to keep office mainly in Paris. It was too dangerous for him in Madrid.

Sam Ross had been my friend and fellow first tenor both at Lawrenceville and at Yale. Sam was from Savannah, Georgia, and both he and I, like so many Southern boys of our generation, were, if I'm allowed to say so, more than simply knowledgeable about the Civil War, we were still living it, and Bowers was himself an expert in the field. A few years before, he'd written a rather sympathetic history of the South following the Civil War, and Sam and I had not only both read it, we could quote from it. Some time into that large and handsome evening, Sam and I introduced ourselves and spoke with Mr. Bowers about his book. You wouldn't have ever heard of it. It was titled *The Tragic Era*. As soon as Mr. Bowers realized that he was talking with a couple of young buffs from the South, he told us, *Come in here with me*. He took us into his personal study and shut the door. How long he absented himself from the party to talk with us, I couldn't say, but it was a long, long time. Thirty minutes?

Then, on July 26th, we went to Valpariso, sang there and departed Chile, sailing up the Pacific coast on the Grace Line steamer *Santa Lucia*. We stopped off, and sang concerts, I believe, in Lima and Quayaquil. Our final concert was in Balboa, as we were passing through the Panama Canal. The *Santa Lucia* then took us on back home to New York.

There's one last thing I want to tell you about those two ships that took us down to South America and back. Late in the war, when I went overseas, we sailed from New York as part of a perfectly huge convoy. We were told it was the largest convoy of the whole war, fifty-two ships. That's not counting the destroyers that seemed to be everywhere, churning past us at flank speed. It seems to me we couldn't ever see more than a quarter of that convoy. With all those ships, and some of them pretty slow, it took us a long, long time—twenty days, something like that—but we made it over safe. The ship just ahead of ours in the convoy was the *Brazil*, the same ship our Glee Club had sailed on, going down to Rio, three and a half years before. But now she was a troop ship, and she was filled to the gunnels with boys just like me, all of us on our way to the war.

On that last afternoon at sea, we'd sailed past miles and miles of high, chalk cliffs lying close at hand to port, until, almost at dark, the whole convoy hove to and dropped anchor, one by one, in some little bay, hard up under the English shore. It was after midnight when our ship up-anchored to cross the Channel to Le Havre. We stood there by our bunks in the dark, wearing life preservers and listening to the constantly repeated dull click and muffled boom of the depth charges the destroyers were dropping all the way over. They were dropping them right there beside us. Only two or three weeks before, one of our troop ships had been torpedoed and sunk when making that same passage, so the Navy wasn't taking chances.

If I failed to mention it, the name of my ship in that convoy going over was the *Santa Rosa*. The *Santa Rosa*, like the *Brazil* and the *Santa Lucia*, had been a passenger liner before the government took her over after Pearl Harbor and converted her to something they could use. The *Santa Rosa* and the *Santa Lucia* had both been Grace Line ships. In fact, the *Santa Rosa* and the *Santa Lucia* were sister ships. That's the same *Santa Lucia* that had carried the Yale Glee Club home from Chile. Right after Pearl Harbor, the government had taken over the *Santa Lucia* and converted her to an amphibious assault vessel. They'd also renamed her and she was the *USS Leedstown* when she was sent to the Mediterranean. She arrived there just in time for the invasion of North Africa but she didn't last long. No sooner had she put her troops and some of her cargo ashore than she was sunk. That happened in November, off Algiers, only fifteen months after she'd brought our glee club safely home all the way from Chile. She was first torpedoed and rendered helpless. Then on the following day a flight of German Stukas set upon her and sent her to the bottom.

Landkjending: Land-Sighting

It wasn't an army band. There wasn't one single thing about it that looked in the least military. No, it was just a bunch of guys who'd taken the subway into Manhattan that morning from out in Flatbush or the Bronx. Some of them might even have come over from Jersey, wearing their everyday clothes and bringing their instruments along. There were about fifteen of them as I recall—an old fashioned dance band would be the best description. And they were playing away like mad. Some Sousa. Some waltzes of course. And lots of the standards the big bands were playing back then. At least, that's what my memory tells me I heard them playing. They'd met us a long way out, after we'd passed The Rockaways and about the time we were sailing past the Statue of Liberty. Oh, yes, she was still there. This all happened long, long before anyone had the foresight even to notice that, one way or another, man would be pretty sure to find a way to turn the planet over to the apes.

This all happened in 1945, what I'm telling you about now. I can tell you the exact day, September 7th, 1945, and it fell on a Friday. I served in the military only three years but that day—well, that day and one other—those two days, they stand out in my memory as more important than all the rest of my time in uniform put together. That joyous day of home-coming and that day in March, almost seven months earlier, when I stood there on that road in Belgium—watching all those aircraft pass by on their way to the Rhine—those were the two days I'll never forget. And no two days could have been more different from each other than those two.

That morning in Belgium, it was cold and bleak and drear. Sullen and ill-boding, like thunder rumbling off somewhere just over the horizon. Even now, whenever I think back on that long-ago, gray morning near the Rhine, I experience the same ineffable sadness, the same sense of loss and bewilderment that I feel whenever I hear those first opening cadences of Mendelssohn's *Scottish* symphony. But on that other morning, the one I'm telling you about now, the morning we sailed into New York harbor, our ship was as sun-dappled as a child's rocking horse and the air was sweet to breathe.

It was one of those gorgeous, warm, late summer mornings when even New York could look inviting. We'd been looking at that wonderful town up ahead for a long time. She was there waiting for us, shimmering in the sun. And when I think of that morning, I think again of Mendelssohn, but this time, it's the immediate joyousness of the first few bars of the *Italian* that I seem to hear.

Only three years in uniform, but my God! how I *did* get around! I can't believe all the places I was stationed. Forget about overseas! I mean just the Army bases here in our own country. I couldn't possibly remember all the places I went while I was in Europe, but I do pretty well remember most of the places I was sent during the time I was here in the States.

Let's see, now. The first place was Fort Devens, in Massachusetts. That's where I was inducted, and I went from there to the Blue Hills Reservation as a private in the Military Police. Then to Fort Sill in Oklahoma and Fort Bragg in North Carolina and Camp Gordon at Augusta, Georgia. That was my longest stay by far—that seven months or so at Gordon with the Tenth Armored. Then to Fort Belvoir in Virginia for a month's course at the Engineer School. I'd already put in for overseas duty, but I was ordered to Rucker instead. So I had to serve a short stint as an officer in a battalion of black combat engineers, first at Camp Rucker outside Enterprise, Alabama, and then at Camp Shelby near Hattiesburg, Mississippi. Then, when my orders to go overseas finally did come through, I stayed a week at some camp in Pennsylvania. It was just outside Hershey, but, for the life of me, I couldn't tell you the name of it. From there, I went with a cadre of replacements to Camp Shanks. Shanks is in New York, just upriver from the City.

I wasn't at Shanks for long, but I can remember being there. Shanks was the main point of embarkation for several whole armies of men headed overseas during the war, more than a million and a quarter of us. I'd been there maybe a week when we were loaded up on trains in the middle of the night and taken down to the docks to board ship. I'll bet there are lots and lots of men still alive today who can remember that short hour's train ride down to their ship from Shanks. And I'll bet that on the way down most of them laughed at the same bit of gallows humor we did.

All during the war the government did everything it could to discourage travel by civilians. In every bus and train station in the country, on every bus and train, even on the streetcars, there were posters of Uncle Sam and he'd be pointing his finger straight at you. He had a question and you'd better have the right answer. *IS THIS TRIP NECESSARY?* That's what Uncle wanted to know, and wouldn't you just know it! When we climbed aboard that troop train, carrying nothing with us but a barracks bag slung over our shoulder, there was Uncle Sam., the first thing we saw, pointing an accusing finger at us from posters everywhere you looked. Naturally, that struck us as very funny indeed. Absolutely hilarious, in fact! Are you kidding? Was *our* trip, the one that for us was just beginning, was that trip really all that necessary after all? Come on, now!

I can clearly remember the laughter in our own railway car and I'm sure that same laughter would have been heard all up and down the whole train. The average age of those boys going over could not have been more than twenty. The men on my ship coming back weren't just a whole lot older than that. Not in years, no. But the mood on board was something altogether different. We weren't laughing as we hung over the ship's rail, listening to that band music coming up to us from that boat that was tugging along beside us.

For us, the war had not long been over but there were already enough of us back in the States, and more coming home all the time, that all the Army could do was put us in temporary storage in camps scattered all over the country until it finally came our turn to be discharged. After I got back, I reported to three different Army camps before being finally sent to Oglethorpe for discharge. The first one was outside Henderson, Kentucky, but so help me, I can't think of the name of it. Then I was transferred to Camp Campbell. Campbell was also in Kentucky, and from there, I was sent to the Infantry School at Fort Benning. That was the second time I'd had orders to go to Benning but that was the first time I actually went.

I'd had plenty of points to get out even before I left the ETO and I sure wasn't interested in a regular commission, but it was just like the Army to enroll me in a heavy-duty, month-long course in logistics, there at Benning. That was the first and only course I was ever exposed to in what I suppose the Army called staff work. Till then, every bit of schooling, all the training and instruction I'd ever received, if it wasn't close order drill or something academic like the Articles of War or the Orders of the Sentry, then it was something related specifically to weapons and combat. But that course I took in logistics was an eye-opener for me. It was one of the most beautifully designed and organized courses I've ever had anywhere. And perfectly executed, as it had two teachers to match. Two tall, full Colonels, each one wearing a slew of ribbons, topped by a DSC. They taught not just by the manual but by example. By anecdote taken from their own experience, so they knew the truth of what they taught. There were about fifty of us in that class. Most of them were captains and majors interested in staying in the service. I went to class every day with two guys wearing Congressional Medals.

Then, at long last, I finally received my orders to go to Fort Oglethorpe and get my discharge. Oglethorpe was also in Georgia, so, at one time or another I was assigned to three different camps, just in Georgia.

Let's see now, if you add that all up, it makes a grand total of fourteen different Army bases here in the States that I graced with my presence. And if you were paying close attention, they were located in no less than ten different states. Just imagine it! A mind-broadening, all-expense-paid tour like that, and all of it at the expense of the tax payers. Never cost me a dime!

I came back home with that tank destroyer battalion I told you about, the 609th. We left from Le Havre, the same port at which I'd arrived in France only some seven months before. We sailed on what was called a Victory ship, and oddly enough, the name of our ship was the *U. S. Victory*. There were about two thousand soldiers on board. But ours was not the only troop ship to arrive in New York that day. No, there were three others that made port the same day we did. And because my father kept records, I know their names. The *William Tilghman*, the *Robert Owen* and the *Marshall Elliott*.

And on that same Friday, three more troop ships arrived in Boston harbor and two more in Newport News. Nine ships on that single day and that was to go on till the end of the year. That'll give you some idea of the enormity of the logistics involved. And the boys out in the Pacific hadn't even started off on their way home.

When I went overseas, I was six feet tall and weighed a hundred and sixty-five or seventy pounds. When I got home, I was still six feet, but I weighed only a hundred and twenty. But I wasn't sick. No, I was in perfectly good health and in great shape. We all were. When my outfit arrived in Garmisch, I'll bet you couldn't have boiled five pounds of fat out of the whole battery.

When the tugs had tucked us in our berth and the gangplanks had been lowered and we'd filed down, the first thing I saw when I touched land was a whole bank of telephones. There must have been twenty-five or thirty of them, and every one of them was there for us to use to call home. And there was a long-distance operator already assigned to each and every one of those phones, just waiting to put us through. When it came your turn, as soon as you picked up the phone, that operator would say, *Welcome Home! Just tell me who to call.* And she'd put your call straight through, no matter what. Other traffic? She'd interrupt it. Line busy? She'd tell them to get off the line. Those women knew just how to get it done. My call to Shreveport had to pass through switchboards in four of five different cities. It had to be handled every time by another long distance operator and every time plugged in by hand. But it didn't take long at all for my call to get through and it didn't cost me a cent either. They did all of that just for us. Well, not just for us, they did it for everybody who'd been over there and was now coming home.

But the biggest thrill—the thing I treasure most—is the sight of that boat with that brass band that came alongside and followed us all the way in. All those people on it, waving up at us and cheering us on. She was just a little low-lying ship of some kind, maybe eighty or a hundred feet long. Her whole top deck was open and it was obvious that she'd been fitted out just to meet the troop ships that came into the harbor bringing the soldiers home. She ran right alongside us, all the way from the Statue of Liberty, past the Battery, clear up until we were about to be berthed. I can see us now, all lined up on the starboard side, looking right down on her. From where I was, she was just a couple of decks below, so she was close. We could see and hear everything and so could they, waving up.

First thing was that band, playing away for all it was worth. Maybe they were paid, I guess they must have been. But it didn't matter, because you could tell they were playing their hearts out for us. And there were all those people down there waving,. At least two or three hundred people down there on that deck where the band was playing. They were just ordinary people. Civilians. Men and women like you'd see anywhere. And I'll guarantee you *they* weren't paid! Hell no, not those civilians! You could see that just as plain as day. They were there because they *wanted* to be. Because they were *proud* of us, and they wanted us to know it. That's why they'd gone to all that trouble.

Now I'm sorry to be telling you this part, but I guess I should. Coming up the river, after about thirty minutes of all that cheering and music, I began to quietly sob away like a woman. I guess I would have been ashamed but for the fact that I wasn't the only one. There were a lot of others doing the same. So I wasn't really ashamed of myself for crying like that. And that was a welcome change in itself. Not being ashamed. No, there were quite a few other creeps like me standing along that rail, tears running down their face. No one seemed to mind it at all—even the ones who stayed dry. But at least the men standing around me, they didn't feel uncomfortable—like they had to move away from me or anything like that. That's something I'd remember if they had.

My feelings at this reception they gave us? Let me just say that it was pride. A feeling of pride. Of enormous, overpowering and utterly silent pride. Not personal pride, mind you. Not pride in myself, it certainly wasn't that. I hadn't done one damn thing in the whole war I could take any particular pride in, for God's sake! Now, some of those guys from the 609th, those tank destroyer guys, they were standing right there beside me and I knew for a fact how much they'd actually done in the war, the high losses they'd taken. But my pride was not really pride in them either. Not in what they'd done, magnificent though it was. No, the pride I felt was in our whole damned country stretched out there to the west. All the people in it. From coast to coast. Pride in how all those individual human beings had managed, for once, to weld themselves together, by God, into an actual country. Our country. My country! When I get discouraged about our country—and I do that a lot—at least I've got that memory to I hang on to. That day we got back from overseas.

You see, that boat that came alongside us, it didn't just meet our ship, it met every ship that came in that day. And every other day, too, for months and months to come. All those people on that boat down there, they'd volunteered themselves aboard just to wave the soldiers home. Just plain American people, that's who I was proud of. People like those who welcomed us, who went to all that trouble every day, week after week and month after month, until all the millions and millions of men who'd gone over there had come back home. Well—at least all those who ever would.

The biggest trouble with getting old is that trouble seems to be all you're able see anymore. I climb up on the levee and all I see around me is trouble. Trouble everywhere, just lying in wait for all my grandchildren and all their grandchildren. Troubles of every kind. And those troubles are not figments of my imagination either. The lanterns are strung out all up and down the river now. The signs are all there for anyone with eyes to see. But maybe—just *maybe*—after I'm gone, things will turn out all right after all. The future's an unknown god, I've always said that. So who's to say?

So I admit it. Maybe I am wrong to be so pessimistic. Despite all the bonfires, all the lanterns lit up all over the place, all the evidence to the contrary, maybe this beautiful, free country of ours, so long now the light of the world, maybe it'll stay strong and free and I'm just blind to it. Maybe she *is* still the same country she was back then, and I'm just too old and too dumb and too ornery to see it. My God! I hope so!

Although all those people were down there cheering their heads off, I remember how quiet those of us on board were. All of us on the U S *Victory*, lined up along her rail coming into New York harbor. How perfectly quiet we all were, scarcely moving.

Anyhow, that's *one* day I'll never forget. That day in the springtime of my life, returning home at the end of the war. A war we'd finally won, but only because almost the whole of our beautiful country had, for once, magically gathered together and joined hands.

The Swan's Song

Since it was you who suggested it, it's only fitting that you be the first to know. Yeah, I've finally decided I'm going to go ahead with it and write some of those stories down. Do it now before I die. Probably my last act before I step off into the night. When one gets old and starts peering out ahead into the unknown—you know, trying to see if there's anything actually out there—one has this feeling that, at best, you're about to find yourself translated into something you don't understand at all. It's rather fun trying to see yourself that way, as becoming a mere fiction of the mind, like the future. Or maybe as being reduced to just a point. A *something*, but a something without dimension. I might just conceivably wind up at a *location* somewhere out there in that curved space, but with nothing to show for it. Nothing left of the old me, the one that everybody knows and loves. I suppose what I've got in the back of my mind is that still point where Eliot tells us time will verge into timelessness.

My memories are the most of me that's left, so I'll just have to plunder them some more for stories. That means a book of ghost stories. But my ghost stories won't be told in the third person, as though by some omniscient writer of elaborate plots. No sir, they'll be told by the ghost himself. By me alone, a living ghost, a revenant to a past that seemed to have no plot and that's long been gone and which, even now, I do not fully understand. A once-upon-a-time of which I am now the lone survivor.

I'm thinking of writing it in folk-style. If I write it as skaz, I'd be saved all the time and bother of giving it any actual thought at all. I can't tell you how many times I've been told, *Lyons, quit thinking! It weakens the team.* Yeah, that's it! I could just start off talking and it wouldn't much matter what I said. It needn't make any sense at all. And the order in which I said it, that wouldn't matter either. And besides, there's a certain cachet attached nowadays to the nonlinear. I'll just start writing stuff down. Let the ink spill out where it will. Let it drip all down the page if it wants to. Like a Pollack splatter painting, or a Rorschach ink blot. There are scads of folks out there nowadays who'll tell you that they can actually make sense out of all that scatter—that there's deep meaning to be found in those fortuitous images. Some of them even go so far as to say that they constitute art! And that *is* encouraging. Someday, someone who's afflicted with palsy and not paying too close attention might think he sees some sign of art in my own indecipherable Southern scrawls. So who knows?

And something else. When I poke around in my limited store of English words and can't find *le mot juste*, I'll just use the French. Just you try to find the English words that express the other-worldly, ineffable dreamy-ness of that simple little phrase, *claire de lune*. English words that at the same time both reproduce the sense of it and set in motion that whole subtle suite of sensibilities it magically provokes. You can't find those words! Not in English, you can't! *Claire de lune* is simply untranslatable. That's why it's sometimes best to think in the original and not even try to translate. And besides, no one has ever faulted Tolstoy for using the French. Certainly not anyone *we* know! Right? So, yes! I'll try to remember to indulge myself in an occasional soupçon of French. Just a suggestion of it, mind! A clove or two sprigged in here and there. When I feel that both me and the book might benefit from a taste of it. That couldn't hurt too awful much, don't you think?

Of course, I'm far too old and feeble now to promote my book myself, to get out and market it the way all those others do. No personal appearances in old curiosity shops. No, I just can't see myself being pawed over—criticized and picked apart on *Antiques Roadshow*. My book will just have to go out there and face the big world all alone. It'll just have to sell itself, that's all there is to it.

The cover's the most important thing, everybody knows that. The picture on the cover, that's what sells a lot of books. What I need is something that grabs the eye. Maybe a—a vaguely romantic figure. One with a garish splash of red in it, there at just the most eye-catching place on the page. We'll have to see about that.

And lots of pictures. People just *love* pictures. As a matter of fact, most people would rather look at the pictures than read the book. All of my own friends would. In fact, both of them have quit reading books altogether. They said it made their lips too tired.

Speaking of pictures, there's one of me I might use. A young friend of mine took it, a fine photographer named Neil Johnson. He shot this at the very end of 1999, late that December. He wanted a picture of me to go with the one thousand, nine hundred and ninety-nine others he took to mark the end of the century. Neil just said *Don't you dress up now! I want to shoot you the way you are.* But I always try to look my best, especially for a big shoot like that, so I couldn't help myself, I got all dressed up anyway. That's why if you didn't know me better, you might think I'm making a fashion statement here. But that's just the way I always try to look—my absolute, dead level best. Here, take a look.

As soon as I got to Neil's studio, he asked me to give him a little something, so that's what I'm doing here in this picture. I'm either waving a hello or waving a goodbye, I'm not sure which. You can read it either way, depending on whether you think I'm coming or going. Actually, that's something about which I've always been a little hazy myself. But now that I look closer, I believe I was actually waving goodbye. Now, whether it was to Godot, as he departed the building, or to the twentieth century, I'm not now exactly sure.

Hello or goodbye, it didn't much matter then but it certainly does now. Because now I'm going to use this photo in my book. Put it somewhere near the end, where people can see for themselves that what I'm doing is waving farewell—and this time to the reader. Maybe add a neat little caption. Something altogether original and totally unexpected like—like, *Auf Wiederschen*.

I've given the title some thought, too. People like to be at least a little surprised by what they find inside, so the title shouldn't give the whole thing away. With that in mind, I've hit on what just may be a pretty nifty idea. Everybody loves to go to the beach, you know that, and what's the first thing they do when they get there? I mean, after they get tired of shaking the sand out of their flip-flops and watching the ladies pop their bikinis. Why, they rusticate! They stretch out and read! I've been hanging out in those book stores a lot lately. Baskins and Robinson, all those book sellers—just watching what people buy. Anybody going to the beach, they're looking for a good book to take along. I hear it all the time. *I'm headed off for the beach, and I was just wondering if you happen to know a good book I could take along. Nothing serious of course. Just some light reading. A page-turner, if you know what I mean.* That's what makes those beach books sell so big—that strenuous intellectual curiosity that overcomes us once we're off on vacation.

Let me ask you something. If a beach book is what they're looking for, then how would a title like this grab you? *A BEACH BOOK*. Just those three magic words, in big, bold, capital letters. Big enough to read all the way across the room. That way, they'd spot my book the moment they walk in. *Well, what do you know! Just what I was looking for—a beach book! This must be my lucky day*! I can hear them saying that plain as day. Then the next thing I can hear is a sound that falls like music on my ears. It's the sweet sound of a cash register out there somewhere, ringing up another sale.

Something else about that title. If lightening *should* strike and I find myself suddenly deluged with demands for the sequel—a nation-wide outcry for the next generation—why then I'll be ready. I'll already have the perfect title for a spin-off. Listen to this. THE SON OF A BEACH BOOK. Pretty nifty, don't you think?

Oh, sure, I know, you don't have to tell me. I'm not *completely* delusional. It doesn't matter a whit what I write, it won't amount to a damn thing. It'll be nothing more than another one of those unsolicited manuscripts that go through the shredder before being remaindered to the dead letter office. A tedious song cycle sung to an empty hall by a slightly dotty and unraveled old man much given over to strange ways.

But that aside, I'm getting so excited about it I think I might even begin work on it tonight. It's highly unlikely that I'll live to finish it, you understand that of course. Come to think of it, I wonder if Levin ever finished that book he was writing? But even if it should fall out that I don't live to get it done, then that'll be all right, too. I'll just have entered a bit too soon the quiet time at the end of the day.

But to be perfectly frank, I've already taken a few stabs at it. Made some preliminary sketches, and the most mysterious, the most exciting thing has already happened. My book already wakes me up in the middle of the night, just the way that once before I was awakened by the characters in a play I was writing. I've got the strange feeling that in large part that book's already been written. That it's already out there somewhere, just waiting for me to come along with pen and ink and put it down on paper.

When you're almost at the end of the road, it's only natural to turn around and look back. To take just one last, long look back down the way you've come. That's what I've been doing for some time now, and when I do that, when I take that sentimental journey back in time, I'm overwhelmed by all the sensations that well up in me. I have this one sensation I can only describe as neither thought nor feeling but both together and all at once, all distinction gone. And the sense of well-being that overcomes me is so powerful, the summing-up so happy, that I'm filled to the overflowing with what I can only describe as elation. A pure and simple joyfulness. I'd share it with you if I could, but I can't. You'd have to have known my parents yourself, but since you never did, it wouldn't make any sense for me even to try.

There now, I hope you don't object too much to these occasional jaunts of mine into, shall I say, into non-sequitur, if not into total irrelevance? Not that there isn't that occasional work of low art in which there's a sense to it that's not readily apparent. That one suspects might possibly lie there somewhere, hidden just out of sight under the jumble, beneath a seeming surface incoherence.

Who'll I get to edit it? Why, I'll edit it myself of course! I don't want anybody to be substituting his voice for mine. That way, they'll know it's me speaking and not some impostor. And besides, I've always taken pride in making my own mistakes. I'm rather good at it, really. It comes with long experience.

Oh, yes, I know. My book will be far too wordy, too over-written and over-wrought. Not to mention, rough-hewn and clumsy. Anything more demanding than homespun would be quite beyond me anyhow. But that's all I can tell you about my book right now. Even that little may be more than I have any right to say. I haven't actually read it yet myself, you know.

Sitting here, I'm minded of my Grandfather Hall. How he'd sit outside for a long time every evening before going in for his supper. He was always so silent, looking out there across Lake Chetek. But what was he thinking about? Was it about all those fish he and his two friends had caught there on that day so long before? No, I don't think it was about fish. Then about his little white dog named Tex? That's getting closer. I think that most of all he was thinking about his childhood, his life growing up on the farm out on Eagle Prairie. About his parents. About his mother, Mary. Mary Scally Hall, who everyone said was the real farmer of the family. And about his father, Michael Hall, who came into that country when little more than a boy and with nothing to his name. And, but for Mary, all alone in that strange land, and who, ten years later, was elected the High Sheriff of the whole of Chippewa County. My grandfather had some things that were worth thinking about.

You've got to forgive me for this, but on those evenings when you're not here and I'm all alone, that's when I go over in my head some of the ten thousand things that make up a person's life. And there are three memories—three in particular—that always come flooding back over me every time. I look over there at her grave and I find myself saying the same thing over and over again, saying it right out loud. *Scout! Scout! Oh, Scout!* That's when I get myself up and go over there and sit by her side a while, before I come back here and pour myself another drink of whiskey.

Then I look out over that glorious garden out there, that sylvan palace my mother made out of nothing but flatwoods. Once raw dirt but now covered over with its carpet of green. I think about my parents. About how blessed I am to have two beautiful people like them to look back on and think about. When I die, I'd like nothing better than to return to the place I came from—which, as best I can tell, was that dream my parents must once have had of me, long, long before I was ever born.

Sorry, I didn't mean to burden you with any more of my personal feelings but that's just the plain truth of it, so there.

But now I've become just like him. Like my Grandfather Hall. Except that I'm not looking out across one of Wisconsin's glaciated lakes the way he used to do. I spend my evenings now looking out across a swimming hole. It's water all right, but it's not at all the same thing as looking across a lake. No, it's just a swimming pool, but it *is* where all my children learned to swim and that means a lot. And right over there is where my mother made her own peaceful garden, so, although I don't have my grandfather's far distant shore to look at, I do have my mother's garden. And I have that gnarly old loblolly pine you see over there, I've got him. He wasn't exactly young sixty years ago when he and I first met, but now he's just another old grandfather, wrapped in the arms of that mulberry tree like the old moon in the arms of the new.

I used to be full of advice for everybody, but now I don't know what I'd say to them if anyone asked. But this new-found ignorance of mine doesn't stop me from worrying. Even though I know perfectly well I shouldn't. I haven't quite got it through my thick skull yet that it'll all be in other hands soon enough.

So although we'll be parting company pretty soon now, I won't be giving you any last minute advice. No, but I do have a little prophecy for you. One of these days, when you grow old like me, you'll find yourself looking back on your own past, the life and times through which you've lived, all that irrational *Sturm und Drang,* and when that time comes, if you don't count yourself as one the luckiest people alive to have lived your life back in the good old days, then the next thing you know you'll be thinking that maybe you'd have been better off not to have lived at all.

But now, there's one more story I'd like for you to hear. It's an important story, too, that's why I've saved it for last. Then you and I will just have to shake hands, turn our backs on each other and walk away. Because that's what all good friends are obliged to do when their good times together come to an end and they just don't have the courage to say good bye. But just so you'll know—when I leave here I'll be going straight in to start work on my book. That book of memories, that omnium gatherum which even from the very first day you've been kind enough to insist that I write.

Opus 9

Pavane for a Dead Prince:
Plot N Row 7 Grave 17

SOMEWHERE IN THE NORTH OF FRANCE (March 18)—On this Sunday afternoon in 1945, I have made of myself a ghost, a mute and invisible revenant to a scene taking place in Company Headquarters, 3264th Signal Company, at which I was not myself present but of which, sixty-five years later, I would be told by one of those two officers you see over there across the room.
Lt. Charlie Higgins—Second Lieutenant Charles Alfred Higgins, Jr. of 906 Dupont Road, Wilmington, Delaware—is talking with another American officer who's come here to the 3264th for a visit with Higgins. That address, 906 Dupont Road, is the home of Higgins' parents. Higgins' father is the President of Hercules Powder Company. Hercules is an enormous munitions company controlled by Dupont. That other officer I see is Lt. Jack Moment—Second Lieutenant John Moment, of 815 Park Avenue, Plainfield, New Jersey. That's the address of the Presbyterian manse in Plainfield, the home of Moment's parents. His father is the Minister of The First Presbyterian Church there. Lt. Higgins is a photographer. That's his job with his Signal Company, taking pictures. Lt. Moment is a paratrooper, an artillery Forward Observer serving with one of the firing batteries of the 17th Airborne Division. In combat, Forward Observers in the artillery are generally to be found up front with the infantry. You can look for him at some coign of vantage from which to best observe the enemy's positions in order to direct the fire of the artillery. That's what Lt. Moment does. That's his job.
Watching the two of them together, even a stranger would have guessed them to be the old friends they are. They're talking hard and fast. Obviously, there's an awful lot they need to talk about. So much to catch up on, and so little time. That the two of them, each in an American military unit wholly unrelated to the other, have somehow managed to be here together, is not nearly so strange as it might at first seem. In fact, the sort of thing we're seeing here

has become a commonplace in the ETO. In the midst of this war, the whereabouts of our friends is a matter of great concern to every one of us who's over here. And if we know their units, then there's always the chance that we can get to them, wherever they are.

The 17th Airborne is a new division, only recently formed back in England. But it has already seen action in the Allied counter-offensive in the southern part of the Bulge. But not yet has Lt. Moment's division made an *airborne* assault. Not yet made a drop into combat. So far, they've just jumped off the back end of a truck.

But now, as I watch and listen, the two of them begin a discussion of some military action in which they have some reason to believe they will both be involved. It's obviously something of considerable magnitude, and, apparently, it might take place very soon. Sixty-five years later, in an e-mail dated March 7, 2005, Jack Moment had this to tell me about his meeting with Charlie Higgins on that Sunday.

"I went up to Charlie Higgins's headquarters a few days before the big drop over the Rhine where he was killed. As a matter of fact we both had an interest in that operation since I was going as a paratrooper and he was going along to photograph the event. He knew a lot more than I did about what was to happen and I got myself in a bit of a jam by hinting that I knew more than I should. Showing off, I suppose. Some army spooks had me on the carpet for quite a while – thinking that perhaps I was about to give the game away."

AN AMERICAN AIR BASE SOMEWHERE IN NORTH-CENTRAL FRANCE (March 24)—At 7:17 a.m. this Saturday morning, after a breakfast of steak and eggs, more than nine thousand men of the 17th Airborne begin their departure for the Rhine. They are leaving on transport aircraft flying out of 17 different airfields scattered about the countryside. A great number of the men, but by no means all, are aboard aircraft which are not tugging gliders. Those aircraft free of gliders number 72 C-46s and 226 C-47s. Lt. Higgins had volunteered for the mission, and he's aboard one of those transports. Its crew chief gives us this early account of Lt. Higgins.

Before the take-off, Lt. Higgins told us that he was not going to wear a flak-suit or parachute. He said, 'The weight and bulkiness of the 'chute and flak-suit will make it impossible for me to get good pictures. I must be able to move about freely.' We told him that the flak-suit was not essential but the 'chute should be worn. I noticed that at the time of the take-off he had neither of them on.

But in addition to those 298 aircraft carrying paratroopers, another 610 C-47s are struggling their way off the ground and slowly climbing out, each towing one or two 906 Waco CG-4A gliders. Lt. Moment is aboard one of those gliders. Three or four enlisted men and a 75mm pack howitzer are with him. At 8:58 a.m. the last of those 908 aircraft that carry the men and equipment of the 17th Airborne breaks ground.

The planes carrying the troopers who are to jump have been holding in a pattern above, waiting for the other transports with their tows of gliders to climb up and join them. Almost two hours have been required to get them all into the air, where, once there, they slowly assemble into a long, thin line. A line of aircraft stretching across the sky to its eastern limits and flying just as passenger pigeons were once seen to fly, patiently following one another in the same slow, painstaking and dutiful way.

But the 17th Airborne is only one-half of this airborne operation, an operation code-named "Operation Varsity." And Varsity itself is only the airborne phase of an enormous joint venture being here begun by the Americans, the British, and the Canadians. That far larger, but no grander, enterprise of which Varsity is a part is code-named *Plunder* and Plunder will, in magnitude, be second only to the Normandy invasion itself.

For at about the same time, from eleven airfields in southeastern England, the British 6th Airborne Division, the "Red Devils", veterans of the D-Day drop into Normandy, is also making its own unhurried way aloft. That done, it will cross the Channel to join the American air armada over Brussels, Belgium, from which city these two airborne divisions will then proceed on together in the same stately fashion the last hundred miles to the drop area in the vicinity of Wesel, a German city just east of the Rhine.

The British lift of its own 6th Airborne consists of 42 Douglas C-54s and 752 C-47s, plus a tow of 420 Airspeed Horsa and General Aircraft Hamilcar gliders, these British gliders being so large and heavy that each has to be towed singly. An escort of 676 fighters from the U.S. Ninth Air Force and 213 fighters of the Royal Air Force is on watch, high up above all these extremely slow and utterly defenseless prop-driven aircraft. This long, thin line stretches a distance of almost 200 miles and its passage requires more than two and a half hours, or so the history of it tells us. But I'm in no need of that history. I saw them myself when they passed. As I believe I told you once—it may even have been on the very first evening we sat down together to talk—I saw that armada myself. I saw the whole thing with my own eyes, so the flight of those planes is not something I have to imagine. All I have to do is remember. Remember the sight of their passage as they made their way past us. How sad it all seemed and slow. *Lento e tristo,* like Massenet's *Élégie*. The sadness that comes with the dying away of bird song and the loss of all gladness forever. *Vous avez fuit pour toujours. Tout est flétri! Pour toujours!*

But these two divisions, nearly 18,000 troopers, though they constitute the vanguard of Plunder, are but two of the *twenty-seven* divisions committed to that attack on the Germans across the Rhine. The forces commanded by Montgomery consist, in addition to these two airborne divisions, seventeen infantry divisions, eight armored divisions, five armored brigades and a Canadian infantry brigade.

Soon now, as the cowcatcher of this sky train reaches the river Rhine, its caboose will still be well west of Brussels, 100 miles to the rear. Including the pilots and crews of all those aircraft, this airborne force numbers some 25,000 men. But there's not one among them who so much as notices our inconsequential little band of Second Louies down there on that dirt road far to the south as we stand around that army six by six. All of us stamping our boots in the cold, cold ground as we gaze up in silence, our eyes riveted on that long sky train rolling by.

A certain Sergeant Gardner is the Crew Chief on the C-47 to which Lt. Higgins was assigned and we've already heard from him about Lt. Higgins at the time of take-off. But now, because Sgt.

Gardner, alone among the four-man crew, managed to survive, we have what only he was left alive to tell. Sgt. Gardiner continues.

Things went along OK until we had dropped the troopers and passed over the DZ (Drop Zone), then all hell broke loose – the flak was very thick and started flying in the jump doors. I threw Lt. Higgins on the floor, covering him with my body and flak-suit to keep him from being injured. All of a sudden, the jump bell rang and I started to bail out. As I stood in the door, ready to jump, I saw him, on his hands and knees, reaching for his 'chute. The next thing I knew, I was in the hospital.

Sgt. Gardner goes on to tell us that when he hooked up to jump, there was a fire burning under the floorboard. That's the last report I have of the part Lt. Higgins played in that big drop across the Rhine.

The next reliable information is that contained in a letter dated May 16, 1945 and written to his mother by a soldier, Corporal Harriss, who, being himself a member of the 3264th Signal Company, knew Lt. Higgins very, very well. Among other things, Cpl. Harriss had this to say in that long belated letter home:

Because of security regulations, I have been unable to mention anything about Lt. Higgins. He was photographing an Airborne operation over the Rhine river; it was a tough assignment and he didn't feel like asking any of us to do the job. Shortly after the mission I went to the front with a searching party, looking for planes and crews. Unfortunately, we had to return before finding the ship he was on. Upon returning to the base, I interviewed the crew chief, and as far as I know the only survivor, on the plane. ...

I don't know what has developed since I left the field but presume that the ship and bodies have been found. It was a tough break; I had grown very fond of him. He was one of the best officers I have ever known and a real pal of all of us. I really admired him.

There exists one more contemporaneous letter, this being one from Janice Hunt to Dr. Allan Heely, at that time Lawrenceville's

Headmaster. Ms. Hunt, though secretary to Lt. Higgins' father, is writing at the request of Lt. Higgins' mother. On June 11, 1945, Ms. Hunt writes to Dr. Heely:

There has been received a letter from Lt. Herod, Commanding Officer of the 3264th Signal Service Company, of which Charlie was a member. According to this letter, Lt. Higgins was 'killed in the Line of Duty near Wesel, Germany on the 24th of March.' Lt. Herod also reports that 'Charles is now resting in a United States Military Cemetery,' and says, 'I knew your son personally . . . and I have the highest respect for him, his ideals and his work with this organization. Charles was an inspiration for the men he worked with and his influence with them was beyond description. Never once have I heard anything other than a compliment for Charles and it was a real pleasure having him in my company.'

There were five people in the plane at the time it was shot down, and from letters received from some of the other families it appears that the pilot, co-pilot and Charlie are reported killed, a sergeant (the radio man) is reported missing, and the one survivor, Sergeant Gardner, has returned to his unit.

This summarizes the most recent information which Mr. and Mrs. Higgins have received.

That book which commemorates the fiftieth reunion of Yale's Class of 1944 has much the same to say. Here it is.

12. Charles Alfred Higgins, Jr. of Wilmington, Delaware, was a member of Davenport College and Delta Kappa Epsilon. He left Yale in September 1943 to join the Army Signal Corps, and earned his commission a year later at Fort Monmouth, New Jersey. He attended the Signal Corps Photography School and served as a photography instructor until July 1944, when he was sent to England and subsequently to France. He was killed in action on March 24, 1945, while photographing an airborne assault over the

Rhine. *After dropping paratroops over the Drop Zone, his plane was hit by heavy flak. The only survivor, who parachuted to safety, later confirmed that Lieutenant Higgins had made a deliberate decision not to wear a parachute that day. To make sure of taking good pictures, he wanted maximum freedom of movement.*

And what of my other roommate, Lt. Moment? What became of him that day? After release from its tow plane, his glider, under heavy German gunfire, did make it to the earth for the controlled crash which, for the military gliders of that era, passed for a highly successful landing, meaning one in which the men aboard all survived more or less intact. And his division *did* accomplish all of their primary missions. It *did* secure the necessary airhead across the Rhine and it *did* clear the enemy from the Diersfordter Forest and it *did* seize the bridges over the Issel River, and thus prevent German reinforcements from reaching the beachhead then being established by the ground forces. Overall, the operation was a tremendous success, with troops and supplies crossing the river and moving easily inland. Casualties? In that action alone, the 17th Airborne suffered 430 killed, 834 wounded and 81 missing.

So that, in brief, is the account of Lt. Moment's first and last airborne combat assault. But, as I said, this was not the first time his division had seen action. Some months prior to the drop on Wesel, the 17th Airborne had been very much involved in the Battle of the Bulge, but about his earlier combat experiences at the Bulge, Moment had almost nothing he cared to tell me before he died.

Well, on Wednesday, March 9, 2005, Jack did send me a brief bit about it—just the kind of thing you'd expect from him.

Doesn't life get stranger and stranger? At Yale I took O'Neill's freshman course in Homer and then, sophomore year, Aristophanes and others with a young instructor whose name I've now forgotten. In that class was a guy called Ben Something-or-other whom I bumped into in Germany in a wheat field that we were using as a temporary airstrip for our liaison planes. Such a surprise! He wasn't the only surprise: there was a young French girl there, in a house by the field, who, when we landed, met our little plane carrying a bouquet of flowers for me — every day. Ah, youth! After the war I bumped into O'Neill a few times, too. I lived right across the street from the Minetta Tavern (locale for The Iceman Cometh*) where he was occasionally seen in the days when he was doing a radio show on public radio or some such. Good God! The stories could go on forever."*

Jack's gone now, but even living on oxygen, as he was when he wrote that, how like him it was to wish to make light of the dark.

    Jack told me that, following Charlie's death, his own parents did what they could to comfort Mr. and Mrs. Higgins, and that in gratitude the Higgins presented a pair of beautiful, silver communion cups which stand there in his father's church to this day. One is inscribed to Charlie Higgins and the other to Jack's own brother, Robert Moment. Robert was also killed in the war. He was a naval aviator flying a PBY. Where he'd been earlier, I don't know, but late in the war, he flying guard duty in the San Francisco Bay area. That was at a time when the formation of the United Nations Organization was taking place there in San Francisco. Robert's plane crashed into a mountain at the north end of the Golden Gate Bridge. If you've never heard of it, the United Nations Organization was the immediate predecessor to the current United Nations.

    When Charlie and I, and Jack Moment and Johnny Green and Bill Flemer were all there together at Lawrenceville, that part of central Jersey in which the school had so happily founded itself was indeed a garden. And for me it was a magical garden. Like my natal home in the South and the other home of my heart in the North, my home there in the East was the last of the three magical gardens in which I'd lived all my life until the war. And I can still see Eden, out there to the west. This country of ours would still be a garden if only we had the eyes to see it and sense enough to keep it green.

    In that part of Jersey, I quite well remember seeing the hunters out walking the fields in the fall. They'd be after pheasants and rabbits, with their guns and their dogs. I still remember helping Flemer, as we went from one to another of those old trees on The Circle. All of them had been planted there by Olmstead himself in 1893, when he was also at work on The Biltmore and The Chicago

World's Fair. We put new tags on every one of them. Brass tags that Bill had made himself and that bore not only their common names, but those that Linnaeus gave them. Bill also remembered that we'd done that. The last thing I heard from him before he died was about how the two of us went around The Circle, putting all those new brass tags on all of Olmstead's trees. I wonder if any of those original old trees are still living. And if they are, I wonder if our tags are still there.

I don't think I've said much about my old friend Bill Flemer. He couldn't stand hanging around after Pearl Harbor for long, so he left school early like so many did. In the war, he was a sergeant in an engineer camouflage battalion that was engaged from D+6 to the end of it. Let me read for you something from one of the painfully handwritten letters I got from Bill before he died.

Like you, I will forever admire Charlie Higgins, who was my room mate freshman year at Yale. After the end of WW II I planted as a memorial to Charlie a grove of rare and unusual oaks. The dedication was attended by Mrs. Higgins and Allan Heely.

I asked him, but Bill seemed not to remember just where it was he planted that grove of oaks. I've made other attempts—all unsuccessful, I'm afraid—to determine its location, because, from the most ancient of times, man has planted sacred groves and if there's such a thing as a *modern* sacred grove, surely this is one. Hard to believe it's gone missing all these years. Perhaps someday it'll turn up again, who knows? Or perhaps not. Because that grove is sacred and likely not to be easily found. Nor entered upon lightly. It's a magical place, a kingdom all its own. A place, like *La Forêt d'Ardennes*, made magical by Shakespeare, but also hallowed by all those who died in those great battles fought there, back and forth, in the two wars that took place in the first half of my own century.

Johnny Green's gone, too. He spent three years in the Navy. He said that although he'd spent more than two of those years at sea, nothing very remarkable ever seemed to happen. After the war, he went to Harvard Law School and served thereafter as the General Counsel and an officer of two family companies, Johnson & Johnson and Richardson-Vicks. I saw Johnny last in 1980. As I say, he's been dead some years now, I think about fifteen.

I might have told you, but that 1980 reunion at Lawrenceville was also the last time I saw Jack Moment. Then, a couple of years back, Jack Moment and I found each other again. We began to talk, this time mostly by e-mail, and it was just as though one of us had only stepped out the room to answer his cell. That's always the way it is with those deep, true friendships of our youth.

Among other things we discussed, Jack and I had a brief exchange about all this talk that's been going around lately about our generation. You've heard it yourself—that ours is *the greatest generation*? I told Jack I'd never liked hearing it. It made me feel self-conscious—like I didn't know which way to turn. Jack felt the same. Here's what he wrote back.

I don't cotton to the greatest generation idea either. I would give credit to the times. A generation seems to rise to meet the challenges it is faced with.

But nowadays, there are a lot of men—especially younger men—who perk up when they learn that I served for a while during the war. Some of them would draw me out, too, if it weren't for fear of treading on tender ground, So they don't probe, but here lately, several of them, four or five, have come up to me and looked me straight in the eye and thanked me for what my generation did in that war back then. Thanked me *personally*! It seems odd, but most of them have been strangers, and that's what seems to unhinge me the most—when a perfect stranger does that to me. You can't imagine how wrenching that is! They should thank *me*? Almost every time that happens, I have to turn away to hide what's welling up. Because I know exactly what it is they're feeling. What they're trying so hard to say. Haven't I felt it myself all these years, for God's sake!

By now, I can recognize one as soon as I see him. He's got his heart in his hand, and he's holding it out to me. You can see that as plain as day. He's wanting desperately for me to look at him. To look him level in the eye, the way he's looking at me, so he can tell me something important—man-to-man. But what I wish he could understand—what I wish I could explain to him is—*Please don't hold your heart out to me, my friend. Don't thank me, save your thanks for Higgins, and all those others over there with him.*

In his letter of June 11, 1945, Lt. Herod wrote this to Mr. and Mrs. Higgins, "*Charles is now resting in a United States Military Cemetery.*" And yes, his body was eventually recovered and buried in a very fitting place. Which is to say, in a military cemetery. That cemetery, I've recently found out, is the Netherlands American Cemetery and Memorial, and it's situated in the town of Margraten, Netherlands. Margraten lies close by Maastricht, and that's a place that's less than forty miles northwest of Verviers. There's a Court of Honor in that cemetery and in it can be found the names—only the *names*, mind you—of 1,723 American soldiers who fought in that war and who are still missing in action and whose graves, if any, lie elsewhere in the immediate area, every one of them unknown and untended. But the bodies of 8,301 *known* American dead *do* lie buried there and almost all of them, as did Lt. Higgins, lost their lives in fighting that took place nearby.

That's a total of 10,024 service men whose sole remains are to be found buried in the cold, chalky soil of that one cemetery. That same number, 10,024, is, as I recall, almost precisely the size of an armored division in World War II. Just imagine, if you can, the whole of the Tenth Armored Division, my old division, lined up out on the parade ground, standing in division review, every man and officer in it, and then, if you can, imagine them all slain in battle, every single one of them suddenly struck dead, and all their bodies—a whole division of dead men, laid out in rows to be buried in that distant place. Because that's just how many of our boys have been buried all these years in that one hallowed ground. All of them dead and buried together, row upon row, there in that Flanders field. A place, I'm told, where poppies grow—made to flourish by the very digging of their graves. And that should give you some sense of the awful magnitude of such a morgue as that.

Now that I know where they buried Higgins, I'd go over there myself, but I'm too old for a trip like that any more. But now, if you should be over there sometime yourself and happen to be in the vicinity of Maastricht, there's something you could do for me.

Just go out to the American military cemetery in Margraten and find Charlie's grave. And if you don't mind, would you just take a second to bend down and tell him I'm still OK? You shouldn't have any trouble at all finding the place. Just go to Plot N Row 7 Grave 17.

AMERICAN BATTLE MONUMENTS COMMISSION

THE WORLD WAR II HONOR ROLL

Charles A. Higgins, Jr.

Second Lieutenant, U.S. Army

Service # O1648625

3264th Signal Company

Entered the Service from: Delaware
Died: 24-Mar-45
Buried at: Plot N Row 7 Grave 17
Netherlands American Cemetery
Margraten, Netherlands

Awards: Silver Star, Purple Heart

There! I'm finally finished.
But Lord! What wouldn't I give,
if only the Fates had dealt him a better hand
and he were sitting here with us now, at the end.

Acknowledgments.

First and last, this book owes its very existence to the infinite patience and loving support of my wife, Peggy McClure Lyons, whose thankless lot it's been to suffer through the near-constant abstraction of her husband, as, turning away from the *here* and the *now*, he stared vacantly back down that long way he'd come, all in order that he might find, buried in shallow graves strewn here and there along the road, the remains of an altogether unremarkable past, and might, as a matter conceivably of interest to his family, if not to the general reader, disinter, bone by dearly remembered bone, at least a few of the memories which the good fortune of a long, happy and active life had leisurely buried there.

Next go my thanks to my daughter, Stafford Lyons, who has not only contributed her own song to the book, and proofread the penultimate text, but has also brought her critical eye and constructive blue pencil to three very early preliminary sketches, thereby qualifying herself as the only thing in the way "editor" this book has ever seen. This book is immeasurably better for her.

Then, too, there is my daughter, Sally Lyons Wood, whom I must thank, because it was Sally who not only retrieved from their ancient repositories and first digitized some of the photographs you've seen in this book but was a more or less constant resource in my perennial problems with my dang-blasted old compooper.

Among the number of pleasant and helpful people I came across for the first time in the course of making this book, at the forefront is my new and most congenial friend, close but never seen, intimate yet otherwise unknown, Jacquelin (Jacqi) Haun, Archivist of The Bunn Library at The Lawrenceville School. I would say more—much more—in praise of her and her extraordinary professional talents but refrain from doing so out of a reasonable respect for her innate modesty, my fear being that, although the words I have in mind using are not in the least intemperate, they might seem so to those who don't know her, thus causing her some unfortunate personal embarrassment should she read this book.

Mr. Evan Thomas, Assistant Managing Editor of Newsweek, is a major writer of history and has generously given me permission to include in my own book of songs a lengthy quote from his very recently published, and much acclaimed, *Sea of Thunder*. You and I have Mr. Thomas to thank for the breathtaking account he has given us, and which I have quoted *in extenso*, of Nick Fellner's attack on history's greatest battleship, Japan's *Yamato*.

Poking through the embers of fires long thought dead, in one such old hearth I turned up, not one but *two* live coals. Nick Fellner and Bill Flemer. From Nick, I've heard extensively and continue to hear, Nick being still very much alive. From Bill, I unfortunately heard less often, and then not at all. Bill died just three months ago, the last to go of those four wonderful friends I made when I went away to school.

Fletcher Thorne-Thomsen, an old friend long, long before this book, has done it a great service by scanning into digital many of the images you've seen here, including, most importantly, the portrait of my mother.

My young friend, the photographer Neil Johnson, did, on his own initiative, both take the picture of me waiving goodbye that appears towards the end of the book and approve my use of it here.

If you imagined that, in the course of writing this book, I must have put myself in touch, either for purposes of confirmation or discovery, with numerous persons who were, or had been, themselves in touch with the persons of this book, or who had knowledge of its events, you would be correct. What you might *not* have imagined is that the information, if any, either confirmed or discovered, failed, more often than not, and for sundry reasons, to make its appearance in the book. Nevertheless, watching the lovely birds that sometimes flew out of those numerous bushes I kicked was always great sleuthing-fun and often, in itself, an act of "bringing the dead to life."

For instance, although my book makes only slight and passing reference to the Sgt. Wister I had known in Battery B, 419th Field Artillery Battalion, I am indebted to two people for making it possible for me to positively identify the person I knew briefly in the service only as "Sgt. Wister." Those two persons are Professor

James A Butler of the Department of English at La Salle University, Philadelphia, and Mrs. Murray J. Belman of Washington, DC. I thank them both so much for their kindnesses to a Southern stranger. My "Sgt. Wister" was, in fact, Charles Kemble Butler Wister, known within his family sometimes as "Carl", and he was indeed a son of Owen Wister, his second son. And I thank Professor Butler and Mrs. Belman also for pointing out the way to Sgt. Wister's son, Charles Kemble Butler Wister, Jr. Owing solely to the two of them, I was able to find Charles in Sun Valley, Idaho, and to have a brief but extremely pleasant e-mail chat with him about his father and the 419th AFA Battalion, with which his father and I had both served for a time. (Coincidentally and parenthetically—and life is certainly full of both, isn't it?—it turned out that Charles is close to the Gene Holmans, old friends of mine who live out around Sun Valley.)

When this book was just a few wisps of smoke seen coming out of my ears, my dear friends, Betsy and Martin Rosen, were early enthusiasts. In fact, when I was first groping about in the dark confines of the subconscious for what might possibly be my true intentions, it was Betsy who, having seen only a dozen pages of some ur-scribblings, instantly, instinctively, and correctly, divined that it was *elegy* that was lying there in wait for me, silent and unseen in the gloom. The instant I saw her word *elegiac*, I knew that hers was the only word that truly expressed the feelings that well up, sweeping over me and turning to tears whenever I look back into the faces and eyes of some of those wonderful people I knew so well and loved so much so long ago.

Another confidence-builder was someone I never met, not face to face. Nor was it by some concatenation of coincidence that our paths would cross, but rather by the purest of serendipities. Serendipity is *not*, as so many think, an event owing itself to sheer, raw luck. No, a serendipitous event is one which, though not at all anticipated, follows in <u>direct</u> and <u>necessary</u> consequence of some purposeful action in which the serendipity finds its springs.

That someone was Mrs. Shearen Elebash, better known as "Tibby". We never did meet, Tibby and I didn't. Only via e-mails but quite a few of them. And once or twice by telephone, the first time being when she called to tell me that her husband—and my friend—Shearen, had died.

It's very strange but I don't think I've even mentioned Shearen. He and Frank Sommer, I suppose, were the closest and warmest of all the new friends I made when I went up to Yale. Even as an undergraduate, Frank had an infectious and all-consuming interest in the Great Questions of cultural and intellectual history, an interest which was to become the story of his life, so it was entirely predictable that, among other admirable activities, he would, after completing graduate work both at Yale and at Cambridge University, founding the Winterthur Program at the H. F. DuPont Museum in Wilmington and serving as its first coordinator, studying for three years with the Jesuits, teaching at the University of Delaware and at Winterthur itself, serving as a professional collector of printed books, manuscripts, drawings, micromedia and photographs for cultural research and serving as a Professor and researcher in the history of American culture and its European origins, finally become the Retired Head Of the Winterthur Library. About thirty-five years ago, I went to Wilmington and spent a day and evening with Frank. He hadn't changed a bit. I thank God for it. Frank never married and never learned to drive an automobile. Too busy.

About a year ago, I had a hand-written letter from Frank. He died last fall. Shearen Elebash had died the fall before that. After Shearen died, that's when I first heard from Tibby. As I say, Shearen and I had not only sung together all the way around South America and through Yale, we'd hung together, too. We were real close. Two Southern boys up North, you know how that is. Shearen contributed a piece about himself to our Fiftieth reunion book and in it he lists six of his most significant personal memories. The very first item on that list is this one. *"Singing in the great opera houses of South America with Charlie Lyons, Sam Ross and Steve Stack."*

In the war, Shearen had been a navigator, both in the ETO and in Burma. After the war, I talked with Shearen a few times on the telephone but saw him once. He'd become, inter alia, a solo entertainer, appearing for hire at large functions here and there around the country. Singing, playing the piano, telling wonderfully funny Southern stories. You'd have loved him. I can say that because he once performed here. At a big appreciation dinner for Barksdale Field, put on by our chamber of commerce. When he called me to tell me he'd be here, I told him not to make a hotel reservation. He could stay with us, we had plenty of room. Which he did. He wound up staying over an extra day and a night, just so we could visit. We had a wonderful time together, most of it around that piano. That, by the way, was the same piano which Nan Merriman would stand around in silence, refusing to join in the song. And if you're still with me, more than fifty years ago, when we lived on Wilder Place, that same piano sat in our living room. For a while, Van Cliburn and his mother were living directly across the street and he could see the children playing in the yard and hear my wife playing on the house, so seeing that, he once or twice walked over and sat down and played that piano a while for the children.

But it was only as Shearen's wife that I was first aware of the name, Tibby. But after she called, it gradually came to light that we had been previously long related and in several ways, all utterly unconnected with Shearen. She was once, in the years when she lived in New Orleans, my father's personal friend and political ally. Delightful herself, she was, again while she lived in New Orleans, the warm friend of my equally delightful cousin, Gordon Ewin and his wife. And finally, she turned out to be a close relative through marriage, and a friend by choice, of Jack and Barbara Moment.

Well, yes—there was one other thing, too, another coincidental relationship. Tibby was born Willey-Gayle Martin, a name so Southern that she simply *must* have, as indeed she did, come off a plantation outside Montgomery, Alabama, the very Seat itself of the Confederacy. Eventually, and solely through the agency of that same continuing serendipity, I was to discover that Tibby had been a friend from girlhood of yet another certain young lady from Montgomery, a vivacious dance partner I first met in the thirties, at the Shipley School in Bryn Mawr, and whom I came to much admire—as who would not, did they but know her?

On August 6, 2006, I had an e-mail from Tibby. She was much interested in my book and wanted to see something, so I'd sent her a copy of the very first song I sang, "Prelude in a Minor Key".

Here's what she said in that e-mail. *Charlton, what a haunting, beautiful song/chapter. Very impressive writing. I've often thought memories are snapshots—and your snapshot of that ghostly, airborne pavane (marvelous simile) is now a double exposure, overlaid with the faces of two friends. Life IS a constant amazement. You are doing a beautiful job and yes, I wish I could join that evening gathering by the pool to hear more. Tibby.*

When I read that, I was ecstatic of course. She wanted to be there! Be there for more of the story-telling! But when the book comes out, Tibby won't be there. Last October 15th she died. But not for me, she didn't! A story teller is never happier than when a stranger walks up and sits down to listen. If you want the back-story, the reason *behind* my book, maybe that's it, right there.

It was nice hearing again from my old friends Phyllis and Bob Oakley, who troubled to confirm all my memories of Vera and Tony and of the terror that lay over Lebanon when I was there.

At the onset of gestation, there were four academics who lent me comfort. My thanks go to all four. To Laura McLemore, the Archivist at Louisiana State University in Shreveport. To Michael Futreal and his wife, Michelle Wolkomir, both of the faculty of Centenary College, Shreveport, Louisiana, and to Marsha Recknagle, of Rice University in Houston, Texas, for each of them, after seeing the first three or four songs—and those few in their most primitive states—gave an encouraging "thumbs-up" to what could then have been no more than the suggestion of the remote possibility that eventually something slightly resembling a "life-literature" might, conceivably, one day arise out of such primordial ooze.

This book owes much to the expertise with images I was lucky to find in Wendy Loy. Wendy is associated with Hilliard Petroleum, the oil company which is a direct descendant of my old outfit, Lyons Petroleum. What was to become "Lyons Petroleum" came into existence in 1927 when my father, recognizing opportunity wherever he saw it, first began to realize that he was no longer altogether in the public practice of law but was gravitating, slowly but inexorably, into the oil business. That he had, in fact, already morphed himself into "an oil man". Hilliard Petroleum, succeeding Lyons Petroleum some twenty years ago, has, first under the leadership of Gene Hilliard, my old friend and business partner of more than fifty years, and now under that of his son, "Gene Three", continued the long tradition. And, if I may be permitted to make such a grand and lofty claim in behalf of my many, many friends, good and old, who've spent their lifetimes there in a common effort to create a bit of new wealth through unflagging pursuit of the humble hydrocarbon—Hilliard Petroleum is now not merely an economic success, but, now recognized as a congenial and productive place to work, may be said to be *un succès d'estime*.

To Melodee Eckerman, Editor of The Chetek Alert, and to Mike McGinnis, also of Chetek, I am indebted for some very early history which enabled me to confirm to my own satisfaction that in 1870 the waters of Lake Chetek were such that Michael and Mary Hall could indeed have got by ox cart around to the lake's north shore and that my great grandfather had indeed made the first traces of that ancient trail that were still visible there, right at the shoreline, when I was a boy and even as a young man there with my children.

And to Patricia Hebert and her niece, Jeanne Hebert, of Chippewa Falls, Wisconsin, I am similarly indebted for their researches involving the early history of the Hall farm out on Eagle Prairie, as well as for other information concerning the early history of that sawmill town to which my great grandparents came with nothing but themselves. That is to say, with nothing but their own two remarkable, pioneering souls. Thanks so very much, Patricia and Jeanne, for going so far out of your way to help a poor wayfaring stranger.

I'm obliged to both Amy Dunagin and T. Sean Maher, archivists for the Yale Glee Club, for their effort, (unfortunately, unsuccessful) to locate the missing first page of excerpts taken from some of the reviews of the Glee Club's concerts, reviews which, in the summer of 1941, appeared in their entirety in quite a number of South American newspapers.

And no, I've not forgotten Jack Moment. But I'm not thanking him. I would not be thanking him even had he lived. He would never have expected thanks from me. We were far too close for far too long for thanks to be needed or even to have any meaning. Some things just need not be said and isn't that nice?

But all that having being said—and at my usual tedious length—there's something I must say again to you, Peggy. This book, first and last, owes its very existence to your infinite patience and loving support, for it has been your thankless lot to suffer through the near-constant abstraction of your husband, as, turning away from the *here* and the *now*, I stared vacantly back down that long way I'd come, all in order that I might find, buried in shallow graves strewn here and there along the road, the remains of an altogether unremarkable past, and might, as a matter conceivably of interest to my family, if not to the general reader, disinter, bone by dearly remembered bone, at least a few of the memories which the good fortune of my long, happy and rather active life had leisurely buried there.

And for the time to do that, dear Peggy, I thank you with all my heart.

Appendices

Appendix A.

The following is the almost complete text of a letter written by the author to Fred Hall Ryan only five days after the formal date for the end of the war in Europe. It was written from the Bavarian village of Bad Heilbrunn and within a very few days of the arrival there of the author's armored artillery firing battery. Fred Ryan was not only the author's first cousin once removed but one of several men who regarded the author as the son they'd never had. This is also the same Fred Ryan who remembered that story *his* grandmother, Mary Scally Hall, had told him about how she had discovered two Indians in full war paint peering at her through a window of her farm house and how she had frightened them away. The "Duke" to whom the letter several times refers was the author's first wife, Susybelle Wilkinson Lyons, whose nickname from childhood was "Duke."

13 May 1945

Dear Fred –

My first mail came two days ago, a luscious packet of 61 letters, about half from Duke and dated as late as 17 April. Ignorance is Purgatory, but I am now released. ...

I got in on the tail-end of the fighting for this division, the last hundred miles or so of rat-race, when we were stopped from point to point by road-blocks, blown bridges and strong points, all covered by fire but lightly held. There wasn't much work for the artillery but it was a wild career, I assure you. But I saw enough, more than enough to slack my curiosity of war. I've spent the bulk of my time traveling, and I've been through the whole of the old front battle grounds from Aachen to Brenner Pass. My battalion holds the Presidential Unit Citation for its defense of Bastogne, where my particular battery was for three days and nights two hundred yards from the front lines. It's impossible to believe some of the things I've heard about Bastogne, things that I know to be true.

My job is that of a forward observer. I realize now that if I had come over with the Div. I would almost certainly have been killed or wounded. [The "Div." referred to is The Tenth Armored Division, the division with which the author had previously served at Camp Gordon, Georgia.] *We can't deceive ourselves about that. This is a terrible thing to discover. And of course don't even allude to danger before Duke. Especially since I may very likely go to the C.B.I. I hope (I am afraid, only fondly) that mortality for armor will not there be so great as here.*

You no doubt wonder how I got back into F.A. and even back into my old division. ["F.A." is Field Artillery, the author having left for overseas as an Engineer officer.] *No doubt. Well, breaks helped me a little, but it was mainly "scrambling", which I learned to do on the golf courses. The principle is the same: one accomplishes by informal, somewhat questionable methods what could not be done customarily. My method briefly was to talk quite casually with the Classification and Assignment Officers at the various Reinforcement Depots I passed through, gaining their unofficial cooperation with the result that I worked my way through the Reinforcement Systems and rear areas of four armies (not including the 7th army, which was my destination) and even down to the very forward battalion which supplied the 10th Armored.*

I had discovered long before that to be reverted back to the F.A. a letter up through channels was necessary and because the need for Engineer Officers was great, there was literally no chance that my application would be approved. So I saw that it would have to be done in another way. When I reported to my most forward battalion (in a town where prisoners were still being taken) I again spoke to the officer handling classification and assignment (this far forward, a 2nd Lt. naturally), persuading him that he could himself reclassify me back to F.A. He didn't know any different and I was F.A. again. Irregularities are nothing in the army since the multitude of regulations is a forest where a man who knows his way about can find it safely. Anyway, there are so many rules that only personalities and opinions mean anything.

You might read this explanation of how I got back to the 10th Armored F.A. (where I have many friends) to Duke and to the folks as I don't think I ever really explained it to them. And I forgot to add not to mention to the folks as well as Duke that in combat my job is as hazardous as the most. May I never get shot at again. It gives you a very annoying feeling that you're not the Invincible Vincent you had thought.

I'll write again shortly and talk about a few other things I wanted to cover. We're occupying now which presents a hundred singular problems in human relations every day.

Love you,

Charlton

Appendix B.

The text, in its entirety, of a very short "society column" which appeared in late December, 1904, in a Chippewa Falls, Wisconsin newspaper. The name of that newspaper is not known to the author but could possibly have been the *Daily Independent.* The "two daughters" of Harry Hall reported in this piece as having "assisted in the entertainment of the guests" were the author's mother, Marjorie Hall, later to become Marjorie Lyons, who was then about nine years old, and Marjorie's sister, Norma, two years younger.

"MR. AND MRS. HALL ENTERTAINERS

Entertained A Company Of Friends
At Their home On Christmas Night.

Mr. and Mrs. Michael Hall very pleasantly entertained a company of their friends at their country home on Christmas night, about twenty-five of their friends partaking of their hospitality. The evening was most agreeably passed in vocal and instrumental music, social converse and partaking of a sumptuous spread. It was a gathering of old friends, all of whom speak in high terms of the host and hostess as entertainers. Harry Hall and his two daughters were present and assisted in the entertainment of the guests. William F. Kirk, of the Milwaukee Sentinel, who is enjoying his Christmas vacation at home, was also present. On the spur of the moment, Mr. Kirk penned the following poem appropriate to the occasion:

We are gathered here tonight,
In a home exceedingly bright,
And our hearts are overflowing with
The joy of Christmas time.
We have come from far and near,
To enjoy the royal cheer
That is found at this old homestead,
And I only write this rhyme
As a sort of feeble toast
To Mike Hall, our dear old host,
Who has shown his hospitality when e'er
We chanced to call.
Let us lift our brimming glasses,
Young and old, lads and lasses,
And just drink to father Michael,
Heaven bless him, that is all."

Appendix C.

The following is the complete text of a piece written by one Thomas McBean, a frequent contributor to the Chippewa Falls, Wisconisn, newspapers. This one appeared in a local paper soon after Michael and Mary Hall had sold the farm and taken up residence on Bridge Street in Chippewa Falls. The author has a copy of the deed by which Michael and Mary conveyed title to the farm and that deed is dated April 1, 1906. The purchase price was $12,000.00. Of particular interest is Mr. McBean's remark, made just in passing, that he had been a Union soldier at the siege of Vicksburg. If true, and there's no reason to doubt that it isn't, then the "early chicken hunt" that Mr. McBean made as a boy, and which he describes in some detail in this piece, must have taken place at least a few years prior to 1865, that being the year in which Michael and Mary first acquired record title to any part of their farm. So from this evidence, it seems probable that Michael and Mary were in possession of the farm—had perhaps even moved onto it—prior obtainin legal title to any of it, with the result that when McBean made his chicken hunt, their farm could possibly have been recognized, even prior to that first deed of acquisition, as "the Hall farm".

Incidentally, if the reader is a bird watcher—even a bad bird watcher—the birds Mr. McBean refers to here as "chickens," though they may have been the pinnated grouse (i.e. the species probably more often called "sharp-tails"), they were much more likely actually to have been one of the prairie chickens, either the greater or the lesser. Prairie chickens in their millions once graced the Great Plains and not so long ago they were to be found here on the prairie that was once southwestern Louisiana. Louisiana's particular brand of prairie-chicken was almost certainly the Attwater's prairie chicken and you could find the Attwater all the way out to the Texas Panhandle. Sadly, the Attwater is now almost extinct.

Long ago, as both boy and young man, the author hunted both sharp-tails and partridge, or ruffed grouse, himself in Wisconsin and elsewhere, and he recalls hearing someone refer to the sharp-tails he shot as "chickens." It might have been Fred Bigler, or possibly it came from Bill Casper or Doc Collins. But the difference in the two species is unmistakable. And, anyway, there were no true prairie-chickens left in that part of Wisconsin seventy years ago. The grouse he did hunt were of two species, sharp-tails and ruffed grouse. But the ruffed grouse was never called ruffed grouse, not in Wisconsin. No, the ruffed grouse was then called *partridge* by everyone up there, as I suspect it still is.

"A PIONEER FARM CHANGES HANDS

An Early Day Chicken Hunt.

The farm lately sold by Mr. M. Hall to Mr. Meagher, is one of the old landmarks of Chippewa County. It is one of the three first farms located on Eagle Prairie on the Chippewa city road. Mr. George Sellers took it under the then preemption law in the early fifties. He sold it to Mr. Hall in 1866, who has resided on it ever since, making it one of the finest farms in the county and under the generous hospitality of Mrs. Hall it has been visited by many Chippewa people who desired to spend a day of leisure in the country.

Mr. Hall and family came to Chippewa Falls in 1859. He has always been an active business man, at one time sheriff of the county; but like all poor frail humanity, he finds that as age creeps on the necessary attention required to maintain the farm and also his city business, was a little too arduous a duty for him, he concluded to part with it, and move into the city, when he could give his whole attention to his office work.

Mr. Hall is one of the few old guards remaining that weathered the hardships and privations of pioneer life nearly half a century ago, of a genial and affable disposition he and his family will be welcomed citizens of the city that he has helped to build.

I cannot close this article without relating a little incident of my boyhood days that happened to me while hunting on this farm. It was my first chicken hunt alone. My father's gun, a Westley Richards, was sacred property to him, he allowed no one to handle it but himself. So I borrowed an old flint lock from Andrew Gregg, who lived in adjoining rooms to us in Battle Row. I think it was originally an old Chinese match-lock of the time of Confucius, and on the invention of the flint-lock it was converted into one. It was a very desirable weapon, the barrel was so long, that in case you could not get near enough to the bird to shoot it, you could knock it down. While hunting over this farm I flushed a covey of chickens, they lighting on a fence. My father had often told me that he considered it equivalent to murder, to shoot a sitting bird, that a true sportsman always shot on the wing, but this was too tempting a shot for a boy. So I got myself in range of the birds along the fence, expecting to rake down a dozen or more. I raised my gun, took good aim, fired, a blaze of fire belched forth before me like the eruption of Mount Pelee, and the report sounded like that of the 100 pound Parrots that I afterwards heard booming when in the army at the siege of

Vicksburg. The air was full of feathers and fence rails; when I came to my senses I was in a ditch, my feet up in the air. I struggled to my feet, found the gun about 20 feet to the rear of me. I picked it up gently, fearing it might go off again, being satisfied that I had had sport enough for one day. I put the old fusee on my shoulder, started for home a wiser and a lamer boy. I learned afterwards that Andrew . . . . [some text is missing here] . . . and old scrap iron, calculating to annihilate the whole Indian tribe at one shot—and I got it.

> Thos. McBean"

Appendix D.

An undated, four page "letter home" written, and illustrated, by Susybelle Lyons while she and her husband were in Havana, Cuba. Although undated, it is clear from internal evidence (corroborated by the author's memory) that this letter would have certainly been written on a May 20th but in a year uncertain, although likely about 1957. May 20 is—or was then—Cuba's national holiday, their Independence Day, their "Fourth of July". Susybelle and Charlton, with their friends, B. F. and Nancy O'Neal, had dined that evening at *La Floridita*, a marvelous restaurant in Old Havana, and they had only to step outside the restaurant to watch the passing parade, the parade which Susybelle describes, and which she illustrates with her own drawings, in such entertaining fashion in this letter. The author ordered Moro crab and remembers that it came with the "house dressing", a mayonnaise the likes of which were then to be found nowhere else in the world.

Hotel Presidente
Operated by Presidente Corporation
Habana, Cuba

ROBERT ACOSTA, MANAGER

P. O. BOX 1249

Sweet girls & my little boy —
We have certainly seen some wonderful sights. Last night we saw a parade that had everybody so beautifully dressed you'd hardly believe it. The men were all dressed up too & were carrying long sticks that had candles in them and sometimes birds. They beat long thin drums and danced all the time. 
They even had some children about your age, Su — who dressed & danced  just like their mamas.
The elevators have tile on the floor just like we have tile on our bathroom floor — and so does our hotel room.

These are Cubans.

The people here are very short, the ladies are all plump, and the men have black moustaches. Lots of the ladies have long black shiny hair. They don't speak English but talk in a very pretty language called Spanish. When I get home I'll teach you how to say "Good-morning, Pa" in Spanish.

One of the strangest things they have here is a little door in a wall. If there is some little baby who doesn't have a mother or father, the neighbors wrap a little cloth around it, wait until it is nighttime, then they go open the door & put the baby in one of the little baskets that is inside the door. When the baby is in the basket a bell rings and then the nuns know that there is another little baby for them to take care of.

They have some beautiful flowers and also some very funny trees that are called palm. They have palm trees in New Orleans, too. They have some other trees that are shaped like this one here →

This is a nun↑

I'll tell you about the rest when I see you. Tomorrow I'm going to buy you all a present. Won't that

— 4 —

be nice! Hope you all are being very very sweet. I love you all oo very much & I miss you, too.

Love,
Mama.

P. S.
Pa says he love you & misses you, too.

Your Popa wants to see his girls and his Charlton. He'll be home probably Tuesday night. And then Pa will give you all a big hug and kiss like this:

Hug   Kiss

Pa

Appendix E.

Appendix E is a "biography" of Charles Richard Spencer as compiled, at a time unknown to the author, by "researcher Professor Richard Sheppard of Magdalen College, Oxford", and sent to the author by Jacqueline Haun with her letter dated August 29, 2005 (which see as first entry in Appendix L, *infra*.)

"Captain Charles R. Spencer

SPENCER, Charles Richard: *b.* 21 June 1903. Second s. of C. St. D. and A. I. Spencer of Llandough, near Cardiff. Clifton. D. 22-26; 2nd English, 26; B. A., 26.

After graduation, Spencer became an assistant master at Stowe School, Buckinghamshire, from September 1926 to January 1930 and Head of English there until July 1932. After Spencer's death, a contemporary at Stowe (P. A. Browne D. 19-22) who later became an Inspector of Schools, left and unusually long and graphic description of his activity there which was published in the School Magazine (*The Stoic*) and is worth quoting *in extenso*.

According to Browne, most members of the School 'would agree that [Spencer] was the most vigorous and exciting of the masters then at the school. His violent and strenuous manner naturally did not endear him to all he came in contact with, but his frank enthusiasm and his warm-hearted sincerity won him countless staunch friends and admirers. He was interesting, approachable, and sympathetic; he respected the individuality of the boys he taught; in fact, he had the first and most important qualities of the successful schoolmaster. That he had also certain defects he himself knew better than anyone; "I'm rebellious and far too casual" he once wrote; and again "There's no doubt that I'm didactic to my finger-tips, a horrid quality".

In one letter he put the case with devastating frankness, in words that in fact describe a great many school-masters but scarcely himself: "I am fed up with myself because I teach without knowing anything, without knowing how to teach, without knowing anything about the minds of the boys I teach, without knowing anything about the world so as to know what ought to be taught". This was no doubt written in one of those moods of depression that in spite of his usual vitality and enthusiasm occasionally attacked him. […] Actually, I suppose anyone who spent a year in Lower V (B) under him would class him as "a very superior teacher".

Certainly he took endless trouble thinking out what to teach his form, and how best to present it. If he sometimes became overwhelmed by the accumulation of uncorrected exercises that lay on his table, it is still true to say that energy and thoroughness were the key-notes of his attitude towards teaching his form.

I have a heap of letters dealing in detail with forthcoming General Papers that he was responsible for; others are concerned with courses of lectures to be given by people from outside, with a careful balancing of subjects and a discussion of the question whether the boys should take notes and if so of what kind. […]

He was as stimulating a companion as he was a teacher. Time spent in his company was never dull. He had the widest interests; perhaps it would be a just criticism to say they were too wide and that he tended to dissipate his energy in too many directions. He was a natural games player, outstanding at Rugger and Cricket; he was above average at bridge, and he constantly lamented the hours he wasted at the billiard table. He was a keen painter, and he once surprised me by announcing in a letter, "I am in the middle of composing a sonata (that is to say one movement is finished) which sounds to me more intolerable every time I stumble through it".

Browne also explained that although Spencer was primarily an English expert, he never lost his love for the Classics and that a Hellenic Tour had made a deep impression on him: 'he wrote a characteristically laconic description – "Glorious time in Greece. Went to bed each night at 2.0 a.m. – got up many mornings at 5 a.m.

to see Stromboli or dawn at Constantinople – a week more of it and I should have a breakdown – fell deeply in love (as always on a ship – remember?) but am heart-whole again, thank goodness – sailed across the Bosphorus in an 8-metre racing yacht and traveled extensively in Asia for 20 minutes –saw many delightful things – and altogether had a charming time. Discovered that they teach you an awful lot of rot about the Classics at school and university – very little sense of proportion in it". […]

His main love was the philosophy of Education, and he was never tired of talking of the aims and methods of school-mastering. For years he worked on a scheme for a super-Public School, and he once came within an ace of putting some of his ideas into practice, when he was offered the Headship of a new Public School in Iraq, though at the last minute the arrangements fell through. […] Throughout his life he was inspired by a divine discontent. He once pointed out to me that one of the best qualities of the average American was his dissatisfaction with things as they are and his determination to better them. This was one of the finest sides of his character. But he carried it, perhaps, to excess. For he would never be content to work to an established routine, or to allow that what should be altered should not necessarily be altered at once and completely. […]

He was himself, in his calmer moments, aware that he was too impatient of restraints and had too little sympathy with those who believed in gradualness; he saw what he thought right with too fierce and logical a clarity to allow himself to be convinced that what he wanted might be more effectively attained by a slower and more roundabout approach. This impatience, naturally, but unfortunately, had an adverse effect on his career. We were sorry, but not surprised, to hear from time to time that he had thrown up a job or expressed his views so indiscreetly that his services were dispensed with.

There were few institutions tolerant enough to give him the rope he needed; it is to the credit of Stowe and of a wise Head Master that he stayed here far longer than in any subsequent job.

He was an engaging and entertaining correspondent, though a highly irregular one. Just as he would descend on us in person after a lapse of years and pick up the threads of intimacy in a few minutes, he would launch a letter describing some piquant scene that had taken his fancy or expounding some brilliant new panacea for the world's ills as if he had been talking to us the day before, though it might have been years since we had seen or heard from him. I saw him three times in America four years ago, and each time he took up the running on the old familiar footing, just as we might have continued a conversation in the Common Room at Stowe that had been begun a few minutes before at the dinner table. [...] His readiness to laugh at himself and his deep humility were among his most endearing qualities. He had the happy knack of pandering to our good opinion of ourselves by asking our advice and of making it seem while he talked to us as if we were the people above all whose judgment he wanted to have. Though he might seem on the surface almost ruthlessly self-confident, at heart he was, I think, never quite sure of himself and he really valued the opinion of the very ordinary people to whom he paid the compliment of asking their advice.

At the same time, these interviews usually developed into a monologue, in which his alert brain played around with arguments and objections; nevertheless, they may perhaps have attained their object if the second party to them assumed the rôle of a patient and sympathetic listener. For it was sympathy and the opportunity of unfolding his mind to another person that he wanted more than advice, and that we were glad enough to be able to give him. His turbulent and restless spirit inspired affection and devotion that no passage of years had power to destroy. [...] He had courage and gaiety and humour, enthusiasm and determination, a fertile and active mind. He accomplished more than most in the short span of his life; he had no fears for the future and his eager spirit is at rest while we that are left lament his loss.'

Another contemporary at Stowe, Patrick G. Hunter, who stayed on there after Browne had left, added supplementary information on events involving Spencer, 'that were part of the very life-blood of

Stowe's development. One is the production of *Comus* in the Summer of 1931, which still surely remains the greatest of Stowe's many fine [pre-war] productions. None who saw that performance can forget it; the fine use of the terrain around the Worthies and the entry by water, the carefully studied detail of every phase and possibility, and what the *Stoic* account at the time called the "astounding effects" of the lighting. Another memory is the Literary Society, an effort perhaps never equaled in any school at any time. For, within little more than a year, papers were read by John Masefield, Edith Sitwell, Walter de la Mare, Ronald Knox and M. R. Ridley. And even Bernard Shaw vouchsafed a written refusal, as opposed to the usual printed one. And at the same time the Society itself was vitally active, for these star performances were punctuated by much internal production. Once more, "Spuggins", with book in hand, stopping at the door of a strange classroom, going in and holding up his hand, "I am not taking you, but wait a minute. Just listen to this", and he read the two verses of a poem he had just discovered. Slightly theatrical perhaps, but that is a petty criticism. Who, that heard it, will ever forget the poem? And who, that met him, will forget Charles Spencer?'

From 1932 to 1934 Spencer was a Commonwealth Fund Fellow in Education, and though based in Chicago and Yale, he traveled widely in the United States. On his return, he seems to have been very unsettled. He was a temporary assistant master at Charterhouse School, Surrey, from autumn 1934 to Easter 1935, and although the school's archive has no record of his employment, the school magazine The Carthusian records him playing Darrell Blake in Denis Johnson's *The Moon in the Yellow River* when it was staged by the staff drama group on 8 December 1934. Everything we know about Spencer indicates why this part would have appealed to him:

'The plot centers around the attempt of Darrell Blake, a revolutionary Irish idealist, to blow up a power house run by a German engineer, who is himself no less of an idealist than Blake. The clash is a fundamental one. The clash between order and disorder; the Teuton and the Celt; collectivism and individualism'.

Spencer then held another temporary post, at Bryanston School, Dorset, for the rest of 1935 and the school magazine, *The Bryanston Saga*, recalls his initiating people in to the rites of village cricket and teaching English, History and Darts. An article on the school's cricketing achievements explains this remark more fully:

'Thanks mainly to the machinations of Mr. C. R. Spencer we have had a good deal of village cricket. A number of evening matches have been played on village greens, and the form of them has been due to the delightfully "leveling" effect of playing cricket in a cow field where carpet drives stop dead at silly point's boots, and the soaring cow-shot gets the runs. At Irwerne Minster the cows had to be persuaded to leave the ground before the game could begin. At Milton Abbas the buttercups were knee-high and at Shillingstone the pitch was about 40 yards x 40 yards in the centre of unshorn hay.

Equality of opportunity was a fact. The sun shone on mug and adept alike as they played on a stretch of river meadow that lapped like a calm green sea against the islands of Hod and Hambledon. The last touch has regularly been sandwiches and liquid refreshment at the local pub, enlivening with a spot of halfpenny-shoving and dart throwing. […] It has been good to watch Mr Spencer's quick and lively work behind the wickets. It is to his counsel and practical exposition that Lee-Barber's improved "keeping" has been largely due'.

During his time at Bryanston, Spencer also gave two talks to the school's Political Society in the autumn term: one entitled 'A Critical survey of America' and the other entitled 'Nazi Germany'. When it is remembered that the Nuremberg Laws, the most comprehensive anti-semitic legislation to be passed in Germany to date, had been announced at the Nazi Party Rally in Nuremberg in 1935, the significance of Spencer role in *The Moon in the Yellow River* becomes even greater and points to an unusual sensitivity to the developments on the Continent of Europe. From 1 January to 12 June 1936 he became an assistant in the Talks Department of the BBC and on 14 March he broadcast a talk entitled 'Topics in the Air

–Gainsborough" in which he criticized that painter for exchanging youthful brilliance for well-paid virtuosity but praised him for leaving such an accurate record of society marked by elegance, good sense and good taste. Judging from Browne's obituary, he left the BBC abruptly and seems then to have been unemployed for six months or so.

But early in 1937 Spencer led an English Speaking Union study group on a 3,000-mile tour on an enquiry into the New Deal and current labour disputes. On 18 April 1937, after this was over, he contacted Allan Heely, the Head Master of Lawrenceville School, New Jersey, 1934-59, whom he had met during his time as a Commonwealth Fund Fellow when Heely was an administrator at Phillips Academy, Andover, Massachusetts. Writing from New York, Spencer proposed a merely friendly visit but made it clear that he was looking for a way of settling down permanently in the USA. As a result of the visit, Heely offered Spencer a job. On 15 May Spencer returned to England to sort out family affairs, and from September 1937 to Spring 1939, he worked at Lawrenceville as a history master and assistant house master. During his time there, Spencer explored the possibility of doing graduate work at nearby Princeton University and spent August 1938 in England. Sensing the approach of war, he made a will in September 1938 leaving all his possessions in the USA (except his financial assets) to Lawrenceville and named Heely as his American executor. But before he left, he had himself given away all his property to American friends, and with hindsight, one senses from his correspondence on this matter that he knew he would not survive the War. During 1930-s, he also found time to publish pieces in the *Times Educational Supplement* and *Universities Review*.
[civilian portrait, half page, vertical]

Captain Charles R. Spencer
Photo 1938: courtesy The Lawrenceville School, New Jersey.
Spencer was commissioned Temporary Second Lieutenant in the Royal Marines on 1 December 1939. He was promoted Acting Temporary Captain on 2 April 1940 and Acting Captain on 1 June

1940 while he was serving with the 2nd Battalion, the 2nd Royal Marine Brigade (which was re-designated the 102nd Royal Marine Brigade in August 1940).

The nucleus of this Brigade had been formed on 1 December 1939 (the date of Spencer's first commission) and the whole Brigade, consisting mainly of temporary officers, conscripts, and older men withdrawn from ships, was assembled at Bisley in Surrey on 1 April 1940 (i.e. the day before Spencer's first promotion). On 1 June 1940 it was sent to the Paignton/Brixham area in Devon for training in boat work, assault landings and infantry tactics; in the event of a German invasion, it would form part of the defense force. Spencer was still part of the same unit in June 1941, but when he died on active service of a gunshot wound, aged 38, on 29 September 1941, he was serving in (and probably commanding) the Transport Company of Mobile Naval Base Defense Organization No. 2.

His death took place in the Portsmouth area (possibly on Hayling Island, where M.N.B.D.O.2 spent much time in 1941). Browne's obituary of Spencer indicates that he had, at some point, served in Africa – but the circumstances of this service in there are unknown. The same obituary also describes him as "a very capable officer who gave infinite thought to the welfare of his men", who, "in spite of a slightly military appearance [...] was anything but cut out for the military life by temperament", who hated the red tape by which he was hedged around, but who, "finding himself an officer [...] devoted himself to the job with all his might".

On 7 November 1941, *The Times* published an obituary which amplifies our picture of Spencer still more: "He had the knack of making friends in a paradoxical way. On one occasion, while motoring in the States, he came into collision with the back of another car and badly damaged it. He rushed up to the driver of the other car and, full of apologies, admitted that it was entirely his own fault, and offered to pay the damages. The driver of the damaged car was so bewildered with this admission and so attracted by this unusual code of courtesy and morals that they became great friends.

At his best Charles was possessed of a gaiety which made the dullest of wits respond to his personality. If in the classroom he was considered 'a joke' he was at least a stimulating jester; he may have moved his class to laughter, but the laughter was genuine, and it had the effect of focusing the attention on the subject. And the subject was Charles's interpretation of the facts. If the intellectuals laughed it meant that they had appreciated his wit. If the dunderheads laughed it meant that they had at least become interested. Lively teachers are not manufactured by the pound at our universities. And when someone like Charles Spencer decides to be a schoolmaster there ought to be a law to prevent him from changing his mind, and a State philosopher to help him always to make the best of himself.

Perhaps Charles was too quick for those who preferred the slower revolutions of progress, too impatient with the present state of affairs – and with himself. But he radiated life; he had a warm heart and a great sense of fun. To laugh with him was to be madly in love with the world". The following poem by a former pupil at Stowe, Robert A. Atthill, who was by then himself teaching at Ampleforth, also appeared in *The Stoic*:

In Memoriam: C. R. Spencer

So on a winter day without a cloud –
for the streamlined wind, leaping over the plain
from the far hills, battered and broke
the grey unwieldy skies, and drove
the last wrack beyond the rim of the sea –
on this November morning the cold printed word
told me of your death, and I was sad
to think how for you the thousand lights of living,
that glittered like frosty stars in the northern night,
were blotted out in the monotone of death.
For you entered our lives with the freshness
of a clean wind that sets the leaves dancing
and stipples the grey streams with passing
beauty that never dies, and though the windows,

where you looked in and smiled, may be closed
against the business of life and the shadow of age,
your laughter lingers in the worn pages of books,
and the pictures on the classroom wall, your bright
glance illuminates the sudden recess of thought
by the winter fire, when thought was strange
adventure into Elysian fields of truth.
There across the midsummer river you threw
the magic dust into our eyes, stronger
than Comus's spells, but not for death.
So, at this moment of your death,
I do not rebel at the event, but only pray
That the daemon reminded you of our debt
outstanding, that none can now repay.
                              Ampleforth, November 1941.

One cannot help wondering how a mercurial, inspirational and memorable teacher like Spencer would have fitted into today's system of state-managed curricula, S.A.T.'s, emasculated syllabuses and invidious league tables, and whether, even, such a system requires personalities like him anymore. Buried: Haslar Royal Naval Cemetery, Hampshire."

Appendix F.

The following text is the transcript of all but the first page of an eight page, single-spaced, typewritten document, containing, in English translation, extracts from many, and perhaps most, of the reviews appearing in South American newspapers of certain of the concerts given throughout South America by The Yale Glee Club in the summer of 1941. Those eight pages were given to the author in the Fall of 1941 by the then Director of the Yale Glee Club, Professor Marshall Bartholomew. Most unfortunately, the author has somehow lost the first page of his copy of those eight pages of reviews. On that first page appeared important quotations from reviews in Rio de Janeiro newspapers that were in addition to the two paragraphs, from an unknown paper and by an unknown reviewer, quoted next below. As stated, each entry is an excerpt taken from newspaper reviews of formal concerts presented by the Yale Glee Club in four South American countries, Brazil, Uruguay, Argentina and Chile, during the Summer of 1941. In addition to those four countries, the Yale Glee Club, dressed in evening clothes (i.e. what is now referred to as "tails") sang other formal concerts in Peru and the Canal Zone, as well as concerts to passengers and crews on board two passenger liners, but no reviews of any of those other concerts exist. Hardly more than mentioned here are the numerous, less formal recitals before school, college and university students which took place during daylight hours, especially in Argentina. Although some of the following reviews may have appeared originally in English language newspapers, most of them, the author believes, are translations into English, either from Portuguese language newspapers published in Brazil or from Spanish language newspapers published elsewhere.

RIO DE JANEIRO

The two paragraphs next following appear at the top of the second page of the author's typescript and are the continuation of a review of the opening concert, which review began on the missing first page and which appeared in some newspaper of uncertain date published in Rio de Janeiro, Brazil.

The propaganda by these students is of the very best: artistic, a perfect performance in the field of choral singing, because it was a most edifying example which might be followed by our university students who choose much less interesting pastimes.
The truth is that in spite of the titanic efforts of Villa-Lobos, we still do not know how to sing in Brazil. And the proof of this, sad as it is, was when the Maestro directed the Brazilian National Anthem and turned toward the audience to lead them, but could find only a half a dozen who could sing it.

[Author's comment. Because it was so briefly mentioned by me in the book itself, I have the following further comment on the appearance of Villa-Lobos at the Glee Club's opening concert in Rio. The review from which these two paragraphs are extracted was of the first, or opening concert of the South American tour. The unknown reviewer reports that "the Maestro" directed the Brazilian National Anthem. Although possibly not made clear, the "Maestro" was in fact the world famous composer, Heitor Villa-Lobos, who was not merely in the audience that night but who, by prearrangement, came up on the stage to conduct the Yale Glee Club in its performance of its first number, the Brazilian National Anthem. And it was during our singing of their National Anthem that Villa-Lobos turned to the audience to conduct the audience as well. The Yale Glee Club <u>did</u> know that country's national anthem—we knew it very, very well and could sing it a splendid version of Portuguese, but the Brazilians did not. I remember the occasion perfectly—well, *almost* perfectly. I have no recollection of the near silence of the audience reported by the reviewer, a silence owing to the fact that only a few could sing it. But, singing my own head off, I would not have heard that silence anyway, would I? No! Certainly not!]

Correio da Manha (July 5)
The best of propaganda is Art because it is universally understood. The presentation of the Yale Glee Club at the Cultura Artistica was an exceptionally artistic event. The date of July 2, 1941 will be engraved in our artistic annals as one of the most friendly, the most interesting, and the most instructive events because of the proof that it gave us of the culture and love of music among American students. The Yale Glee Club is a model for any country. It is an invaluable institution. Its success was complete and it makes a great victory for the Cultura Artistica.

O Jornal (July 4) - Ayres de Andrade
Hollywood never told us that in the United States there exists a chorus as perfect as the Yale Glee Club. Made up of students of Yale University, the Glee Club can be favorably compared to any professional chorus in the whole world. The expressive flexibility of the ensemble is really remarkable. Rigorous discipline and the good

taste revealed in the choice of program brought to the audience moments of great beauty and deep emotion."

Jornal do Commercio (July 9) - Andrade Muricy
The first concert of the Yale Glee Club was a performance of the highest artistic attainment. From this first contact with the public these young singers immediately touched the artistic sensibility of the audience and conquered their sympathies. Their welcome among us is guaranteed.

Choral singing is not new to us and for this reason it is easy to make comparisons which yesterday were entirely in favor of the students.

The Yale Glee Club brings from North America a message which will have profound repercussions, for it touches the emotions and the artistic appreciation of the Brazilians.

<u>SÃO PAULO</u>

Although São Paulo is now the largest city south of the equator, the Glee Club sang only one concert there, leaving that same night by special train for Santos, where it re-boarded the *Brazil*.

Diario de São Paulo (July 5)
The discipline, perfect pitch, perfect taste with which the program was chosen deserve the highest praise. A beautiful concert and even more a beautiful lesson to us.

Correio Paulistano (July 5)
Much was expected of this chorus for its fame had proceeded it from the United States and there were excellent reports of its concerts in Rio. Yet this performance far surpassed all expectations and each number called forth a thunder of applause. The theatre yesterday was too small to hold the multitudes that wished to attend this concert. The enthusiasm and applause lasted through the entire performance.

MONTEVIDEO

El Dia (July 8)

It should be pointed out that the presence of this chorus in Montevideo is one of the most pleasing and the most positive aspects of the cultural exchange which is taking place between Uruguay and the United States. The Yale students are typical exponents of the North American colleges. Tall, gay, with an air of tranquil ease, they showed by their manners the characteristic freedom and poise of the North American. Even while still on board ship, waiting to land, they sang several beautiful songs of their country.

This is a university chorus, a chorus composed of students; that is of amateurs who have reached a perfection and training in no way inferior to the best male choirs we have heard. These are the fresh young voices of sixty young men who sing with the skill of professionals, but, because they are not professionals, they sing even with more ardor, with more devotion and more enthusiasm. They have voices remarkably well trained and selected, skillfully balanced and harmonized, that constitute an admirable instrument.

The Yale Glee Club revealed in yesterday's audition extreme vivacity and flexibility in the interpretation of various kinds of compositions. It possesses an unique mastery, a finished control of the choral technique which manifests itself in the assurance of the attack, in the preciseness and vigor of its rhythms, and the perfection of the crescendos, in the admirable pianissimo, in the clearness of its expression which reached the most ample gamut of tone shading and gives to all the numbers a very interesting and fine musical quality.

This attractive student choir was vigorously applauded and they were obliged to give frequent encores. The impression they made was excellent and there is no doubt that there will be a full house at the second and final concert tomorrow.

El Diario (July 8)

An original and pleasant note, not lacking in artistic values, was given to Montevideo by these young and well trained North American students who compose the Yale Glee Club and whose presentation at the Estudio Auditorio yesterday afternoon assembled a large audience. A vast program created a real enthusiasm. The audience applauded heartily both singers and director.

El Dia(July 9)

North American and Uruguayian students were gathered together yesterday in the University in a beautiful act of brotherhood. The Yale Glee Club in a public function organized by the Uruguay Student Federation, was welcomed and honored in the university assembly hall. Our students wished to express the pleasure which they feel in the visit of these boys who have come to Montevideo to bring an example of the spirit of American youth, a pleasant mission of cultural exchange.

It ought to be said that we have never seen such a large crowd as gathered yesterday in the assembly hall of the university. Students from all schools and departments, from private schools such as the Crandon Institute and Licee Francais, came in great numbers to welcome these friendly guests. The orchestra and the gallery were filled to the top and even the entrance stairways were crowded. When the Yale students appeared on the platform the unanimous ovation lasting for several minutes expressed the respect of these Uruguayian colleagues.

A student, Anibal Radellino, spoke in English on behalf of the Uruguayian Federation of University Students, pointing out that the Uruguayian students acknowledge with great satisfaction the presence of the representatives of one of the world's most famous and honored universities. He said that this brotherhood of students among American nations, geographically so far apart, is a faithful expression of the spirit of solidarity that moves the youth of the American hemisphere toward the defense of our liberties and our rights, so endangered at this time. Donald S. Devor, Jr., President of the Yale Glee Club, answered with heartfelt and cordial words, pointing out the democratic motives that brought the Yale students to Uruguay.

Then the chorus gave a series of admirable renditions of North American folk tunes. They sang in English but the spiritual vibration of these songs crossed over the language difference and reached the public as an exact expression of the spirit of a young, *powerful and idealistic nation. A unanimous ovation greeted this performance and the Yale students as they left the hall and fused with the crowd that surrounded them and accompanied them with lively indications of friendship.*

BUENOS AIRES

La Prensa (July 16)

This panorama of choral music, made up of about twenty-six compositions, was interpreted by the Yale Club with perfect pitch, richness and variety of tone, and impeccable musical taste. Each one of these numbers became, thanks to the indeed remarkable skill of the conductor and the discipline and personal qualities so finely assembled in this group of Yale students, a rendition of unusually high rank that never weakened in spite of the wide range, the variety in style, manner, spiritual level and expression.

Beautiful songs of the sea, literary or folkloric South American songs, sung with good diction in Spanish or Portuguese, such as Alberto William's "Canción del mal tiempo", expressed with infinite poetry, or Hector Villa-Lobos' "O tremsinho" a humorous and imitative page, filled with priceless good humor; admirable negro spirituals in the interpretation of which the choir seemed like a really human organ, an organ because of its sonority and human because of its emotion. Almost everyone of these had to be repeated.

There were gay student songs, sacred music which brought out evidence of the choir being a polyphonic group of high rank. Everything contributed to make this concert an outstanding artistic event which honors the leader and his supporters and which the audience applauded most enthusiastically. The second concert will take place tomorrow.

La Nación (July 11)

Throughout the unfolding of this program, the chorus gave evidence of those qualities which make of it an organization of rare merit in its class, not only on account of its discipline and homogeneity, and of the flexibility with which it follows the slightest indications of its conductor but also because of the variety of resources that it is able to display.

Besides faultless pitch and adjustment, the Yale Glee Club has some voices of excellent timbre (particularly a tenor and a baritone), who contributed interest to the solo parts. Very felicitous likewise are the humming effects, the imitation of instruments, and onomatopoeias, etc. From the standpoint of interpretation they sing with equal efficacy both gay and light popular tunes as well as the serene melodies of poetic atmosphere, or compositions of greater depth and artistic value.

A large audience which followed with interest the progress of this program received the brilliant performance with continued signs of approval. The Yale Glee Club because of the public's insistence had to repeat many of the numbers and add others as encores."

El Mundo (July 11)
The chorus of Yale University which last night appeared at the Odeón is a group of excellent merit. This is shown by its homogeneity, its tone quality, its discipline and its ability to give each work the shape and modulation which determines its quality. This group of selected young voices which as a result of its good discipline is able to compete with professional choruses and which lends to its interpretations the enthusiasm and energy of those who generously give their gifts to the service of art, obtained last night the most enthusiastic reception of a large audience.

Libertad (July 11)
Last night appeared in the Odeón theatre the Yale Glee Club and obtained an excellent artistic success before a large audience. It is, as we have written, a group which comes on an artistic tour and as a spiritual brotherhood, without any utilitarian purpose whatever.

Critica (July 11)
The Yale Glee Club made yesterday in its first concert an unsurpassable impression. It is not just a good student choir, it is a

really perfect organization which interprets with musical judgment and adaptability the style of each composition; traditional songs as well as the sacred music of Victoria or of di Lasso; the folkloric expression of the Americas, as well as student songs from all over the world.

The choir impresses one by the vigor and freshness of the voices, by the variety of its resources, by the enthusiasm of each of its members, and by the excellent direction and discipline of their leader.

The choir sang with good diction and correct style songs of Argentina, Brazil, etc. The way in which they have assimilated the peculiarities of the Argentinian and Brazilian folklore is really remarkable.

May the example of this great North American University and of these students who sing with fervor and good taste, with the souls of real artists, spread into our atmosphere and give rise to the formation of similar choirs for the benefit of our own culture.

La Razon (July 11)
Last night Marshall Bartholomew had the satisfaction of seeing once again the success of his chorus. The audience of the Odeón accorded them the most cordial and most enthusiastic reception. The chorus showed charming quality and had to repeat several numbers. [We were constantly being required everywhere to repeat certain songs: they would simply refuse to let us go on.]

El Diario (July 12)
The Yale Glee Club is a group of young men who love to sing and are perfectly trained. The North American Chorus showed an exquisite musical sensitiveness, a freshness of voices and perfect pitch, sometimes sounding like marvelous musical instruments of incomparable sonority and exactness rather than just a chorus of human voices. We admired in some of the compositions the humming which gave the impression of a murmur accompanying the song; in others we applauded the sustained open notes which were a counterpoint to the melodies. The conductor used these resources with moderation and good taste. Some of the soloists were unusual –

the tenor and the baritone have really excellent voices, well timbred, well adjusted to the interpretation of the music.

El Pueblo (July 15)
After all we have already said about this matter there is very little we could add with respect to this excellent choral group, the Yale Glee Club, which has just given with extraordinary success its third concert.

These ambassadors of North American artistic culture show very well that in this great Northern country the adoration of sports and of jazz is not everything. They had to give a number of encores.

La Prensa (July 17)
The Yale Glee Club seems to be more than just a student choir, it is a group of professionals who still preserve their youthful enthusiasm and have not yet been mechanized by the daily work in an opera house. Their songs were interpreted with a musical sense, artistic fervor, and discipline.

The Argentine audience showed their appreciation of these qualities by offering these North American students and their leader the warmest reception and the most affectionate farewell.

ROSARIO

La Capital (July 15)
Throughout this program the chorus demonstrates qualities not often found in an organization of this kind, outstanding in unity and balance, making their program – so varied in style, spirit, and sentiment – particularly attractive and with an accuracy of pitch that is difficult to surpass.

MENDOZA

Los Andes (July 19)
It is easy for us to admit that this is the most extraordinary choral group that has ever visited our Republic. The discipline of its members, their perfect homogeneity, the unique skill with which they

achieve onomatopoeic sound effects, the complete balance of voices, raised this program to a high level and gave complete musical values to the compositions which composed it.

These young singers from Yale are indeed advanced scholars of beauty and art. They are ambassadors of that hemispheric fraternity which can be achieved by means of music. The audience rendered enthusiastic and warm ovations to these charming guests.

SANTIAGO de CHILE

El Imparcial (July 20)
They sing with refined taste, with perfect pitch, the audience applauded warmly and called for encores. They are missionaries of the songs of their country, and as such they deserve the affectionate welcome extended to them, extended without any reservations by the youth of Chile.

VALPARAISO

El Mercurio (July 25)
The visit of the Yale Glee Club to South America at the very moment in which all the nations of the western hemisphere are united in a supreme ideal of liberty is not only a spiritual bond between our peoples but also the most beautiful message of fraternal understanding. We heard yesterday these heralds of friendship singing the language of humanity, expressed in passage of folkloric music, compositions of classic polyphony, sacred numbers, student songs, choral selections from all over the world.

We could not classify them just as another choral group of first class quality. There is something different here. The boys of the Yale Glee Club – in our opinion – are part of the spirit of North America; they have that naturalness which permits them to interpret anything that has beauty and poetry.

Seeing Mr. Bartholomew conduct produces a sensation of watching a strange organist who with miraculous hands manipulates the keys of sound, sure of his results. [This description of Barty's conducting is just as the author so clearly remembers it.]

La Union (July 25)

These young men arrived as artistic emissaries. They came and they succeeded because this is a magnificent group whose discipline, homogeneity, and skill remind us of other great choirs which have visited us in the past. And one must point out that the core, the soul of this group, is the personality of its conductor in whom one may appreciate the musician with a real vocation fully accomplishing his duties.

The simplicity of these interpretations -- let us not forget that they are students and not professionals -- imparts a personal and sincere flavor to each composition. At the same time the quality of shading obtained and the exquisite poetic feeling revealed sensitiveness and temperament.

This artistic mission has served to show us that what the movies and the radio are spreading is not all that the United States produces in music.

Appendix G.

The following text is that of what clearly appears to have been a press release. It was undated but issued around the time, late in August of 1945, when the 609th Tank Destroyer Battalion, whose officers included the author, was departing from Camp Atlanta, in France, for Le Havre to board the Victory ship, *U. S. Victory*, for return to the States. The author recently discovered an original of this press release in a scrapbook which had been kept by his father during the war.

"HEADQUARTERS
ASSEMBLY AREA COMMAND
UNITED STATES FORCES, EUROPEAN THEATRE
FAMOUS PATTON UNIT BOASTS Shreveport SOLDIER

ASSEMBLY AREA COMMAND, France – More of General George S. Patton's Third Army heroes are heading for home. Newest Patton spearheading outfit to pass through Assembly Area Command redeployment at Camp Atlanta, near Chalons,

France, is the 609th Tank Destroyer Battalion, well known in combat as the "Claws of the 10th Armored Division Tigers."

With this battalion is <u>1st Lt. Charlton H. Lyons</u>, of <u>1075 Erie Street, Shreveport, La</u>.

The 609th, now commanded by Major William E. Hatina of St. Louis, Missouri, first gained fame in the assault on Metz, although their performance around Bastogne during the historic German breakthrough of General Von Runstedt's Panzers really highlights combat achievements.

Major Hatina's TDs effected the assault crossing of the Moselle River for the drive which cut off supply routes to Metz. This lead to the surrender of that city, with its surrounding forts. From there, the 609th raced into Germany with the 10th Armored, the first Third Army troops to enter Naziland.

Bastogne battling covered the TDs with glory. They were among the first sent in to stop the Nazi thrust. One self-propelled 76mm. gun alone knocked out five German tanks with six shots. Numerous German Mark IVs and Vs were smashed.

The 609th drive into the Moselle-Saar culminated in the capture of Trier, which at that time was the biggest German city to fall into American hands. The battalion drove from Mannheim to cut off the forces defending Heilbronn, and then raced into the famed Redoubt Area, finishing at Garmisch-Partenkirchen, scene of the 1936 Winter Olympics.

In combat 165 days, the TDs destroyed 37 tanks, 5 self-propelled guns, 7 artillery batteries, 2 airplanes, 21 anti-tank guns, 10 anti-aircraft guns, 36 trucks, 77 pill boxes, 8 machine gun nests, an ammo dump and a locomotive. They captured 1,542 prisoners and handled the wholesale surrender of thousands.

Awards and decorations totaled 389, including 217 Purple Hearts.

END"

<u>Appendix H</u>.

The following text is that of an Associated Press release which was prominently displayed in the New Orleans morning newspaper, *The*

Times-Picayune, of September 8, 1945. The author's father had cut it out of the paper that day and squirreled it away in that same scrapbook in which he'd kept so much else during the war. The author's father would have heard from his son the name of the ship, the *U. S. Victory*, on which his son was to sail from Le Havre. The author's memory has it that they were permitted to send one wire (telegrams were then often called "wires") home to family, advising of the ship they'd be taking home. So his father would have been watching every day for news just such as this, announcing the port and date of each ship's arrival. The arrival on September 7th of the *U. S. Victory* is clearly marked with a penciled arrow on this clipping. The principal interest of this piece lies in the fact that it exemplifies the enormous importance that was attached by the people of this country to the daily return of their service men from overseas, a return which required the better part of a year to accomplish in full. The reader will not see here any arrivals scheduled for ports on the West Coast, of course. The war in the Pacific had ended, but it had only just ended, and it ended so suddenly and unexpectedly that most of the boys out there were a long, long time ever getting home.

"Homecoming Units

A total of 2251 American troops are scheduled to arrive at east coast ports from Europe today [September 8, 1945] aboard eight troop-carrying vessels.

Three of the vessels are scheduled to dock at New York, four at Newport News and one at Boston.

Army units and troop designations include:

At New York—(Aboard Lightning) 27 troops, units undesignated. (Aboard Feinstone) 28 troops, units undesignated. (Aboard Aztec) 21 troops, units undesignated.

At Newport News—(Aboard Griswold) 137 troops, units undesignated. (Aboard Montclair Victory, originally scheduled to arrive yesterday) 1957 troops, including elements of the 388th Fighter Squad; 404th Fighter Group; 506th, 507th, 508th Fighter Squads; 90th Troop Carrier Squad; headquarters and headquarters squad, 91st Air Depot Group; headquarters and headquarters squad, 94th Air Depot Group; 818th Medical Air Evacuation Squad, and the 908th Signal Deport Company. (Aboard Pollock) 41 troops, undesignated units. (Aboard W. Paca) 16 troops, undesignated unit.

At Boston—(Aboard Joseph H. Martion) 24 troops, including men of the air force mobile training unit No. 182, personnel for reassignment and miscellaneous air force personnel.

The following army units arrived in the United States Friday:
→→At New York—(Aboard U. S. Victory) 1918 troops, mainly for reassignment. (Aboard William Tilghman) 21 troops, Office of Strategic Personnel. (Aboard Robert Owen) 710 troops, including the 336th Depot Repair Squadron; 1373rd Signal Company, wing; 37th Medical Supply Platoon, wing; advance group, 474th Quartermaster Platoon. (Aboard Marshall Elliott) 709 troops for reassignment.

At Boston—(Aboard Claymount Victory) 1243 troops, including the 406th Coast Artillery Gun Detachment; 422nd Anti-Aircraft Artillery Gun Detachment; 419th AAA (Automatic Weapons) Battery; 8th Airways Squad; 309th Station Hospital; Company Q, 470th Infantry Battalion; Company B. 1st Platoon, Company C, Company D, all of the 470th Infantry Battalion Communications Platoon, 470th Infantry Battalion; Searchlight Platoon, Headquarters Battery, 24th Coast Artillery; Batteries A, D, and F, 24th Coast Artillery Battalion, and 417 AAA (Automatic Weapons) Battery. (Aboard Jacob S. Fassett) 49 miscellaneous and personnel for discharge. (Aboard John W. Garrett) 25 surplus personnel and men from the 835th Engineer Aviation Battalion.

At Newport News—(Aboard B. Juarez) 44 miscellaneous troops. (Aboard Cape Pembroke) 55 troops, miscellaneous. (Aboard N. Aldrich) 27 troops, units undesignated."

Appendix I.

On Monday, March 7, 2005 there began an e-mail colloquy between Jack Moment and the author which went briskly back and forth for several days. In an e-mail dated March 7th, Jack had written about his meeting with Charlie Higgins at Charlie's headquarters, only mentioning what he termed "the big drop over the Rhine." In another e-mail sent the following day, March 8th, Moment described that "big drop" in considerable detail and directed the author to websites wherein *The Airborne Bridge Across the Rhine* was even more generously described. In response to this news of that event, on March 9, 2005, the author sent Moment the following e-mail:

From: Charlton Lyons
To: Jack Moment
Sent: Wednesday, March 09, 2005 11:50 AM
Subject: None

Good afternoon, Jack —

When the war ended, I came home, went to law school at Tulane and then to work in the oil business. Like almost every one of my contemporaries here, after a year or two I put the war behind me, never thought about it, never talked about it. Until, that is, about ten or twelve years ago when, television having become full of it (especially the History Channel), I became aware of a large, general and growing interest in it by so many people of younger generations.

On those rare occasions when I did speak of the war, I was most apt to recall the most impressive sight I ever beheld over there. And what was that? It was a passage over me of what I believed must certainly [have been] every Allied aircraft in the ETO. Jack, I knew, absolutely <u>knew</u>, that the text you sent to me would only confirm what I already knew. You see, Jack, at that time in late March I was near the town of Verviers, Belgium and that sky train, which stretched nearly 200 miles and took two hours and 37 minutes to pass any given point, the sky train which had you and Charlie aboard it, was the very same air armada of which I myself had seen the passage, not directly over me but out there to the North, and on about the same date. None of us who watched it for those two plus hours had ever seen anything like it. Oh, yes, we'd seen lots of planes, of course, flights of 50 or 100 but this was something so different in degree as to be different in kind. That was <u>your</u> sky train, yours and Charlie's, there could have been no mistake.

So, Jack, when you passed by up there on your way to the Rhine, I was down there, down there on the ground <u>below</u> you, Jack, and I <u>saw</u> you and Charlie as you passed by, only just minutes before the Rhine. But I didn't know that it was the two of you up there, Jack, not until now.
Charlton

<u>Appendix J</u>.

Here, on the pages next following, are three documents relating to one of the closest friends and dearest people of the author's life, Charles Alfred Higgins, Jr. The first, the text of a letter to the author from Jacqueline Haun dated August 29, 2005, relates also to Charles Richard Spencer.

THE LAWRENCEVILLE SCHOOL

August 29, 2005

THE BUNN LIBRARY

Charlton H. Lyons, Jr.
6336 Querbes Drive
Shreveport, LA 71106

Dear Mr. Lyons:

Charles Higgins' World War II file, originally kept by Mrs. Heely and now in the Archives, contained correspondence that filled out details of the story of his death. I have photocopied those items for you. I hope they will answer some of your questions.

I also was able to locate online Lt. Higgins' burial place. The American Battle Monuments Commission, which handles American overseas war burials, has the following listing for him in their database.

Charles A. Higgins, Jr.
Second Lieutenant, U.S. Army
Service # O1648625
3264th Signal Company
Entered the Service from: Delaware
Died: 24-Mar-45
Buried at: Plot N Row 7 Grave 17
Netherlands American Cemetery
Margraten, Netherlands
Awards: Silver Star, Purple Heart

I've also enclosed a copy of Charles Spencer's biography as compiled recently by researcher Professor Richard Sheppard from Magdalen College, Oxford. It focuses both on Mr. Spencer's academic career and his military career. While his death by suicide is not spelled out explicitly, particularly since the biography is intended for publication in a college history, Mr. Sheppard told me in the cover letter that he sent with the biography that that was his understanding of what had happened.

I hope you find this information helpful.

Regards,

Jacqueline Haun
Archivist

Glad Shreveport seems to be safe from Katrina — my thoughts are with all of Lt — Jacqi Haun

C. A. HIGGINS
Box 1071
Wilmington, Delaware
June 11, 1945

Dr. Allan V. Heely
The Lawrenceville School
Lawrenceville, New Jersey

Dear Dr. Heely:

Following up previous letters from Mr. Groff, and in accordance with Mrs. Higgins' request, I am enclosing the attached excerpt.

There has been received a letter from Lt. Herod, Commanding Officer of the 3264th Signal Service Company, of which Charlie was a member. According to this letter, Lt. Higgins was "killed in the Line of Duty near Wesel, Germany on the 24th of March." Lt. Herod also reports that "Charles is now resting in a United States Military Cemetery," and says, "I knew your son personally . . . and I have the highest respect for him, his ideals and his work with this organization. Charles was an inspiration for the men he worked with and his influence with them was beyond description. Never once have I heard anything other than a compliment for Charles and it was a real pleasure having him in my company."

There were five people in the plane at the time it was shot down, and from letters received from some of the other families it appears that the pilot, co-pilot and Charlie are reported killed, a sergeant (the radio man) is reported missing, and the one survivor, Sergeant Gardner, has returned to his unit.

This summarizes the most recent information which Mr. and Mrs. Higgins have received.

Very truly yours,
S/ Janice Hunt, Secretary

NB: the following was attached to the letter dated June 11, 1945.

Paragraph from letter of Corporal Harriss to his mother, dated May 16, 1945. Corporal Harriss was a member of Charlie's unit.

Because of security regulations, I have been unable to mention anything about Lt. Higgins. He was photographing an Airborne operation over the Rhine river; it was a tough assignment and he didn't feel like asking any of us to do the job. Shortly after the mission I went to the front with a searching party, looking for planes and crews. Unfortunately, we had to return before finding the ship he was on. Upon returning to the base, I interviewed the crew chief, and as far as I know the only survivor, on the plane. Here is the story as he told it to me.

'Before the take-off, Lt. Higgins told us that he was not going to wear a flak-suit or parachute. He said, 'The weight and bulkiness of the 'chute and flak-suit will make it impossible for me to get good pictures. I must be able to move about freely.' We told him that the flak-suit was not essential but the 'chute should be worn. I noticed that at the time of the take-off he had neither of them on.
Things went along OK until we had dropped the troopers and passed over the DZ (Drop Zone), then all hell broke loose – the flak was very thick and started flying in the jump doors. I threw Lt. Higgins on the floor, covering him with my body and flak-suit to keep him from being injured. All of a sudden, the jump bell rang and I started to bail out. As I stood in the door, ready to jump, I saw him, on his hands and knees, reaching for his 'chute. The next thing I knew, I was in the hospital.' Sergeant Grober* went on to say that there was a fire under the floorboard when he left the plane. I don't know what has developed since I left the field but presume that the ship and bodies have been found. It was a tough break; I had grown very fond of him He was one of the best officers I have ever known and a real pal of all of us. I really admired him.
*This should probably be "Gardner".
Copied 6/11/45 Jh